The Go Programming Language

The Go Programming Language

Alan A. A. Donovan
Google Inc.

Brian W. Kernighan
Princeton University

✦✦Addison-Wesley

New York • Boston • Indianapolis • San Francisco
Toronto • Montreal • London • Munich • Paris • Madrid
Capetown • Sydney • Tokyo • Singapore • Mexico City

For information about buying this title in bulk quantities, or for special sales opportunities (which may include electronic versions; custom cover designs; and content particular to your business, training goals, marketing focus, or branding interests), please contact our corporate sales department at corpsales@pearsoned.com or (800) 382-3419.

For government sales inquiries, please contact governmentsales@pearsoned.com.

For questions about sales outside the United States, please contact international@pearsoned.com.

Visit us on the Web: informit.com/aw

Library of Congress Control Number: 2015950709

Front cover: Millau Viaduct, Tarn valley, southern France. A paragon of simplicity in modern engineering design, the viaduct replaced a convoluted path from capital to coast with a direct route over the clouds. © Jean-Pierre Lescourret/Corbis.

Back cover: the original Go gopher. © 2009 Renée French. Used under Creative Commons Attributions 3.0 license.

Typeset by the authors in Minion Pro, Lato, and Consolas, using Go, groff, ghostscript, and a host of other open-source Unix tools. Figures were created in Google Drawings.

ISBN-13: 978-0-13-419044-0
ISBN-10: 0-13-419044-0
Text printed in the United States on recycled paper at RR Donnelley in Crawfordsville, Indiana.
Third printing, January 2016

For Leila and Meg

Contents

Preface   **xi**

   The Origins of Go   xii

   The Go Project   xiii

   Organization of the Book   xv

   Where to Find More Information   xvi

   Acknowledgments   xvii

1. Tutorial   **1**

   1.1. Hello, World   1

   1.2. Command-Line Arguments   4

   1.3. Finding Duplicate Lines   8

   1.4. Animated GIFs   13

   1.5. Fetching a URL   15

   1.6. Fetching URLs Concurrently   17

   1.7. A Web Server   19

   1.8. Loose Ends   23

2. Program Structure   **27**

   2.1. Names   27

   2.2. Declarations   28

   2.3. Variables   30

   2.4. Assignments   36

   2.5. Type Declarations   39

   2.6. Packages and Files   41

   2.7. Scope   45

3. Basic Data Types   **51**
   3.1. Integers   51
   3.2. Floating-Point Numbers   56
   3.3. Complex Numbers   61
   3.4. Booleans   63
   3.5. Strings   64
   3.6. Constants   75

4. Composite Types   **81**
   4.1. Arrays   81
   4.2. Slices   84
   4.3. Maps   93
   4.4. Structs   99
   4.5. JSON   107
   4.6. Text and HTML Templates   113

5. Functions   **119**
   5.1. Function Declarations   119
   5.2. Recursion   121
   5.3. Multiple Return Values   124
   5.4. Errors   127
   5.5. Function Values   132
   5.6. Anonymous Functions   135
   5.7. Variadic Functions   142
   5.8. Deferred Function Calls   143
   5.9. Panic   148
   5.10. Recover   151

6. Methods   **155**
   6.1. Method Declarations   155
   6.2. Methods with a Pointer Receiver   158
   6.3. Composing Types by Struct Embedding   161
   6.4. Method Values and Expressions   164
   6.5. Example: Bit Vector Type   165
   6.6. Encapsulation   168

7. Interfaces   **171**
   7.1. Interfaces as Contracts   171
   7.2. Interface Types   174
   7.3. Interface Satisfaction   175
   7.4. Parsing Flags with `flag.Value`   179
   7.5. Interface Values   181

7.6. Sorting with `sort.Interface`   186
7.7. The `http.Handler` Interface   191
7.8. The `error` Interface   196
7.9. Example: Expression Evaluator   197
7.10. Type Assertions   205
7.11. Discriminating Errors with Type Assertions   206
7.12. Querying Behaviors with Interface Type Assertions   208
7.13. Type Switches   210
7.14. Example: Token-Based XML Decoding   213
7.15. A Few Words of Advice   216

8. Goroutines and Channels   **217**
8.1. Goroutines   217
8.2. Example: Concurrent Clock Server   219
8.3. Example: Concurrent Echo Server   222
8.4. Channels   225
8.5. Looping in Parallel   234
8.6. Example: Concurrent Web Crawler   239
8.7. Multiplexing with `select`   244
8.8. Example: Concurrent Directory Traversal   247
8.9. Cancellation   251
8.10. Example: Chat Server   253

9. Concurrency with Shared Variables   **257**
9.1. Race Conditions   257
9.2. Mutual Exclusion: `sync.Mutex`   262
9.3. Read/Write Mutexes: `sync.RWMutex`   266
9.4. Memory Synchronization   267
9.5. Lazy Initialization: `sync.Once`   268
9.6. The Race Detector   271
9.7. Example: Concurrent Non-Blocking Cache   272
9.8. Goroutines and Threads   280

10. Packages and the Go Tool   **283**
10.1. Introduction   283
10.2. Import Paths   284
10.3. The Package Declaration   285
10.4. Import Declarations   285
10.5. Blank Imports   286
10.6. Packages and Naming   289
10.7. The Go Tool   290

11. Testing   **301**
  11.1. The go test Tool   302
  11.2. Test Functions   302
  11.3. Coverage   318
  11.4. Benchmark Functions   321
  11.5. Profiling   323
  11.6. Example Functions   326

12. Reflection   **329**
  12.1. Why Reflection?   329
  12.2. reflect.Type and reflect.Value   330
  12.3. Display, a Recursive Value Printer   333
  12.4. Example: Encoding S-Expressions   338
  12.5. Setting Variables with reflect.Value   341
  12.6. Example: Decoding S-Expressions   344
  12.7. Accessing Struct Field Tags   348
  12.8. Displaying the Methods of a Type   351
  12.9. A Word of Caution   352

13. Low-Level Programming   **353**
  13.1. unsafe.Sizeof, Alignof, and Offsetof   354
  13.2. unsafe.Pointer   356
  13.3. Example: Deep Equivalence   358
  13.4. Calling C Code with cgo   361
  13.5. Another Word of Caution   366

Index   **367**

Preface

"Go is an open source programming language that makes it easy to build simple, reliable, and efficient software." (From the Go web site at `golang.org`)

Go was conceived in September 2007 by Robert Griesemer, Rob Pike, and Ken Thompson, all at Google, and was announced in November 2009. The goals of the language and its accompanying tools were to be expressive, efficient in both compilation and execution, and effective in writing reliable and robust programs.

Go bears a surface similarity to C and, like C, is a tool for professional programmers, achieving maximum effect with minimum means. But it is much more than an updated version of C. It borrows and adapts good ideas from many other languages, while avoiding features that have led to complexity and unreliable code. Its facilities for concurrency are new and efficient, and its approach to data abstraction and object-oriented programming is unusually flexible. It has automatic memory management or *garbage collection*.

Go is especially well suited for building infrastructure like networked servers, and tools and systems for programmers, but it is truly a general-purpose language and finds use in domains as diverse as graphics, mobile applications, and machine learning. It has become popular as a replacement for untyped scripting languages because it balances expressiveness with safety: Go programs typically run faster than programs written in dynamic languages and suffer far fewer crashes due to unexpected type errors.

Go is an open-source project, so source code for its compiler, libraries, and tools is freely available to anyone. Contributions to the project come from an active worldwide community. Go runs on Unix-like systems—Linux, FreeBSD, OpenBSD, Mac OS X—and on Plan 9 and Microsoft Windows. Programs written in one of these environments generally work without modification on the others.

This book is meant to help you start using Go effectively right away and to use it well, taking full advantage of Go's language features and standard libraries to write clear, idiomatic, and efficient programs.

The Origins of Go

Like biological species, successful languages beget offspring that incorporate the advantages of their ancestors; interbreeding sometimes leads to surprising strengths; and, very occasionally, a radical new feature arises without precedent. We can learn a lot about why a language is the way it is and what environment it has been adapted for by looking at these influences.

The figure below shows the most important influences of earlier programming languages on the design of Go.

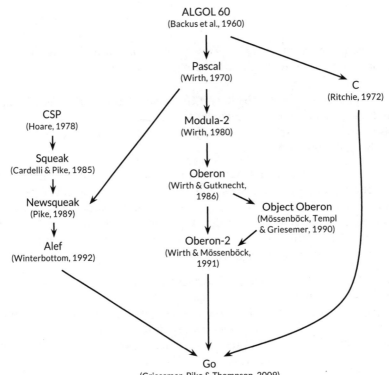

Go is sometimes described as a "C-like language," or as "C for the 21st century." From C, Go inherited its expression syntax, control-flow statements, basic data types, call-by-value parameter passing, pointers, and above all, C's emphasis on programs that compile to efficient machine code and cooperate naturally with the abstractions of current operating systems.

But there are other ancestors in Go's family tree. One major stream of influence comes from languages by Niklaus Wirth, beginning with Pascal. Modula-2 inspired the package concept. Oberon eliminated the distinction between module interface files and module implementation files. Oberon-2 influenced the syntax for packages, imports, and declarations, and Object Oberon provided the syntax for method declarations.

Another lineage among Go's ancestors, and one that makes Go distinctive among recent programming languages, is a sequence of little-known research languages developed at Bell Labs, all inspired by the concept of *communicating sequential processes* (CSP) from Tony Hoare's seminal 1978 paper on the foundations of concurrency. In CSP, a program is a parallel composition of processes that have no shared state; the processes communicate and synchronize using channels. But Hoare's CSP was a formal language for describing the fundamental concepts of concurrency, not a programming language for writing executable programs.

Rob Pike and others began to experiment with CSP implementations as actual languages. The first was called Squeak ("A language for communicating with mice"), which provided a language for handling mouse and keyboard events, with statically created channels. This was followed by Newsqueak, which offered C-like statement and expression syntax and Pascal-like type notation. It was a purely functional language with garbage collection, again aimed at managing keyboard, mouse, and window events. Channels became first-class values, dynamically created and storable in variables.

The Plan 9 operating system carried these ideas forward in a language called Alef. Alef tried to make Newsqueak a viable system programming language, but its omission of garbage collection made concurrency too painful.

Other constructions in Go show the influence of non-ancestral genes here and there; for example iota is loosely from APL, and lexical scope with nested functions is from Scheme (and most languages since). Here too we find novel mutations. Go's innovative slices provide dynamic arrays with efficient random access but also permit sophisticated sharing arrangements reminiscent of linked lists. And the defer statement is new with Go.

The Go Project

All programming languages reflect the programming philosophy of their creators, which often includes a significant component of reaction to the perceived shortcomings of earlier languages. The Go project was born of frustration with several software systems at Google that were suffering from an explosion of complexity. (This problem is by no means unique to Google.)

As Rob Pike put it, "complexity is multiplicative": fixing a problem by making one part of the system more complex slowly but surely adds complexity to other parts. With constant pressure to add features and options and configurations, and to ship code quickly, it's easy to neglect simplicity, even though in the long run simplicity is the key to good software.

Simplicity requires more work at the beginning of a project to reduce an idea to its essence and more discipline over the lifetime of a project to distinguish good changes from bad or pernicious ones. With sufficient effort, a good change can be accommodated without compromising what Fred Brooks called the "conceptual integrity" of the design but a bad change cannot, and a pernicious change trades simplicity for its shallow cousin, convenience. Only through simplicity of design can a system remain stable, secure, and coherent as it grows.

The Go project includes the language itself, its tools and standard libraries, and last but not least, a cultural agenda of radical simplicity. As a recent high-level language, Go has the benefit of hindsight, and the basics are done well: it has garbage collection, a package system, first-class functions, lexical scope, a system-call interface, and immutable strings in which text is generally encoded in UTF-8. But it has comparatively few features and is unlikely to add more. For instance, it has no implicit numeric conversions, no constructors or destructors, no operator overloading, no default parameter values, no inheritance, no generics, no exceptions, no macros, no function annotations, and no thread-local storage. The language is mature and stable, and guarantees backwards compatibility: older Go programs can be compiled and run with newer versions of compilers and standard libraries.

Go has enough of a type system to avoid most of the careless mistakes that plague programmers in dynamic languages, but it has a simpler type system than comparable typed languages. This approach can sometimes lead to isolated pockets of "untyped" programming within a broader framework of types, and Go programmers do not go to the lengths that C++ or Haskell programmers do to express safety properties as type-based proofs. But in practice Go gives programmers much of the safety and run-time performance benefits of a relatively strong type system without the burden of a complex one.

Go encourages an awareness of contemporary computer system design, particularly the importance of locality. Its built-in data types and most library data structures are crafted to work naturally without explicit initialization or implicit constructors, so relatively few memory allocations and memory writes are hidden in the code. Go's aggregate types (structs and arrays) hold their elements directly, requiring less storage and fewer allocations and pointer indirections than languages that use indirect fields. And since the modern computer is a parallel machine, Go has concurrency features based on CSP, as mentioned earlier. The variable-size stacks of Go's lightweight threads or *goroutines* are initially small enough that creating one goroutine is cheap and creating a million is practical.

Go's standard library, often described as coming with "batteries included," provides clean building blocks and APIs for I/O, text processing, graphics, cryptography, networking, and distributed applications, with support for many standard file formats and protocols. The libraries and tools make extensive use of convention to reduce the need for configuration and explanation, thus simplifying program logic and making diverse Go programs more similar to each other and thus easier to learn. Projects built using the go tool use only file and identifier names and an occasional special comment to determine all the libraries, executables, tests, benchmarks, examples, platform-specific variants, and documentation for a project; the Go source itself contains the build specification.

Organization of the Book

We assume that you have programmed in one or more other languages, whether compiled like C, C++, and Java, or interpreted like Python, Ruby, and JavaScript, so we won't spell out everything as if for a total beginner. Surface syntax will be familiar, as will variables and constants, expressions, control flow, and functions.

Chapter 1 is a tutorial on the basic constructs of Go, introduced through a dozen programs for everyday tasks like reading and writing files, formatting text, creating images, and communicating with Internet clients and servers.

Chapter 2 describes the structural elements of a Go program—declarations, variables, new types, packages and files, and scope. Chapter 3 discusses numbers, booleans, strings, and constants, and explains how to process Unicode. Chapter 4 describes composite types, that is, types built up from simpler ones using arrays, maps, structs, and *slices*, Go's approach to dynamic lists. Chapter 5 covers functions and discusses error handling, panic and recover, and the defer statement.

Chapters 1 through 5 are thus the basics, things that are part of any mainstream imperative language. Go's syntax and style sometimes differ from other languages, but most programmers will pick them up quickly. The remaining chapters focus on topics where Go's approach is less conventional: methods, interfaces, concurrency, packages, testing, and reflection.

Go has an unusual approach to object-oriented programming. There are no class hierarchies, or indeed any classes; complex object behaviors are created from simpler ones by composition, not inheritance. Methods may be associated with any user-defined type, not just structures, and the relationship between concrete types and abstract types (*interfaces*) is implicit, so a concrete type may satisfy an interface that the type's designer was unaware of. Methods are covered in Chapter 6 and interfaces in Chapter 7.

Chapter 8 presents Go's approach to concurrency, which is based on the idea of communicating sequential processes (CSP), embodied by goroutines and channels. Chapter 9 explains the more traditional aspects of concurrency based on shared variables.

Chapter 10 describes packages, the mechanism for organizing libraries. This chapter also shows how to make effective use of the go tool, which provides for compilation, testing, benchmarking, program formatting, documentation, and many other tasks, all within a single command.

Chapter 11 deals with testing, where Go takes a notably lightweight approach, avoiding abstraction-laden frameworks in favor of simple libraries and tools. The testing libraries provide a foundation atop which more complex abstractions can be built if necessary.

Chapter 12 discusses reflection, the ability of a program to examine its own representation during execution. Reflection is a powerful tool, though one to be used carefully; this chapter explains finding the right balance by showing how it is used to implement some important Go libraries. Chapter 13 explains the gory details of low-level programming that uses the unsafe package to step around Go's type system, and when that is appropriate.

Each chapter has a number of exercises that you can use to test your understanding of Go, and to explore extensions and alternatives to the examples from the book.

All but the most trivial code examples in the book are available for download from the public Git repository at gopl.io. Each example is identified by its package import path and may be conveniently fetched, built, and installed using the go get command. You'll need to choose a directory to be your Go workspace and set the GOPATH environment variable to point to it. The go tool will create the directory if necessary. For example:

```
$ export GOPATH=$HOME/gobook      # choose workspace directory
$ go get gopl.io/ch1/helloworld   # fetch, build, install
$ $GOPATH/bin/helloworld          # run
Hello, 世界
```

To run the examples, you will need at least version 1.5 of Go.

```
$ go version
go version go1.5 linux/amd64
```

Follow the instructions at https://golang.org/doc/install if the go tool on your computer is older or missing.

Where to Find More Information

The best source for more information about Go is the official web site, https://golang.org, which provides access to the documentation, including the *Go Programming Language Specification*, standard packages, and the like. There are also tutorials on how to write Go and how to write it well, and a wide variety of online text and video resources that will be valuable complements to this book. The Go Blog at blog.golang.org publishes some of the best writing on Go, with articles on the state of the language, plans for the future, reports on conferences, and in-depth explanations of a wide variety of Go-related topics.

One of the most useful aspects of online access to Go (and a regrettable limitation of a paper book) is the ability to run Go programs from the web pages that describe them. This functionality is provided by the Go Playground at play.golang.org, and may be embedded within other pages, such as the home page at golang.org or the documentation pages served by the godoc tool.

The Playground makes it convenient to perform simple experiments to check one's understanding of syntax, semantics, or library packages with short programs, and in many ways takes the place of a *read-eval-print loop* (REPL) in other languages. Its persistent URLs are great for sharing snippets of Go code with others, for reporting bugs or making suggestions.

Built atop the Playground, the Go Tour at tour.golang.org is a sequence of short interactive lessons on the basic ideas and constructions of Go, an orderly walk through the language.

The primary shortcoming of the Playground and the Tour is that they allow only standard libraries to be imported, and many library features—networking, for example—are restricted for practical or security reasons. They also require access to the Internet to compile and run each program. So for more elaborate experiments, you will have to run Go programs on your own computer. Fortunately the download process is straightforward, so it should not take more than a few minutes to fetch the Go distribution from `golang.org` and start writing and running Go programs of your own.

Since Go is an open-source project, you can read the code for any type or function in the standard library online at `https://golang.org/pkg`; the same code is part of the downloaded distribution. Use this to figure out how something works, or to answer questions about details, or merely to see how experts write really good Go.

Acknowledgments

Rob Pike and Russ Cox, core members of the Go team, read the manuscript several times with great care; their comments on everything from word choice to overall structure and organization have been invaluable. While preparing the Japanese translation, Yoshiki Shibata went far beyond the call of duty; his meticulous eye spotted numerous inconsistencies in the English text and errors in the code. We greatly appreciate thorough reviews and critical comments on the entire manuscript from Brian Goetz, Corey Kosak, Arnold Robbins, Josh Bleecher Snyder, and Peter Weinberger.

We are indebted to Sameer Ajmani, Ittai Balaban, David Crawshaw, Billy Donahue, Jonathan Feinberg, Andrew Gerrand, Robert Griesemer, John Linderman, Minux Ma, Bryan Mills, Bala Natarajan, Cosmos Nicolaou, Paul Staniforth, Nigel Tao, and Howard Trickey for many helpful suggestions. We also thank David Brailsford and Raph Levien for typesetting advice, and Chris Loper for explaining many mysteries of e-book production.

Our editor Greg Doench at Addison-Wesley got the ball rolling originally and has been continuously helpful ever since. The AW production team—John Fuller, Dayna Isley, Julie Nahil, Chuti Prasertsith, and Barbara Wood—has been outstanding; authors could not hope for better support.

Alan Donovan wishes to thank: Sameer Ajmani, Chris Demetriou, Walt Drummond, and Reid Tatge at Google for allowing him time to write; Stephen Donovan, for his advice and timely encouragement; and above all, his wife Leila Kazemi, for her unhesitating enthusiasm and unwavering support for this project, despite the long hours of distraction and absenteeism from family life that it entailed.

Brian Kernighan is deeply grateful to friends and colleagues for their patience and forbearance as he moved slowly along the path to understanding, and especially to his wife Meg, who has been unfailingly supportive of book-writing and so much else.

New York
October 2015

1

Tutorial

This chapter is a tour of the basic components of Go. We hope to provide enough information and examples to get you off the ground and doing useful things as quickly as possible. The examples here, and indeed in the whole book, are aimed at tasks that you might have to do in the real world. In this chapter we'll try to give you a taste of the diversity of programs that one might write in Go, ranging from simple file processing and a bit of graphics to concurrent Internet clients and servers. We certainly won't explain everything in the first chapter, but studying such programs in a new language can be an effective way to get started.

When you're learning a new language, there's a natural tendency to write code as you would have written it in a language you already know. Be aware of this bias as you learn Go and try to avoid it. We've tried to illustrate and explain how to write good Go, so use the code here as a guide when you're writing your own.

1.1. Hello, World

We'll start with the now-traditional "hello, world" example, which appears at the beginning of *The C Programming Language*, published in 1978. C is one of the most direct influences on Go, and "hello, world" illustrates a number of central ideas.

gopl.io/ch1/helloworld   / cf xvi

```
package main

import "fmt"

func main() {
    fmt.Println("Hello, 世界")
}
```

1

Go is a compiled language. The Go toolchain converts a source program and the things it depends on into instructions in the native machine language of a computer. These tools are accessed through a single command called go that has a number of subcommands. The simplest of these subcommands is run, which compiles the source code from one or more source files whose names end in .go, links it with libraries, then runs the resulting executable file. (We will use $ as the command prompt throughout the book.)

```
$ go run helloworld.go
```

Not surprisingly, this prints

```
Hello, 世界
```

Go natively handles Unicode, so it can process text in all the world's languages.

If the program is more than a one-shot experiment, it's likely that you would want to compile it once and save the compiled result for later use. That is done with go build:

```
$ go build helloworld.go
```

This creates an executable binary file called helloworld that can be run any time without further processing:

```
$ ./helloworld
Hello, 世界
```

We have labeled each significant example as a reminder that you can obtain the code from the book's source code repository at gopl.io:

gopl.io/ch1/helloworld $GOPATH/src/gopl.io/ch1/helloworld

If you run go get gopl.io/ch1/helloworld, it will fetch the source code and place it in the corresponding directory. There's more about this topic in Section 2.6 and Section 10.7.

Let's now talk about the program itself. Go code is organized into packages, which are similar to libraries or modules in other languages. A package consists of one or more .go source files in a single directory that define what the package does. Each source file begins with a package declaration, here package main, that states which package the file belongs to, followed by a list of other packages that it imports, and then the declarations of the program that are stored in that file.

The Go standard library has over 100 packages for common tasks like input and output, sorting, and text manipulation. For instance, the fmt package contains functions for printing formatted output and scanning input. Println is one of the basic output functions in fmt; it prints one or more values, separated by spaces, with a newline character at the end so that the values appear as a single line of output.

Package main is special. It defines a standalone executable program, not a library. Within package main the _function_ main is also special—it's where execution of the program begins. Whatever main does is what the program does. Of course, main will normally call upon functions in other packages to do much of the work, such as the function fmt.Println.

We must tell the compiler what packages are needed by this source file; that's the role of the `import` declaration that follows the `package` declaration. The "hello, world" program uses only one function from one other package, but most programs will import more packages.

You must import exactly the packages you need. A program will not compile if there are missing imports or if there are unnecessary ones. This strict requirement prevents references to unused packages from accumulating as programs evolve.

The `import` declarations must follow the `package` declaration. After that, a program consists of the declarations of functions, variables, constants, and types (introduced by the keywords `func`, `var`, `const`, and `type`); for the most part, the order of declarations does not matter. This program is about as short as possible since it declares only one function, which in turn calls only one other function. To save space, we will sometimes not show the `package` and `import` declarations when presenting examples, but they are in the source file and must be there to compile the code.

A function declaration consists of the keyword `func`, the name of the function, a parameter list (empty for `main`), a result list (also empty here), and the body of the function—the statements that define what it does—enclosed in braces. We'll take a closer look at functions in Chapter 5.

Go does not require semicolons at the ends of statements or declarations, except where two or more appear on the same line. In effect, newlines following certain tokens are converted into semicolons, so where newlines are placed matters to proper parsing of Go code. For instance, the opening brace `{` of the function must be on the same line as the end of the `func` declaration, not on a line by itself, and in the expression x + y, a newline is permitted after but not before the + operator.

Go takes a strong stance on code formatting. The `gofmt` tool rewrites code into the standard format, and the go tool's `fmt` subcommand applies `gofmt` to all the files in the specified package, or the ones in the current directory by default. All Go source files in the book have been run through `gofmt`, and you should get into the habit of doing the same for your own code. Declaring a standard format by fiat eliminates a lot of pointless debate about trivia and, more importantly, enables a variety of automated source code transformations that would be infeasible if arbitrary formatting were allowed.

Many text editors can be configured to run `gofmt` each time you save a file, so that your source code is always properly formatted. A related tool, `goimports`, additionally manages the insertion and removal of import declarations as needed. It is not part of the standard distribution but you can obtain it with this command:

```
$ go get golang.org/x/tools/cmd/goimports
```

For most users, the usual way to download and build packages, run their tests, show their documentation, and so on, is with the go tool, which we'll look at in Section 10.7.

1.2. Command-Line Arguments

Most programs process some input to produce some output; that's pretty much the definition of computing. But how does a program get input data on which to operate? Some programs generate their own data, but more often, input comes from an external source: a file, a network connection, the output of another program, a user at a keyboard, command-line arguments, or the like. The next few examples will discuss some of these alternatives, starting with command-line arguments.

✳ The os package provides functions and other values for dealing with the operating system in a platform-independent fashion. Command-line arguments are available to a program in a variable named Args that is part of the os package; thus its name anywhere outside the os package is os.Args.

The variable os.Args is a *slice* of strings. Slices are a fundamental notion in Go, and we'll talk a lot more about them soon. For now, think of a slice as a dynamically sized sequence s of array elements where individual elements can be accessed as s[i] and a contiguous subsequence as s[m:n]. The number of elements is given by len(s). As in most other programming languages, all indexing in Go uses *half-open* intervals that include the first index but exclude the last, because it simplifies logic. For example, the slice s[m:n], where $0 \leq m \leq n \leq$ len(s), contains n-m elements.

The first element of os.Args, os.Args[0], is the name of the command itself; the other elements are the arguments that were presented to the program when it started execution. A slice expression of the form s[m:n] yields a slice that refers to elements m through n-1, so the elements we need for our next example are those in the slice os.Args[1:len(os.Args)]. If m or n is omitted, it defaults to 0 or len(s) respectively, so we can abbreviate the desired slice as os.Args[1:].

Here's an implementation of the Unix echo command, which prints its command-line arguments on a single line. It imports two packages, which are given as a parenthesized list rather than as individual import declarations. Either form is legal, but conventionally the list form is used. The order of imports doesn't matter; the gofmt tool sorts the package names into alphabetical order. (When there are several versions of an example, we will often number them so you can be sure of which one we're talking about.)

gopl.io/ch1/echo1
```
// Echo1 prints its command-line arguments.
package main

import (
    "fmt"
    "os"
)
```

```
func main() {
    var s, sep string
    for i := 1; i < len(os.Args); i++ {
        s += sep + os.Args[i]
        sep = " "
    }
    fmt.Println(s)
}
```

// s, sep are variables of type string
// no parens, Note := , a short var.decl

Comments begin with //. All text from a // to the end of the line is commentary for programmers and is ignored by the compiler. By convention, we describe each package in a comment immediately preceding its package declaration; for a main package, this comment is one or more complete sentences that describe the program as a whole.

The var declaration declares two variables s and sep, of type string. A variable can be initialized as part of its declaration. If it is not explicitly initialized, it is implicitly initialized to the *zero value* for its type, which is 0 for numeric types and the empty string "" for strings. Thus in this example, the declaration implicitly initializes s and sep to empty strings. We'll have more to say about variables and declarations in Chapter 2.

For numbers, Go provides the usual arithmetic and logical operators. When applied to strings, however, the + operator *concatenates* the values, so the expression

```
sep + os.Args[i]
```

represents the concatenation of the strings sep and os.Args[i]. The statement we used in the program,

```
s += sep + os.Args[i]
```

is an *assignment statement* that concatenates the old value of s with sep and os.Args[i] and assigns it back to s; it is equivalent to

```
s = s + sep + os.Args[i]
```

The operator += is an *assignment operator*. Each arithmetic and logical operator like + or * has a corresponding assignment operator.

The echo program could have printed its output in a loop one piece at a time, but this version instead builds up a string by repeatedly appending new text to the end. The string s starts life empty, that is, with value "", and each trip through the loop adds some text to it; after the first iteration, a space is also inserted so that when the loop is finished, there is one space between each argument. This is a quadratic process that could be costly if the number of arguments is large, but for echo, that's unlikely. We'll show a number of improved versions of echo in this chapter and the next that will deal with any real inefficiency.

The loop index variable i is declared in the first part of the for loop. The := symbol is part of a *short variable declaration*, a statement that declares one or more variables and gives them appropriate types based on the initializer values; there's more about this in the next chapter.

The increment statement i++ adds 1 to i; it's equivalent to i += 1 which is in turn equivalent to i = i + 1. There's a corresponding decrement statement i-- that subtracts 1. These are statements, not expressions as they are in most languages in the C family, so `j = i++` is illegal, and they are postfix only, so `--i` is not legal either.

The `for` loop is the only loop statement in Go. It has a number of forms, one of which is illustrated here:

```
for initialization; condition; post {
    // zero or more statements
}
```

Parentheses are never used around the three components of a `for` loop. The braces are mandatory, however, and the opening brace must be on the same line as the *post* statement.

The optional *initialization* statement is executed before the loop starts. If it is present, it must be a *simple statement*, that is, a short variable declaration, an increment or assignment statement, or a function call. The *condition* is a boolean expression that is evaluated at the beginning of each iteration of the loop; if it evaluates to `true`, the statements controlled by the loop are executed. The *post* statement is executed after the body of the loop, then the condition is evaluated again. The loop ends when the condition becomes false.

Any of these parts may be omitted. If there is no *initialization* and no *post*, the semicolons may also be omitted:

```
// a traditional "while" loop
for condition {
    // ...
}
```

If the condition is omitted entirely in any of these forms, for example in

```
// a traditional infinite loop
for {
    // ...
}
```

the loop is infinite, though loops of this form may be terminated in some other way, like a `break` or `return` statement.

Another form of the `for` loop iterates over a *range* of values from a data type like a string or a slice. To illustrate, here's a second version of echo:

gopl.io/ch1/echo2

```
// Echo2 prints its command-line arguments.
package main

import (
    "fmt"
    "os"
)
```

```go
func main() {
    s, sep := "", ""
    for _, arg := range os.Args[1:] {        // _, arg get 1,arg1, 2,arg2 succ'ly
        s += sep + arg
        sep = " "
    }
    fmt.Println(s)
}
```

In each iteration of the loop, range produces a pair of values: the index and the value of the   ✗
element at that index. In this example, we don't need the index, but the syntax of a range loop
requires that if we deal with the element, we must deal with the index too. One idea would be
to assign the index to an obviously temporary variable like temp and ignore its value, but Go
does not permit unused local variables, so this would result in a compilation error.

The solution is to use the *blank identifier*, whose name is _ (that is, an underscore). The blank   ✗
identifier may be used whenever syntax requires a variable name but program logic does not,
for instance to discard an unwanted loop index when we require only the element value. Most
Go programmers would likely use range and _ to write the echo program as above, since the
indexing over os.Args is implicit, not explicit, and thus easier to get right.

This version of the program uses a short variable declaration to declare and initialize s and
sep, but we could equally well have declared the variables separately. There are several ways
to declare a string variable; these are all equivalent:

```go
s := ""                      } Recommended
var s string
var s = ""
var s string = ""
```

Why should you prefer one form to another? The first form, a short variable declaration, is
the most compact, but it may be used only within a function, not for package-level variables.
The second form relies on default initialization to the zero value for strings, which is "". The
third form is rarely used except when declaring multiple variables. The fourth form is explicit
about the variable's type, which is redundant when it is the same as that of the initial value but
necessary in other cases where they are not of the same type. In practice, you should generally
use one of the first two forms, with explicit initialization to say that the initial value is
important and implicit initialization to say that the initial value doesn't matter.

As noted above, each time around the loop, the string s gets completely new contents. The +=
statement makes a new string by concatenating the old string, a space character, and the next
argument, then assigns the new string to s. The old contents of s are no longer in use, so they
will be garbage-collected in due course.

If the amount of data involved is large, this could be costly. A simpler and more efficient
solution would be to use the Join function from the strings package:

package "strings"

gopl.io/ch1/echo3
```
func main() {
    fmt.Println(strings.Join(os.Args[1:], " "))
}
```
slice

Finally, if we don't care about format but just want to see the values, perhaps for debugging, we can let Println format the results for us:

```
fmt.Println(os.Args[1:])
```

The output of this statement is like what we would get from strings.Join, but with surrounding brackets. Any slice may be printed this way.

Exercise 1.1: Modify the echo program to also print os.Args[0], the name of the command that invoked it.

Exercise 1.2: Modify the echo program to print the index and value of each of its arguments, one per line.

Exercise 1.3: Experiment to measure the difference in running time between our potentially inefficient versions and the one that uses strings.Join. (Section 1.6 illustrates part of the time package, and Section 11.4 shows how to write benchmark tests for systematic performance evaluation.) *321*

1.3. Finding Duplicate Lines

Programs for file copying, printing, searching, sorting, counting, and the like all have a similar structure: a loop over the input, some computation on each element, and generation of output on the fly or at the end. We'll show three variants of a program called dup; it is partly inspired by the Unix uniq command, which looks for adjacent duplicate lines. The structures and packages used are models that can be easily adapted.

The first version of dup prints each line that appears more than once in the standard input, preceded by its count. This program introduces the if statement, the map data type, and the bufio package.

gopl.io/ch1/dup1
```
// Dup1 prints the text of each line that appears more than
// once in the standard input, preceded by its count.
package main

import (
    "bufio"
    "fmt"
    "os"
)
```

package "bufio."
"fmt"

bufio

```
func main() {
    counts := make(map[string]int)
    input := bufio.NewScanner(os.Stdin)
    for input.Scan() {
        counts[input.Text()]++
    }
    // NOTE: ignoring potential errors from input.Err()
    for line, n := range counts {
        if n > 1 {
            fmt.Printf("%d\t%s\n", n, line)
        }
    }
}
```

ⓐ
for:6 condition only

ⓑ

ⓒ *16*

for *16 condition only*

As with for, parentheses are never used around the condition in an if statement, but braces are required for the body. There can be an optional else part that is executed if the condition is false.

A *map* holds a set of key/value pairs and provides constant-time operations to store, retrieve, or test for an item in the set. The key may be of any type whose values can be compared with ==, strings being the most common example; the value may be of any type at all. In this example, the keys are strings and the values are ints. The built-in function make creates a new empty map; it has other uses too. Maps are discussed at length in Section 4.3.

map

Each time dup reads a line of input, the line is used as a key into the map and the corresponding value is incremented. The statement counts[input.Text()]++ is equivalent to these two statements:

```
line := input.Text()
counts[line] = counts[line] + 1
```

It's not a problem if the map doesn't yet contain that key. The first time a new line is seen, the expression counts[line] on the right-hand side evaluates to the zero value for its type, which is 0 for int.

To print the results, we use another range-based for loop, this time over the counts map. As before, each iteration produces two results, a key and the value of the map element for that key. The order of map iteration is not specified, but in practice it is random, varying from one run to another. This design is intentional, since it prevents programs from relying on any particular ordering where none is guaranteed.

ⓑ

Onward to the bufio package, which helps make input and output efficient and convenient. One of its most useful features is a type called Scanner that reads input and breaks it into lines or words; it's often the easiest way to process input that comes naturally in lines.

ⓐ

The program uses a short variable declaration to create a new variable input that refers to a bufio.Scanner:

```
input := bufio.NewScanner(os.Stdin)
```

The scanner reads from the program's standard input. Each call to `input.Scan()` reads the next line and removes the newline character from the end; the result can be retrieved by calling `input.Text()`. The Scan function returns `true` if there is a line and `false` when there is no more input.

The function `fmt.Printf`, like `printf` in C and other languages, produces formatted output from a list of expressions. Its first argument is a format string that specifies how subsequent arguments should be formatted. The format of each argument is determined by a conversion character, a letter following a percent sign. For example, `%d` formats an integer operand using decimal notation, and `%s` expands to the value of a string operand.

Printf has over a dozen such conversions, which Go programmers call *verbs*. This table is far from a complete specification but illustrates many of the features that are available:

%d	decimal integer
%x, %o, %b	integer in hexadecimal, octal, binary
%f, %g, %e	floating-point number: 3.141593 3.141592653589793 3.141593e+00
%t	boolean: true or false
%c	rune (Unicode code point)
%s	string
%q	quoted string "abc" or rune 'c'
%v	any value in a natural format
%T	type of any value
%%	literal percent sign (no operand)

The format string in dup1 also contains a tab \t and a newline \n. String literals may contain such *escape sequences* for representing otherwise invisible characters. Printf does not write a newline by default. By convention, formatting functions whose names end in f, such as `log.Printf` and `fmt.Errorf`, use the formatting rules of `fmt.Printf`, whereas those whose names end in ln follow Println, formatting their arguments as if by %v, followed by a newline.

Many programs read either from their standard input, as above, or from a sequence of named files. The next version of dup can read from the standard input or handle a list of file names, using `os.Open` to open each one:

gopl.io/ch1/dup2
```go
// Dup2 prints the count and text of lines that appear more than once
// in the input.  It reads from stdin or from a list of named files.
package main

import (
    "bufio"
    "fmt"
    "os"
)
```

```go
func main() {
    counts := make(map[string]int)
    files := os.Args[1:]
    if len(files) == 0 {
        countLines(os.Stdin, counts)
    } else {
        for _, arg := range files {
            f, err := os.Open(arg)
            if err != nil {
                fmt.Fprintf(os.Stderr, "dup2: %v\n", err)
                continue
            }
            countLines(f, counts)
            f.Close()
        }
    }
    for line, n := range counts {
        if n > 1 {
            fmt.Printf("%d\t%s\n", n, line)
        }
    }
}

func countLines(f *os.File, counts map[string]int) {
    input := bufio.NewScanner(f)
    for input.Scan() {
        counts[input.Text()]++
    }
    // NOTE: ignoring potential errors from input.Err()
}
```

(handwritten annotations: " Command-line args", "os.Args", "type *os.File, "open file"", "f, err := os.open(arg)", "os.Stdin", "// may produce error", "err")*

The function os.Open returns two values. The first is an open file (*os.File) that is used in subsequent reads by the Scanner.

The second result of os.Open is a value of the built-in error type. If err equals the special built-in value nil, the file was opened successfully. The file is read, and when the end of the input is reached, Close closes the file and releases any resources. On the other hand, if err is not nil, something went wrong. In that case, the error value describes the problem. Our simple-minded error handling prints a message on the standard error stream using Fprintf and the verb %v, which displays a value of any type in a default format, and dup then carries on with the next file; the continue statement goes to the next iteration of the enclosing for loop.

In the interests of keeping code samples to a reasonable size, our early examples are intentionally somewhat cavalier about error handling. Clearly we must check for an error from os.Open; however, we are ignoring the less likely possibility that an error could occur while reading the file with input.Scan. We will note places where we've skipped error checking, and we will go into the details of error handling in Section 5.4.

Notice that the call to countLines precedes its declaration. Functions and other package-level entities may be declared in any order.

A map is a *reference* to the data structure created by make. When a map is passed to a function, the function receives a copy of the reference, so any changes the called function makes to the underlying data structure will be visible through the caller's map reference too. In our example, the values inserted into the counts map by countLines are seen by main.

The versions of dup above operate in a "streaming" mode in which input is read and broken into lines as needed, so in principle these programs can handle an arbitrary amount of input. An alternative approach is to read the entire input into memory in one big gulp, split it into lines all at once, then process the lines. The following version, dup3, operates in that fashion. It introduces the function ReadFile (from the io/ioutil package), which reads the entire contents of a named file, and strings.Split, which splits a string into a slice of substrings. (Split is the opposite of strings.Join, which we saw earlier.)

We've simplified dup3 somewhat. First, it only reads named files, not the standard input, since ReadFile requires a file name argument. Second, we moved the counting of the lines back into main, since it is now needed in only one place.

gopl.io/ch1/dup3

```go
// Dup3 prints the count and text of lines that
// appear more than once in the named input files.
package main

import (
    "fmt"
    "io/ioutil"
    "os"
    "strings"
)

func main() {
    counts := make(map[string]int)
    for _, filename := range os.Args[1:] {
        data, err := ioutil.ReadFile(filename)
        if err != nil {
            fmt.Fprintf(os.Stderr, "dup3: %v\n", err)
            continue
        }
        for _, line := range strings.Split(string(data), "\n") {
            counts[line]++
        }
    }
    for line, n := range counts {
        if n > 1 {
            fmt.Printf("%d\t%s\n", n, line)
        }
    }
}
```

ReadFile returns a byte slice that must be converted into a string so it can be split by strings.Split. We will discuss strings and byte slices at length in Section 3.5.4.

Under the covers, `bufio.Scanner`, `ioutil.ReadFile`, and `ioutil.WriteFile` use the `Read` and `Write` methods of `*os.File`, but it's rare that most programmers need to access those lower-level routines directly. The higher-level functions like those from `bufio` and `io/ioutil` are easier to use.

Exercise 1.4: Modify `dup2` to print the names of all files in which each duplicated line occurs.

1.4. Animated GIFs

The next program demonstrates basic usage of Go's standard image packages, which we'll use to create a sequence of bit-mapped images and then encode the sequence as a GIF animation. The images, called *Lissajous figures*, were a staple visual effect in sci-fi films of the 1960s. They are the parametric curves produced by harmonic oscillation in two dimensions, such as two sine waves fed into the x and y inputs of an oscilloscope. Figure 1.1 shows some examples.

Figure 1.1. Four Lissajous figures.

There are several new constructs in this code, including `const` declarations, struct types, and composite literals. Unlike most of our examples, this one also involves floating-point computations. We'll discuss these topics only briefly here, pushing most details off to later chapters, since the primary goal right now is to give you an idea of what Go looks like and the kinds of things that can be done easily with the language and its libraries.

gopl.io/ch1/lissajous

```
// Lissajous generates GIF animations of random Lissajous figures.
package main

import (
    "image"
    "image/color"
    "image/gif"
    "io"
    "math"
    "math/rand"
    "os"
)
```

(a)

```go
    var palette = []color.Color{color.White, color.Black}        // slice

    const (
        whiteIndex = 0 // first color in palette
        blackIndex = 1 // next color in palette
    )

    func main() {
        lissajous(os.Stdout)
    }

    func lissajous(out io.Writer) {
        const (
            cycles  = 5     // number of complete x oscillator revolutions
            res     = 0.001 // angular resolution
            size    = 100   // image canvas covers [-size..+size]
            nframes = 64    // number of animation frames
            delay   = 8     // delay between frames in 10ms units
        )
        freq := rand.Float64() * 3.0 // relative frequency of y oscillator
        anim := gif.GIF{LoopCount: nframes}    // struct
        phase := 0.0 // phase difference
        for i := 0; i < nframes; i++ {
            rect := image.Rect(0, 0, 2*size+1, 2*size+1)    image size  201 x 201
            img := image.NewPaletted(rect, palette)
            for t := 0.0; t < cycles*2*math.Pi; t += res {
                x := math.Sin(t)
                y := math.Sin(t*freq + phase)
                img.SetColorIndex(size+int(x*size+0.5), size+int(y*size+0.5),
                    blackIndex)      Set pixel computed loc to black
            }
            phase += 0.1
            anim.Delay = append(anim.Delay, delay)
            anim.Image = append(anim.Image, img)
        }
        gif.EncodeAll(out, &anim) // NOTE: ignoring encoding errors
    }
```

(a) (b) 15

After importing a package whose path has multiple components, like image/color, we refer to the package with a name that comes from the last component. Thus the variable color.White belongs to the image/color package and gif.GIF belongs to image/gif.

Const

A const declaration (§3.6) gives names to constants, that is, values that are fixed at compile time, such as the numerical parameters for cycles, frames, and delay. Like var declarations, const declarations may appear at package level (so the names are visible throughout the package) or within a function (so the names are visible only within that function). The value of a constant must be a number, string, or boolean.

(a)

The expressions []color.Color{...} and gif.GIF{...} are *composite literals* (§4.2, §4.4.1), a compact notation for instantiating any of Go's composite types from a sequence of element values. Here, the first one is a slice and the second one is a *struct*.

The type gif.GIF is a struct type (§4.4). A struct is a group of values called *fields*, often of different types, that are collected together in a single object that can be treated as a unit. The variable anim is a struct of type gif.GIF. The struct literal creates a struct value whose Loop-Count field is set to nframes; all other fields have the zero value for their type. The individual fields of a struct can be accessed using dot notation, as in the final two assignments which explicitly update the Delay and Image fields of anim.

The lissajous function has two nested loops. The outer loop runs for 64 iterations, each producing a single frame of the animation. It creates a new 201×201 image with a palette of two colors, white and black. All pixels are initially set to the palette's zero value (the zeroth color in the palette), which we set to white. Each pass through the outer loop generates a new image by setting some pixels to black. The result is appended, using the built-in append function (§4.2.1), to a list of frames in anim, along with a specified delay of 80ms. Finally the sequence of frames and delays is encoded into GIF format and written to the output stream out. The type of out is io.Writer, which lets us write to a wide range of possible destinations, as we'll show soon.

The inner loop runs the two oscillators. The x oscillator is just the sine function. The y oscillator is also a sinusoid, but its frequency relative to the x oscillator is a random number between 0 and 3, and its phase relative to the x oscillator is initially zero but increases with each frame of the animation. The loop runs until the x oscillator has completed five full cycles. At each step, it calls SetColorIndex to color the pixel corresponding to (x, y) black, which is at position 1 in the palette.

The main function calls the lissajous function, directing it to write to the standard output, so this command produces an animated GIF with frames like those in Figure 1.1:

```
$ go build gopl.io/ch1/lissajous
$ ./lissajous >out.gif
```

Exercise 1.5: Change the Lissajous program's color palette to green on black, for added authenticity. To create the web color #RRGGBB, use color.RGBA{0xRR, 0xGG, 0xBB, 0xff}, where each pair of hexadecimal digits represents the intensity of the red, green, or blue component of the pixel.

Exercise 1.6: Modify the Lissajous program to produce images in multiple colors by adding more values to palette and then displaying them by changing the third argument of Set-ColorIndex in some interesting way.

1.5. Fetching a URL

For many applications, access to information from the Internet is as important as access to the local file system. Go provides a collection of packages, grouped under net, that make it easy to send and receive information through the Internet, make low-level network connections, and set up servers, for which Go's concurrency features (introduced in Chapter 8) are particularly useful.

To illustrate the minimum necessary to retrieve information over HTTP, here's a simple program called `fetch` that fetches the content of each specified URL and prints it as uninterpreted text; it's inspired by the invaluable utility `curl`. Obviously one would usually do more with such data, but this shows the basic idea. We will use this program frequently in the book.

gopl.io/ch1/fetch

```go
// Fetch prints the content found at each specified URL.
package main

import (
    "fmt"
    "io/ioutil"
    "net/http"
    "os"
)

func main() {
    for _, url := range os.Args[1:] {
        resp, err := http.Get(url)
        if err != nil {
            fmt.Fprintf(os.Stderr, "fetch: %v\n", err)
            os.Exit(1)
        }
        b, err := ioutil.ReadAll(resp.Body)
        resp.Body.Close()
        if err != nil {
            fmt.Fprintf(os.Stderr, "fetch: reading %s: %v\n", url, err)
            os.Exit(1)
        }
        fmt.Printf("%s", b)
    }
}
```

This program introduces functions from two packages, `net/http` and `io/ioutil`. The `http.Get` function makes an HTTP request and, if there is no error, returns the result in the response struct `resp`. The `Body` field of `resp` contains the server response as a readable stream. Next, `ioutil.ReadAll` reads the entire response; the result is stored in `b`. The `Body` stream is closed to avoid leaking resources, and `Printf` writes the response to the standard output.

```
$ go build gopl.io/ch1/fetch
$ ./fetch http://gopl.io
<html>
<head>
<title>The Go Programming Language</title>
...
```

If the HTTP request fails, `fetch` reports the failure instead:

```
$ ./fetch http://bad.gopl.io
fetch: Get http://bad.gopl.io: dial tcp: lookup bad.gopl.io: no such host
```

In either error case, os.Exit(1) causes the process to exit with a status code of 1.

Exercise 1.7: The function call io.Copy(dst, src) reads from src and writes to dst. Use it instead of ioutil.ReadAll to copy the response body to os.Stdout without requiring a buffer large enough to hold the entire stream. Be sure to check the error result of io.Copy.

Exercise 1.8: Modify fetch to add the prefix http:// to each argument URL if it is missing. You might want to use strings.HasPrefix.

Exercise 1.9: Modify fetch to also print the HTTP status code, found in resp.Status.

1.6. Fetching URLs Concurrently

One of the most interesting and novel aspects of Go is its support for concurrent programming. This is a large topic, to which Chapter 8 and Chapter 9 are devoted, so for now we'll give you just a taste of Go's main concurrency mechanisms, goroutines and channels.

The next program, fetchall, does the same fetch of a URL's contents as the previous example, but it fetches many URLs, all concurrently, so that the process will take no longer than the longest fetch rather than the sum of all the fetch times. This version of fetchall discards the responses but reports the size and elapsed time for each one:

gopl.io/ch1/fetchall

```go
// Fetchall fetches URLs in parallel and reports their times and sizes.
package main

import (
    "fmt"
    "io"
    "io/ioutil"
    "net/http"
    "os"
    "time"
)

func main() {
    start := time.Now()
    ch := make(chan string)
    for _, url := range os.Args[1:] {
        go fetch(url, ch) // start a goroutine
    }
    for range os.Args[1:] {
        fmt.Println(<-ch) // receive from channel ch
    }
    fmt.Printf("%.2fs elapsed\n", time.Since(start).Seconds())
}
```

```
func fetch(url string, ch chan<- string) {
    start := time.Now()
    resp, err := http.Get(url)
    if err != nil {
        ch <- fmt.Sprint(err) // send to channel ch
        return
    }

    nbytes, err := io.Copy(ioutil.Discard, resp.Body)
    resp.Body.Close() // don't leak resources
    if err != nil {
        ch <- fmt.Sprintf("while reading %s: %v", url, err)
        return
    }
    secs := time.Since(start).Seconds()
    ch <- fmt.Sprintf("%.2fs  %7d  %s", secs, nbytes, url)
}
```

Here's an example:

```
$ go build gopl.io/ch1/fetchall
$ ./fetchall https://golang.org http://gopl.io https://godoc.org
0.14s     6852   https://godoc.org
0.16s     7261   https://golang.org
0.48s     2475   http://gopl.io
0.48s elapsed
```

A *goroutine* is a concurrent function execution. A *channel* is a communication mechanism that allows one goroutine to pass values of a specified type to another goroutine. The function main runs in a goroutine and the go statement creates additional goroutines.

The main function creates a channel of strings using make. For each command-line argument, the go statement in the first range loop starts a new goroutine that calls fetch asynchronously to fetch the URL using http.Get. The io.Copy function reads the body of the response and discards it by writing to the ioutil.Discard output stream. Copy returns the byte count, along with any error that occurred. As each result arrives, fetch sends a summary line on the channel ch. The second range loop in main receives and prints those lines.

When one goroutine attempts a send or receive on a channel, it blocks until another goroutine attempts the corresponding receive or send operation, at which point the value is transferred and both goroutines proceed. In this example, each fetch sends a value (ch <- *expression*) on the channel ch, and main receives all of them (<-ch). Having main do all the printing ensures that output from each goroutine is processed as a unit, with no danger of interleaving if two goroutines finish at the same time.

Exercise 1.10: Find a web site that produces a large amount of data. Investigate caching by running fetchall twice in succession to see whether the reported time changes much. Do you get the same content each time? Modify fetchall to print its output to a file so it can be examined.

Exercise 1.11: Try `fetchall` with longer argument lists, such as samples from the top million web sites available at `alexa.com`. How does the program behave if a web site just doesn't respond? (Section 8.9 describes mechanisms for coping in such cases.)

1.7. A Web Server

Go's library makes it easy to write a web server that responds to client requests like those made by `fetch`. In this section, we'll show a minimal server that returns the path component of the URL used to access the server. That is, if the request is for `http://localhost:8000/hello`, the response will be `URL.Path = "/hello"`.

gopl.io/ch1/server1

```go
// Server1 is a minimal "echo" server.
package main

import (
    "fmt"
    "log"
    "net/http"
)

func main() {
    http.HandleFunc("/", handler) // each request calls handler
    log.Fatal(http.ListenAndServe("localhost:8000", nil))
}

// handler echoes the Path component of the requested URL.
func handler(w http.ResponseWriter, r *http.Request) {
    fmt.Fprintf(w, "URL.Path = %q\n", r.URL.Path)
}
```

The program is only a handful of lines long because library functions do most of the work. The `main` function connects a handler function to incoming URLs whose path begins with /, which is all URLs, and starts a server listening for incoming requests on port 8000. A request is represented as a struct of type `http.Request`, which contains a number of related fields, one of which is the URL of the incoming request. When a request arrives, it is given to the handler function, which extracts the path component (`/hello`) from the request URL and sends it back as the response, using `fmt.Fprintf`. Web servers will be explained in detail in Section 7.7.

Let's start the server in the background. On Mac OS X or Linux, add an ampersand (&) to the command; on Microsoft Windows, you will need to run the command without the ampersand in a separate command window.

```
$ go run src/gopl.io/ch1/server1/main.go &
```

We can then make client requests from the command line:

```
$ go build gopl.io/ch1/fetch
$ ./fetch http://localhost:8000
URL.Path = "/"
$ ./fetch http://localhost:8000/help
URL.Path = "/help"
```

Alternatively, we can access the server from a web browser, as shown in Figure 1.2.

Figure 1.2. A response from the echo server.

It's easy to add features to the server. One useful addition is a specific URL that returns a status of some sort. For example, this version does the same echo but also counts the number of requests; a request to the URL /count returns the count so far, excluding /count requests themselves:

gopl.io/ch1/server2
```
// Server2 is a minimal "echo" and counter server.
package main

import (
    "fmt"
    "log"
    "net/http"
    "sync"
)

var mu sync.Mutex
var count int

func main() {
    http.HandleFunc("/", handler)
    http.HandleFunc("/count", counter)
    log.Fatal(http.ListenAndServe("localhost:8000", nil))
}

// handler echoes the Path component of the requested URL.
func handler(w http.ResponseWriter, r *http.Request) {
    mu.Lock()
    count++
    mu.Unlock()
    fmt.Fprintf(w, "URL.Path = %q\n", r.URL.Path)
}
```

```
// counter echoes the number of calls so far.
func counter(w http.ResponseWriter, r *http.Request) {
    mu.Lock()
    fmt.Fprintf(w, "Count %d\n", count)
    mu.Unlock()
}
```

The server has two handlers, and the request URL determines which one is called: a request for /count invokes counter and all others invoke handler. A handler pattern that ends with a slash matches any URL that has the pattern as a prefix. Behind the scenes, the server runs the handler for each incoming request in a separate goroutine so that it can serve multiple requests simultaneously. However, if two concurrent requests try to update count at the same time, it might not be incremented consistently; the program would have a serious bug called a *race condition* (§9.1). To avoid this problem, we must ensure that at most one goroutine accesses the variable at a time, which is the purpose of the mu.Lock() and mu.Unlock() calls that bracket each access of count. We'll look more closely at concurrency with shared variables in Chapter 9.

As a richer example, the handler function can report on the headers and form data that it receives, making the server useful for inspecting and debugging requests:

gopl.io/ch1/server3
```
// handler echoes the HTTP request.
func handler(w http.ResponseWriter, r *http.Request) {
    fmt.Fprintf(w, "%s %s %s\n", r.Method, r.URL, r.Proto)
    for k, v := range r.Header {
        fmt.Fprintf(w, "Header[%q] = %q\n", k, v)
    }
    fmt.Fprintf(w, "Host = %q\n", r.Host)
    fmt.Fprintf(w, "RemoteAddr = %q\n", r.RemoteAddr)
    if err := r.ParseForm(); err != nil {
        log.Print(err)
    }
    for k, v := range r.Form {
        fmt.Fprintf(w, "Form[%q] = %q\n", k, v)
    }
}
```

This uses the fields of the http.Request struct to produce output like this:
```
GET /?q=query HTTP/1.1
Header["Accept-Encoding"] = ["gzip, deflate, sdch"]
Header["Accept-Language"] = ["en-US,en;q=0.8"]
Header["Connection"] = ["keep-alive"]
Header["Accept"] = ["text/html,application/xhtml+xml,application/xml;..."]
Header["User-Agent"] = ["Mozilla/5.0 (Macintosh; Intel Mac OS X 10_7_5)..."]
Host = "localhost:8000"
RemoteAddr = "127.0.0.1:59911"
Form["q"] = ["query"]
```

Notice how the call to ParseForm is nested within an if statement. Go allows a simple statement such as a local variable declaration to precede the if condition, which is particularly
useful for error handling as in this example. We could have written it as

```
err := r.ParseForm()
if err != nil {
    log.Print(err)
}
```

but combining the statements is shorter and reduces the scope of the variable err, which is
good practice. We'll define scope in Section 2.7.

In these programs, we've seen three very different types used as output streams. The fetch
program copied HTTP response data to os.Stdout, a file, as did the lissajous program.
The fetchall program threw the response away (while counting its length) by copying it to
the trivial sink ioutil.Discard. And the web server above used fmt.Fprintf to write to an
http.ResponseWriter representing the web browser.

Although these three types differ in the details of what they do, they all satisfy a common
interface, allowing any of them to be used wherever an output stream is needed. That interface, called io.Writer, is discussed in Section 7.1.

Go's interface mechanism is the topic of Chapter 7, but to give an idea of what it's capable of,
let's see how easy it is to combine the web server with the lissajous function so that animated GIFs are written not to the standard output, but to the HTTP client. Just add these
lines to the web server:

```
handler := func(w http.ResponseWriter, r *http.Request) {
    lissajous(w)
}
http.HandleFunc("/", handler)
```

or equivalently:

```
http.HandleFunc("/", func(w http.ResponseWriter, r *http.Request) {
    lissajous(w)
})
```

The second argument to the HandleFunc function call immediately above is a *function literal*,
that is, an anonymous function defined at its point of use. We will explain it further in
Section 5.6.

Once you've made this change, visit http://localhost:8000 in your browser. Each time you
load the page, you'll see a new animation like the one in Figure 1.3.

Exercise 1.12: Modify the Lissajous server to read parameter values from the URL. For example, you might arrange it so that a URL like http://localhost:8000/?cycles=20 sets the
number of cycles to 20 instead of the default 5. Use the strconv.Atoi function to convert the
string parameter into an integer. You can see its documentation with go doc strconv.Atoi.

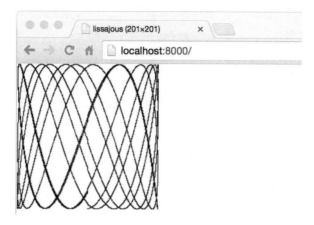

Figure 1.3. Animated Lissajous figures in a browser.

1.8. Loose Ends

There is a lot more to Go than we've covered in this quick introduction. Here are some topics we've barely touched upon or omitted entirely, with just enough discussion that they will be familiar when they make brief appearances before the full treatment.

Control flow: We covered the two fundamental control-flow statements, if and for, but not the switch statement, which is a multi-way branch. Here's a small example:

switch w. operand

```
switch coinflip() {
case "heads":
    heads++
case "tails":
    tails++
default:
    fmt.Println("landed on edge!")
}
```

The result of calling coinflip is compared to the value of each case. Cases are evaluated from top to bottom, so the first matching one is executed. The optional default case matches if none of the other cases does; it may be placed anywhere. Cases do not fall through from one to the next as in C-like languages (though there is a rarely used fallthrough statement that overrides this behavior).

A switch does not need an operand; it can just list the cases, each of which is a boolean expression:

switch w- no operand

```
func Signum(x int) int {
    switch {
    case x > 0:
        return +1
    default:
        return 0
    case x < 0:
        return -1
    }
}
```

This form is called a *tagless switch*; it's equivalent to switch true.

b 22   Like the for and if statements, a switch may include an optional simple statement—a short variable declaration, an increment or assignment statement, or a function call—that can be used to set a value before it is tested.

The break and continue statements modify the flow of control. A break causes control to resume at the next statement after the innermost for, switch, or select statement (which we'll see later), and as we saw in Section 1.3, a continue causes the innermost for loop to start its next iteration. Statements may be labeled so that break and continue can refer to them, for instance to break out of several nested loops at once or to start the next iteration of the outermost loop. There is even a goto statement, though it's intended for machine-generated code, not regular use by programmers.

Named types: A type declaration makes it possible to give a name to an existing type. Since struct types are often long, they are nearly always named. A familiar example is the definition of a Point type for a 2-D graphics system:

```
type Point struct {
    X, Y int
}
var p Point
```

Type declarations and named types are covered in Chapter 2.

27

Pointers: Go provides pointers, that is, values that contain the address of a variable. In some languages, notably C, pointers are relatively unconstrained. In other languages, pointers are disguised as "references," and there's not much that can be done with them except pass them around. Go takes a position somewhere in the middle. Pointers are explicitly visible. The & operator yields the address of a variable, and the * operator retrieves the variable that the pointer refers to, but there is no pointer arithmetic. We'll explain pointers in Section 2.3.2.

Methods and interfaces: A method is a function associated with a named type; Go is unusual in that methods may be attached to almost any named type. Methods are covered in Chapter 6. Interfaces are abstract types that let us treat different concrete types in the same way based on what methods they have, not how they are represented or implemented. Interfaces are the subject of Chapter 7.

155

171

Packages: Go comes with an extensive standard library of useful packages, and the Go community has created and shared many more. Programming is often more about using existing packages than about writing original code of one's own. Throughout the book, we will point out a couple of dozen of the most important standard packages, but there are many more we don't have space to mention, and we cannot provide anything remotely like a complete reference for any package.

Before you embark on any new program, it's a good idea to see if packages already exist that might help you get your job done more easily. You can find an index of the standard library packages at `https://golang.org/pkg` and the packages contributed by the community at `https://godoc.org`. The `go doc` tool makes these documents easily accessible from the command line:

```
$ go doc http.ListenAndServe
package http // import "net/http"

func ListenAndServe(addr string, handler Handler) error

    ListenAndServe listens on the TCP network address addr and then
    calls Serve with handler to handle requests on incoming connections.
...
```

Comments: We have already mentioned documentation comments at the beginning of a program or package. It's also good style to write a comment before the declaration of each function to specify its behavior. These conventions are important, because they are used by tools like go doc and godoc to locate and display documentation (§10.7.4).

For comments that span multiple lines or appear within an expression or statement, there is also the /* ... */ notation familiar from other languages. Such comments are sometimes used at the beginning of a file for a large block of explanatory text to avoid a // on every line. Within a comment, // and /* have no special meaning, so comments do not nest.

2

Program Structure

In Go, as in any other programming language, one builds large programs from a small set of basic constructs. Variables store values. Simple expressions are combined into larger ones with operations like addition and subtraction. Basic types are collected into aggregates like arrays and structs. Expressions are used in statements whose execution order is determined by control-flow statements like `if` and `for`. Statements are grouped into functions for isolation and reuse. Functions are gathered into source files and packages.

We saw examples of most of these in the previous chapter. In this chapter, we'll go into more detail about the basic structural elements of a Go program. The example programs are intentionally simple, so we can focus on the language without getting sidetracked by complicated algorithms or data structures.

2.1. Names

The names of Go functions, variables, constants, types, statement labels, and packages follow a simple rule: a name begins with a letter (that is, anything that Unicode deems a letter) or an underscore and may have any number of additional letters, digits, and underscores. Case matters: `heapSort` and `Heapsort` are different names.

Go has 25 *keywords* like `if` and `switch` that may be used only where the syntax permits; they can't be used as names.

break	default	func	interface	select
case	defer	go	map	struct
chan	else	goto	package	switch
const	fallthrough	if	range	type
continue	for	import	return	var

In addition, there are about three dozen *predeclared* names like int and true for built-in constants, types, and functions:

Constants: true false iota nil

Types: int int8 int16 int32 int64
                    uint uint8 uint16 uint32 uint64 uintptr
                    float32 float64 complex128 complex64
                    bool byte rune string error

Functions: make len cap new append copy close delete
                    complex real imag
                    panic recover

These names are not reserved, so you may use them in declarations. We'll see a handful of places where redeclaring one of them makes sense, but beware of the potential for confusion.

If an entity is declared within a function, it is *local* to that function. If declared outside of a function, however, it is visible in all files of the package to which it belongs. The case of the first letter of a name determines its visibility across package boundaries. If the name begins with an upper-case letter, it is *exported*, which means that it is visible and accessible outside of its own package and may be referred to by other parts of the program, as with Printf in the fmt package. Package names themselves are always in lower case.

There is no limit on name length, but convention and style in Go programs lean toward short names, especially for local variables with small scopes; you are much more likely to see variables named i than theLoopIndex. Generally, the larger the scope of a name, the longer and more meaningful it should be.

Stylistically, Go programmers use "camel case" when forming names by combining words; that is, interior capital letters are preferred over interior underscores. Thus the standard libraries have functions with names like QuoteRuneToASCII and parseRequestLine but never quote_rune_to_ASCII or parse_request_line. The letters of acronyms and initialisms like ASCII and HTML are always rendered in the same case, so a function might be called htmlEscape, HTMLEscape, or escapeHTML, but not escapeHtml.

2.2. Declarations

A *declaration* names a program entity and specifies some or all of its properties. There are four major kinds of declarations: var, const, type, and func. We'll talk about variables and types in this chapter, constants in Chapter 3, and functions in Chapter 5.

A Go program is stored in one or more files whose names end in .go. Each file begins with a package declaration that says what package the file is part of. The package declaration is followed by any import declarations, and then a sequence of *package-level* declarations of types, variables, constants, and functions, in any order. For example, this program declares a constant, a function, and a couple of variables:

gopl.io/ch2/boiling

```
// Boiling prints the boiling point of water.
package main

import "fmt"

const boilingF = 212.0

func main() {
    var f = boilingF
    var c = (f - 32) * 5 / 9
    fmt.Printf("boiling point = %g°F or %g°C\n", f, c)
    // Output:
    // boiling point = 212°F or 100°C
}
```

The constant boilingF is a package-level declaration (as is main), whereas the variables f and c are local to the function main. The name of each package-level entity is visible not only throughout the source file that contains its declaration, but throughout all the files of the package. By contrast, local declarations are visible only within the function in which they are declared and perhaps only within a small part of it.

A function declaration has a name, a list of parameters (the variables whose values are provided by the function's callers), an optional list of results, and the function body, which contains the statements that define what the function does. The result list is omitted if the function does not return anything. Execution of the function begins with the first statement and continues until it encounters a return statement or reaches the end of a function that has no results. Control and any results are then returned to the caller.

We've seen a fair number of functions already and there are lots more to come, including an extensive discussion in Chapter 5, so this is only a sketch. The function fToC below encapsulates the temperature conversion logic so that it is defined only once but may be used from multiple places. Here main calls it twice, using the values of two different local constants:

gopl.io/ch2/ftoc

```
// Ftoc prints two Fahrenheit-to-Celsius conversions.
package main

import "fmt"

func main() {
    const freezingF, boilingF = 32.0, 212.0
    fmt.Printf("%g°F = %g°C\n", freezingF, fToC(freezingF)) // "32°F = 0°C"
    fmt.Printf("%g°F = %g°C\n", boilingF, fToC(boilingF))   // "212°F = 100°C"
}

func fToC(f float64) float64 {
    return (f - 32) * 5 / 9
}
```

2.3. Variables

A `var` declaration creates a variable of a particular type, attaches a name to it, and sets its initial value. Each declaration has the general form

```
var name type = expression
```

Either the type or the `= expression` part may be omitted, but not both. If the type is omitted, it is determined by the initializer expression. If the expression is omitted, the initial value is the *zero value* for the type, which is `0` for numbers, `false` for booleans, `""` for strings, and `nil` for interfaces and reference types (slice, pointer, map, channel, function). The zero value of an aggregate type like an array or a struct has the zero value of all of its elements or fields.

The zero-value mechanism ensures that a variable always holds a well-defined value of its type; in Go there is no such thing as an uninitialized variable. This simplifies code and often ensures sensible behavior of boundary conditions without extra work. For example,

```
var s string
fmt.Println(s) // ""
```

prints an empty string, rather than causing some kind of error or unpredictable behavior. Go programmers often go to some effort to make the zero value of a more complicated type meaningful, so that variables begin life in a useful state.

It is possible to declare and optionally initialize a set of variables in a single declaration, with a matching list of expressions. Omitting the type allows declaration of multiple variables of different types:

```
var i, j, k int                    // int, int, int
var b, f, s = true, 2.3, "four" // bool, float64, string
```

Initializers may be literal values or arbitrary expressions. Package-level variables are initialized before `main` begins (§2.6.2), and local variables are initialized as their declarations are encountered during function execution.

A set of variables can also be initialized by calling a function that returns multiple values:

```
var f, err = os.Open(name) // os.Open returns a file and an error
```

2.3.1. Short Variable Declarations

Within a function, an alternate form called a *short variable declaration* may be used to declare and initialize local variables. It takes the form *name* := *expression*, and the type of *name* is determined by the type of *expression*. Here are three of the many short variable declarations in the `lissajous` function (§1.4):

```
anim := gif.GIF{LoopCount: nframes}
freq := rand.Float64() * 3.0
t := 0.0
```

Because of their brevity and flexibility, short variable declarations are used to declare and initialize the majority of local variables. A var declaration tends to be reserved for local variables that need an explicit type that differs from that of the initializer expression, or for when the variable will be assigned a value later and its initial value is unimportant.

```
i := 100                    // an int
var boiling float64 = 100 // a float64

var names []string
var err error
var p Point
```

As with var declarations, multiple variables may be declared and initialized in the same short variable declaration,

```
i, j := 0, 1
```

but declarations with multiple initializer expressions should be used only when they help readability, such as for short and natural groupings like the initialization part of a for loop.

Keep in mind that := is a declaration, whereas = is an assignment. A multi-variable declaration should not be confused with a *tuple assignment* (§2.4.1), in which each variable on the left-hand side is assigned the corresponding value from the right-hand side:

```
i, j = j, i // swap values of i and j
```

Like ordinary var declarations, short variable declarations may be used for calls to functions like os.Open that return two or more values:

```
f, err := os.Open(name)
if err != nil {
    return err
}
// ...use f...
f.Close()
```

One subtle but important point: a short variable declaration does not necessarily *declare* all the variables on its left-hand side. If some of them were already declared in the *same* lexical block (§2.7), then the short variable declaration acts like an *assignment* to those variables.

In the code below, the first statement declares both in and err. The second declares out but only assigns a value to the existing err variable.

```
in, err := os.Open(infile)
// ...
out, err := os.Create(outfile)
```

A short variable declaration must declare at least one new variable, however, so this code will not compile:

```
f, err := os.Open(infile)
// ...
f, err := os.Create(outfile) // compile error: no new variables
```

The fix is to use an ordinary assignment for the second statement.

A short variable declaration acts like an assignment only to variables that were already declared in the same lexical block; declarations in an outer block are ignored. We'll see examples of this at the end of the chapter.

2.3.2. Pointers

A *variable* is a piece of storage containing a value. Variables created by declarations are identified by a name, such as x, but many variables are identified only by expressions like x[i] or x.f. All these expressions read the value of a variable, except when they appear on the left-hand side of an assignment, in which case a new value is assigned to the variable.

A *pointer* value is the *address* of a variable. A pointer is thus the location at which a value is stored. Not every value has an address, but every variable does. With a pointer, we can read or update the value of a variable *indirectly*, without using or even knowing the name of the variable, if indeed it has a name.

If a variable is declared var x int, the expression &x ("address of x") yields a pointer to an integer variable, that is, a value of type *int, which is pronounced "pointer to int." If this value is called p, we say "p points to x," or equivalently "p contains the address of x." The variable to which p points is written *p. The expression *p yields the value of that variable, an int, but since *p denotes a variable, it may also appear on the left-hand side of an assignment, in which case the assignment updates the variable.

```
x := 1
p := &x          // p, of type *int, points to x
fmt.Println(*p) // "1"
*p = 2           // equivalent to x = 2
fmt.Println(x)  // "2"
```

Each component of a variable of aggregate type—a field of a struct or an element of an array—is also a variable and thus has an address too.

Variables are sometimes described as *addressable* values. Expressions that denote variables are the only expressions to which the *address-of* operator & may be applied.

The zero value for a pointer of any type is nil. The test p != nil is true if p points to a variable. Pointers are comparable; two pointers are equal if and only if they point to the same variable or both are nil.

```
var x, y int
fmt.Println(&x == &x, &x == &y, &x == nil) // "true false false"
```

It is perfectly safe for a function to return the address of a local variable. For instance, in the code below, the local variable v created by this particular call to f will remain in existence even after the call has returned, and the pointer p will still refer to it:

```
var p = f()

func f() *int {
    v := 1
    return &v
}
```

Each call of f returns a distinct value:

```
fmt.Println(f() == f()) // "false"
```

Because a pointer contains the address of a variable, passing a pointer argument to a function makes it possible for the function to update the variable that was indirectly passed. For example, this function increments the variable that its argument points to and returns the new value of the variable so it may be used in an expression:

```
func incr(p *int) int {
    *p++ // increments what p points to; does not change p
    return *p
}

v := 1
incr(&v)                // side effect: v is now 2
fmt.Println(incr(&v)) // "3" (and v is 3)
```

Each time we take the address of a variable or copy a pointer, we create new *aliases* or ways to identify the same variable. For example, *p is an alias for v. Pointer aliasing is useful because it allows us to access a variable without using its name, but this is a double-edged sword: to find all the statements that access a variable, we have to know all its aliases. It's not just pointers that create aliases; aliasing also occurs when we copy values of other reference types like slices, maps, and channels, and even structs, arrays, and interfaces that contain these types.

Pointers are key to the flag package, which uses a program's command-line arguments to set the values of certain variables distributed throughout the program. To illustrate, this variation on the earlier echo command takes two optional flags: -n causes echo to omit the trailing newline that would normally be printed, and -s sep causes it to separate the output arguments by the contents of the string sep instead of the default single space. Since this is our fourth version, the package is called gopl.io/ch2/echo4.

gopl.io/ch2/echo4
```
// Echo4 prints its command-line arguments.
package main

import (
    "flag"
    "fmt"
    "strings"
)

var n = flag.Bool("n", false, "omit trailing newline")
var sep = flag.String("s", " ", "separator")
```

```
func main() {
    flag.Parse()
    fmt.Print(strings.Join(flag.Args(), *sep))
    if !*n {
        fmt.Println()
    }
}
```

The function `flag.Bool` creates a new flag variable of type `bool`. It takes three arguments: the name of the flag (`"n"`), the variable's default value (`false`), and a message that will be printed if the user provides an invalid argument, an invalid flag, or `-h` or `-help`. Similarly, `flag.String` takes a name, a default value, and a message, and creates a `string` variable. The variables `sep` and `n` are pointers to the flag variables, which must be accessed indirectly as `*sep` and `*n`.

When the program is run, it must call `flag.Parse` before the flags are used, to update the flag variables from their default values. The non-flag arguments are available from `flag.Args()` as a slice of strings. If `flag.Parse` encounters an error, it prints a usage message and calls `os.Exit(2)` to terminate the program.

Let's run some test cases on echo:

```
$ go build gopl.io/ch2/echo4
$ ./echo4 a bc def
a bc def
$ ./echo4 -s / a bc def
a/bc/def
$ ./echo4 -n a bc def
a bc def$
$ ./echo4 -help
Usage of ./echo4:
  -n        omit trailing newline
  -s string
            separator (default " ")
```

2.3.3. The new Function

Another way to create a variable is to use the built-in function `new`. The expression `new(T)` creates an *unnamed variable* of type `T`, initializes it to the zero value of `T`, and returns its address, which is a value of type `*T`.

```
p := new(int)    // p, of type *int, points to an unnamed int variable
fmt.Println(*p)  // "0"
*p = 2           // sets the unnamed int to 2
fmt.Println(*p)  // "2"
```

A variable created with `new` is no different from an ordinary local variable whose address is taken, except that there's no need to invent (and declare) a dummy name, and we can use `new(T)` in an expression. Thus `new` is only a syntactic convenience, not a fundamental notion:

the two newInt functions below have identical behaviors.

```
func newInt() *int {              func newInt() *int {
    return new(int)                   var dummy int
}                                     return &dummy
                                  }
```

Each call to new returns a distinct variable with a unique address:

```
p := new(int)
q := new(int)
fmt.Println(p == q) // "false"
```

There is one exception to this rule: two variables whose type carries no information and is therefore of size zero, such as struct{} or [0]int, may, depending on the implementation, have the same address.

The new function is relatively rarely used because the most common unnamed variables are of struct types, for which the struct literal syntax (§4.4.1) is more flexible.

Since new is a predeclared function, not a keyword, it's possible to redefine the name for something else within a function, for example:

```
func delta(old, new int) int { return new - old }
```

Of course, within delta, the built-in new function is unavailable.

2.3.4. Lifetime of Variables

The *lifetime* of a variable is the interval of time during which it exists as the program executes. The lifetime of a package-level variable is the entire execution of the program. By contrast, local variables have dynamic lifetimes: a new instance is created each time the declaration statement is executed, and the variable lives on until it becomes *unreachable*, at which point its storage may be recycled. Function parameters and results are local variables too; they are created each time their enclosing function is called.

For example, in this excerpt from the Lissajous program of Section 1.4,

```
for t := 0.0; t < cycles*2*math.Pi; t += res {
    x := math.Sin(t)
    y := math.Sin(t*freq + phase)
    img.SetColorIndex(size+int(x*size+0.5), size+int(y*size+0.5),
        blackIndex)
}
```

the variable t is created each time the for loop begins, and new variables x and y are created on each iteration of the loop.

How does the garbage collector know that a variable's storage can be reclaimed? The full story is much more detailed than we need here, but the basic idea is that every package-level variable, and every local variable of each currently active function, can potentially be the start or root of a path to the variable in question, following pointers and other kinds of references that ultimately lead to the variable. If no such path exists, the variable has become unreachable, so it can no longer affect the rest of the computation.

Because the lifetime of a variable is determined only by whether or not it is reachable, a local variable may outlive a single iteration of the enclosing loop. It may continue to exist even after its enclosing function has returned.

A compiler may choose to allocate local variables on the heap or on the stack but, perhaps surprisingly, this choice is not determined by whether var or new was used to declare the variable.

```
var global *int

func f() {                      func g() {
    var x int                       y := new(int)
    x = 1                           *y = 1
    global = &x                 }
}
```

Here, x must be heap-allocated because it is still reachable from the variable global after f has returned, despite being declared as a local variable; we say x *escapes from* f. Conversely, when g returns, the variable *y becomes unreachable and can be recycled. Since *y does not escape from g, it's safe for the compiler to allocate *y on the stack, even though it was allocated with new. In any case, the notion of escaping is not something that you need to worry about in order to write correct code, though it's good to keep in mind during performance optimization, since each variable that escapes requires an extra memory allocation.

Garbage collection is a tremendous help in writing correct programs, but it does not relieve you of the burden of thinking about memory. You don't need to explicitly allocate and free memory, but to write efficient programs you still need to be aware of the lifetime of variables. For example, keeping unnecessary pointers to short-lived objects within long-lived objects, especially global variables, will prevent the garbage collector from reclaiming the short-lived objects.

2.4. Assignments

The value held by a variable is updated by an assignment statement, which in its simplest form has a variable on the left of the = sign and an expression on the right.

```
x = 1                           // named variable
*p = true                       // indirect variable
person.name = "bob"             // struct field
count[x] = count[x] * scale     // array or slice or map element
```

Each of the arithmetic and bitwise binary operators has a corresponding *assignment operator* allowing, for example, the last statement to be rewritten as

```
count[x] *= scale
```

which saves us from having to repeat (and re-evaluate) the expression for the variable.

Numeric variables can also be incremented and decremented by ++ and - - statements:

```
v := 1
v++     // same as v = v + 1; v becomes 2
v--     // same as v = v - 1; v becomes 1 again
```

2.4.1. Tuple Assignment

Another form of assignment, known as *tuple assignment*, allows several variables to be assigned at once. All of the right-hand side expressions are evaluated before any of the variables are updated, making this form most useful when some of the variables appear on both sides of the assignment, as happens, for example, when swapping the values of two variables:

```
x, y = y, x
a[i], a[j] = a[j], a[i]
```

or when computing the greatest common divisor (GCD) of two integers:

```
func gcd(x, y int) int {
    for y != 0 {
        x, y = y, x%y
    }
    return x
}
```

or when computing the *n*-th Fibonacci number iteratively:

```
func fib(n int) int {
    x, y := 0, 1
    for i := 0; i < n; i++ {
        x, y = y, x+y
    }
    return x
}
```

Tuple assignment can also make a sequence of trivial assignments more compact,

```
i, j, k = 2, 3, 5
```

though as a matter of style, avoid the tuple form if the expressions are complex; a sequence of separate statements is easier to read.

Certain expressions, such as a call to a function with multiple results, produce several values. When such a call is used in an assignment statement, the left-hand side must have as many variables as the function has results.

```
f, err = os.Open("foo.txt")   // function call returns two values
```

Often, functions use these additional results to indicate some kind of error, either by returning an error as in the call to os.Open, or a bool, usually called ok. As we'll see in later chapters, there are three operators that sometimes behave this way too. If a map lookup (§4.3), type assertion (§7.10), or channel receive (§8.4.2) appears in an assignment in which two results are expected, each produces an additional boolean result:

```
v, ok = m[key]              // map lookup
v, ok = x.(T)               // type assertion
v, ok = <-ch                // channel receive
```

As with variable declarations, we can assign unwanted values to the blank identifier:

```
_, err = io.Copy(dst, src) // discard byte count
_, ok = x.(T)               // check type but discard result
```

2.4.2. Assignability

Assignment statements are an explicit form of assignment, but there are many places in a program where an assignment occurs *implicitly*: a function call implicitly assigns the argument values to the corresponding parameter variables; a return statement implicitly assigns the return operands to the corresponding result variables; and a literal expression for a composite type (§4.2) such as this slice:

```
medals := []string{"gold", "silver", "bronze"}
```

implicitly assigns each element, as if it had been written like this:

```
medals[0] = "gold"
medals[1] = "silver"
medals[2] = "bronze"
```

The elements of maps and channels, though not ordinary variables, are also subject to similar implicit assignments.

An assignment, explicit or implicit, is always legal if the left-hand side (the variable) and the right-hand side (the value) have the same type. More generally, the assignment is legal only if the value is *assignable* to the type of the variable.

The rule for *assignability* has cases for various types, so we'll explain the relevant case as we introduce each new type. For the types we've discussed so far, the rules are simple: the types must exactly match, and nil may be assigned to any variable of interface or reference type. Constants (§3.6) have more flexible rules for assignability that avoid the need for most explicit conversions.

Whether two values may be compared with == and != is related to assignability: in any comparison, the first operand must be assignable to the type of the second operand, or vice versa. As with assignability, we'll explain the relevant cases for *comparability* when we present each new type.

2.5. Type Declarations

The type of a variable or expression defines the characteristics of the values it may take on, such as their size (number of bits or number of elements, perhaps), how they are represented internally, the intrinsic operations that can be performed on them, and the methods associated with them.

In any program there are variables that share the same representation but signify very different concepts. For instance, an int could be used to represent a loop index, a timestamp, a file descriptor, or a month; a float64 could represent a velocity in meters per second or a temperature in one of several scales; and a string could represent a password or the name of a color.

A type declaration defines a new *named type* that has the same *underlying type* as an existing type. The named type provides a way to separate different and perhaps incompatible uses of the underlying type so that they can't be mixed unintentionally.

```
type name underlying-type
```

Type declarations most often appear at package level, where the named type is visible throughout the package, and if the name is exported (it starts with an upper-case letter), it's accessible from other packages as well.

To illustrate type declarations, let's turn the different temperature scales into different types:

gopl.io/ch2/tempconv0

```go
// Package tempconv performs Celsius and Fahrenheit temperature computations.
package tempconv

import "fmt"

type Celsius float64
type Fahrenheit float64

const (
    AbsoluteZeroC Celsius = -273.15
    FreezingC     Celsius = 0
    BoilingC      Celsius = 100
)

func CToF(c Celsius) Fahrenheit { return Fahrenheit(c*9/5 + 32) }

func FToC(f Fahrenheit) Celsius { return Celsius((f - 32) * 5 / 9) }
```

This package defines two types, Celsius and Fahrenheit, for the two units of temperature. Even though both have the same underlying type, float64, they are not the same type, so they cannot be compared or combined in arithmetic expressions. Distinguishing the types makes it possible to avoid errors like inadvertently combining temperatures in the two different scales; an explicit type *conversion* like Celsius(t) or Fahrenheit(t) is required to convert from a float64. Celsius(t) and Fahrenheit(t) are conversions, not function calls. They don't change the value or representation in any way, but they make the change of meaning explicit. On the other hand, the functions CToF and FToC convert between the two scales; they *do* return different values.

For every type T, there is a corresponding conversion operation T(x) that converts the value x to type T. A conversion from one type to another is allowed if both have the same underlying type, or if both are unnamed pointer types that point to variables of the same underlying type; these conversions change the type but not the representation of the value. If x is assignable to T, a conversion is permitted but is usually redundant.

Conversions are also allowed between numeric types, and between string and some slice types, as we will see in the next chapter. These conversions may change the representation of the value. For instance, converting a floating-point number to an integer discards any fractional part, and converting a string to a [ ]byte slice allocates a copy of the string data. In any case, a conversion never fails at run time.

The underlying type of a named type determines its structure and representation, and also the set of intrinsic operations it supports, which are the same as if the underlying type had been used directly. That means that arithmetic operators work the same for Celsius and Fahrenheit as they do for float64, as you might expect.

```
fmt.Printf("%g\n", BoilingC-FreezingC) // "100" °C
boilingF := CToF(BoilingC)
fmt.Printf("%g\n", boilingF-CToF(FreezingC)) // "180" °F
fmt.Printf("%g\n", boilingF-FreezingC)        // compile error: type mismatch
```

Comparison operators like == and < can also be used to compare a value of a named type to another of the same type, or to a value of the underlying type. But two values of different named types cannot be compared directly:

```
var c Celsius
var f Fahrenheit
fmt.Println(c == 0)          // "true"
fmt.Println(f >= 0)          // "true"
fmt.Println(c == f)          // compile error: type mismatch
fmt.Println(c == Celsius(f)) // "true"!
```

Note the last case carefully. In spite of its name, the type conversion Celsius(f) does not change the value of its argument, just its type. The test is true because c and f are both zero.

A named type may provide notational convenience if it helps avoid writing out complex types over and over again. The advantage is small when the underlying type is simple like float64, but big for complicated types, as we will see when we discuss structs.

Named types also make it possible to define new behaviors for values of the type. These behaviors are expressed as a set of functions associated with the type, called the type's *methods*. We'll look at methods in detail in Chapter 6 but will give a taste of the mechanism here.

The declaration below, in which the Celsius parameter c appears before the function name, associates with the Celsius type a method named String that returns c's numeric value followed by °C:

```
func (c Celsius) String() string { return fmt.Sprintf("%g°C", c) }
```

Many types declare a `String` method of this form because it controls how values of the type appear when printed as a string by the `fmt` package, as we will see in Section 7.1.

```
c := FToC(212.0)
fmt.Println(c.String()) // "100°C"
fmt.Printf("%v\n", c)   // "100°C"; no need to call String explicitly
fmt.Printf("%s\n", c)   // "100°C"
fmt.Println(c)          // "100°C"
fmt.Printf("%g\n", c)   // "100"; does not call String
fmt.Println(float64(c)) // "100"; does not call String
```

2.6. Packages and Files

Packages in Go serve the same purposes as libraries or modules in other languages, supporting modularity, encapsulation, separate compilation, and reuse. The source code for a package resides in one or more `.go` files, usually in a directory whose name ends with the import path; for instance, the files of the `gopl.io/ch1/helloworld` package are stored in directory `$GOPATH/src/gopl.io/ch1/helloworld`.

Each package serves as a separate *name space* for its declarations. Within the `image` package, for example, the identifier `Decode` refers to a different function than does the same identifier in the `unicode/utf16` package. To refer to a function from outside its package, we must *qualify* the identifier to make explicit whether we mean `image.Decode` or `utf16.Decode`.

Packages also let us hide information by controlling which names are visible outside the package, or *exported*. In Go, a simple rule governs which identifiers are exported and which are not: exported identifiers start with an upper-case letter.

To illustrate the basics, suppose that our temperature conversion software has become popular and we want to make it available to the Go community as a new package. How do we do that?

Let's create a package called `gopl.io/ch2/tempconv`, a variation on the previous example. (Here we've made an exception to our usual rule of numbering examples in sequence, so that the package path can be more realistic.) The package itself is stored in two files to show how declarations in separate files of a package are accessed; in real life, a tiny package like this would need only one file.

We have put the declarations of the types, their constants, and their methods in `tempconv.go`:

gopl.io/ch2/tempconv
```
// Package tempconv performs Celsius and Fahrenheit conversions.
package tempconv

import "fmt"

type Celsius float64
type Fahrenheit float64
```

```
const (
    AbsoluteZeroC Celsius = -273.15
    FreezingC     Celsius = 0
    BoilingC      Celsius = 100
)

func (c Celsius) String() string    { return fmt.Sprintf("%g°C", c) }
func (f Fahrenheit) String() string { return fmt.Sprintf("%g°F", f) }
```

and the conversion functions in conv.go:

```
package tempconv

// CToF converts a Celsius temperature to Fahrenheit.
func CToF(c Celsius) Fahrenheit { return Fahrenheit(c*9/5 + 32) }

// FToC converts a Fahrenheit temperature to Celsius.
func FToC(f Fahrenheit) Celsius { return Celsius((f - 32) * 5 / 9) }
```

Each file starts with a package declaration that defines the package name. When the package is imported, its members are referred to as tempconv.CToF and so on. Package-level names like the types and constants declared in one file of a package are visible to all the other files of the package, as if the source code were all in a single file. Note that tempconv.go imports fmt, but conv.go does not, because it does not use anything from fmt.

Because the package-level const names begin with upper-case letters, they too are accessible with qualified names like tempconv.AbsoluteZeroC:

```
fmt.Printf("Brrrr! %v\n", tempconv.AbsoluteZeroC) // "Brrrr! -273.15°C"
```

To convert a Celsius temperature to Fahrenheit in a package that imports gopl.io/ch2/tempconv, we can write the following code:

```
fmt.Println(tempconv.CToF(tempconv.BoilingC)) // "212°F"
```

The *doc comment* (§10.7.4) immediately preceding the package declaration documents the package as a whole. Conventionally, it should start with a summary sentence in the style illustrated. Only one file in each package should have a package doc comment. Extensive doc comments are often placed in a file of their own, conventionally called doc.go.

Exercise 2.1: Add types, constants, and functions to tempconv for processing temperatures in the Kelvin scale, where zero Kelvin is −273.15°C and a difference of 1K has the same magnitude as 1°C.

2.6.1. Imports

Within a Go program, every package is identified by a unique string called its *import path*. These are the strings that appear in an import declaration like "gopl.io/ch2/tempconv". The language specification doesn't define where these strings come from or what they mean; it's up to the tools to interpret them. When using the go tool (Chapter 10), an import path denotes a directory containing one or more Go source files that together make up the package.

In addition to its import path, each package has a *package name*, which is the short (and not necessarily unique) name that appears in its `package` declaration. By convention, a package's name matches the last segment of its import path, making it easy to predict that the package name of `gopl.io/ch2/tempconv` is `tempconv`.

To use `gopl.io/ch2/tempconv`, we must import it:

gopl.io/ch2/cf
```go
// Cf converts its numeric argument to Celsius and Fahrenheit.
package main

import (
    "fmt"
    "os"
    "strconv"

    "gopl.io/ch2/tempconv"
)

func main() {
    for _, arg := range os.Args[1:] {
        t, err := strconv.ParseFloat(arg, 64)
        if err != nil {
            fmt.Fprintf(os.Stderr, "cf: %v\n", err)
            os.Exit(1)
        }
        f := tempconv.Fahrenheit(t)
        c := tempconv.Celsius(t)
        fmt.Printf("%s = %s, %s = %s\n",
            f, tempconv.FToC(f), c, tempconv.CToF(c))
    }
}
```

The import declaration binds a short name to the imported package that may be used to refer to its contents throughout the file. The `import` above lets us refer to names within `gopl.io/ch2/tempconv` by using a *qualified identifier* like `tempconv.CToF`. By default, the short name is the package name—`tempconv` in this case—but an import declaration may specify an alternative name to avoid a conflict (§10.4).

The `cf` program converts a single numeric command-line argument to its value in both Celsius and Fahrenheit:

```
$ go build gopl.io/ch2/cf
$ ./cf 32
32°F = 0°C, 32°C = 89.6°F
$ ./cf 212
212°F = 100°C, 212°C = 413.6°F
$ ./cf -40
-40°F = -40°C, -40°C = -40°F
```

It is an error to import a package and then not refer to it. This check helps eliminate dependencies that become unnecessary as the code evolves, although it can be a nuisance during debugging, since commenting out a line of code like log.Print("got here!") may remove the sole reference to the package name log, causing the compiler to emit an error. In this situation, you need to comment out or delete the unnecessary import.

Better still, use the golang.org/x/tools/cmd/goimports tool, which automatically inserts and removes packages from the import declaration as necessary; most editors can be configured to run goimports each time you save a file. Like the gofmt tool, it also pretty-prints Go source files in the canonical format.

Exercise 2.2: Write a general-purpose unit-conversion program analogous to cf that reads numbers from its command-line arguments or from the standard input if there are no arguments, and converts each number into units like temperature in Celsius and Fahrenheit, length in feet and meters, weight in pounds and kilograms, and the like.

2.6.2. Package Initialization

Package initialization begins by initializing package-level variables in the order in which they are declared, except that dependencies are resolved first:

```
var a = b + c     // a initialized third, to 3
var b = f()       // b initialized second, to 2, by calling f
var c = 1         // c initialized first, to 1

func f() int { return c + 1 }
```

If the package has multiple .go files, they are initialized in the order in which the files are given to the compiler; the go tool sorts .go files by name before invoking the compiler.

Each variable declared at package level starts life with the value of its initializer expression, if any, but for some variables, like tables of data, an initializer expression may not be the simplest way to set its initial value. In that case, the init function mechanism may be simpler. Any file may contain any number of functions whose declaration is just

```
func init() { /* ... */ }
```

Such init functions can't be called or referenced, but otherwise they are normal functions. Within each file, init functions are automatically executed when the program starts, in the order in which they are declared.

One package is initialized at a time, in the order of imports in the program, dependencies first, so a package p importing q can be sure that q is fully initialized before p's initialization begins. Initialization proceeds from the bottom up; the main package is the last to be initialized. In this manner, all packages are fully initialized before the application's main function begins.

The package below defines a function PopCount that returns the number of set bits, that is, bits whose value is 1, in a uint64 value, which is called its *population count*. It uses an init function to precompute a table of results, pc, for each possible 8-bit value so that the PopCount function needn't take 64 steps but can just return the sum of eight table lookups. (This is definitely *not* the fastest algorithm for counting bits, but it's convenient for illustrating init functions, and for showing how to precompute a table of values, which is often a useful programming technique.)

gopl.io/ch2/popcount

```
package popcount

// pc[i] is the population count of i.
var pc [256]byte

func init() {
    for i := range pc {
        pc[i] = pc[i/2] + byte(i&1)
    }
}

// PopCount returns the population count (number of set bits) of x.
func PopCount(x uint64) int {
    return int(pc[byte(x>>(0*8))] +
        pc[byte(x>>(1*8))] +
        pc[byte(x>>(2*8))] +
        pc[byte(x>>(3*8))] +
        pc[byte(x>>(4*8))] +
        pc[byte(x>>(5*8))] +
        pc[byte(x>>(6*8))] +
        pc[byte(x>>(7*8))])
}
```

Note that the range loop in init uses only the index; the value is unnecessary and thus need not be included. The loop could also have been written as

```
for i, _ := range pc {
```

We'll see other uses of init functions in the next section and in Section 10.5.

Exercise 2.3: Rewrite PopCount to use a loop instead of a single expression. Compare the performance of the two versions. (Section 11.4 shows how to compare the performance of different implementations systematically.)

Exercise 2.4: Write a version of PopCount that counts bits by shifting its argument through 64 bit positions, testing the rightmost bit each time. Compare its performance to the table-lookup version.

Exercise 2.5: The expression x&(x-1) clears the rightmost non-zero bit of x. Write a version of PopCount that counts bits by using this fact, and assess its performance.

2.7. Scope

A declaration associates a name with a program entity, such as a function or a variable. The *scope* of a declaration is the part of the source code where a use of the declared name refers to that declaration.

Don't confuse scope with lifetime. The scope of a declaration is a region of the program text; it is a compile-time property. The lifetime of a variable is the range of time during execution when the variable can be referred to by other parts of the program; it is a run-time property.

A syntactic *block* is a sequence of statements enclosed in braces like those that surround the body of a function or loop. A name declared inside a syntactic block is not visible outside that block. The block encloses its declarations and determines their scope. We can generalize this notion of blocks to include other groupings of declarations that are not explicitly surrounded by braces in the source code; we'll call them all *lexical blocks*. There is a lexical block for the entire source code, called the *universe block*; for each package; for each file; for each for, if, and switch statement; for each case in a switch or select statement; and, of course, for each explicit syntactic block.

A declaration's lexical block determines its scope, which may be large or small. The declarations of built-in types, functions, and constants like int, len, and true are in the universe block and can be referred to throughout the entire program. Declarations outside any function, that is, at *package level*, can be referred to from any file in the same package. Imported packages, such as fmt in the tempconv example, are declared at the *file level*, so they can be referred to from the same file, but not from another file in the same package without another import. Many declarations, like that of the variable c in the tempconv.CToF function, are *local*, so they can be referred to only from within the same function or perhaps just a part of it.

The scope of a control-flow label, as used by break, continue, and goto statements, is the entire enclosing function.

A program may contain multiple declarations of the same name so long as each declaration is in a different lexical block. For example, you can declare a local variable with the same name as a package-level variable. Or, as shown in Section 2.3.3, you can declare a function parameter called new, even though a function of this name is predeclared in the universe block. Don't overdo it, though; the larger the scope of the redeclaration, the more likely you are to surprise the reader.

When the compiler encounters a reference to a name, it looks for a declaration, starting with the innermost enclosing lexical block and working up to the universe block. If the compiler finds no declaration, it reports an "undeclared name" error. If a name is declared in both an outer block and an inner block, the inner declaration will be found first. In that case, the inner declaration is said to *shadow* or *hide* the outer one, making it inaccessible:

```
func f() {}

var g = "g"

func main() {
    f := "f"
    fmt.Println(f) // "f"; local var f shadows package-level func f
    fmt.Println(g) // "g"; package-level var
    fmt.Println(h) // compile error: undefined: h
}
```

Within a function, lexical blocks may be nested to arbitrary depth, so one local declaration can shadow another. Most blocks are created by control-flow constructs like if statements and for loops. The program below has three different variables called x because each declaration appears in a different lexical block. (This example illustrates scope rules, not good style!)

```go
func main() {
    x := "hello!"
    for i := 0; i < len(x); i++ {
        x := x[i]
        if x != '!' {
            x := x + 'A' - 'a'
            fmt.Printf("%c", x) // "HELLO" (one letter per iteration)
        }
    }
}
```

The expressions x[i] and x + 'A' - 'a' each refer to a declaration of x from an outer block; we'll explain that in a moment. (Note that the latter expression is *not* equivalent to unicode.ToUpper.)

As mentioned above, not all lexical blocks correspond to explicit brace-delimited sequences of statements; some are merely implied. The for loop above creates two lexical blocks: the explicit block for the loop body, and an implicit block that additionally encloses the variables declared by the initialization clause, such as i. The scope of a variable declared in the implicit block is the condition, post-statement (i++), and body of the for statement.

The example below also has three variables named x, each declared in a different block—one in the function body, one in the for statement's block, and one in the loop body—but only two of the blocks are explicit:

```go
func main() {
    x := "hello"
    for _, x := range x {
        x := x + 'A' - 'a'
        fmt.Printf("%c", x) // "HELLO" (one letter per iteration)
    }
}
```

Like for loops, if statements and switch statements also create implicit blocks in addition to their body blocks. The code in the following if-else chain shows the scope of x and y:

```go
if x := f(); x == 0 {
    fmt.Println(x)
} else if y := g(x); x == y {
    fmt.Println(x, y)
} else {
    fmt.Println(x, y)
}
fmt.Println(x, y) // compile error: x and y are not visible here
```

The second if statement is nested within the first, so variables declared within the first statement's initializer are visible within the second. Similar rules apply to each case of a switch statement: there is a block for the condition and a block for each case body.

At the package level, the order in which declarations appear has no effect on their scope, so a declaration may refer to itself or to another that follows it, letting us declare recursive or mutually recursive types and functions. The compiler will report an error if a constant or variable declaration refers to itself, however.

In this program:

```
if f, err := os.Open(fname); err != nil { // compile error: unused: f
    return err
}
f.ReadByte() // compile error: undefined f
f.Close()    // compile error: undefined f
```

the scope of f is just the if statement, so f is not accessible to the statements that follow, resulting in compiler errors. Depending on the compiler, you may get an additional error reporting that the local variable f was never used.

Thus it is often necessary to declare f before the condition so that it is accessible after:

```
f, err := os.Open(fname)
if err != nil {
    return err
}
f.ReadByte()
f.Close()
```

You may be tempted to avoid declaring f and err in the outer block by moving the calls to ReadByte and Close inside an else block:

```
if f, err := os.Open(fname); err != nil {
    return err
} else {
    // f and err are visible here too
    f.ReadByte()
    f.Close()
}
```

but normal practice in Go is to deal with the error in the if block and then return, so that the successful execution path is not indented.

Short variable declarations demand an awareness of scope. Consider the program below, which starts by obtaining its current working directory and saving it in a package-level variable. This could be done by calling os.Getwd in function main, but it might be better to separate this concern from the primary logic, especially if failing to get the directory is a fatal error. The function log.Fatalf prints a message and calls os.Exit(1).

```
    var cwd string

    func init() {
        cwd, err := os.Getwd() // compile error: unused: cwd
        if err != nil {
            log.Fatalf("os.Getwd failed: %v", err)
        }
    }
```

Since neither cwd nor err is already declared in the init function's block, the := statement declares both of them as local variables. The inner declaration of cwd makes the outer one inaccessible, so the statement does not update the package-level cwd variable as intended.

Current Go compilers detect that the local cwd variable is never used and report this as an error, but they are not strictly required to perform this check. Furthermore, a minor change, such as the addition of a logging statement that refers to the local cwd would defeat the check.

```
    var cwd string

    func init() {
        cwd, err := os.Getwd() // NOTE: wrong!
        if err != nil {
            log.Fatalf("os.Getwd failed: %v", err)
        }
        log.Printf("Working directory = %s", cwd)
    }
```

The global cwd variable remains uninitialized, and the apparently normal log output obfuscates the bug.

There are a number of ways to deal with this potential problem. The most direct is to avoid := by declaring err in a separate var declaration:

```
    var cwd string

    func init() {
        var err error
        cwd, err = os.Getwd()
        if err != nil {
            log.Fatalf("os.Getwd failed: %v", err)
        }
    }
```

We've now seen how packages, files, declarations, and statements express the structure of programs. In the next two chapters, we'll look at the structure of data.

3

Basic Data Types

It's all bits at the bottom, of course, but computers operate fundamentally on fixed-size numbers called *words*, which are interpreted as integers, floating-point numbers, bit sets, or memory addresses, then combined into larger aggregates that represent packets, pixels, portfolios, poetry, and everything else. Go offers a variety of ways to organize data, with a spectrum of data types that at one end match the features of the hardware and at the other end provide what programmers need to conveniently represent complicated data structures.

Go's types fall into four categories: *basic types*, *aggregate types*, *reference types*, and *interface types*. Basic types, the topic of this chapter, include numbers, strings, and booleans. Aggregate types—arrays (§4.1) and structs (§4.4)—form more complicated data types by combining values of several simpler ones. Reference types are a diverse group that includes pointers (§2.3.2), slices (§4.2), maps (§4.3), functions (Chapter 5), and channels (Chapter 8), but what they have in common is that they all refer to program variables or state *indirectly*, so that the effect of an operation applied to one reference is observed by all copies of that reference. Finally, we'll talk about interface types in Chapter 7.

3.1. Integers

Go's numeric data types include several sizes of integers, floating-point numbers, and complex numbers. Each numeric type determines the size and signedness of its values. Let's begin with integers.

Go provides both signed and unsigned integer arithmetic. There are four distinct sizes of signed integers—8, 16, 32, and 64 bits—represented by the types int8, int16, int32, and int64, and corresponding unsigned versions uint8, uint16, uint32, and uint64.

There are also two types called just int and uint that are the natural or most efficient size for signed and unsigned integers on a particular platform; int is by far the most widely used numeric type. Both these types have the same size, either 32 or 64 bits, but one must not make assumptions about which; different compilers may make different choices even on identical hardware.

The type rune is a synonym for int32 and conventionally indicates that a value is a Unicode code point. The two names may be used interchangeably. Similarly, the type byte is a synonym for uint8, and emphasizes that the value is a piece of raw data rather than a small numeric quantity.

Finally, there is an unsigned integer type uintptr, whose width is not specified but is sufficient to hold all the bits of a pointer value. The uintptr type is used only for low-level programming, such as at the boundary of a Go program with a C library or an operating system. We'll see examples of this when we deal with the unsafe package in Chapter 13.

Regardless of their size, int, uint, and uintptr are different types from their explicitly sized siblings. Thus int is not the same type as int32, even if the natural size of integers is 32 bits, and an explicit conversion is required to use an int value where an int32 is needed, and vice versa.

Signed numbers are represented in 2's-complement form, in which the high-order bit is reserved for the sign of the number and the range of values of an n-bit number is from -2^{n-1} to $2^{n-1}-1$. Unsigned integers use the full range of bits for non-negative values and thus have the range 0 to 2^n-1. For instance, the range of int8 is -128 to 127, whereas the range of uint8 is 0 to 255.

Go's binary operators for arithmetic, logic, and comparison are listed here in order of decreasing precedence:

```
*    /    %    <<    >>    &    &^
+    -    |    ^
==   !=   <    <=    >     >=
&&
||
```

There are only five levels of precedence for binary operators. Operators at the same level associate to the left, so parentheses may be required for clarity, or to make the operators evaluate in the intended order in an expression like mask & (1 << 28).

Each operator in the first two lines of the table above, for instance +, has a corresponding *assignment operator* like += that may be used to abbreviate an assignment statement.

The integer arithmetic operators +, -, *, and / may be applied to integer, floating-point, and complex numbers, but the remainder operator % applies only to integers. The behavior of % for negative numbers varies across programming languages. In Go, the sign of the remainder is always the same as the sign of the dividend, so -5%3 and -5%-3 are both -2. The behavior of / depends on whether its operands are integers, so 5.0/4.0 is 1.25, but 5/4 is 1 because integer division truncates the result toward zero.

If the result of an arithmetic operation, whether signed or unsigned, has more bits than can be represented in the result type, it is said to *overflow*. The high-order bits that do not fit are silently discarded. If the original number is a signed type, the result could be negative if the leftmost bit is a 1, as in the int8 example here:

```
var u uint8 = 255
fmt.Println(u, u+1, u*u) // "255 0 1"

var i int8 = 127
fmt.Println(i, i+1, i*i) // "127 -128 1"
```

Two integers of the same type may be compared using the binary comparison operators below; the type of a comparison expression is a boolean.

==	equal to
!=	not equal to
<	less than
<=	less than or equal to
>	greater than
>=	greater than or equal to

In fact, all values of basic type—booleans, numbers, and strings—are *comparable*, meaning that two values of the same type may be compared using the == and != operators. Furthermore, integers, floating-point numbers, and strings are *ordered* by the comparison operators. The values of many other types are not comparable, and no other types are ordered. As we encounter each type, we'll present the rules governing the *comparability* of its values.

There are also unary addition and subtraction operators:

+	unary positive (no effect)
-	unary negation

For integers, +x is a shorthand for 0+x and -x is a shorthand for 0-x; for floating-point and complex numbers, +x is just x and -x is the negation of x.

Go also provides the following bitwise binary operators, the first four of which treat their operands as bit patterns with no concept of arithmetic carry or sign:

&	bitwise AND
|	bitwise OR
^	bitwise XOR
&^	bit clear (AND NOT)
<<	left shift
>>	right shift

The operator ^ is bitwise exclusive OR (XOR) when used as a binary operator, but when used as a unary prefix operator it is bitwise negation or complement; that is, it returns a value with each bit in its operand inverted. The &^ operator is bit clear (AND NOT): in the expression z = x &^ y, each bit of z is 0 if the corresponding bit of y is 1; otherwise it equals the corresponding bit of x.

The code below shows how bitwise operations can be used to interpret a `uint8` value as a compact and efficient set of 8 independent bits. It uses `Printf`'s `%b` verb to print a number's binary digits; `08` modifies `%b` (an adverb!) to pad the result with zeros to exactly 8 digits.

```go
var x uint8 = 1<<1 | 1<<5
var y uint8 = 1<<1 | 1<<2

fmt.Printf("%08b\n", x)    // "00100010", the set {1, 5}
fmt.Printf("%08b\n", y)    // "00000110", the set {1, 2}

fmt.Printf("%08b\n", x&y)  // "00000010", the intersection {1}
fmt.Printf("%08b\n", x|y)  // "00100110", the union {1, 2, 5}
fmt.Printf("%08b\n", x^y)  // "00100100", the symmetric difference {2, 5}
fmt.Printf("%08b\n", x&^y) // "00100000", the difference {5}

for i := uint(0); i < 8; i++ {
    if x&(1<<i) != 0 { // membership test
        fmt.Println(i) // "1", "5"
    }
}

fmt.Printf("%08b\n", x<<1) // "01000100", the set {2, 6}
fmt.Printf("%08b\n", x>>1) // "00010001", the set {0, 4}
```

(Section 6.5 shows an implementation of integer sets that can be much bigger than a byte.)

In the shift operations `x<<n` and `x>>n`, the `n` operand determines the number of bit positions to shift and must be unsigned; the `x` operand may be unsigned or signed. Arithmetically, a left shift `x<<n` is equivalent to multiplication by 2^n and a right shift `x>>n` is equivalent to the floor of division by 2^n.

Left shifts fill the vacated bits with zeros, as do right shifts of unsigned numbers, but right shifts of signed numbers fill the vacated bits with copies of the sign bit. For this reason, it is important to use unsigned arithmetic when you're treating an integer as a bit pattern.

Although Go provides unsigned numbers and arithmetic, we tend to use the signed `int` form even for quantities that can't be negative, such as the length of an array, though `uint` might seem a more obvious choice. Indeed, the built-in `len` function returns a signed `int`, as in this loop which announces prize medals in reverse order:

```go
medals := []string{"gold", "silver", "bronze"}
for i := len(medals) - 1; i >= 0; i-- {
    fmt.Println(medals[i]) // "bronze", "silver", "gold"
}
```

The alternative would be calamitous. If `len` returned an unsigned number, then `i` too would be a `uint`, and the condition `i >= 0` would always be true by definition. After the third iteration, in which `i == 0`, the `i--` statement would cause `i` to become not -1, but the maximum uint value (for example, $2^{64}-1$), and the evaluation of `medals[i]` would fail at run time, or *panic* (§5.9), by attempting to access an element outside the bounds of the slice.

For this reason, unsigned numbers tend to be used only when their bitwise operators or peculiar arithmetic operators are required, as when implementing bit sets, parsing binary file formats, or for hashing and cryptography. They are typically not used for merely non-negative quantities.

In general, an explicit conversion is required to convert a value from one type to another, and binary operators for arithmetic and logic (except shifts) must have operands of the same type. Although this occasionally results in longer expressions, it also eliminates a whole class of problems and makes programs easier to understand.

As an example familiar from other contexts, consider this sequence:

```
var apples int32 = 1
var oranges int16 = 2
var compote int = apples + oranges // compile error
```

Attempting to compile these three declarations produces an error message:

```
invalid operation: apples + oranges (mismatched types int32 and int16)
```

This type mismatch can be fixed in several ways, most directly by converting everything to a common type:

```
var compote = int(apples) + int(oranges)
```

As described in Section 2.5, for every type T, the conversion operation T(x) converts the value x to type T if the conversion is allowed. Many integer-to-integer conversions do not entail any change in value; they just tell the compiler how to interpret a value. But a conversion that narrows a big integer into a smaller one, or a conversion from integer to floating-point or vice versa, may change the value or lose precision:

```
f := 3.141 // a float64
i := int(f)
fmt.Println(f, i)   // "3.141 3"
f = 1.99
fmt.Println(int(f)) // "1"
```

Float to integer conversion discards any fractional part, truncating toward zero. You should avoid conversions in which the operand is out of range for the target type, because the behavior depends on the implementation:

```
f := 1e100  // a float64
i := int(f) // result is implementation-dependent
```

Integer literals of any size and type can be written as ordinary decimal numbers, or as octal numbers if they begin with 0, as in 0666, or as hexadecimal if they begin with 0x or 0X, as in 0xdeadbeef. Hex digits may be upper or lower case. Nowadays octal numbers seem to be used for exactly one purpose—file permissions on POSIX systems—but hexadecimal numbers are widely used to emphasize the bit pattern of a number over its numeric value.

When printing numbers using the fmt package, we can control the radix and format with the %d, %o, and %x verbs, as shown in this example:

```
o := 0666
fmt.Printf("%d %[1]o %#[1]o\n", o) // "438 666 0666"
x := int64(0xdeadbeef)
fmt.Printf("%d %[1]x %#[1]x %#[1]X\n", x)
// Output:
// 3735928559 deadbeef 0xdeadbeef 0XDEADBEEF
```

Note the use of two `fmt` tricks. Usually a `Printf` format string containing multiple % verbs would require the same number of extra operands, but the `[1]` "adverbs" after % tell `Printf` to use the first operand over and over again. Second, the # adverb for %o or %x or %X tells `Printf` to emit a 0 or 0x or 0X prefix respectively.

Rune literals are written as a character within single quotes. The simplest example is an ASCII character like `'a'`, but it's possible to write any Unicode code point either directly or with numeric escapes, as we will see shortly.

Runes are printed with %c, or with %q if quoting is desired:

```
ascii := 'a'
unicode := '国'
newline := '\n'
fmt.Printf("%d %[1]c %[1]q\n", ascii)   // "97 a 'a'"
fmt.Printf("%d %[1]c %[1]q\n", unicode) // "22269 国 '国'"
fmt.Printf("%d %[1]q\n", newline)       // "10 '\n'"
```

3.2. Floating-Point Numbers

Go provides two sizes of floating-point numbers, `float32` and `float64`. Their arithmetic properties are governed by the IEEE 754 standard implemented by all modern CPUs.

Values of these numeric types range from tiny to huge. The limits of floating-point values can be found in the `math` package. The constant `math.MaxFloat32`, the largest `float32`, is about `3.4e38`, and `math.MaxFloat64` is about `1.8e308`. The smallest positive values are near `1.4e-45` and `4.9e-324`, respectively.

A `float32` provides approximately six decimal digits of precision, whereas a `float64` provides about 15 digits; `float64` should be preferred for most purposes because `float32` computations accumulate error rapidly unless one is quite careful, and the smallest positive integer that cannot be exactly represented as a `float32` is not large:

```
var f float32 = 16777216 // 1 << 24
fmt.Println(f == f+1)    // "true"!
```

Floating-point numbers can be written literally using decimals, like this:

```
const e = 2.71828 // (approximately)
```

Digits may be omitted before the decimal point (`.707`) or after it (`1.`). Very small or very large numbers are better written in scientific notation, with the letter e or E preceding the decimal exponent:

```
const Avogadro = 6.02214129e23
const Planck   = 6.62606957e-34
```

Floating-point values are conveniently printed with Printf's %g verb, which chooses the most compact representation that has adequate precision, but for tables of data, the %e (exponent) or %f (no exponent) forms may be more appropriate. All three verbs allow field width and numeric precision to be controlled.

```
for x := 0; x < 8; x++ {
    fmt.Printf("x = %d   eˣ = %8.3f\n", x, math.Exp(float64(x)))
}
```

The code above prints the powers of e with three decimal digits of precision, aligned in an eight-character field:

```
x = 0   eˣ =    1.000
x = 1   eˣ =    2.718
x = 2   eˣ =    7.389
x = 3   eˣ =   20.086
x = 4   eˣ =   54.598
x = 5   eˣ =  148.413
x = 6   eˣ =  403.429
x = 7   eˣ = 1096.633
```

In addition to a large collection of the usual mathematical functions, the math package has functions for creating and detecting the special values defined by IEEE 754: the positive and negative infinities, which represent numbers of excessive magnitude and the result of division by zero; and NaN ("not a number"), the result of such mathematically dubious operations as 0/0 or Sqrt(-1).

```
var z float64
fmt.Println(z, -z, 1/z, -1/z, z/z) //  "0 -0 +Inf -Inf NaN"
```

The function math.IsNaN tests whether its argument is a not-a-number value, and math.NaN returns such a value. It's tempting to use NaN as a sentinel value in a numeric computation, but testing whether a specific computational result is equal to NaN is fraught with peril because any comparison with NaN *always* yields false:

```
nan := math.NaN()
fmt.Println(nan == nan, nan < nan, nan > nan) // "false false false"
```

If a function that returns a floating-point result might fail, it's better to report the failure separately, like this:

```
func compute() (value float64, ok bool) {
    // ...
    if failed {
        return 0, false
    }
    return result, true
}
```

The next program illustrates floating-point graphics computation. It plots a function of two variables z = f(x, y) as a wire mesh 3-D surface, using Scalable Vector Graphics (SVG), a standard XML notation for line drawings. Figure 3.1 shows an example of its output for the function sin(r)/r, where r is sqrt(x*x+y*y).

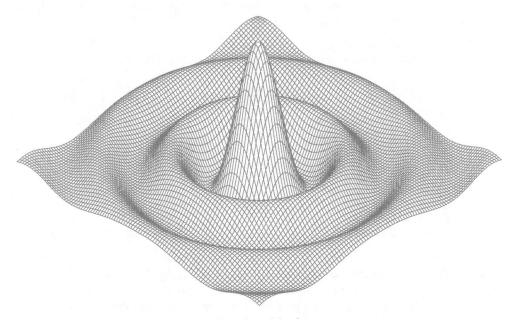

Figure 3.1. A surface plot of the function sin(r)/r.

gopl.io/ch3/surface

```go
// Surface computes an SVG rendering of a 3-D surface function.
package main

import (
    "fmt"
    "math"
)

const (
    width, height = 600, 320            // canvas size in pixels
    cells         = 100                 // number of grid cells
    xyrange       = 30.0                // axis ranges (-xyrange..+xyrange)
    xyscale       = width / 2 / xyrange // pixels per x or y unit
    zscale        = height * 0.4        // pixels per z unit
    angle         = math.Pi / 6         // angle of x, y axes (=30°)
)

var sin30, cos30 = math.Sin(angle), math.Cos(angle) // sin(30°), cos(30°)
```

```go
func main() {
    fmt.Printf("<svg xmlns='http://www.w3.org/2000/svg' "+
        "style='stroke: grey; fill: white; stroke-width: 0.7' "+
        "width='%d' height='%d'>", width, height)
    for i := 0; i < cells; i++ {
        for j := 0; j < cells; j++ {
            ax, ay := corner(i+1, j)
            bx, by := corner(i, j)
            cx, cy := corner(i, j+1)
            dx, dy := corner(i+1, j+1)
            fmt.Printf("<polygon points='%g,%g %g,%g %g,%g %g,%g'/>\n",
                ax, ay, bx, by, cx, cy, dx, dy)
        }
    }
    fmt.Println("</svg>")
}

func corner(i, j int) (float64, float64) {
    // Find point (x,y) at corner of cell (i,j).
    x := xyrange * (float64(i)/cells - 0.5)
    y := xyrange * (float64(j)/cells - 0.5)

    // Compute surface height z.
    z := f(x, y)

    // Project (x,y,z) isometrically onto 2-D SVG canvas (sx,sy).
    sx := width/2 + (x-y)*cos30*xyscale
    sy := height/2 + (x+y)*sin30*xyscale - z*zscale
    return sx, sy
}

func f(x, y float64) float64 {
    r := math.Hypot(x, y) // distance from (0,0)
    return math.Sin(r) / r
}
```

Notice that the function corner returns two values, the coordinates of the corner of the cell.

The explanation of how the program works requires only basic geometry, but it's fine to skip over it, since the point is to illustrate floating-point computation. The essence of the program is mapping between three different coordinate systems, shown in Figure 3.2. The first is a 2-D grid of 100×100 cells identified by integer coordinates (i, j), starting at $(0, 0)$ in the far back corner. We plot from the back to the front so that background polygons may be obscured by foreground ones.

The second coordinate system is a mesh of 3-D floating-point coordinates (x, y, z), where x and y are linear functions of i and j, translated so that the origin is in the center, and scaled by the constant xyrange. The height z is the value of the surface function $f(x, y)$.

The third coordinate system is the 2-D image canvas, with $(0, 0)$ in the top left corner. Points in this plane are denoted (sx, sy). We use an isometric projection to map each 3-D point

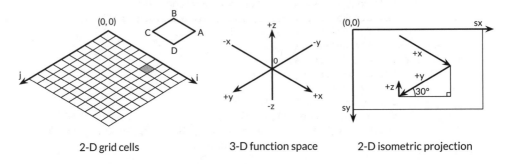

Figure 3.2. Three different coordinate systems.

(x, y, z) onto the 2-D canvas. A point appears farther to the right on the canvas the greater its x value or the *smaller* its y value. And a point appears farther down the canvas the greater its x value *or* y value, and the smaller its z value. The vertical and horizontal scale factors for x and y are derived from the sine and cosine of a 30° angle. The scale factor for z, 0.4, is an arbitrary parameter.

For each cell in the 2-D grid, the main function computes the coordinates on the image canvas of the four corners of the polygon *ABCD*, where *B* corresponds to (i, j) and *A*, *C*, and *D* are its neighbors, then prints an SVG instruction to draw it.

Exercise 3.1: If the function `f` returns a non-finite `float64` value, the SVG file will contain invalid `<polygon>` elements (although many SVG renderers handle this gracefully). Modify the program to skip invalid polygons.

Exercise 3.2: Experiment with visualizations of other functions from the `math` package. Can you produce an egg box, moguls, or a saddle?

Exercise 3.3: Color each polygon based on its height, so that the peaks are colored red (`#ff0000`) and the valleys blue (`#0000ff`).

Exercise 3.4: Following the approach of the Lissajous example in Section 1.7, construct a web server that computes surfaces and writes SVG data to the client. The server must set the Content-Type header like this:

```
w.Header().Set("Content-Type", "image/svg+xml")
```

(This step was not required in the Lissajous example because the server uses standard heuristics to recognize common formats like PNG from the first 512 bytes of the response, and generates the proper header.) Allow the client to specify values like height, width, and color as HTTP request parameters.

3.3. Complex Numbers

Go provides two sizes of complex numbers, `complex64` and `complex128`, whose components are `float32` and `float64` respectively. The built-in function `complex` creates a complex number from its real and imaginary components, and the built-in `real` and `imag` functions extract those components:

```
var x complex128 = complex(1, 2) // 1+2i
var y complex128 = complex(3, 4) // 3+4i
fmt.Println(x*y)                 // "(-5+10i)"
fmt.Println(real(x*y))           // "-5"
fmt.Println(imag(x*y))           // "10"
```

If a floating-point literal or decimal integer literal is immediately followed by i, such as `3.141592i` or `2i`, it becomes an *imaginary literal*, denoting a complex number with a zero real component:

```
fmt.Println(1i * 1i) // "(-1+0i)", i² = -1
```

Under the rules for constant arithmetic, complex constants can be added to other numeric constants (integer or floating point, real or imaginary), allowing us to write complex numbers naturally, like `1+2i` or, equivalently, `2i+1`. The declarations of x and y above can be simplified:

```
x := 1 + 2i
y := 3 + 4i
```

Complex numbers may be compared for equality with `==` and `!=`. Two complex numbers are equal if their real parts are equal and their imaginary parts are equal.

The `math/cmplx` package provides library functions for working with complex numbers, such as the complex square root and exponentiation functions.

```
fmt.Println(cmplx.Sqrt(-1)) // "(0+1i)"
```

The following program uses `complex128` arithmetic to generate a Mandelbrot set.

gopl.io/ch3/mandelbrot
```
// Mandelbrot emits a PNG image of the Mandelbrot fractal.
package main

import (
    "image"
    "image/color"
    "image/png"
    "math/cmplx"
    "os"
)
```

```go
func main() {
    const (
        xmin, ymin, xmax, ymax = -2, -2, +2, +2
        width, height          = 1024, 1024
    )

    img := image.NewRGBA(image.Rect(0, 0, width, height))
    for py := 0; py < height; py++ {
        y := float64(py)/height*(ymax-ymin) + ymin
        for px := 0; px < width; px++ {
            x := float64(px)/width*(xmax-xmin) + xmin
            z := complex(x, y)
            // Image point (px, py) represents complex value z.
            img.Set(px, py, mandelbrot(z))
        }
    }
    png.Encode(os.Stdout, img) // NOTE: ignoring errors
}

func mandelbrot(z complex128) color.Color {
    const iterations = 200
    const contrast = 15

    var v complex128
    for n := uint8(0); n < iterations; n++ {
        v = v*v + z
        if cmplx.Abs(v) > 2 {
            return color.Gray{255 - contrast*n}
        }
    }
    return color.Black
}
```

The two nested loops iterate over each point in a 1024×1024 grayscale raster image representing the −2 to +2 portion of the complex plane. The program tests whether repeatedly squaring and adding the number that point represents eventually "escapes" the circle of radius 2. If so, the point is shaded by the number of iterations it took to escape. If not, the value belongs to the Mandelbrot set, and the point remains black. Finally, the program writes to its standard output the PNG-encoded image of the iconic fractal, shown in Figure 3.3.

Exercise 3.5: Implement a full-color Mandelbrot set using the function image.NewRGBA and the type color.RGBA or color.YCbCr.

Exercise 3.6: Supersampling is a technique to reduce the effect of pixelation by computing the color value at several points within each pixel and taking the average. The simplest method is to divide each pixel into four "subpixels." Implement it.

Exercise 3.7: Another simple fractal uses Newton's method to find complex solutions to a function such as $z^4-1 = 0$. Shade each starting point by the number of iterations required to get close to one of the four roots. Color each point by the root it approaches.

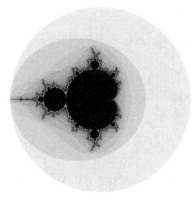

Figure 3.3. The Mandelbrot set.

Exercise 3.8: Rendering fractals at high zoom levels demands great arithmetic precision. Implement the same fractal using four different representations of numbers: `complex64`, `complex128`, `big.Float`, and `big.Rat`. (The latter two types are found in the `math/big` package. `Float` uses arbitrary but bounded-precision floating-point; `Rat` uses unbounded-precision rational numbers.) How do they compare in performance and memory usage? At what zoom levels do rendering artifacts become visible?

Exercise 3.9: Write a web server that renders fractals and writes the image data to the client. Allow the client to specify the x, y, and zoom values as parameters to the HTTP request.

3.4. Booleans

A value of type `bool`, or *boolean*, has only two possible values, `true` and `false`. The conditions in `if` and `for` statements are booleans, and comparison operators like `==` and `<` produce a boolean result. The unary operator `!` is logical negation, so `!true` is `false`, or, one might say, `(!true==false)==true`, although as a matter of style, we always simplify redundant boolean expressions like `x==true` to `x`.

Boolean values can be combined with the `&&` (AND) and `||` (OR) operators, which have *short-circuit* behavior: if the answer is already determined by the value of the left operand, the right operand is not evaluated, making it safe to write expressions like this:

```
s != "" && s[0] == 'x'
```

where `s[0]` would panic if applied to an empty string.

Since `&&` has higher precedence than `||` (mnemonic: `&&` is boolean multiplication, `||` is boolean addition), no parentheses are required for conditions of this form:

```
if 'a' <= c && c <= 'z' ||
    'A' <= c && c <= 'Z' ||
    '0' <= c && c <= '9' {
    // ...ASCII letter or digit...
}
```

There is no implicit conversion from a boolean value to a numeric value like 0 or 1, or vice versa. It's necessary to use an explicit if, as in

```
i := 0
if b {
    i = 1
}
```

It might be worth writing a conversion function if this operation were needed often:

```
// btoi returns 1 if b is true and 0 if false.
func btoi(b bool) int {
    if b {
        return 1
    }
    return 0
}
```

The inverse operation is so simple that it doesn't warrant a function, but for symmetry here it is:

```
// itob reports whether i is non-zero.
func itob(i int) bool { return i != 0 }
```

3.5. Strings

A string is an immutable sequence of bytes. Strings may contain arbitrary data, including bytes with value 0, but usually they contain human-readable text. Text strings are conventionally interpreted as UTF-8-encoded sequences of Unicode code points (runes), which we'll explore in detail very soon.

The built-in len function returns the number of bytes (not runes) in a string, and the *index* operation s[i] retrieves the *i*-th byte of string s, where $0 \le i < len(s)$.

```
s := "hello, world"
fmt.Println(len(s))      // "12"
fmt.Println(s[0], s[7]) // "104 119"  ('h' and 'w')
```

Attempting to access a byte outside this range results in a panic:

```
c := s[len(s)] // panic: index out of range
```

The *i*-th byte of a string is not necessarily the *i*-th *character* of a string, because the UTF-8 encoding of a non-ASCII code point requires two or more bytes. Working with characters is discussed shortly.

The *substring* operation s[i:j] yields a new string consisting of the bytes of the original string starting at index i and continuing up to, but not including, the byte at index j. The result contains j-i bytes.

```
fmt.Println(s[0:5]) // "hello"
```

Again, a panic results if either index is out of bounds or if j is less than i.

Either or both of the i and j operands may be omitted, in which case the default values of 0 (the start of the string) and len(s) (its end) are assumed, respectively.

```
fmt.Println(s[:5]) // "hello"
fmt.Println(s[7:]) // "world"
fmt.Println(s[:])  // "hello, world"
```

The + operator makes a new string by concatenating two strings:

```
fmt.Println("goodbye" + s[5:]) // "goodbye, world"
```

Strings may be compared with comparison operators like == and <; the comparison is done byte by byte, so the result is the natural lexicographic ordering.

String values are immutable: the byte sequence contained in a string value can never be changed, though of course we can assign a new value to a string *variable*. To append one string to another, for instance, we can write

```
s := "left foot"
t := s
s += ", right foot"
```

This does not modify the string that s originally held but causes s to hold the new string formed by the += statement; meanwhile, t still contains the old string.

```
fmt.Println(s) // "left foot, right foot"
fmt.Println(t) // "left foot"
```

Since strings are immutable, constructions that try to modify a string's data in place are not allowed:

```
s[0] = 'L' // compile error: cannot assign to s[0]
```

Immutability means that it is safe for two copies of a string to share the same underlying memory, making it cheap to copy strings of any length. Similarly, a string s and a substring like s[7:] may safely share the same data, so the substring operation is also cheap. No new memory is allocated in either case. Figure 3.4 illustrates the arrangement of a string and two of its substrings sharing the same underlying byte array.

3.5.1. String Literals

A string value can be written as a *string literal*, a sequence of bytes enclosed in double quotes:

```
"Hello, 世界"
```

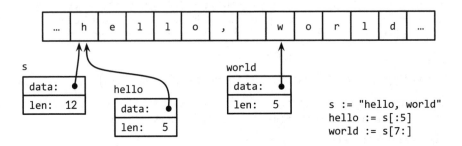

Figure 3.4. The string "hello, world" and two substrings.

Because Go source files are always encoded in UTF-8 and Go text strings are conventionally interpreted as UTF-8, we can include Unicode code points in string literals.

Within a double-quoted string literal, *escape sequences* that begin with a backslash \ can be used to insert arbitrary byte values into the string. One set of escapes handles ASCII control codes like newline, carriage return, and tab:

\a	"alert" or bell
\b	backspace
\f	form feed
\n	newline
\r	carriage return
\t	tab
\v	vertical tab
\'	single quote (only in the rune literal '\'')
\"	double quote (only within "..." literals)
\\	backslash

Arbitrary bytes can also be included in literal strings using hexadecimal or octal escapes. A *hexadecimal escape* is written \x*hh*, with exactly two hexadecimal digits *h* (in upper or lower case). An *octal escape* is written \ooo with exactly three octal digits *o* (0 through 7) not exceeding \377. Both denote a single byte with the specified value. Later, we'll see how to encode Unicode code points numerically in string literals.

A *raw string literal* is written ` ...`, using backquotes instead of double quotes. Within a raw string literal, no escape sequences are processed; the contents are taken literally, including backslashes and newlines, so a raw string literal may spread over several lines in the program source. The only processing is that carriage returns are deleted so that the value of the string is the same on all platforms, including those that conventionally put carriage returns in text files.

Raw string literals are a convenient way to write regular expressions, which tend to have lots of backslashes. They are also useful for HTML templates, JSON literals, command usage messages, and the like, which often extend over multiple lines.

```
const GoUsage = `Go is a tool for managing Go source code.

Usage:
    go command [arguments]
...`
```

3.5.2. Unicode

Long ago, life was simple and there was, at least in a parochial view, only one character set to deal with: ASCII, the American Standard Code for Information Interchange. ASCII, or more precisely US-ASCII, uses 7 bits to represent 128 "characters": the upper- and lower-case letters of English, digits, and a variety of punctuation and device-control characters. For much of the early days of computing, this was adequate, but it left a very large fraction of the world's population unable to use their own writing systems in computers. With the growth of the Internet, data in myriad languages has become much more common. How can this rich variety be dealt with at all and, if possible, efficiently?

The answer is Unicode (unicode.org), which collects all of the characters in all of the world's writing systems, plus accents and other diacritical marks, control codes like tab and carriage return, and plenty of esoterica, and assigns each one a standard number called a *Unicode code point* or, in Go terminology, a *rune*.

Unicode version 8 defines code points for over 120,000 characters in well over 100 languages and scripts. How are these represented in computer programs and data? The natural data type to hold a single rune is int32, and that's what Go uses; it has the synonym rune for precisely this purpose.

We could represent a sequence of runes as a sequence of int32 values. In this representation, which is called UTF-32 or UCS-4, the encoding of each Unicode code point has the same size, 32 bits. This is simple and uniform, but it uses much more space than necessary since most computer-readable text is in ASCII, which requires only 8 bits or 1 byte per character. All the characters in widespread use still number fewer than 65,536, which would fit in 16 bits. Can we do better?

3.5.3. UTF-8

UTF-8 is a variable-length encoding of Unicode code points as bytes. UTF-8 was invented by Ken Thompson and Rob Pike, two of the creators of Go, and is now a Unicode standard. It uses between 1 and 4 bytes to represent each rune, but only 1 byte for ASCII characters, and only 2 or 3 bytes for most runes in common use. The high-order bits of the first byte of the encoding for a rune indicate how many bytes follow. A high-order 0 indicates 7-bit ASCII, where each rune takes only 1 byte, so it is identical to conventional ASCII. A high-order 110 indicates that the rune takes 2 bytes; the second byte begins with 10. Larger runes have analogous encodings.

```
0xxxxxxx                              runes 0–127    (ASCII)
110xxxxx 10xxxxxx                     128–2047       (values <128 unused)
1110xxxx 10xxxxxx 10xxxxxx            2048–65535     (values <2048 unused)
11110xxx 10xxxxxx 10xxxxxx 10xxxxxx   65536–0x10ffff (other values unused)
```

A variable-length encoding precludes direct indexing to access the n-th character of a string, but UTF-8 has many desirable properties to compensate. The encoding is compact, compatible with ASCII, and self-synchronizing: it's possible to find the beginning of a character by backing up no more than three bytes. It's also a prefix code, so it can be decoded from left to right without any ambiguity or lookahead. No rune's encoding is a substring of any other, or even of a sequence of others, so you can search for a rune by just searching for its bytes, without worrying about the preceding context. The lexicographic byte order equals the Unicode code point order, so sorting UTF-8 works naturally. There are no embedded NUL (zero) bytes, which is convenient for programming languages that use NUL to terminate strings.

Go source files are always encoded in UTF-8, and UTF-8 is the preferred encoding for text strings manipulated by Go programs. The unicode package provides functions for working with individual runes (such as distinguishing letters from numbers, or converting an upper-case letter to a lower-case one), and the unicode/utf8 package provides functions for encoding and decoding runes as bytes using UTF-8.

Many Unicode characters are hard to type on a keyboard or to distinguish visually from similar-looking ones; some are even invisible. Unicode escapes in Go string literals allow us to specify them by their numeric code point value. There are two forms, \u*hhhh* for a 16-bit value and \U*hhhhhhhh* for a 32-bit value, where each *h* is a hexadecimal digit; the need for the 32-bit form arises very infrequently. Each denotes the UTF-8 encoding of the specified code point. Thus, for example, the following string literals all represent the same six-byte string:

```
"世界"
"\xe4\xb8\x96\xe7\x95\x8c"
"\u4e16\u754c"
"\U00004e16\U0000754c"
```

The three escape sequences above provide alternative notations for the first string, but the values they denote are identical.

Unicode escapes may also be used in rune literals. These three literals are equivalent:

```
'世'   '\u4e16'   '\U00004e16'
```

A rune whose value is less than 256 may be written with a single hexadecimal escape, such as '\x41' for 'A', but for higher values, a \u or \U escape must be used. Consequently, '\xe4\xb8\x96' is not a legal rune literal, even though those three bytes are a valid UTF-8 encoding of a single code point.

Thanks to the nice properties of UTF-8, many string operations don't require decoding. We can test whether one string contains another as a prefix:

```
func HasPrefix(s, prefix string) bool {
    return len(s) >= len(prefix) && s[:len(prefix)] == prefix
}
```

or as a suffix:

```
func HasSuffix(s, suffix string) bool {
    return len(s) >= len(suffix) && s[len(s)-len(suffix):] == suffix
}
```

or as a substring:

```
func Contains(s, substr string) bool {
    for i := 0; i < len(s); i++ {
        if HasPrefix(s[i:], substr) {
            return true
        }
    }
    return false
}
```

using the same logic for UTF-8-encoded text as for raw bytes. This is not true for other encodings. (The functions above are drawn from the strings package, though its implementation of Contains uses a hashing technique to search more efficiently.)

On the other hand, if we really care about the individual Unicode characters, we have to use other mechanisms. Consider the string from our very first example, which includes two East Asian characters. Figure 3.5 illustrates its representation in memory. The string contains 13 bytes, but interpreted as UTF-8, it encodes only nine code points or runes:

```
import "unicode/utf8"

s := "Hello, 世界"
fmt.Println(len(s))                    // "13"
fmt.Println(utf8.RuneCountInString(s)) // "9"
```

To process those characters, we need a UTF-8 decoder. The unicode/utf8 package provides one that we can use like this:

```
for i := 0; i < len(s); {
    r, size := utf8.DecodeRuneInString(s[i:])
    fmt.Printf("%d\t%c\n", i, r)
    i += size
}
```

Each call to DecodeRuneInString returns r, the rune itself, and size, the number of bytes occupied by the UTF-8 encoding of r. The size is used to update the byte index i of the next rune in the string. But this is clumsy, and we need loops of this kind all the time. Fortunately, Go's range loop, when applied to a string, performs UTF-8 decoding implicitly. The output of the loop below is also shown in Figure 3.5; notice how the index jumps by more than 1 for each non-ASCII rune.

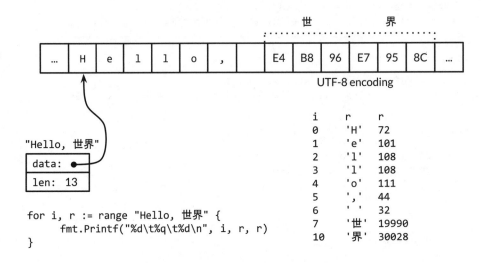

Figure 3.5. A range loop decodes a UTF-8-encoded string.

```
for i, r := range "Hello, 世界" {
    fmt.Printf("%d\t%q\t%d\n", i, r, r)
}
```

We could use a simple `range` loop to count the number of runes in a string, like this:

```
n := 0
for _, _ = range s {
    n++
}
```

As with the other forms of `range` loop, we can omit the variables we don't need:

```
n := 0
for range s {
    n++
}
```

Or we can just call `utf8.RuneCountInString(s)`.

We mentioned earlier that it is mostly a matter of convention in Go that text strings are interpreted as UTF-8-encoded sequences of Unicode code points, but for correct use of `range` loops on strings, it's more than a convention, it's a necessity. What happens if we range over a string containing arbitrary binary data or, for that matter, UTF-8 data containing errors?

Each time a UTF-8 decoder, whether explicit in a call to `utf8.DecodeRuneInString` or implicit in a `range` loop, consumes an unexpected input byte, it generates a special Unicode *replacement character*, `'\uFFFD'`, which is usually printed as a white question mark inside a black hexagonal or diamond-like shape �. When a program encounters this rune value, it's often a sign that some upstream part of the system that generated the string data has been careless in its treatment of text encodings.

UTF-8 is exceptionally convenient as an interchange format but within a program runes may be more convenient because they are of uniform size and are thus easily indexed in arrays and slices.

A []rune conversion applied to a UTF-8-encoded string returns the sequence of Unicode code points that the string encodes:

```
// "program" in Japanese katakana
s := "プログラム"
fmt.Printf("% x\n", s) // "e3 83 97 e3 83 ad e3 82 b0 e3 83 a9 e3 83 a0"
r := []rune(s)
fmt.Printf("%x\n", r)  // "[30d7 30ed 30b0 30e9 30e0]"
```

(The verb % x in the first Printf inserts a space between each pair of hex digits.)

If a slice of runes is converted to a string, it produces the concatenation of the UTF-8 encodings of each rune:

```
fmt.Println(string(r)) // "プログラム"
```

Converting an integer value to a string interprets the integer as a rune value, and yields the UTF-8 representation of that rune:

```
fmt.Println(string(65))     // "A", not "65"
fmt.Println(string(0x4eac)) // "京"
```

If the rune is invalid, the replacement character is substituted:

```
fmt.Println(string(1234567)) // "�"
```

3.5.4. Strings and Byte Slices

Four standard packages are particularly important for manipulating strings: bytes, strings, strconv, and unicode. The strings package provides many functions for searching, replacing, comparing, trimming, splitting, and joining strings.

The bytes package has similar functions for manipulating slices of bytes, of type []byte, which share some properties with strings. Because strings are immutable, building up strings incrementally can involve a lot of allocation and copying. In such cases, it's more efficient to use the bytes.Buffer type, which we'll show in a moment.

The strconv package provides functions for converting boolean, integer, and floating-point values to and from their string representations, and functions for quoting and unquoting strings.

The unicode package provides functions like IsDigit, IsLetter, IsUpper, and IsLower for classifying runes. Each function takes a single rune argument and returns a boolean. Conversion functions like ToUpper and ToLower convert a rune into the given case if it is a letter. All these functions use the Unicode standard categories for letters, digits, and so on. The strings package has similar functions, also called `ToUpper` and `ToLower`, that return a new string with the specified transformation applied to each character of the original string.

The `basename` function below was inspired by the Unix shell utility of the same name. In our version, `basename(s)` removes any prefix of s that looks like a file system path with components separated by slashes, and it removes any suffix that looks like a file type:

```
fmt.Println(basename("a/b/c.go")) // "c"
fmt.Println(basename("c.d.go"))   // "c.d"
fmt.Println(basename("abc"))      // "abc"
```

The first version of `basename` does all the work without the help of libraries:

gopl.io/ch3/basename1

```
// basename removes directory components and a .suffix.
// e.g., a => a, a.go => a, a/b/c.go => c, a/b.c.go => b.c
func basename(s string) string {
    // Discard last '/' and everything before.
    for i := len(s) - 1; i >= 0; i-- {
        if s[i] == '/' {
            s = s[i+1:]
            break
        }
    }
    // Preserve everything before last '.'.
    for i := len(s) - 1; i >= 0; i-- {
        if s[i] == '.' {
            s = s[:i]
            break
        }
    }
    return s
}
```

A simpler version uses the `strings.LastIndex` library function:

gopl.io/ch3/basename2

```
func basename(s string) string {
    slash := strings.LastIndex(s, "/") // -1 if "/" not found
    s = s[slash+1:]
    if dot := strings.LastIndex(s, "."); dot >= 0 {
        s = s[:dot]
    }
    return s
}
```

The `path` and `path/filepath` packages provide a more general set of functions for manipulating hierarchical names. The `path` package works with slash-delimited paths on any platform. It shouldn't be used for file names, but it is appropriate for other domains, like the path component of a URL. By contrast, `path/filepath` manipulates file names using the rules for the host platform, such as `/foo/bar` for POSIX or `c:\foo\bar` on Microsoft Windows.

Let's continue with another substring example. The task is to take a string representation of an integer, such as "12345", and insert commas every three places, as in "12,345". This version only works for integers; handling floating-point numbers is left as a exercise.

gopl.io/ch3/comma

```
// comma inserts commas in a non-negative decimal integer string.
func comma(s string) string {
    n := len(s)
    if n <= 3 {
        return s
    }
    return comma(s[:n-3]) + "," + s[n-3:]
}
```

The argument to comma is a string. If its length is less than or equal to 3, no comma is necessary. Otherwise, comma calls itself recursively with a substring consisting of all but the last three characters, and appends a comma and the last three characters to the result of the recursive call.

A string contains an array of bytes that, once created, is immutable. By contrast, the elements of a byte slice can be freely modified.

Strings can be converted to byte slices and back again:

```
s  := "abc"
b  := []byte(s)
s2 := string(b)
```

Conceptually, the []byte(s) conversion allocates a new byte array holding a copy of the bytes of s, and yields a slice that references the entirety of that array. An optimizing compiler may be able to avoid the allocation and copying in some cases, but in general copying is required to ensure that the bytes of s remain unchanged even if those of b are subsequently modified. The conversion from byte slice back to string with string(b) also makes a copy, to ensure immutability of the resulting string s2.

To avoid conversions and unnecessary memory allocation, many of the utility functions in the bytes package directly parallel their counterparts in the strings package. For example, here are half a dozen functions from strings:

```
func Contains(s, substr string) bool
func Count(s, sep string) int
func Fields(s string) []string
func HasPrefix(s, prefix string) bool
func Index(s, sep string) int
func Join(a []string, sep string) string
```

and the corresponding ones from bytes:

```
func Contains(b, subslice []byte) bool
func Count(s, sep []byte) int
func Fields(s []byte) [][]byte
func HasPrefix(s, prefix []byte) bool
func Index(s, sep []byte) int
func Join(s [][]byte, sep []byte) []byte
```

The only difference is that strings have been replaced by byte slices.

The bytes package provides the Buffer type for efficient manipulation of byte slices. A Buffer starts out empty but grows as data of types like string, byte, and []byte are written to it. As the example below shows, a bytes.Buffer variable requires no initialization because its zero value is usable:

gopl.io/ch3/printints
```
// intsToString is like fmt.Sprint(values) but adds commas.
func intsToString(values []int) string {
    var buf bytes.Buffer
    buf.WriteByte('[')
    for i, v := range values {
        if i > 0 {
            buf.WriteString(", ")
        }
        fmt.Fprintf(&buf, "%d", v)
    }
    buf.WriteByte(']')
    return buf.String()
}

func main() {
    fmt.Println(intsToString([]int{1, 2, 3})) // "[1, 2, 3]"
}
```

When appending the UTF-8 encoding of an arbitrary rune to a bytes.Buffer, it's best to use bytes.Buffer's WriteRune method, but WriteByte is fine for ASCII characters such as '[' and ']'.

The bytes.Buffer type is extremely versatile, and when we discuss interfaces in Chapter 7, we'll see how it may be used as a replacement for a file whenever an I/O function requires a sink for bytes (io.Writer) as Fprintf does above, or a source of bytes (io.Reader).

Exercise 3.10: Write a non-recursive version of comma, using bytes.Buffer instead of string concatenation.

Exercise 3.11: Enhance comma so that it deals correctly with floating-point numbers and an optional sign.

Exercise 3.12: Write a function that reports whether two strings are anagrams of each other, that is, they contain the same letters in a different order.

3.5.5. Conversions between Strings and Numbers

In addition to conversions between strings, runes, and bytes, it's often necessary to convert between numeric values and their string representations. This is done with functions from the strconv package.

To convert an integer to a string, one option is to use fmt.Sprintf; another is to use the function strconv.Itoa ("integer to ASCII"):

```
x := 123
y := fmt.Sprintf("%d", x)
fmt.Println(y, strconv.Itoa(x)) // "123 123"
```

FormatInt and FormatUint can be used to format numbers in a different base:

```
fmt.Println(strconv.FormatInt(int64(x), 2)) // "1111011"
```

The fmt.Printf verbs %b, %d, %u, and %x are often more convenient than Format functions, especially if we want to include additional information besides the number:

```
s := fmt.Sprintf("x=%b", x) // "x=1111011"
```

To parse a string representing an integer, use the strconv functions Atoi or ParseInt, or ParseUint for unsigned integers:

```
x, err := strconv.Atoi("123")            // x is an int
y, err := strconv.ParseInt("123", 10, 64) // base 10, up to 64 bits
```

The third argument of ParseInt gives the size of the integer type that the result must fit into; for example, 16 implies int16, and the special value of 0 implies int. In any case, the type of the result y is always int64, which you can then convert to a smaller type.

Sometimes fmt.Scanf is useful for parsing input that consists of orderly mixtures of strings and numbers all on a single line, but it can be inflexible, especially when handling incomplete or irregular input.

3.6. Constants

Constants are expressions whose value is known to the compiler and whose evaluation is guaranteed to occur at compile time, not at run time. The underlying type of every constant is a basic type: boolean, string, or number.

A const declaration defines named values that look syntactically like variables but whose value is constant, which prevents accidental (or nefarious) changes during program execution. For instance, a constant is more appropriate than a variable for a mathematical constant like pi, since its value won't change:

```
const pi = 3.14159 // approximately; math.Pi is a better approximation
```

As with variables, a sequence of constants can appear in one declaration; this would be appropriate for a group of related values:

```
const (
    e  = 2.71828182845904523536028747135266249775724709369995957496696763
    pi = 3.14159265358979323846264338327950288419716939937510582097494459
)
```

Many computations on constants can be completely evaluated at compile time, reducing the work necessary at run time and enabling other compiler optimizations. Errors ordinarily detected at run time can be reported at compile time when their operands are constants, such as integer division by zero, string indexing out of bounds, and any floating-point operation that would result in a non-finite value.

The results of all arithmetic, logical, and comparison operations applied to constant operands are themselves constants, as are the results of conversions and calls to certain built-in functions such as len, cap, real, imag, complex, and unsafe.Sizeof (§13.1).

Since their values are known to the compiler, constant expressions may appear in types, specifically as the length of an array type:

```
const IPv4Len = 4

// parseIPv4 parses an IPv4 address (d.d.d.d).
func parseIPv4(s string) IP {
    var p [IPv4Len]byte
    // ...
}
```

A constant declaration may specify a type as well as a value, but in the absence of an explicit type, the type is inferred from the expression on the right-hand side. In the following, time.Duration is a named type whose underlying type is int64, and time.Minute is a constant of that type. Both of the constants declared below thus have the type time.Duration as well, as revealed by %T:

```
const noDelay time.Duration = 0
const timeout = 5 * time.Minute
fmt.Printf("%T %[1]v\n", noDelay)      // "time.Duration 0"
fmt.Printf("%T %[1]v\n", timeout)      // "time.Duration 5m0s"
fmt.Printf("%T %[1]v\n", time.Minute)  // "time.Duration 1m0s"
```

When a sequence of constants is declared as a group, the right-hand side expression may be omitted for all but the first of the group, implying that the previous expression and its type should be used again. For example:

```
const (
    a = 1
    b
    c = 2
    d
)

fmt.Println(a, b, c, d) // "1 1 2 2"
```

This is not very useful if the implicitly copied right-hand side expression always evaluates to the same thing. But what if it could vary? This brings us to `iota`.

3.6.1. The Constant Generator `iota`

A `const` declaration may use the *constant generator* `iota`, which is used to create a sequence of related values without spelling out each one explicitly. In a `const` declaration, the value of `iota` begins at zero and increments by one for each item in the sequence.

Here's an example from the `time` package, which defines named constants of type `Weekday` for the days of the week, starting with zero for `Sunday`. Types of this kind are often called *enumerations*, or *enums* for short.

```
type Weekday int

const (
    Sunday Weekday = iota
    Monday
    Tuesday
    Wednesday
    Thursday
    Friday
    Saturday
)
```

This declares `Sunday` to be 0, `Monday` to be 1, and so on.

We can use `iota` in more complex expressions too, as in this example from the `net` package where each of the lowest 5 bits of an unsigned integer is given a distinct name and boolean interpretation:

```
type Flags uint

const (
    FlagUp Flags = 1 << iota // is up
    FlagBroadcast            // supports broadcast access capability
    FlagLoopback             // is a loopback interface
    FlagPointToPoint         // belongs to a point-to-point link
    FlagMulticast            // supports multicast access capability
)
```

As `iota` increments, each constant is assigned the value of `1 << iota`, which evaluates to successive powers of two, each corresponding to a single bit. We can use these constants within functions that test, set, or clear one or more of these bits:

```
gopl.io/ch3/netflag
func IsUp(v Flags) bool     { return v&FlagUp == FlagUp }
func TurnDown(v *Flags)     { *v &^= FlagUp }
func SetBroadcast(v *Flags) { *v |= FlagBroadcast }
func IsCast(v Flags) bool   { return v&(FlagBroadcast|FlagMulticast) != 0 }
```

```
func main() {
    var v Flags = FlagMulticast | FlagUp
    fmt.Printf("%b %t\n", v, IsUp(v)) // "10001 true"
    TurnDown(&v)
    fmt.Printf("%b %t\n", v, IsUp(v)) // "10000 false"
    SetBroadcast(&v)
    fmt.Printf("%b %t\n", v, IsUp(v))   // "10010 false"
    fmt.Printf("%b %t\n", v, IsCast(v)) // "10010 true"
}
```

As a more complex example of iota, this declaration names the powers of 1024:

```
const (
    _ = 1 << (10 * iota)
    KiB // 1024
    MiB // 1048576
    GiB // 1073741824
    TiB // 1099511627776                 (exceeds 1 << 32)
    PiB // 1125899906842624
    EiB // 1152921504606846976
    ZiB // 1180591620717411303424        (exceeds 1 << 64)
    YiB // 1208925819614629174706176
)
```

The iota mechanism has its limits. For example, it's not possible to generate the more familiar powers of 1000 (KB, MB, and so on) because there is no exponentiation operator.

Exercise 3.13: Write const declarations for KB, MB, up through YB as compactly as you can.

3.6.2. Untyped Constants

Constants in Go are a bit unusual. Although a constant can have any of the basic data types
like int or float64, including named basic types like time.Duration, many constants are
not committed to a particular type. The compiler represents these uncommitted constants
with much greater numeric precision than values of basic types, and arithmetic on them is
more precise than machine arithmetic; you may assume at least 256 bits of precision. There
are six flavors of these uncommitted constants, called *untyped* boolean, untyped integer,
untyped rune, untyped floating-point, untyped complex, and untyped string.

By deferring this commitment, untyped constants not only retain their higher precision until
later, but they can participate in many more expressions than committed constants without
requiring conversions. For example, the values ZiB and YiB in the example above are too big
to store in any integer variable, but they are legitimate constants that may be used in expressions like this one:

```
fmt.Println(YiB/ZiB) // "1024"
```

As another example, the floating-point constant math.Pi may be used wherever any floating-
point or complex value is needed:

```
var x float32 = math.Pi
var y float64 = math.Pi
var z complex128 = math.Pi
```

If `math.Pi` had been committed to a specific type such as `float64`, the result would not be as precise, and type conversions would be required to use it when a `float32` or `complex128` value is wanted:

```
const Pi64 float64 = math.Pi

var x float32 = float32(Pi64)
var y float64 = Pi64
var z complex128 = complex128(Pi64)
```

For literals, syntax determines flavor. The literals `0`, `0.0`, `0i`, and `'\u0000'` all denote constants of the same value but different flavors: untyped integer, untyped floating-point, untyped complex, and untyped rune, respectively. Similarly, `true` and `false` are untyped booleans and string literals are untyped strings.

Recall that `/` may represent integer or floating-point division depending on its operands. Consequently, the choice of literal may affect the result of a constant division expression:

```
var f float64 = 212
fmt.Println((f - 32) * 5 / 9)     // "100"; (f - 32) * 5 is a float64
fmt.Println(5 / 9 * (f - 32))     // "0";   5/9 is an untyped integer, 0
fmt.Println(5.0 / 9.0 * (f - 32)) // "100"; 5.0/9.0 is an untyped float
```

Only constants can be untyped. When an untyped constant appears on the right-hand side of a variable declaration with an explicit type, as in the first statement below, or is assigned to a variable, as in the other three statements, the constant is implicitly converted to the type of that variable if possible.

```
var f float64 = 3 + 0i // untyped complex -> float64
f = 2                  // untyped integer -> float64
f = 1e123              // untyped floating-point -> float64
f = 'a'                // untyped rune -> float64
```

The statements above are thus equivalent to these:

```
var f float64 = float64(3 + 0i)
f = float64(2)
f = float64(1e123)
f = float64('a')
```

Whether implicit or explicit, converting a constant from one type to another requires that the target type can represent the original value. Rounding is allowed for real and complex floating-point numbers:

```
const (
    deadbeef = 0xdeadbeef // untyped int with value 3735928559
    a = uint32(deadbeef)  // uint32 with value 3735928559
    b = float32(deadbeef) // float32 with value 3735928576 (rounded up)
    c = float64(deadbeef) // float64 with value 3735928559 (exact)
    d = int32(deadbeef)   // compile error: constant overflows int32
    e = float64(1e309)    // compile error: constant overflows float64
    f = uint(-1)          // compile error: constant underflows uint
)
```

In a variable declaration without an explicit type (including short variable declarations), the flavor of the untyped constant implicitly determines the default type of the variable, as in these examples:

```
i := 0      // untyped integer;        implicit int(0)
r := '\000' // untyped rune;           implicit rune('\000')
f := 0.0    // untyped floating-point; implicit float64(0.0)
c := 0i     // untyped complex;        implicit complex128(0i)
```

Note the asymmetry: untyped integers are converted to int, whose size is not guaranteed, but untyped floating-point and complex numbers are converted to the explicitly sized types float64 and complex128. The language has no unsized float and complex types analogous to unsized int, because it is very difficult to write correct numerical algorithms without knowing the size of one's floating-point data types.

To give the variable a different type, we must explicitly convert the untyped constant to the desired type or state the desired type in the variable declaration, as in these examples:

```
var i = int8(0)
var i int8 = 0
```

These defaults are particularly important when converting an untyped constant to an interface value (see Chapter 7) since they determine its dynamic type.

```
fmt.Printf("%T\n", 0)       // "int"
fmt.Printf("%T\n", 0.0)     // "float64"
fmt.Printf("%T\n", 0i)      // "complex128"
fmt.Printf("%T\n", '\000')  // "int32" (rune)
```

We've now covered the basic data types of Go. The next step is to show how they can be combined into larger groupings like arrays and structs, and then into data structures for solving real programming problems; that is the topic of Chapter 4.

4
Composite Types

In Chapter 3 we discussed the basic types that serve as building blocks for data structures in a Go program; they are the atoms of our universe. In this chapter, we'll take a look at *composite* types, the molecules created by combining the basic types in various ways. We'll talk about four such types—arrays, slices, maps, and structs—and at the end of the chapter, we'll show how structured data using these types can be encoded as and parsed from JSON data and used to generate HTML from templates.

Arrays and structs are *aggregate* types; their values are concatenations of other values in memory. Arrays are homogeneous—their elements all have the same type—whereas structs are heterogeneous. Both arrays and structs are fixed size. In contrast, slices and maps are dynamic data structures that grow as values are added.

4.1. Arrays

An array is a fixed-length sequence of zero or more elements of a particular type. Because of their fixed length, arrays are rarely used directly in Go. Slices, which can grow and shrink, are much more versatile, but to understand slices we must understand arrays first.

Individual array elements are accessed with the conventional subscript notation, where subscripts run from zero to one less than the array length. The built-in function `len` returns the number of elements in the array.

```
var a [3]int            // array of 3 integers
fmt.Println(a[0])       // print the first element
fmt.Println(a[len(a)-1]) // print the last element, a[2]
```

```
// Print the indices and elements.
for i, v := range a {
    fmt.Printf("%d %d\n", i, v)
}

// Print the elements only.
for _, v := range a {
    fmt.Printf("%d\n", v)
}
```

By default, the elements of a new array variable are initially set to the zero value for the element type, which is 0 for numbers. We can use an *array literal* to initialize an array with a list of values:

```
var q [3]int = [3]int{1, 2, 3}
var r [3]int = [3]int{1, 2}
fmt.Println(r[2]) // "0"
```

In an array literal, if an ellipsis "..." appears in place of the length, the array length is determined by the number of initializers. The definition of q can be simplified to

```
q := [...]int{1, 2, 3}
fmt.Printf("%T\n", q) // "[3]int"
```

The size of an array is part of its type, so [3]int and [4]int are different types. The size must be a constant expression, that is, an expression whose value can be computed as the program is being compiled.

```
q := [3]int{1, 2, 3}
q = [4]int{1, 2, 3, 4} // compile error: cannot assign [4]int to [3]int
```

As we'll see, the literal syntax is similar for arrays, slices, maps, and structs. The specific form above is a list of values in order, but it is also possible to specify a list of index and value pairs, like this:

```
type Currency int

const (
    USD Currency = iota
    EUR
    GBP
    RMB
)

symbol := [...]string{USD: "$", EUR: "€", GBP: "£", RMB: "¥"}

fmt.Println(RMB, symbol[RMB]) // "3 ¥"
```

In this form, indices can appear in any order and some may be omitted; as before, unspecified values take on the zero value for the element type. For instance,

```
r := [...]int{99: -1}
```

defines an array r with 100 elements, all zero except for the last, which has value -1.

If an array's element type is *comparable* then the array type is comparable too, so we may directly compare two arrays of that type using the == operator, which reports whether all corresponding elements are equal. The != operator is its negation.

```
a := [2]int{1, 2}
b := [...]int{1, 2}
c := [2]int{1, 3}
fmt.Println(a == b, a == c, b == c) // "true false false"
d := [3]int{1, 2}
fmt.Println(a == d) // compile error: cannot compare [2]int == [3]int
```

As a more plausible example, the function Sum256 in the crypto/sha256 package produces the SHA256 cryptographic hash or *digest* of a message stored in an arbitrary byte slice. The digest has 256 bits, so its type is [32]byte. If two digests are the same, it is extremely likely that the two messages are the same; if the digests differ, the two messages are different. This program prints and compares the SHA256 digests of "x" and "X":

gopl.io/ch4/sha256
```
import "crypto/sha256"

func main() {
    c1 := sha256.Sum256([]byte("x"))
    c2 := sha256.Sum256([]byte("X"))
    fmt.Printf("%x\n%x\n%t\n%T\n", c1, c2, c1 == c2, c1)
    // Output:
    // 2d711642b726b04401627ca9fbac32f5c8530fb1903cc4db02258717921a4881
    // 4b68ab3847feda7d6c62c1fbcbeebfa35eab7351ed5e78f4ddadea5df64b8015
    // false
    // [32]uint8
}
```

The two inputs differ by only a single bit, but approximately half the bits are different in the digests. Notice the Printf verbs: %x to print all the elements of an array or slice of bytes in hexadecimal, %t to show a boolean, and %T to display the type of a value.

When a function is called, a copy of each argument value is assigned to the corresponding parameter variable, so the function receives a copy, not the original. Passing large arrays in this way can be inefficient, and any changes that the function makes to array elements affect only the copy, not the original. In this regard, Go treats arrays like any other type, but this behavior is different from languages that implicitly pass arrays *by reference*.

Of course, we can explicitly pass a pointer to an array so that any modifications the function makes to array elements will be visible to the caller. This function zeroes the contents of a [32]byte array:

```
func zero(ptr *[32]byte) {
    for i := range ptr {
        ptr[i] = 0
    }
}
```

The array literal [32]byte{} yields an array of 32 bytes. Each element of the array has the zero value for byte, which is zero. We can use that fact to write a different version of zero:

```
func zero(ptr *[32]byte) {
    *ptr = [32]byte{}
}
```

Using a pointer to an array is efficient and allows the called function to mutate the caller's variable, but arrays are still inherently inflexible because of their fixed size. The zero function will not accept a pointer to a [16]byte variable, for example, nor is there any way to add or remove array elements. For these reasons, other than special cases like SHA256's fixed-size hash, arrays are seldom used as function parameters; instead, we use slices.

Exercise 4.1: Write a function that counts the number of bits that are different in two SHA256 hashes. (See PopCount from Section 2.6.2.)

Exercise 4.2: Write a program that prints the SHA256 hash of its standard input by default but supports a command-line flag to print the SHA384 or SHA512 hash instead.

4.2. Slices

Slices represent variable-length sequences whose elements all have the same type. A slice type is written []T, where the elements have type T; it looks like an array type without a size.

Arrays and slices are intimately connected. A slice is a lightweight data structure that gives access to a subsequence (or perhaps all) of the elements of an array, which is known as the slice's *underlying array*. A slice has three components: a pointer, a length, and a capacity. The pointer points to the first element of the array that is reachable through the slice, which is not necessarily the array's first element. The length is the number of slice elements; it can't exceed the capacity, which is usually the number of elements between the start of the slice and the end of the underlying array. The built-in functions len and cap return those values.

Multiple slices can share the same underlying array and may refer to overlapping parts of that array. Figure 4.1 shows an array of strings for the months of the year, and two overlapping slices of it. The array is declared as

```
months := [...]string{1: "January", /* ... */, 12: "December"}
```

so January is months[1] and December is months[12]. Ordinarily, the array element at index 0 would contain the first value, but because months are always numbered from 1, we can leave it out of the declaration and it will be initialized to an empty string.

The *slice operator* s[i:j], where $0 \le i \le j \le cap(s)$, creates a new slice that refers to elements i through j-1 of the sequence s, which may be an array variable, a pointer to an array, or another slice. The resulting slice has j-i elements. If i is omitted, it's 0, and if j is omitted, it's len(s). Thus the slice months[1:13] refers to the whole range of valid months, as does the slice months[1:]; the slice months[:] refers to the whole array. Let's define overlapping slices for the second quarter and the northern summer:

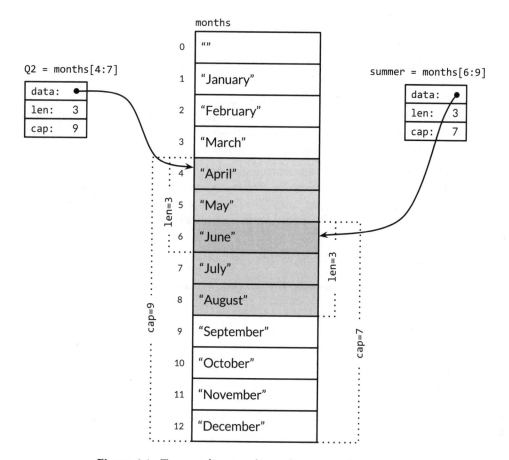

Figure 4.1. Two overlapping slices of an array of months.

```
Q2 := months[4:7]
summer := months[6:9]
fmt.Println(Q2)     // ["April" "May" "June"]
fmt.Println(summer) // ["June" "July" "August"]
```

June is included in each and is the sole output of this (inefficient) test for common elements:

```
for _, s := range summer {
    for _, q := range Q2 {
        if s == q {
            fmt.Printf("%s appears in both\n", s)
        }
    }
}
```

Slicing beyond `cap(s)` causes a panic, but slicing beyond `len(s)` extends the slice, so the result may be longer than the original:

```
fmt.Println(summer[:20]) // panic: out of range

endlessSummer := summer[:5] // extend a slice (within capacity)
fmt.Println(endlessSummer)  // "[June July August September October]"
```

As an aside, note the similarity of the substring operation on strings to the slice operator on `[]byte` slices. Both are written x[m:n], and both return a subsequence of the original bytes, sharing the underlying representation so that both operations take constant time. The expression x[m:n] yields a string if x is a string, or a `[]byte` if x is a `[]byte`.

Since a slice contains a pointer to an element of an array, passing a slice to a function permits the function to modify the underlying array elements. In other words, copying a slice creates an *alias* (§2.3.2) for the underlying array. The function `reverse` reverses the elements of an `[]int` slice in place, and it may be applied to slices of any length.

gopl.io/ch4/rev
```
// reverse reverses a slice of ints in place.
func reverse(s []int) {
    for i, j := 0, len(s)-1; i < j; i, j = i+1, j-1 {
        s[i], s[j] = s[j], s[i]
    }
}
```

Here we reverse the whole array a:

```
a := [...]int{0, 1, 2, 3, 4, 5}
reverse(a[:])
fmt.Println(a) // "[5 4 3 2 1 0]"
```

A simple way to *rotate* a slice left by *n* elements is to apply the `reverse` function three times, first to the leading *n* elements, then to the remaining elements, and finally to the whole slice. (To rotate to the right, make the third call first.)

```
s := []int{0, 1, 2, 3, 4, 5}
// Rotate s left by two positions.
reverse(s[:2])
reverse(s[2:])
reverse(s)
fmt.Println(s) // "[2 3 4 5 0 1]"
```

Notice how the expression that initializes the slice s differs from that for the array a. A *slice literal* looks like an array literal, a sequence of values separated by commas and surrounded by braces, but the size is not given. This implicitly creates an array variable of the right size and yields a slice that points to it. As with array literals, slice literals may specify the values in order, or give their indices explicitly, or use a mix of the two styles.

Unlike arrays, slices are not comparable, so we cannot use == to test whether two slices contain the same elements. The standard library provides the highly optimized `bytes.Equal` function for comparing two slices of bytes (`[]byte`), but for other types of slice, we must do the comparison ourselves:

```
func equal(x, y []string) bool {
    if len(x) != len(y) {
        return false
    }
    for i := range x {
        if x[i] != y[i] {
            return false
        }
    }
    return true
}
```

Given how natural this "deep" equality test is, and that it is no more costly at run time than the == operator for arrays of strings, it may be puzzling that slice comparisons do not also work this way. There are two reasons why deep equivalence is problematic. First, unlike array elements, the elements of a slice are indirect, making it possible for a slice to contain itself. Although there are ways to deal with such cases, none is simple, efficient, and most importantly, obvious.

Second, because slice elements are indirect, a fixed slice value may contain different elements at different times as the contents of the underlying array are modified. Because a hash table such as Go's map type makes only shallow copies of its keys, it requires that equality for each key remain the same throughout the lifetime of the hash table. Deep equivalence would thus make slices unsuitable for use as map keys. For reference types like pointers and channels, the == operator tests *reference identity*, that is, whether the two entities refer to the same thing. An analogous "shallow" equality test for slices could be useful, and it would solve the problem with maps, but the inconsistent treatment of slices and arrays by the == operator would be confusing. The safest choice is to disallow slice comparisons altogether.

The only legal slice comparison is against nil, as in

```
if summer == nil { /* ... */ }
```

The zero value of a slice type is nil. A nil slice has no underlying array. The nil slice has length and capacity zero, but there are also non-nil slices of length and capacity zero, such as []int{} or make([]int, 3)[3:]. As with any type that can have nil values, the nil value of a particular slice type can be written using a conversion expression such as []int(nil).

```
var s []int     // len(s) == 0, s == nil
s = nil         // len(s) == 0, s == nil
s = []int(nil)  // len(s) == 0, s == nil
s = []int{}     // len(s) == 0, s != nil
```

So, if you need to test whether a slice is empty, use len(s) == 0, not s == nil. Other than comparing equal to nil, a nil slice behaves like any other zero-length slice; reverse(nil) is perfectly safe, for example. Unless clearly documented to the contrary, Go functions should treat all zero-length slices the same way, whether nil or non-nil.

The built-in function make creates a slice of a specified element type, length, and capacity. The capacity argument may be omitted, in which case the capacity equals the length.

```
make([]T, len)
make([]T, len, cap) // same as make([]T, cap)[:len]
```

Under the hood, make creates an unnamed array variable and returns a slice of it; the array is accessible only through the returned slice. In the first form, the slice is a view of the entire array. In the second, the slice is a view of only the array's first len elements, but its capacity includes the entire array. The additional elements are set aside for future growth.

4.2.1. The append Function

The built-in append function appends items to slices:

```
var runes []rune
for _, r := range "Hello, 世界" {
    runes = append(runes, r)
}
fmt.Printf("%q\n", runes) // "['H' 'e' 'l' 'l' 'o' ',' ' ' '世' '界']"
```

The loop uses append to build the slice of nine runes encoded by the string literal, although this specific problem is more conveniently solved by using the built-in conversion []rune("Hello, 世界").

The append function is crucial to understanding how slices work, so let's take a look at what is going on. Here's a version called appendInt that is specialized for []int slices:

gopl.io/ch4/append
```
func appendInt(x []int, y int) []int {
    var z []int
    zlen := len(x) + 1
    if zlen <= cap(x) {
        // There is room to grow.  Extend the slice.
        z = x[:zlen]
    } else {
        // There is insufficient space.  Allocate a new array.
        // Grow by doubling, for amortized linear complexity.
        zcap := zlen
        if zcap < 2*len(x) {
            zcap = 2 * len(x)
        }
        z = make([]int, zlen, zcap)
        copy(z, x) // a built-in function; see text
    }
    z[len(x)] = y
    return z
}
```

Each call to appendInt must check whether the slice has sufficient capacity to hold the new elements in the existing array. If so, it extends the slice by defining a larger slice (still within the original array), copies the element y into the new space, and returns the slice. The input x and the result z share the same underlying array.

If there is insufficient space for growth, appendInt must allocate a new array big enough to hold the result, copy the values from x into it, then append the new element y. The result z now refers to a different underlying array than the array that x refers to.

It would be straightforward to copy the elements with explicit loops, but it's easier to use the built-in function copy, which copies elements from one slice to another of the same type. Its first argument is the destination and its second is the source, resembling the order of operands in an assignment like dst = src. The slices may refer to the same underlying array; they may even overlap. Although we don't use it here, copy returns the number of elements actually copied, which is the smaller of the two slice lengths, so there is no danger of running off the end or overwriting something out of range.

For efficiency, the new array is usually somewhat larger than the minimum needed to hold x and y. Expanding the array by doubling its size at each expansion avoids an excessive number of allocations and ensures that appending a single element takes constant time on average. This program demonstrates the effect:

```go
func main() {
    var x, y []int
    for i := 0; i < 10; i++ {
        y = appendInt(x, i)
        fmt.Printf("%d  cap=%d\t%v\n", i, cap(y), y)
        x = y
    }
}
```

Each change in capacity indicates an allocation and a copy:

```
0   cap=1    [0]
1   cap=2    [0 1]
2   cap=4    [0 1 2]
3   cap=4    [0 1 2 3]
4   cap=8    [0 1 2 3 4]
5   cap=8    [0 1 2 3 4 5]
6   cap=8    [0 1 2 3 4 5 6]
7   cap=8    [0 1 2 3 4 5 6 7]
8   cap=16   [0 1 2 3 4 5 6 7 8]
9   cap=16   [0 1 2 3 4 5 6 7 8 9]
```

Let's take a closer look at the i=3 iteration. The slice x contains the three elements [0 1 2] but has capacity 4, so there is a single element of slack at the end, and appendInt of the element 3 may proceed without reallocating. The resulting slice y has length and capacity 4, and has the same underlying array as the original slice x, as Figure 4.2 shows.

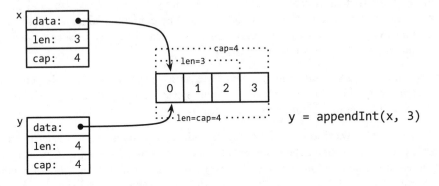

Figure 4.2. Appending with room to grow.

On the next iteration, i=4, there is no slack at all, so appendInt allocates a new array of size 8, copies the four elements [0 1 2 3] of x, and appends 4, the value of i. The resulting slice y has a length of 5 but a capacity of 8; the slack of 3 will save the next three iterations from the need to reallocate. The slices y and x are views of different arrays. This operation is depicted in Figure 4.3.

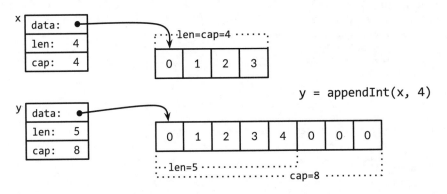

Figure 4.3. Appending without room to grow.

The built-in append function may use a more sophisticated growth strategy than appendInt's simplistic one. Usually we don't know whether a given call to append will cause a reallocation, so we can't assume that the original slice refers to the same array as the resulting slice, nor that it refers to a different one. Similarly, we must not assume that assignments to elements of the old slice will (or will not) be reflected in the new slice. Consequently, it's usual to assign the result of a call to append to the same slice variable whose value we passed to append:

```
runes = append(runes, r)
```

Updating the slice variable is required not just when calling append, but for any function that may change the length or capacity of a slice or make it refer to a different underlying array. To use slices correctly, it's important to bear in mind that although the elements of the underlying array are indirect, the slice's pointer, length, and capacity are not. To update them requires an assignment like the one above. In this respect, slices are not "pure" reference types but resemble an aggregate type such as this struct:

```
type IntSlice struct {
    ptr      *int
    len, cap int
}
```

Our appendInt function adds a single element to a slice, but the built-in append lets us add more than one new element, or even a whole slice of them.

```
var x []int
x = append(x, 1)
x = append(x, 2, 3)
x = append(x, 4, 5, 6)
x = append(x, x...) // append the slice x
fmt.Println(x)      // "[1 2 3 4 5 6 1 2 3 4 5 6]"
```

With the small modification shown below, we can match the behavior of the built-in append. The ellipsis "..." in the declaration of appendInt makes the function *variadic*: it accepts any number of final arguments. The corresponding ellipsis in the call above to append shows how to supply a list of arguments from a slice. We'll explain this mechanism in detail in Section 5.7.

```
func appendInt(x []int, y ...int) []int {
    var z []int
    zlen := len(x) + len(y)
    // ...expand z to at least zlen...
    copy(z[len(x):], y)
    return z
}
```

The logic to expand z's underlying array remains unchanged and is not shown.

4.2.2. In-Place Slice Techniques

Let's see more examples of functions that, like rotate and reverse, modify the elements of a slice in place. Given a list of strings, the nonempty function returns the non-empty ones:

gopl.io/ch4/nonempty

```
// Nonempty is an example of an in-place slice algorithm.
package main

import "fmt"
```

```
// nonempty returns a slice holding only the non-empty strings.
// The underlying array is modified during the call.
func nonempty(strings []string) []string {
    i := 0
    for _, s := range strings {
        if s != "" {
            strings[i] = s
            i++
        }
    }
    return strings[:i]
}
```

The subtle part is that the input slice and the output slice share the same underlying array.
This avoids the need to allocate another array, though of course the contents of data are partly
overwritten, as evidenced by the second print statement:

```
data := []string{"one", "", "three"}
fmt.Printf("%q\n", nonempty(data)) // `["one" "three"]`
fmt.Printf("%q\n", data)           // `["one" "three" "three"]`
```

Thus we would usually write: data = nonempty(data).

The nonempty function can also be written using append:

```
func nonempty2(strings []string) []string {
    out := strings[:0] // zero-length slice of original
    for _, s := range strings {
        if s != "" {
            out = append(out, s)
        }
    }
    return out
}
```

Whichever variant we use, reusing an array in this way requires that at most one output value
is produced for each input value, which is true of many algorithms that filter out elements of a
sequence or combine adjacent ones. Such intricate slice usage is the exception, not the rule,
but it can be clear, efficient, and useful on occasion.

A slice can be used to implement a stack. Given an initially empty slice stack, we can push a
new value onto the end of the slice with append:

```
stack = append(stack, v) // push v
```

The top of the stack is the last element:

```
top := stack[len(stack)-1] // top of stack
```

and shrinking the stack by popping that element is

```
stack = stack[:len(stack)-1] // pop
```

To remove an element from the middle of a slice, preserving the order of the remaining elements, use copy to slide the higher-numbered elements down by one to fill the gap:

```
func remove(slice []int, i int) []int {
    copy(slice[i:], slice[i+1:])
    return slice[:len(slice)-1]
}
func main() {
    s := []int{5, 6, 7, 8, 9}
    fmt.Println(remove(s, 2)) // "[5 6 8 9]"
}
```

And if we don't need to preserve the order, we can just move the last element into the gap:

```
func remove(slice []int, i int) []int {
    slice[i] = slice[len(slice)-1]
    return slice[:len(slice)-1]
}
func main() {
    s := []int{5, 6, 7, 8, 9}
    fmt.Println(remove(s, 2)) // "[5 6 9 8]
}
```

Exercise 4.3: Rewrite reverse to use an array pointer instead of a slice.

Exercise 4.4: Write a version of rotate that operates in a single pass.

Exercise 4.5: Write an in-place function to eliminate adjacent duplicates in a []string slice.

Exercise 4.6: Write an in-place function that squashes each run of adjacent Unicode spaces (see unicode.IsSpace) in a UTF-8-encoded []byte slice into a single ASCII space.

Exercise 4.7: Modify reverse to reverse the characters of a []byte slice that represents a UTF-8-encoded string, in place. Can you do it without allocating new memory?

4.3. Maps

The hash table is one of the most ingenious and versatile of all data structures. It is an unordered collection of key/value pairs in which all the keys are distinct, and the value associated with a given key can be retrieved, updated, or removed using a constant number of key comparisons on the average, no matter how large the hash table.

In Go, a *map* is a reference to a hash table, and a map type is written map[K]V, where K and V are the types of its keys and values. All of the keys in a given map are of the same type, and all of the values are of the same type, but the keys need not be of the same type as the values. The key type K must be comparable using ==, so that the map can test whether a given key is equal to one already within it. Though floating-point numbers are comparable, it's a bad idea to compare floats for equality and, as we mentioned in Chapter 3, especially bad if NaN is a possible value. There are no restrictions on the value type V.

The built-in function make can be used to create a map:

```
ages := make(map[string]int) // mapping from strings to ints
```

We can also use a *map literal* to create a new map populated with some initial key/value pairs:

```
ages := map[string]int{
    "alice":   31,
    "charlie": 34,
}
```

This is equivalent to

```
ages := make(map[string]int)
ages["alice"] = 31
ages["charlie"] = 34
```

so an alternative expression for a new empty map is map[string]int{}.

Map elements are accessed through the usual subscript notation:

```
ages["alice"] = 32
fmt.Println(ages["alice"]) // "32"
```

and removed with the built-in function delete:

```
delete(ages, "alice") // remove element ages["alice"]
```

All of these operations are safe even if the element isn't in the map; a map lookup using a key that isn't present returns the zero value for its type, so, for instance, the following works even when "bob" is not yet a key in the map because the value of ages["bob"] will be 0.

```
ages["bob"] = ages["bob"] + 1 // happy birthday!
```

The shorthand assignment forms x += y and x++ also work for map elements, so we can rewrite the statement above as

```
ages["bob"] += 1
```

or even more concisely as

```
ages["bob"]++
```

But a map element is not a variable, and we cannot take its address:

```
_ = &ages["bob"] // compile error: cannot take address of map element
```

One reason that we can't take the address of a map element is that growing a map might cause rehashing of existing elements into new storage locations, thus potentially invalidating the address.

To enumerate all the key/value pairs in the map, we use a range-based for loop similar to those we saw for slices. Successive iterations of the loop cause the name and age variables to be set to the next key/value pair:

```
for name, age := range ages {
    fmt.Printf("%s\t%d\n", name, age)
}
```

The order of map iteration is unspecified, and different implementations might use a different hash function, leading to a different ordering. In practice, the order is random, varying from one execution to the next. This is intentional; making the sequence vary helps force programs to be robust across implementations. To enumerate the key/value pairs in order, we must sort the keys explicitly, for instance, using the `Strings` function from the `sort` package if the keys are strings. This is a common pattern:

```
import "sort"

var names []string
for name := range ages {
    names = append(names, name)
}
sort.Strings(names)
for _, name := range names {
    fmt.Printf("%s\t%d\n", name, ages[name])
}
```

Since we know the final size of `names` from the outset, it is more efficient to allocate an array of the required size up front. The statement below creates a slice that is initially empty but has sufficient capacity to hold all the keys of the `ages` map:

```
names := make([]string, 0, len(ages))
```

In the first `range` loop above, we require only the keys of the `ages` map, so we omit the second loop variable. In the second loop, we require only the elements of the `names` slice, so we use the blank identifier _ to ignore the first variable, the index.

The zero value for a map type is `nil`, that is, a reference to no hash table at all.

```
var ages map[string]int
fmt.Println(ages == nil)    // "true"
fmt.Println(len(ages) == 0) // "true"
```

Most operations on maps, including lookup, `delete`, `len`, and `range` loops, are safe to perform on a nil map reference, since it behaves like an empty map. But storing to a nil map causes a panic:

```
ages["carol"] = 21 // panic: assignment to entry in nil map
```

You must allocate the map before you can store into it.

Accessing a map element by subscripting always yields a value. If the key is present in the map, you get the corresponding value; if not, you get the zero value for the element type, as we saw with `ages["bob"]`. For many purposes that's fine, but sometimes you need to know whether the element was really there or not. For example, if the element type is numeric, you might have to distinguish between a nonexistent element and an element that happens to have the value zero, using a test like this:

```
age, ok := ages["bob"]
if !ok { /* "bob" is not a key in this map; age == 0. */ }
```

You'll often see these two statements combined, like this:

```
if age, ok := ages["bob"]; !ok { /* ... */ }
```

Subscripting a map in this context yields two values; the second is a boolean that reports whether the element was present. The boolean variable is often called ok, especially if it is immediately used in an if condition.

As with slices, maps cannot be compared to each other; the only legal comparison is with nil. To test whether two maps contain the same keys and the same associated values, we must write a loop:

```
func equal(x, y map[string]int) bool {
    if len(x) != len(y) {
        return false
    }
    for k, xv := range x {
        if yv, ok := y[k]; !ok || yv != xv {
            return false
        }
    }
    return true
}
```

Observe how we use !ok to distinguish the "missing" and "present but zero" cases. Had we naïvely written xv != y[k], the call below would incorrectly report its arguments as equal:

```
// True if equal is written incorrectly.
equal(map[string]int{"A": 0}, map[string]int{"B": 42})
```

Go does not provide a set type, but since the keys of a map are distinct, a map can serve this purpose. To illustrate, the program dedup reads a sequence of lines and prints only the first occurrence of each distinct line. (It's a variant of the dup program that we showed in Section 1.3.) The dedup program uses a map whose keys represent the set of lines that have already appeared to ensure that subsequent occurrences are not printed.

gopl.io/ch4/dedup
```
func main() {
    seen := make(map[string]bool) // a set of strings
    input := bufio.NewScanner(os.Stdin)
    for input.Scan() {
        line := input.Text()
        if !seen[line] {
            seen[line] = true
            fmt.Println(line)
        }
    }
```

```
        if err := input.Err(); err != nil {
            fmt.Fprintf(os.Stderr, "dedup: %v\n", err)
            os.Exit(1)
        }
    }
```

Go programmers often describe a map used in this fashion as a "set of strings" without further ado, but beware, not all map[string]bool values are simple sets; some may contain both true and false values.

Sometimes we need a map or set whose keys are slices, but because a map's keys must be comparable, this cannot be expressed directly. However, it can be done in two steps. First we define a helper function k that maps each key to a string, with the property that k(x) == k(y) if and only if we consider x and y equivalent. Then we create a map whose keys are strings, applying the helper function to each key before we access the map.

The example below uses a map to record the number of times Add has been called with a given list of strings. It uses fmt.Sprintf to convert a slice of strings into a single string that is a suitable map key, quoting each slice element with %q to record string boundaries faithfully:

```
var m = make(map[string]int)

func k(list []string) string { return fmt.Sprintf("%q", list) }

func Add(list []string)       { m[k(list)]++ }
func Count(list []string) int { return m[k(list)] }
```

The same approach can be used for any non-comparable key type, not just slices. It's even useful for comparable key types when you want a definition of equality other than ==, such as case-insensitive comparisons for strings. And the type of k(x) needn't be a string; any comparable type with the desired equivalence property will do, such as integers, arrays, or structs.

Here's another example of maps in action, a program that counts the occurrences of each distinct Unicode code point in its input. Since there are a large number of possible characters, only a small fraction of which would appear in any particular document, a map is a natural way to keep track of just the ones that have been seen and their corresponding counts.

gopl.io/ch4/charcount

```
// Charcount computes counts of Unicode characters.
package main

import (
    "bufio"
    "fmt"
    "io"
    "os"
    "unicode"
    "unicode/utf8"
)
```

```go
func main() {
    counts := make(map[rune]int)    // counts of Unicode characters
    var utflen [utf8.UTFMax + 1]int // count of lengths of UTF-8 encodings
    invalid := 0                    // count of invalid UTF-8 characters

    in := bufio.NewReader(os.Stdin)
    for {
        r, n, err := in.ReadRune() // returns rune, nbytes, error
        if err == io.EOF {
            break
        }
        if err != nil {
            fmt.Fprintf(os.Stderr, "charcount: %v\n", err)
            os.Exit(1)
        }
        if r == unicode.ReplacementChar && n == 1 {
            invalid++
            continue
        }
        counts[r]++
        utflen[n]++
    }
    fmt.Printf("rune\tcount\n")
    for c, n := range counts {
        fmt.Printf("%q\t%d\n", c, n)
    }
    fmt.Print("\nlen\tcount\n")
    for i, n := range utflen {
        if i > 0 {
            fmt.Printf("%d\t%d\n", i, n)
        }
    }
    if invalid > 0 {
        fmt.Printf("\n%d invalid UTF-8 characters\n", invalid)
    }
}
```

The ReadRune method performs UTF-8 decoding and returns three values: the decoded rune, the length in bytes of its UTF-8 encoding, and an error value. The only error we expect is end-of-file. If the input was not a legal UTF-8 encoding of a rune, the returned rune is unicode.ReplacementChar and the length is 1.

The charcount program also prints a count of the lengths of the UTF-8 encodings of the runes that appeared in the input. A map is not the best data structure for that; since encoding lengths range only from 1 to utf8.UTFMax (which has the value 4), an array is more compact.

As an experiment, we ran charcount on this book itself at one point. Although it's mostly in English, of course, it does have a fair number of non-ASCII characters. Here are the top ten:

° 27 世 15 界 14 é 13 ˣ 10 ≤ 5 × 5 国 4 ɡ 4 □ 3 and here is the distribution of the lengths of all the UTF-8 encodings:

```
len count
1   765391
2   60
3   70
4   0
```

The value type of a map can itself be a composite type, such as a map or slice. In the following code, the key type of graph is string and the value type is map[string]bool, representing a set of strings. Conceptually, graph maps a string to a set of related strings, its successors in a directed graph.

gopl.io/ch4/graph

```go
var graph = make(map[string]map[string]bool)

func addEdge(from, to string) {
    edges := graph[from]
    if edges == nil {
        edges = make(map[string]bool)
        graph[from] = edges
    }
    edges[to] = true
}

func hasEdge(from, to string) bool {
    return graph[from][to]
}
```

The addEdge function shows the idiomatic way to populate a map lazily, that is, to initialize each value as its key appears for the first time. The hasEdge function shows how the zero value of a missing map entry is often put to work: even if neither from nor to is present, graph[from][to] will always give a meaningful result.

Exercise 4.8: Modify charcount to count letters, digits, and so on in their Unicode categories, using functions like unicode.IsLetter.

Exercise 4.9: Write a program wordfreq to report the frequency of each word in an input text file. Call input.Split(bufio.ScanWords) before the first call to Scan to break the input into words instead of lines.

4.4. Structs

A *struct* is an aggregate data type that groups together zero or more named values of arbitrary types as a single entity. Each value is called a *field*. The classic example of a struct from data processing is the employee record, whose fields are a unique ID, the employee's name, address, date of birth, position, salary, manager, and the like. All of these fields are collected into a single entity that can be copied as a unit, passed to functions and returned by them, stored in arrays, and so on.

These two statements declare a struct type called `Employee` and a variable called `dilbert` that is an instance of an `Employee`:

```
type Employee struct {
    ID          int
    Name        string
    Address     string
    DoB         time.Time
    Position    string
    Salary      int
    ManagerID int
}

var dilbert Employee
```

The individual fields of `dilbert` are accessed using dot notation like `dilbert.Name` and `dilbert.DoB`. Because `dilbert` is a variable, its fields are variables too, so we may assign to a field:

```
dilbert.Salary -= 5000 // demoted, for writing too few lines of code
```

or take its address and access it through a pointer:

```
position := &dilbert.Position
*position = "Senior " + *position // promoted, for outsourcing to Elbonia
```

The dot notation also works with a pointer to a struct:

```
var employeeOfTheMonth *Employee = &dilbert
employeeOfTheMonth.Position += " (proactive team player)"
```

The last statement is equivalent to

```
(*employeeOfTheMonth).Position += " (proactive team player)"
```

Given an employee's unique ID, the function `EmployeeByID` returns a pointer to an `Employee` struct. We can use the dot notation to access its fields:

```
func EmployeeByID(id int) *Employee { /* ... */ }

fmt.Println(EmployeeByID(dilbert.ManagerID).Position) // "Pointy-haired boss"

id := dilbert.ID
EmployeeByID(id).Salary = 0 // fired for... no real reason
```

The last statement updates the `Employee` struct that is pointed to by the result of the call to `EmployeeByID`. If the result type of `EmployeeByID` were changed to `Employee` instead of `*Employee`, the assignment statement would not compile since its left-hand side would not identify a variable.

Fields are usually written one per line, with the field's name preceding its type, but consecutive fields of the same type may be combined, as with `Name` and `Address` here:

```
type Employee struct {
    ID              int
    Name, Address   string
    DoB             time.Time
    Position        string
    Salary          int
    ManagerID       int
}
```

Field order is significant to type identity. Had we also combined the declaration of the Position field (also a string), or interchanged Name and Address, we would be defining a different
struct type. Typically we only combine the declarations of related fields.

The name of a struct field is exported if it begins with a capital letter; this is Go's main access
control mechanism. A struct type may contain a mixture of exported and unexported fields.

Struct types tend to be verbose because they often involve a line for each field. Although we
could write out the whole type each time it is needed, the repetition would get tiresome.
Instead, struct types usually appear within the declaration of a named type like Employee.

A named struct type S can't declare a field of the same type S: an aggregate value cannot contain itself. (An analogous restriction applies to arrays.) But S may declare a field of the
pointer type *S, which lets us create recursive data structures like linked lists and trees. This is
illustrated in the code below, which uses a binary tree to implement an insertion sort:

gopl.io/ch4/treesort

```
type tree struct {
    value       int
    left, right *tree
}
// Sort sorts values in place.
func Sort(values []int) {
    var root *tree
    for _, v := range values {
        root = add(root, v)
    }
    appendValues(values[:0], root)
}

// appendValues appends the elements of t to values in order
// and returns the resulting slice.
func appendValues(values []int, t *tree) []int {
    if t != nil {
        values = appendValues(values, t.left)
        values = append(values, t.value)
        values = appendValues(values, t.right)
    }
    return values
}
```

```
func add(t *tree, value int) *tree {
    if t == nil {
        // Equivalent to return &tree{value: value}.
        t = new(tree)
        t.value = value
        return t
    }
    if value < t.value {
        t.left = add(t.left, value)
    } else {
        t.right = add(t.right, value)
    }
    return t
}
```

The zero value for a struct is composed of the zero values of each of its fields. It is usually desirable that the zero value be a natural or sensible default. For example, in bytes.Buffer, the initial value of the struct is a ready-to-use empty buffer, and the zero value of sync.Mutex, which we'll see in Chapter 9, is a ready-to-use unlocked mutex. Sometimes this sensible initial behavior happens for free, but sometimes the type designer has to work at it.

The struct type with no fields is called the *empty struct*, written struct{}. It has size zero and carries no information but may be useful nonetheless. Some Go programmers use it instead of bool as the value type of a map that represents a set, to emphasize that only the keys are significant, but the space saving is marginal and the syntax more cumbersome, so we generally avoid it.

```
seen := make(map[string]struct{}) // set of strings
// ...
if _, ok := seen[s]; !ok {
    seen[s] = struct{}{}
    // ...first time seeing s...
}
```

4.4.1. Struct Literals

A value of a struct type can be written using a *struct literal* that specifies values for its fields.

```
type Point struct{ X, Y int }

p := Point{1, 2}
```

There are two forms of struct literal. The first form, shown above, requires that a value be specified for *every* field, in the right order. It burdens the writer (and reader) with remembering exactly what the fields are, and it makes the code fragile should the set of fields later grow or be reordered. Accordingly, this form tends to be used only within the package that defines the struct type, or with smaller struct types for which there is an obvious field ordering convention, like image.Point{x, y} or color.RGBA{red, green, blue, alpha}.

More often, the second form is used, in which a struct value is initialized by listing some or all of the field names and their corresponding values, as in this statement from the Lissajous program of Section 1.4:

```
anim := gif.GIF{LoopCount: nframes}
```

If a field is omitted in this kind of literal, it is set to the zero value for its type. Because names are provided, the order of fields doesn't matter.

The two forms cannot be mixed in the same literal. Nor can you use the (order-based) first form of literal to sneak around the rule that unexported identifiers may not be referred to from another package.

```
package p
type T struct{ a, b int } // a and b are not exported

package q
import "p"
var _ = p.T{a: 1, b: 2} // compile error: can't reference a, b
var _ = p.T{1, 2}       // compile error: can't reference a, b
```

Although the last line above doesn't mention the unexported field identifiers, it's really using them implicitly, so it's not allowed.

Struct values can be passed as arguments to functions and returned from them. For instance, this function scales a Point by a specified factor:

```
func Scale(p Point, factor int) Point {
    return Point{p.X * factor, p.Y * factor}
}

fmt.Println(Scale(Point{1, 2}, 5)) // "{5 10}"
```

For efficiency, larger struct types are usually passed to or returned from functions indirectly using a pointer,

```
func Bonus(e *Employee, percent int) int {
    return e.Salary * percent / 100
}
```

and this is required if the function must modify its argument, since in a call-by-value language like Go, the called function receives only a copy of an argument, not a reference to the original argument.

```
func AwardAnnualRaise(e *Employee) {
    e.Salary = e.Salary * 105 / 100
}
```

Because structs are so commonly dealt with through pointers, it's possible to use this shorthand notation to create and initialize a struct variable and obtain its address:

```
pp := &Point{1, 2}
```

It is exactly equivalent to

```
pp := new(Point)
*pp = Point{1, 2}
```

but &Point{1, 2} can be used directly within an expression, such as a function call.

4.4.2. Comparing Structs

If all the fields of a struct are comparable, the struct itself is comparable, so two expressions of that type may be compared using == or !=. The == operation compares the corresponding fields of the two structs in order, so the two printed expressions below are equivalent:

```
type Point struct{ X, Y int }

p := Point{1, 2}
q := Point{2, 1}
fmt.Println(p.X == q.X && p.Y == q.Y) // "false"
fmt.Println(p == q)                    // "false"
```

Comparable struct types, like other comparable types, may be used as the key type of a map.

```
type address struct {
    hostname string
    port     int
}

hits := make(map[address]int)
hits[address{"golang.org", 443}]++
```

4.4.3. Struct Embedding and Anonymous Fields

In this section, we'll see how Go's unusual *struct embedding* mechanism lets us use one named struct type as an *anonymous field* of another struct type, providing a convenient syntactic shortcut so that a simple dot expression like x.f can stand for a chain of fields like x.d.e.f.

Consider a 2-D drawing program that provides a library of shapes, such as rectangles, ellipses, stars, and wheels. Here are two of the types it might define:

```
type Circle struct {
    X, Y, Radius int
}

type Wheel struct {
    X, Y, Radius, Spokes int
}
```

A Circle has fields for the X and Y coordinates of its center, and a Radius. A Wheel has all the features of a Circle, plus Spokes, the number of inscribed radial spokes. Let's create a wheel:

```
var w Wheel
w.X = 8
w.Y = 8
w.Radius = 5
w.Spokes = 20
```

As the set of shapes grows, we're bound to notice similarities and repetition among them, so it may be convenient to factor out their common parts:

```
type Point struct {
    X, Y int
}

type Circle struct {
    Center Point
    Radius int
}

type Wheel struct {
    Circle Circle
    Spokes int
}
```

The application may be clearer for it, but this change makes accessing the fields of a Wheel more verbose:

```
var w Wheel
w.Circle.Center.X = 8
w.Circle.Center.Y = 8
w.Circle.Radius = 5
w.Spokes = 20
```

Go lets us declare a field with a type but no name; such fields are called *anonymous fields*. The type of the field must be a named type or a pointer to a named type. Below, Circle and Wheel have one anonymous field each. We say that a Point is *embedded* within Circle, and a Circle is embedded within Wheel.

```
type Circle struct {
    Point
    Radius int
}

type Wheel struct {
    Circle
    Spokes int
}
```

Thanks to embedding, we can refer to the names at the leaves of the implicit tree without giving the intervening names:

```
var w Wheel
w.X = 8            // equivalent to w.Circle.Point.X = 8
w.Y = 8            // equivalent to w.Circle.Point.Y = 8
w.Radius = 5       // equivalent to w.Circle.Radius = 5
w.Spokes = 20
```

The explicit forms shown in the comments above are still valid, however, showing that "anonymous field" is something of a misnomer. The fields `Circle` and `Point` do have names—that of the named type—but those names are optional in dot expressions. We may omit any or all of the anonymous fields when selecting their subfields.

Unfortunately, there's no corresponding shorthand for the struct literal syntax, so neither of these will compile:

```
w = Wheel{8, 8, 5, 20}                              // compile error: unknown fields
w = Wheel{X: 8, Y: 8, Radius: 5, Spokes: 20} // compile error: unknown fields
```

The struct literal must follow the shape of the type declaration, so we must use one of the two forms below, which are equivalent to each other:

gopl.io/ch4/embed

```
w = Wheel{Circle{Point{8, 8}, 5}, 20}

w = Wheel{
    Circle: Circle{
        Point:  Point{X: 8, Y: 8},
        Radius: 5,
    },
    Spokes: 20, // NOTE: trailing comma necessary here (and at Radius)
}

fmt.Printf("%#v\n", w)
// Output:
// Wheel{Circle:Circle{Point:Point{X:8, Y:8}, Radius:5}, Spokes:20}

w.X = 42

fmt.Printf("%#v\n", w)
// Output:
// Wheel{Circle:Circle{Point:Point{X:42, Y:8}, Radius:5}, Spokes:20}
```

Notice how the # adverb causes `Printf`'s %v verb to display values in a form similar to Go syntax. For struct values, this form includes the name of each field.

Because "anonymous" fields do have implicit names, you can't have two anonymous fields of the same type since their names would conflict. And because the name of the field is implicitly determined by its type, so too is the visibility of the field. In the examples above, the `Point` and `Circle` anonymous fields are exported. Had they been unexported (`point` and `circle`), we could still use the shorthand form

```
w.X = 8 // equivalent to w.circle.point.X = 8
```

but the explicit long form shown in the comment would be forbidden outside the declaring package because `circle` and `point` would be inaccessible.

What we've seen so far of struct embedding is just a sprinkling of syntactic sugar on the dot notation used to select struct fields. Later, we'll see that anonymous fields need not be struct types; any named type or pointer to a named type will do. But why would you want to embed a type that has no subfields?

The answer has to do with methods. The shorthand notation used for selecting the fields of an embedded type works for selecting its methods as well. In effect, the outer struct type gains not just the fields of the embedded type but its methods too. This mechanism is the main way that complex object behaviors are composed from simpler ones. *Composition* is central to object-oriented programming in Go, and we'll explore it further in Section 6.3.

4.5. JSON

JavaScript Object Notation (JSON) is a standard notation for sending and receiving structured information. JSON is not the only such notation. XML (§7.14), ASN.1, and Google's Protocol Buffers serve similar purposes and each has its niche, but because of its simplicity, readability, and universal support, JSON is the most widely used.

Go has excellent support for encoding and decoding these formats, provided by the standard library packages `encoding/json`, `encoding/xml`, `encoding/asn1`, and so on, and these packages all have similar APIs. This section gives a brief overview of the most important parts of the `encoding/json` package.

JSON is an encoding of JavaScript values—strings, numbers, booleans, arrays, and objects—as Unicode text. It's an efficient yet readable representation for the basic data types of Chapter 3 and the composite types of this chapter—arrays, slices, structs, and maps.

The basic JSON types are numbers (in decimal or scientific notation), booleans (`true` or `false`), and strings, which are sequences of Unicode code points enclosed in double quotes, with backslash escapes using a similar notation to Go, though JSON's \U*hhhh* numeric escapes denote UTF-16 codes, not runes.

These basic types may be combined recursively using JSON arrays and objects. A JSON array is an ordered sequence of values, written as a comma-separated list enclosed in square brackets; JSON arrays are used to encode Go arrays and slices. A JSON object is a mapping from strings to values, written as a sequence of `name:value` pairs separated by commas and surrounded by braces; JSON objects are used to encode Go maps (with string keys) and structs. For example:

```
boolean       true
number        -273.15
string        "She said \"Hello, 世界\""
array         ["gold", "silver", "bronze"]
object        {"year": 1980,
               "event": "archery",
               "medals": ["gold", "silver", "bronze"]}
```

Consider an application that gathers movie reviews and offers recommendations. Its Movie data type and a typical list of values are declared below. (The string literals after the Year and Color field declarations are *field tags*; we'll explain them in a moment.)

gopl.io/ch4/movie

```
type Movie struct {
    Title  string
    Year   int  `json:"released"`
    Color  bool `json:"color,omitempty"`
    Actors []string
}

var movies = []Movie{
    {Title: "Casablanca", Year: 1942, Color: false,
        Actors: []string{"Humphrey Bogart", "Ingrid Bergman"}},
    {Title: "Cool Hand Luke", Year: 1967, Color: true,
        Actors: []string{"Paul Newman"}},
    {Title: "Bullitt", Year: 1968, Color: true,
        Actors: []string{"Steve McQueen", "Jacqueline Bisset"}},
    // ...
}
```

Data structures like this are an excellent fit for JSON, and it's easy to convert in both directions. Converting a Go data structure like movies to JSON is called *marshaling*. Marshaling is done by json.Marshal:

```
data, err := json.Marshal(movies)
if err != nil {
    log.Fatalf("JSON marshaling failed: %s", err)
}
fmt.Printf("%s\n", data)
```

Marshal produces a byte slice containing a very long string with no extraneous white space; we've folded the lines so it fits:

```
[{"Title":"Casablanca","released":1942,"Actors":["Humphrey Bogart","Ingr
id Bergman"]},{"Title":"Cool Hand Luke","released":1967,"color":true,"Ac
tors":["Paul Newman"]},{"Title":"Bullitt","released":1968,"color":true,"
Actors":["Steve McQueen","Jacqueline Bisset"]}]
```

This compact representation contains all the information but it's hard to read. For human consumption, a variant called json.MarshalIndent produces neatly indented output. Two additional arguments define a prefix for each line of output and a string for each level of indentation:

```
data, err := json.MarshalIndent(movies, "", "    ")
if err != nil {
    log.Fatalf("JSON marshaling failed: %s", err)
}
fmt.Printf("%s\n", data)
```

The code above prints

```
[
    {
        "Title": "Casablanca",
        "released": 1942,
        "Actors": [
            "Humphrey Bogart",
            "Ingrid Bergman"
        ]
    },
    {
        "Title": "Cool Hand Luke",
        "released": 1967,
        "color": true,
        "Actors": [
            "Paul Newman"
        ]
    },
    {
        "Title": "Bullitt",
        "released": 1968,
        "color": true,
        "Actors": [
            "Steve McQueen",
            "Jacqueline Bisset"
        ]
    }
]
```

Marshaling uses the Go struct field names as the field names for the JSON objects (through *reflection*, as we'll see in Section 12.6). Only exported fields are marshaled, which is why we chose capitalized names for all the Go field names.

You may have noticed that the name of the Year field changed to released in the output, and Color changed to color. That's because of the *field tags*. A field tag is a string of metadata associated at compile time with the field of a struct:

```
Year  int  `json:"released"`
Color bool `json:"color,omitempty"`
```

A field tag may be any literal string, but it is conventionally interpreted as a space-separated list of key:"value" pairs; since they contain double quotation marks, field tags are usually written with raw string literals. The json key controls the behavior of the encoding/json package, and other encoding/... packages follow this convention. The first part of the json field tag specifies an alternative JSON name for the Go field. Field tags are often used to specify an idiomatic JSON name like total_count for a Go field named TotalCount. The tag for Color has an additional option, omitempty, which indicates that no JSON output should be produced if the field has the zero value for its type (false, here) or is otherwise empty. Sure enough, the JSON output for *Casablanca*, a black-and-white movie, has no color field.

The inverse operation to marshaling, decoding JSON and populating a Go data structure, is called *unmarshaling*, and it is done by `json.Unmarshal`. The code below unmarshals the JSON movie data into a slice of structs whose only field is `Title`. By defining suitable Go data structures in this way, we can select which parts of the JSON input to decode and which to discard. When `Unmarshal` returns, it has filled in the slice with the `Title` information; other names in the JSON are ignored.

```
var titles []struct{ Title string }
if err := json.Unmarshal(data, &titles); err != nil {
    log.Fatalf("JSON unmarshaling failed: %s", err)
}
fmt.Println(titles) // "[{Casablanca} {Cool Hand Luke} {Bullitt}]"
```

Many web services provide a JSON interface—make a request with HTTP and back comes the desired information in JSON format. To illustrate, let's query the GitHub issue tracker using its web-service interface. First we'll define the necessary types and constants:

gopl.io/ch4/github

```
// Package github provides a Go API for the GitHub issue tracker.
// See https://developer.github.com/v3/search/#search-issues.
package github

import "time"

const IssuesURL = "https://api.github.com/search/issues"

type IssuesSearchResult struct {
    TotalCount int `json:"total_count"`
    Items      []*Issue
}

type Issue struct {
    Number    int
    HTMLURL   string `json:"html_url"`
    Title     string
    State     string
    User      *User
    CreatedAt time.Time `json:"created_at"`
    Body      string    // in Markdown format
}

type User struct {
    Login   string
    HTMLURL string `json:"html_url"`
}
```

As before, the names of all the struct fields must be capitalized even if their JSON names are not. However, the matching process that associates JSON names with Go struct names during unmarshaling is case-insensitive, so it's only necessary to use a field tag when there's an underscore in the JSON name but not in the Go name. Again, we are being selective about which fields to decode; the GitHub search response contains considerably more information than we show here.

The SearchIssues function makes an HTTP request and decodes the result as JSON. Since the query terms presented by a user could contain characters like ? and & that have special meaning in a URL, we use url.QueryEscape to ensure that they are taken literally.

gopl.io/ch4/github

```go
package github

import (
    "encoding/json"
    "fmt"
    "net/http"
    "net/url"
    "strings"
)

// SearchIssues queries the GitHub issue tracker.
func SearchIssues(terms []string) (*IssuesSearchResult, error) {
    q := url.QueryEscape(strings.Join(terms, " "))
    resp, err := http.Get(IssuesURL + "?q=" + q)
    if err != nil {
        return nil, err
    }

    // We must close resp.Body on all execution paths.
    // (Chapter 5 presents 'defer', which makes this simpler.)
    if resp.StatusCode != http.StatusOK {
        resp.Body.Close()
        return nil, fmt.Errorf("search query failed: %s", resp.Status)
    }

    var result IssuesSearchResult
    if err := json.NewDecoder(resp.Body).Decode(&result); err != nil {
        resp.Body.Close()
        return nil, err
    }
    resp.Body.Close()
    return &result, nil
}
```

The earlier examples used json.Unmarshal to decode the entire contents of a byte slice as a single JSON entity. For variety, this example uses the *streaming* decoder, json.Decoder, which allows several JSON entities to be decoded in sequence from the same stream, although we don't need that feature here. As you might expect, there is a corresponding streaming encoder called json.Encoder.

The call to Decode populates the variable result. There are various ways we can format its value nicely. The simplest, demonstrated by the issues command below, is as a text table with fixed-width columns, but in the next section we'll see a more sophisticated approach based on templates.

gopl.io/ch4/issues

```go
// Issues prints a table of GitHub issues matching the search terms.
package main

import (
    "fmt"
    "log"
    "os"

    "gopl.io/ch4/github"
)

func main() {
    result, err := github.SearchIssues(os.Args[1:])
    if err != nil {
        log.Fatal(err)
    }
    fmt.Printf("%d issues:\n", result.TotalCount)
    for _, item := range result.Items {
        fmt.Printf("#%-5d %9.9s %.55s\n",
            item.Number, item.User.Login, item.Title)
    }
}
```

The command-line arguments specify the search terms. The command below queries the Go project's issue tracker for the list of open bugs related to JSON decoding:

```
$ go build gopl.io/ch4/issues
$ ./issues repo:golang/go is:open json decoder
13 issues:
#5680     eaigner encoding/json: set key converter on en/decoder
#6050   gopherbot encoding/json: provide tokenizer
#8658   gopherbot encoding/json: use bufio
#8462   kortschak encoding/json: UnmarshalText confuses json.Unmarshal
#5901         rsc encoding/json: allow override type marshaling
#9812   klauspost encoding/json: string tag not symmetric
#7872   extempora encoding/json: Encoder internally buffers full output
#9650     cespare encoding/json: Decoding gives errPhase when unmarshalin
#6716   gopherbot encoding/json: include field name in unmarshal error me
#6901   lukescott encoding/json, encoding/xml: option to treat unknown fi
#6384     joeshaw encoding/json: encode precise floating point integers u
#6647     btracey x/tools/cmd/godoc: display type kind of each named type
#4237   gjemiller encoding/base64: URLEncoding padding is optional
```

The GitHub web-service interface at https://developer.github.com/v3/ has many more features than we have space for here.

Exercise 4.10: Modify issues to report the results in age categories, say less than a month old, less than a year old, and more than a year old.

Exercise 4.11: Build a tool that lets users create, read, update, and delete GitHub issues from the command line, invoking their preferred text editor when substantial text input is required.

Exercise 4.12: The popular web comic *xkcd* has a JSON interface. For example, a request to `https://xkcd.com/571/info.0.json` produces a detailed description of comic 571, one of many favorites. Download each URL (once!) and build an offline index. Write a tool `xkcd` that, using this index, prints the URL and transcript of each comic that matches a search term provided on the command line.

Exercise 4.13: The JSON-based web service of the Open Movie Database lets you search `https://omdbapi.com/` for a movie by name and download its poster image. Write a tool `poster` that downloads the poster image for the movie named on the command line.

4.6. Text and HTML Templates

The previous example does only the simplest possible formatting, for which `Printf` is entirely adequate. But sometimes formatting must be more elaborate, and it's desirable to separate the format from the code more completely. This can be done with the `text/template` and `html/template` packages, which provide a mechanism for substituting the values of variables into a text or HTML template.

A template is a string or file containing one or more portions enclosed in double braces, `{{...}}`, called *actions*. Most of the string is printed literally, but the actions trigger other behaviors. Each action contains an expression in the template language, a simple but powerful notation for printing values, selecting struct fields, calling functions and methods, expressing control flow such as `if-else` statements and `range` loops, and instantiating other templates. A simple template string is shown below:

gopl.io/ch4/issuesreport

```
const templ = `{{.TotalCount}} issues:
{{range .Items}}----------------------------------------
Number: {{.Number}}
User:   {{.User.Login}}
Title:  {{.Title | printf "%.64s"}}
Age:    {{.CreatedAt | daysAgo}} days
{{end}}`
```

This template first prints the number of matching issues, then prints the number, user, title, and age in days of each one. Within an action, there is a notion of the current value, referred to as "dot" and written as ".", a period. The dot initially refers to the template's parameter, which will be a `github.IssuesSearchResult` in this example. The `{{.TotalCount}}` action expands to the value of the `TotalCount` field, printed in the usual way. The `{{range .Items}}` and `{{end}}` actions create a loop, so the text between them is expanded multiple times, with dot bound to successive elements of `Items`.

Within an action, the | notation makes the result of one operation the argument of another, analogous to a Unix shell pipeline. In the case of `Title`, the second operation is the `printf` function, which is a built-in synonym for `fmt.Sprintf` in all templates. For `Age`, the second operation is the following function, `daysAgo`, which converts the `CreatedAt` field into an elapsed time, using `time.Since`:

```
func daysAgo(t time.Time) int {
    return int(time.Since(t).Hours() / 24)
}
```

Notice that the type of `CreatedAt` is `time.Time`, not `string`. In the same way that a type may control its string formatting (§2.5) by defining certain methods, a type may also define methods to control its JSON marshaling and unmarshaling behavior. The JSON-marshaled value of a `time.Time` is a string in a standard format.

Producing output with a template is a two-step process. First we must parse the template into a suitable internal representation, and then execute it on specific inputs. Parsing need be done only once. The code below creates and parses the template `templ` defined above. Note the chaining of method calls: the `New` function from the `text/template` package creates and returns a template; `Funcs` adds `daysAgo` to the set of functions accessible within this template, then returns that template; finally, `Parse` is called on the result.

```
report, err := template.New("report").
    Funcs(template.FuncMap{"daysAgo": daysAgo}).
    Parse(templ)
if err != nil {
    log.Fatal(err)
}
```

Because templates are usually fixed at compile time, failure to parse a template indicates a fatal bug in the program. The `template.Must` helper function makes error handling more convenient: it accepts a template and an error, checks that the error is nil (and panics otherwise), and then returns the template. We'll come back to this idea in Section 5.9.

Once the template has been created, augmented with `daysAgo`, parsed, and checked, we can execute it using a `github.IssuesSearchResult` as the data source and `os.Stdout` as the destination:

```
var report = template.Must(template.New("issuelist").
    Funcs(template.FuncMap{"daysAgo": daysAgo}).
    Parse(templ))

func main() {
    result, err := github.SearchIssues(os.Args[1:])
    if err != nil {
        log.Fatal(err)
    }
    if err := report.Execute(os.Stdout, result); err != nil {
        log.Fatal(err)
    }
}
```

The program prints a plain text report like this:

```
$ go build gopl.io/ch4/issuesreport
$ ./issuesreport repo:golang/go is:open json decoder
13 issues:
----------------------------------------
Number: 5680
User:   eaigner
Title:  encoding/json: set key converter on en/decoder
Age:    750 days
----------------------------------------
Number: 6050
User:   gopherbot
Title:  encoding/json: provide tokenizer
Age:    695 days
----------------------------------------
...
```

Now let's turn to the html/template package. It uses the same API and expression language as text/template but adds features for automatic and context-appropriate escaping of strings appearing within HTML, JavaScript, CSS, or URLs. These features can help avoid a perennial security problem of HTML generation, an *injection attack*, in which an adversary crafts a string value like the title of an issue to include malicious code that, when improperly escaped by a template, gives them control over the page.

The template below prints the list of issues as an HTML table. Note the different import:

gopl.io/ch4/issueshtml
```
import "html/template"

var issueList = template.Must(template.New("issuelist").Parse(`
<h1>{{.TotalCount}} issues</h1>
<table>
<tr style='text-align: left'>
  <th>#</th>
  <th>State</th>
  <th>User</th>
  <th>Title</th>
</tr>
{{range .Items}}
<tr>
  <td><a href='{{.HTMLURL}}'>{{.Number}}</td>
  <td>{{.State}}</td>
  <td><a href='{{.User.HTMLURL}}'>{{.User.Login}}</a></td>
  <td><a href='{{.HTMLURL}}'>{{.Title}}</a></td>
</tr>
{{end}}
</table>
`))
```

The command below executes the new template on the results of a slightly different query:

```
$ go build gopl.io/ch4/issueshtml
$ ./issueshtml repo:golang/go commenter:gopherbot json encoder >issues.html
```

Figure 4.4 shows the appearance of the table in a web browser. The links connect to the appropriate web pages at GitHub.

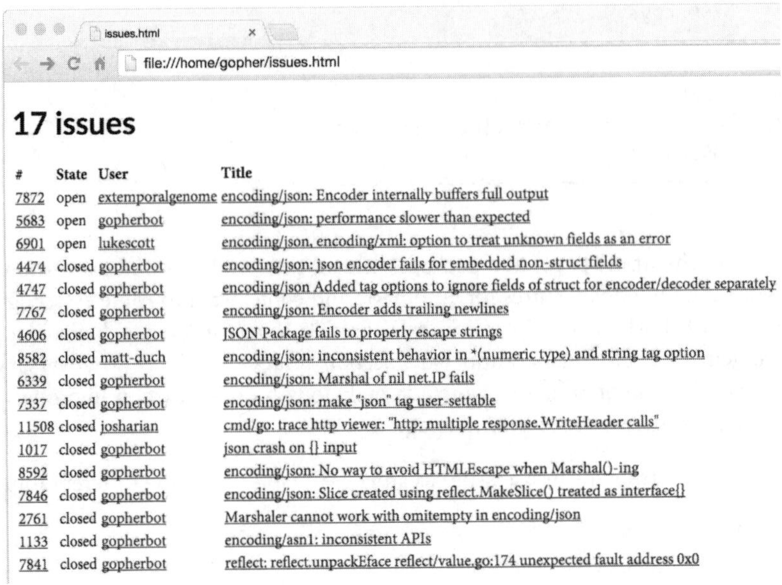

17 issues

#	State	User	Title
7872	open	extemporalgenome	encoding/json: Encoder internally buffers full output
5683	open	gopherbot	encoding/json: performance slower than expected
6901	open	lukescott	encoding/json, encoding/xml: option to treat unknown fields as an error
4474	closed	gopherbot	encoding/json: json encoder fails for embedded non-struct fields
4747	closed	gopherbot	encoding/json Added tag options to ignore fields of struct for encoder/decoder separately
7767	closed	gopherbot	encoding/json: Encoder adds trailing newlines
4606	closed	gopherbot	JSON Package fails to properly escape strings
8582	closed	matt-duch	encoding/json: inconsistent behavior in *(numeric type) and string tag option
6339	closed	gopherbot	encoding/json: Marshal of nil net.IP fails
7337	closed	gopherbot	encoding/json: make "json" tag user-settable
11508	closed	josharian	cmd/go: trace http viewer: "http: multiple response.WriteHeader calls"
1017	closed	gopherbot	json crash on {} input
8592	closed	gopherbot	encoding/json: No way to avoid HTMLEscape when Marshal()-ing
7846	closed	gopherbot	encoding/json: Slice created using reflect.MakeSlice() treated as interface{}
2761	closed	gopherbot	Marshaler cannot work with omitempty in encoding/json
1133	closed	gopherbot	encoding/asn1: inconsistent APIs
7841	closed	gopherbot	reflect: reflect.unpackEface reflect/value.go:174 unexpected fault address 0x0

Figure 4.4. An HTML table of Go project issues relating to JSON encoding.

None of the issues in Figure 4.4 pose a challenge for HTML, but we can see the effect more clearly with issues whose titles contain HTML metacharacters like & and <. We've selected two such issues for this example:

```
$ ./issueshtml repo:golang/go 3133 10535 >issues2.html
```

Figure 4.5 shows the result of this query. Notice that the html/template package automatically HTML-escaped the titles so that they appear literally. Had we used the text/template package by mistake, the four-character string "<" would have been rendered as a less-than character '<', and the string "<link>" would have become a link element, changing the structure of the HTML document and perhaps compromising its security.

We can suppress this auto-escaping behavior for fields that contain trusted HTML data by using the named string type template.HTML instead of string. Similar named types exist for trusted JavaScript, CSS, and URLs. The program below demonstrates the principle by using two fields with the same value but different types: A is a string and B is a template.HTML.

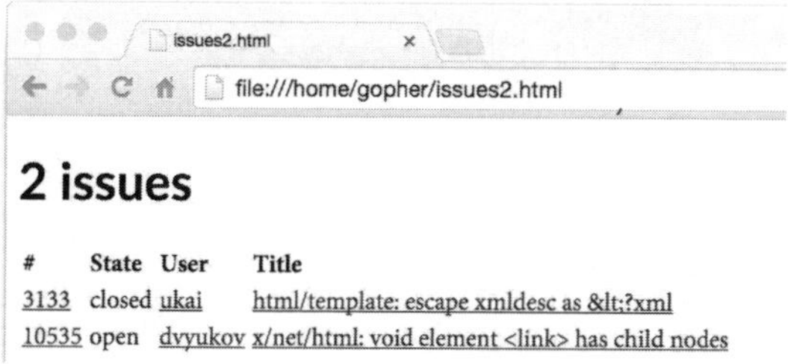

Figure 4.5. HTML metacharacters in issue titles are correctly displayed.

gopl.io/ch4/autoescape

```
func main() {
    const templ = `<p>A: {{.A}}</p><p>B: {{.B}}</p>`
    t := template.Must(template.New("escape").Parse(templ))
    var data struct {
        A string        // untrusted plain text
        B template.HTML // trusted HTML
    }
    data.A = "<b>Hello!</b>"
    data.B = "<b>Hello!</b>"
    if err := t.Execute(os.Stdout, data); err != nil {
        log.Fatal(err)
    }
}
```

Figure 4.6 shows the template's output as it appears in a browser. We can see that A was subject to escaping but B was not.

Figure 4.6. String values are HTML-escaped but `template.HTML` values are not.

We have space here to show only the most basic features of the template system. As always, for more information, consult the package documentation:

```
$ go doc text/template
$ go doc html/template
```

Exercise 4.14: Create a web server that queries GitHub once and then allows navigation of the list of bug reports, milestones, and users.

5

Functions

A function lets us wrap up a sequence of statements as a unit that can be called from elsewhere in a program, perhaps multiple times. Functions make it possible to break a big job into smaller pieces that might well be written by different people separated by both time and space. A function hides its implementation details from its users. For all of these reasons, functions are a critical part of any programming language.

We've seen many functions already. Now let's take time for a more thorough discussion. The running example of this chapter is a web crawler, that is, the component of a web search engine responsible for fetching web pages, discovering the links within them, fetching the pages identified by those links, and so on. A web crawler gives us ample opportunity to explore recursion, anonymous functions, error handling, and aspects of functions that are unique to Go.

5.1. Function Declarations

A function declaration has a name, a list of parameters, an optional list of results, and a body:

```
func name(parameter-list) (result-list) {
    body
}
```

The parameter list specifies the names and types of the function's *parameters*, which are the local variables whose values or *arguments* are supplied by the caller. The result list specifies the types of the values that the function returns. If the function returns one unnamed result or no results at all, parentheses are optional and usually omitted. Leaving off the result list entirely declares a function that does not return any value and is called only for its effects. In the hypot function,

```
func hypot(x, y float64) float64 {
    return math.Sqrt(x*x + y*y)
}

fmt.Println(hypot(3, 4)) // "5"
```

x and y are parameters in the declaration, 3 and 4 are arguments of the call, and the function returns a float64 value.

Like parameters, results may be named. In that case, each name declares a local variable initialized to the zero value for its type.

A function that has a result list must end with a return statement unless execution clearly cannot reach the end of the function, perhaps because the function ends with a call to panic or an infinite for loop with no break.

As we saw with hypot, a sequence of parameters or results of the same type can be factored so that the type itself is written only once. These two declarations are equivalent:

```
func f(i, j, k int, s, t string)                 { /* ... */ }
func f(i int, j int, k int, s string, t string) { /* ... */ }
```

Here are four ways to declare a function with two parameters and one result, all of type int. The blank identifier can be used to emphasize that a parameter is unused.

```
func add(x int, y int) int   { return x + y }
func sub(x, y int) (z int)    { z = x - y; return }
func first(x int, _ int) int { return x }
func zero(int, int) int       { return 0 }

fmt.Printf("%T\n", add)   // "func(int, int) int"
fmt.Printf("%T\n", sub)   // "func(int, int) int"
fmt.Printf("%T\n", first) // "func(int, int) int"
fmt.Printf("%T\n", zero)  // "func(int, int) int"
```

The type of a function is sometimes called its *signature*. Two functions have the same type or signature if they have the same sequence of parameter types and the same sequence of result types. The names of parameters and results don't affect the type, nor does whether or not they were declared using the factored form.

Every function call must provide an argument for each parameter, in the order in which the parameters were declared. Go has no concept of default parameter values, nor any way to specify arguments by name, so the names of parameters and results don't matter to the caller except as documentation.

Parameters are local variables within the body of the function, with their initial values set to the arguments supplied by the caller. Function parameters and named results are variables in the same lexical block as the function's outermost local variables.

Arguments are passed *by value*, so the function receives a copy of each argument; modifications to the copy do not affect the caller. However, if the argument contains some kind of reference, like a pointer, slice, map, function, or channel, then the caller may be affected by any modifications the function makes to variables *indirectly* referred to by the argument.

You may occasionally encounter a function declaration without a body, indicating that the function is implemented in a language other than Go. Such a declaration defines the function signature.

```
package math

func Sin(x float64) float64 // implemented in assembly language
```

5.2. Recursion

Functions may be *recursive*, that is, they may call themselves, either directly or indirectly. Recursion is a powerful technique for many problems, and of course it's essential for process-ing recursive data structures. In Section 4.4, we used recursion over a tree to implement a simple insertion sort. In this section, we'll use it again for processing HTML documents.

The example program below uses a non-standard package, golang.org/x/net/html, which provides an HTML parser. The golang.org/x/... repositories hold packages designed and maintained by the Go team for applications such as networking, internationalized text processing, mobile platforms, image manipulation, cryptography, and developer tools. These packages are not in the standard library because they're still under development or because they're rarely needed by the majority of Go programmers.

The parts of the golang.org/x/net/html API that we'll need are shown below. The function html.Parse reads a sequence of bytes, parses them, and returns the root of the HTML doc-ument tree, which is an html.Node. HTML has several kinds of nodes—text, comments, and so on—but here we are concerned only with *element* nodes of the form <name key='value'>.

```
golang.org/x/net/html
    package html

    type Node struct {
        Type                      NodeType
        Data                      string
        Attr                      []Attribute
        FirstChild, NextSibling   *Node
    }

    type NodeType int32

    const (
        ErrorNode NodeType = iota
        TextNode
        DocumentNode
        ElementNode
        CommentNode
        DoctypeNode
    )
```

```go
type Attribute struct {
    Key, Val string
}

func Parse(r io.Reader) (*Node, error)
```

The main function parses the standard input as HTML, extracts the links using a recursive
visit function, and prints each discovered link:

gopl.io/ch5/findlinks1

```go
// Findlinks1 prints the links in an HTML document read from standard input.
package main

import (
    "fmt"
    "os"

    "golang.org/x/net/html"
)

func main() {
    doc, err := html.Parse(os.Stdin)
    if err != nil {
        fmt.Fprintf(os.Stderr, "findlinks1: %v\n", err)
        os.Exit(1)
    }
    for _, link := range visit(nil, doc) {
        fmt.Println(link)
    }
}
```

The visit function traverses an HTML node tree, extracts the link from the href attribute of
each *anchor* element <a href='...'>, appends the links to a slice of strings, and returns the
resulting slice:

```go
// visit appends to links each link found in n and returns the result.
func visit(links []string, n *html.Node) []string {
    if n.Type == html.ElementNode && n.Data == "a" {
        for _, a := range n.Attr {
            if a.Key == "href" {
                links = append(links, a.Val)
            }
        }
    }
    for c := n.FirstChild; c != nil; c = c.NextSibling {
        links = visit(links, c)
    }
    return links
}
```

To descend the tree for a node n, visit recursively calls itself for each of n's children, which
are held in the FirstChild linked list.

Let's run `findlinks` on the Go home page, piping the output of `fetch` (§1.5) to the input of `findlinks`. We've edited the output slightly for brevity.

```
$ go build gopl.io/ch1/fetch
$ go build gopl.io/ch5/findlinks1
$ ./fetch https://golang.org | ./findlinks1
#
/doc/
/pkg/
/help/
/blog/
http://play.golang.org/
//tour.golang.org/
https://golang.org/dl/
//blog.golang.org/
/LICENSE
/doc/tos.html
http://www.google.com/intl/en/policies/privacy/
```

Notice the variety of forms of links that appear in the page. Later we'll see how to resolve them relative to the base URL, `https://golang.org`, to make absolute URLs.

The next program uses recursion over the HTML node tree to print the structure of the tree in outline. As it encounters each element, it pushes the element's tag onto a stack, then prints the stack.

gopl.io/ch5/outline

```
func main() {
    doc, err := html.Parse(os.Stdin)
    if err != nil {
        fmt.Fprintf(os.Stderr, "outline: %v\n", err)
        os.Exit(1)
    }
    outline(nil, doc)
}
func outline(stack []string, n *html.Node) {
    if n.Type == html.ElementNode {
        stack = append(stack, n.Data) // push tag
        fmt.Println(stack)
    }
    for c := n.FirstChild; c != nil; c = c.NextSibling {
        outline(stack, c)
    }
}
```

Note one subtlety: although `outline` "pushes" an element on `stack`, there is no corresponding pop. When `outline` calls itself recursively, the callee receives a copy of `stack`. Although the callee may append elements to this slice, modifying its underlying array and perhaps even allocating a new array, it doesn't modify the initial elements that are visible to the caller, so when the function returns, the caller's `stack` is as it was before the call.

Here's the outline of `https://golang.org`, again edited for brevity:

```
$ go build gopl.io/ch5/outline
$ ./fetch https://golang.org | ./outline
[html]
[html head]
[html head meta]
[html head title]
[html head link]
[html body]
[html body div]
[html body div]
[html body div div]
[html body div div form]
[html body div div form div]
[html body div div form div a]
...
```

As you can see by experimenting with `outline`, most HTML documents can be processed with only a few levels of recursion, but it's not hard to construct pathological web pages that require extremely deep recursion.

Many programming language implementations use a fixed-size function call stack; sizes from 64KB to 2MB are typical. Fixed-size stacks impose a limit on the depth of recursion, so one must be careful to avoid a *stack overflow* when traversing large data structures recursively; fixed-size stacks may even pose a security risk. In contrast, typical Go implementations use variable-size stacks that start small and grow as needed up to a limit on the order of a gigabyte. This lets us use recursion safely and without worrying about overflow.

Exercise 5.1: Change the `findlinks` program to traverse the `n.FirstChild` linked list using recursive calls to `visit` instead of a loop.

Exercise 5.2: Write a function to populate a mapping from element names—p, div, span, and so on—to the number of elements with that name in an HTML document tree.

Exercise 5.3: Write a function to print the contents of all text nodes in an HTML document tree. Do not descend into `<script>` or `<style>` elements, since their contents are not visible in a web browser.

Exercise 5.4: Extend the `visit` function so that it extracts other kinds of links from the document, such as images, scripts, and style sheets.

5.3. Multiple Return Values

A function can return more than one result. We've seen many examples of functions from standard packages that return two values, the desired computational result and an error value or boolean that indicates whether the computation worked. The next example shows how to write one of our own.

The program below is a variation of findlinks that makes the HTTP request itself so that we no longer need to run fetch. Because the HTTP and parsing operations can fail, findLinks declares two results: the list of discovered links and an error. Incidentally, the HTML parser can usually recover from bad input and construct a document containing error nodes, so Parse rarely fails; when it does, it's typically due to underlying I/O errors.

`gopl.io/ch5/findlinks2`

```go
func main() {
    for _, url := range os.Args[1:] {
        links, err := findLinks(url)
        if err != nil {
            fmt.Fprintf(os.Stderr, "findlinks2: %v\n", err)
            continue
        }
        for _, link := range links {
            fmt.Println(link)
        }
    }
}

// findLinks performs an HTTP GET request for url, parses the
// response as HTML, and extracts and returns the links.
func findLinks(url string) ([]string, error) {
    resp, err := http.Get(url)
    if err != nil {
        return nil, err
    }
    if resp.StatusCode != http.StatusOK {
        resp.Body.Close()
        return nil, fmt.Errorf("getting %s: %s", url, resp.Status)
    }
    doc, err := html.Parse(resp.Body)
    resp.Body.Close()
    if err != nil {
        return nil, fmt.Errorf("parsing %s as HTML: %v", url, err)
    }
    return visit(nil, doc), nil
}
```

There are four return statements in findLinks, each of which returns a pair of values. The first three returns cause the function to pass the underlying errors from the http and html packages on to the caller. In the first case, the error is returned unchanged; in the second and third, it is augmented with additional context information by fmt.Errorf (§7.8). If find-Links is successful, the final return statement returns the slice of links, with no error.

We must ensure that resp.Body is closed so that network resources are properly released even in case of error. Go's garbage collector recycles unused memory, but do not assume it will release unused operating system resources like open files and network connections. They should be closed explicitly.

The result of calling a multi-valued function is a tuple of values. The caller of such a function must explicitly assign the values to variables if any of them are to be used:

```
links, err := findLinks(url)
```

To ignore one of the values, assign it to the blank identifier:

```
links, _ := findLinks(url) // errors ignored
```

The result of a multi-valued call may itself be returned from a (multi-valued) calling function, as in this function that behaves like findLinks but logs its argument:

```
func findLinksLog(url string) ([]string, error) {
    log.Printf("findLinks %s", url)
    return findLinks(url)
}
```

A multi-valued call may appear as the sole argument when calling a function of multiple parameters. Although rarely used in production code, this feature is sometimes convenient during debugging since it lets us print all the results of a call using a single statement. The two print statements below have the same effect.

```
log.Println(findLinks(url))

links, err := findLinks(url)
log.Println(links, err)
```

Well-chosen names can document the significance of a function's results. Names are particularly valuable when a function returns multiple results of the same type, like

```
func Size(rect image.Rectangle) (width, height int)
func Split(path string) (dir, file string)
func HourMinSec(t time.Time) (hour, minute, second int)
```

but it's not always necessary to name multiple results solely for documentation. For instance, convention dictates that a final bool result indicates success; an error result often needs no explanation.

In a function with named results, the operands of a return statement may be omitted. This is called a *bare return*.

```
// CountWordsAndImages does an HTTP GET request for the HTML
// document url and returns the number of words and images in it.
func CountWordsAndImages(url string) (words, images int, err error) {
    resp, err := http.Get(url)
    if err != nil {
        return
    }
```

```
        doc, err := html.Parse(resp.Body)
        resp.Body.Close()
        if err != nil {
            err = fmt.Errorf("parsing HTML: %s", err)
            return
        }
        words, images = countWordsAndImages(doc)
        return
    }
    func countWordsAndImages(n *html.Node) (words, images int) { /* ... */ }
```

A bare return is a shorthand way to return each of the named result variables in order, so in the function above, each return statement is equivalent to

```
    return words, images, err
```

In functions like this one, with many return statements and several results, bare returns can reduce code duplication, but they rarely make code easier to understand. For instance, it's not obvious at first glance that the two early returns are equivalent to return 0, 0, err (because the result variables words and images are initialized to their zero values) and that the final return is equivalent to return words, images, nil. For this reason, bare returns are best used sparingly.

Exercise 5.5: Implement countWordsAndImages. (See Exercise 4.9 for word-splitting.)

Exercise 5.6: Modify the corner function in gopl.io/ch3/surface (§3.2) to use named results and a bare return statement.

5.4. Errors

Some functions always succeed at their task. For example, strings.Contains and strconv.FormatBool have well-defined results for all possible argument values and cannot fail—barring catastrophic and unpredictable scenarios like running out of memory, where the symptom is far from the cause and from which there's little hope of recovery.

Other functions always succeed so long as their preconditions are met. For example, the time.Date function always constructs a time.Time from its components—year, month, and so on—unless the last argument (the time zone) is nil, in which case it panics. This panic is a sure sign of a bug in the calling code and should never happen in a well-written program.

For many other functions, even in a well-written program, success is not assured because it depends on factors beyond the programmer's control. Any function that does I/O, for example, must confront the possibility of error, and only a naïve programmer believes a simple read or write cannot fail. Indeed, it's when the most reliable operations fail unexpectedly that we most need to know why.

Errors are thus an important part of a package's API or an application's user interface, and failure is just one of several expected behaviors. This is the approach Go takes to error handling.

A function for which failure is an expected behavior returns an additional result, conventionally the last one. If the failure has only one possible cause, the result is a boolean, usually called ok, as in this example of a cache lookup that always succeeds unless there was no entry for that key:

```
value, ok := cache.Lookup(key)
if !ok {
    // ...cache[key] does not exist...
}
```

More often, and especially for I/O, the failure may have a variety of causes for which the caller will need an explanation. In such cases, the type of the additional result is error.

The built-in type error is an interface type. We'll see more of what this means and its implications for error handling in Chapter 7. For now it's enough to know that an error may be nil or non-nil, that nil implies success and non-nil implies failure, and that a non-nil error has an error message string which we can obtain by calling its Error method or print by calling fmt.Println(err) or fmt.Printf("%v", err).

Usually when a function returns a non-nil error, its other results are undefined and should be ignored. However, a few functions may return partial results in error cases. For example, if an error occurs while reading from a file, a call to Read returns the number of bytes it was able to read *and* an error value describing the problem. For correct behavior, some callers may need to process the incomplete data before handling the error, so it is important that such functions clearly document their results.

Go's approach sets it apart from many other languages in which failures are reported using *exceptions*, not ordinary values. Although Go does have an exception mechanism of sorts, as we will see in Section 5.9, it is used only for reporting truly unexpected errors that indicate a bug, not the routine errors that a robust program should be built to expect.

The reason for this design is that exceptions tend to entangle the description of an error with the control flow required to handle it, often leading to an undesirable outcome: routine errors are reported to the end user in the form of an incomprehensible stack trace, full of information about the structure of the program but lacking intelligible context about what went wrong.

By contrast, Go programs use ordinary control-flow mechanisms like if and return to respond to errors. This style undeniably demands that more attention be paid to error-handling logic, but that is precisely the point.

5.4.1. Error-Handling Strategies

When a function call returns an error, it's the caller's responsibility to check it and take appropriate action. Depending on the situation, there may be a number of possibilities. Let's take a look at five of them.

First, and most common, is to *propagate* the error, so that a failure in a subroutine becomes a failure of the calling routine. We saw examples of this in the findLinks function of Section 5.3. If the call to http.Get fails, findLinks returns the HTTP error to the caller without further ado:

```
resp, err := http.Get(url)
if err != nil {
    return nil, err
}
```

In contrast, if the call to html.Parse fails, findLinks does not return the HTML parser's error directly because it lacks two crucial pieces of information: that the error occurred in the parser, and the URL of the document that was being parsed. In this case, findLinks constructs a new error message that includes both pieces of information as well as the underlying parse error:

```
doc, err := html.Parse(resp.Body)
resp.Body.Close()
if err != nil {
    return nil, fmt.Errorf("parsing %s as HTML: %v", url, err)
}
```

The fmt.Errorf function formats an error message using fmt.Sprintf and returns a new error value. We use it to build descriptive errors by successively prefixing additional context information to the original error message. When the error is ultimately handled by the program's main function, it should provide a clear causal chain from the root problem to the overall failure, reminiscent of a NASA accident investigation:

```
genesis: crashed: no parachute: G-switch failed: bad relay orientation
```

Because error messages are frequently chained together, message strings should not be capitalized and newlines should be avoided. The resulting errors may be long, but they will be self-contained when found by tools like grep.

When designing error messages, be deliberate, so that each one is a meaningful description of the problem with sufficient and relevant detail, and be consistent, so that errors returned by the same function or by a group of functions in the same package are similar in form and can be dealt with in the same way.

For example, the os package guarantees that every error returned by a file operation, such as os.Open or the Read, Write, or Close methods of an open file, describes not just the nature of the failure (permission denied, no such directory, and so on) but also the name of the file, so the caller needn't include this information in the error message it constructs.

In general, the call f(x) is responsible for reporting the attempted operation f and the argument value x as they relate to the context of the error. The caller is responsible for adding further information that it has but the call f(x) does not, such as the URL in the call to html.Parse above.

Let's move on to the second strategy for handling errors. For errors that represent transient or unpredictable problems, it may make sense to *retry* the failed operation, possibly with a delay between tries, and perhaps with a limit on the number of attempts or the time spent trying before giving up entirely.

gopl.io/ch5/wait

```
// WaitForServer attempts to contact the server of a URL.
// It tries for one minute using exponential back-off.
// It reports an error if all attempts fail.
func WaitForServer(url string) error {
    const timeout = 1 * time.Minute
    deadline := time.Now().Add(timeout)
    for tries := 0; time.Now().Before(deadline); tries++ {
        _, err := http.Head(url)
        if err == nil {
            return nil // success
        }
        log.Printf("server not responding (%s); retrying...", err)
        time.Sleep(time.Second << uint(tries)) // exponential back-off
    }
    return fmt.Errorf("server %s failed to respond after %s", url, timeout)
}
```

Third, if progress is impossible, the caller can print the error and stop the program gracefully, but this course of action should generally be reserved for the main package of a program. Library functions should usually propagate errors to the caller, unless the error is a sign of an internal inconsistency—that is, a bug.

```
// (In function main.)
if err := WaitForServer(url); err != nil {
    fmt.Fprintf(os.Stderr, "Site is down: %v\n", err)
    os.Exit(1)
}
```

A more convenient way to achieve the same effect is to call `log.Fatalf`. As with all the `log` functions, by default it prefixes the time and date to the error message.

```
if err := WaitForServer(url); err != nil {
    log.Fatalf("Site is down: %v\n", err)
}
```

The default format is helpful in a long-running server, but less so for an interactive tool:

```
2006/01/02 15:04:05 Site is down: no such domain: bad.gopl.io
```

For a more attractive output, we can set the prefix used by the `log` package to the name of the command, and suppress the display of the date and time:

```
log.SetPrefix("wait: ")
log.SetFlags(0)
```

Fourth, in some cases, it's sufficient just to log the error and then continue, perhaps with reduced functionality. Again there's a choice between using the log package, which adds the usual prefix:

```
if err := Ping(); err != nil {
    log.Printf("ping failed: %v; networking disabled", err)
}
```

and printing directly to the standard error stream:

```
if err := Ping(); err != nil {
    fmt.Fprintf(os.Stderr, "ping failed: %v; networking disabled\n", err)
}
```

(All log functions append a newline if one is not already present.)

And fifth and finally, in rare cases we can safely ignore an error entirely:

```
dir, err := ioutil.TempDir("", "scratch")
if err != nil {
    return fmt.Errorf("failed to create temp dir: %v", err)
}

// ...use temp dir...

os.RemoveAll(dir) // ignore errors; $TMPDIR is cleaned periodically
```

The call to os.RemoveAll may fail, but the program ignores it because the operating system periodically cleans out the temporary directory. In this case, discarding the error was intentional, but the program logic would be the same had we forgotten to deal with it. Get into the habit of considering errors after every function call, and when you deliberately ignore one, document your intention clearly.

Error handling in Go has a particular rhythm. After checking an error, failure is usually dealt with before success. If failure causes the function to return, the logic for success is not indented within an else block but follows at the outer level. Functions tend to exhibit a common structure, with a series of initial checks to reject errors, followed by the substance of the function at the end, minimally indented.

5.4.2. End of File (EOF)

Usually, the variety of errors that a function may return is interesting to the end user but not to the intervening program logic. On occasion, however, a program must take different actions depending on the kind of error that has occurred. Consider an attempt to read n bytes of data from a file. If n is chosen to be the length of the file, any error represents a failure. On the other hand, if the caller repeatedly tries to read fixed-size chunks until the file is exhausted, the caller must respond differently to an end-of-file condition than it does to all other errors. For this reason, the io package guarantees that any read failure caused by an end-of-file condition is always reported by a distinguished error, io.EOF, which is defined as follows:

```
package io

import "errors"

// EOF is the error returned by Read when no more input is available.
var EOF = errors.New("EOF")
```

The caller can detect this condition using a simple comparison, as in the loop below, which reads runes from the standard input. (The charcount program in Section 4.3 provides a more complete example.)

```
in := bufio.NewReader(os.Stdin)
for {
    r, _, err := in.ReadRune()
    if err == io.EOF {
        break // finished reading
    }
    if err != nil {
        return fmt.Errorf("read failed: %v", err)
    }
    // ...use r...
}
```

Since in an end-of-file condition there is no information to report besides the fact of it, io.EOF has a fixed error message, "EOF". For other errors, we may need to report both the quality and quantity of the error, so to speak, so a fixed error value will not do. In Section 7.11, we'll present a more systematic way to distinguish certain error values from others.

5.5. Function Values

Functions are *first-class values* in Go: like other values, function values have types, and they may be assigned to variables or passed to or returned from functions. A function value may be called like any other function. For example:

```
func square(n int) int     { return n * n }
func negative(n int) int   { return -n }
func product(m, n int) int { return m * n }

f := square
fmt.Println(f(3)) // "9"

f = negative
fmt.Println(f(3))      // "-3"
fmt.Printf("%T\n", f) // "func(int) int"

f = product // compile error: can't assign func(int,int) int to func(int) int
```

The zero value of a function type is nil. Calling a nil function value causes a panic:

```
var f func(int) int
f(3) // panic: call of nil function
```

Function values may be compared with `nil`:

```
var f func(int) int
if f != nil {
    f(3)
}
```

but they are not comparable, so they may not be compared against each other or used as keys in a map.

Function values let us parameterize our functions over not just data, but behavior too. The standard libraries contain many examples. For instance, `strings.Map` applies a function to each character of a string, joining the results to make another string.

```
func add1(r rune) rune { return r + 1 }

fmt.Println(strings.Map(add1, "HAL-9000")) // "IBM.:111"
fmt.Println(strings.Map(add1, "VMS"))      // "WNT"

fmt.Println(strings.Map(add1, "Admix"))    // "Benjy"
```

The `findLinks` function from Section 5.2 uses a helper function, `visit`, to visit all the nodes in an HTML document and apply an action to each one. Using a function value, we can separate the logic for tree traversal from the logic for the action to be applied to each node, letting us reuse the traversal with different actions.

gopl.io/ch5/outline2
```
// forEachNode calls the functions pre(x) and post(x) for each node
// x in the tree rooted at n. Both functions are optional.
// pre is called before the children are visited (preorder) and
// post is called after (postorder).
func forEachNode(n *html.Node, pre, post func(n *html.Node)) {
    if pre != nil {
        pre(n)
    }

    for c := n.FirstChild; c != nil; c = c.NextSibling {
        forEachNode(c, pre, post)
    }

    if post != nil {
        post(n)
    }
}
```

The `forEachNode` function accepts two function arguments, one to call before a node's children are visited and one to call after. This arrangement gives the caller a great deal of flexibility. For example, the functions `startElement` and `endElement` print the start and end tags of an HTML element like `<b>...</b>`:

```
var depth int
```

```
func startElement(n *html.Node) {
    if n.Type == html.ElementNode {
        fmt.Printf("%*s<%s>\n", depth*2, "", n.Data)
        depth++
    }
}
func endElement(n *html.Node) {
    if n.Type == html.ElementNode {
        depth--
        fmt.Printf("%*s</%s>\n", depth*2, "", n.Data)
    }
}
```

The functions also indent the output using another `fmt.Printf` trick. The `*` adverb in `%*s` prints a string padded with a variable number of spaces. The width and the string are provided by the arguments `depth*2` and `""`.

If we call `forEachNode` on an HTML document, like this:

```
forEachNode(doc, startElement, endElement)
```

we get a more elaborate variation on the output of our earlier `outline` program:

```
$ go build gopl.io/ch5/outline2
$ ./outline2 http://gopl.io
<html>
  <head>
    <meta>
    </meta>
    <title>
    </title>
    <style>
    </style>
  </head>
  <body>
    <table>
      <tbody>
        <tr>
          <td>
            <a>
              <img>
              </img>
  ...
```

Exercise 5.7: Develop `startElement` and `endElement` into a general HTML pretty-printer. Print comment nodes, text nodes, and the attributes of each element (`<a href='...'>`). Use short forms like `<img/>` instead of `<img></img>` when an element has no children. Write a test to ensure that the output can be parsed successfully. (See Chapter 11.)

Exercise 5.8: Modify `forEachNode` so that the pre and post functions return a boolean result indicating whether to continue the traversal. Use it to write a function `ElementByID` with the following signature that finds the first HTML element with the specified id attribute. The function should stop the traversal as soon as a match is found.

```
func ElementByID(doc *html.Node, id string) *html.Node
```

Exercise 5.9: Write a function expand(s string, f func(string) string) string that replaces each substring "$foo" within s by the text returned by f("foo").

5.6. Anonymous Functions

Named functions can be declared only at the package level, but we can use a *function literal* to denote a function value within any expression. A function literal is written like a function declaration, but without a name following the func keyword. It is an expression, and its value is called an *anonymous function*.

Function literals let us define a function at its point of use. As an example, the earlier call to strings.Map can be rewritten as

```
strings.Map(func(r rune) rune { return r + 1 }, "HAL-9000")
```

More importantly, functions defined in this way have access to the entire lexical environment, so the inner function can refer to variables from the enclosing function, as this example shows:

gopl.io/ch5/squares
```
// squares returns a function that returns
// the next square number each time it is called.
func squares() func() int {
    var x int
    return func() int {
        x++
        return x * x
    }
}
func main() {
    f := squares()
    fmt.Println(f()) // "1"
    fmt.Println(f()) // "4"
    fmt.Println(f()) // "9"
    fmt.Println(f()) // "16"
}
```

The function squares returns another function, of type func() int. A call to squares creates a local variable x and returns an anonymous function that, each time it is called, increments x and returns its square. A second call to squares would create a second variable x and return a new anonymous function which increments that variable.

The squares example demonstrates that function values are not just code but can have state. The anonymous inner function can access and update the local variables of the enclosing function squares. These hidden variable references are why we classify functions as reference types and why function values are not comparable. Function values like these are implemented using a technique called *closures*, and Go programmers often use this term for function values.

Here again we see an example where the lifetime of a variable is not determined by its scope: the variable x exists after squares has returned within main, even though x is hidden inside f.

As a somewhat academic example of anonymous functions, consider the problem of computing a sequence of computer science courses that satisfies the prerequisite requirements of each one. The prerequisites are given in the prereqs table below, which is a mapping from each course to the list of courses that must be completed before it.

gopl.io/ch5/toposort

```
// prereqs maps computer science courses to their prerequisites.
var prereqs = map[string][]string{
    "algorithms": {"data structures"},
    "calculus":   {"linear algebra"},

    "compilers": {
        "data structures",
        "formal languages",
        "computer organization",
    },

    "data structures":       {"discrete math"},
    "databases":             {"data structures"},
    "discrete math":         {"intro to programming"},
    "formal languages":      {"discrete math"},
    "networks":              {"operating systems"},
    "operating systems":     {"data structures", "computer organization"},
    "programming languages": {"data structures", "computer organization"},
}
```

This kind of problem is known as topological sorting. Conceptually, the prerequisite information forms a directed graph with a node for each course and edges from each course to the courses that it depends on. The graph is acyclic: there is no path from a course that leads back to itself. We can compute a valid sequence using depth-first search through the graph with the code below:

```
func main() {
    for i, course := range topoSort(prereqs) {
        fmt.Printf("%d:\t%s\n", i+1, course)
    }
}

func topoSort(m map[string][]string) []string {
    var order []string
    seen := make(map[string]bool)
    var visitAll func(items []string)
```

```
    visitAll = func(items []string) {
        for _, item := range items {
            if !seen[item] {
                seen[item] = true
                visitAll(m[item])
                order = append(order, item)
            }
        }
    }
    var keys []string
    for key := range m {
        keys = append(keys, key)
    }
    sort.Strings(keys)
    visitAll(keys)
    return order
}
```

When an anonymous function requires recursion, as in this example, we must first declare a variable, and then assign the anonymous function to that variable. Had these two steps been combined in the declaration, the function literal would not be within the scope of the variable visitAll so it would have no way to call itself recursively:

```
visitAll := func(items []string) {
    // ...
    visitAll(m[item]) // compile error: undefined: visitAll
    // ...
}
```

The output of the toposort program is shown below. It is deterministic, an often-desirable property that doesn't always come for free. Here, the values of the prereqs map are slices, not more maps, so their iteration order is deterministic, and we sorted the keys of prereqs before making the initial calls to visitAll.

```
 1:      intro to programming
 2:      discrete math
 3:      data structures
 4:      algorithms
 5:      linear algebra
 6:      calculus
 7:      formal languages
 8:      computer organization
 9:      compilers
10:      databases
11:      operating systems
12:      networks
13:      programming languages
```

Let's return to our findLinks example. We've moved the link-extraction function links.Extract to its own package, since we'll use it again in Chapter 8. We replaced the

visit function with an anonymous function that appends to the links slice directly, and used
forEachNode to handle the traversal. Since Extract needs only the pre function, it passes
nil for the post argument.

gopl.io/ch5/links

```go
// Package links provides a link-extraction function.
package links

import (
    "fmt"
    "net/http"

    "golang.org/x/net/html"
)

// Extract makes an HTTP GET request to the specified URL, parses
// the response as HTML, and returns the links in the HTML document.
func Extract(url string) ([]string, error) {
    resp, err := http.Get(url)
    if err != nil {
        return nil, err
    }
    if resp.StatusCode != http.StatusOK {
        resp.Body.Close()
        return nil, fmt.Errorf("getting %s: %s", url, resp.Status)
    }

    doc, err := html.Parse(resp.Body)
    resp.Body.Close()
    if err != nil {
        return nil, fmt.Errorf("parsing %s as HTML: %v", url, err)
    }

    var links []string
    visitNode := func(n *html.Node) {
        if n.Type == html.ElementNode && n.Data == "a" {
            for _, a := range n.Attr {
                if a.Key != "href" {
                    continue
                }
                link, err := resp.Request.URL.Parse(a.Val)
                if err != nil {
                    continue // ignore bad URLs
                }
                links = append(links, link.String())
            }
        }
    }
    forEachNode(doc, visitNode, nil)
    return links, nil
}
```

Instead of appending the raw `href` attribute value to the `links` slice, this version parses it as a URL relative to the base URL of the document, `resp.Request.URL`. The resulting `link` is in absolute form, suitable for use in a call to `http.Get`.

Crawling the web is, at its heart, a problem of graph traversal. The `topoSort` example showed a depth-first traversal; for our web crawler, we'll use breadth-first traversal, at least initially. In Chapter 8, we'll explore concurrent traversal.

The function below encapsulates the essence of a breadth-first traversal. The caller provides an initial list `worklist` of items to visit and a function value `f` to call for each item. Each item is identified by a string. The function `f` returns a list of new items to append to the worklist. The `breadthFirst` function returns when all items have been visited. It maintains a set of strings to ensure that no item is visited twice.

gopl.io/ch5/findlinks3
```
// breadthFirst calls f for each item in the worklist.
// Any items returned by f are added to the worklist.
// f is called at most once for each item.
func breadthFirst(f func(item string) []string, worklist []string) {
    seen := make(map[string]bool)
    for len(worklist) > 0 {
        items := worklist
        worklist = nil
        for _, item := range items {
            if !seen[item] {
                seen[item] = true
                worklist = append(worklist, f(item)...)
            }
        }
    }
}
```

As we explained in passing in Chapter 3, the argument "`f(item)...`" causes all the items in the list returned by `f` to be appended to the worklist.

In our crawler, items are URLs. The `crawl` function we'll supply to `breadthFirst` prints the URL, extracts its links, and returns them so that they too are visited.

```
func crawl(url string) []string {
    fmt.Println(url)
    list, err := links.Extract(url)
    if err != nil {
        log.Print(err)
    }
    return list
}
```

To start the crawler off, we'll use the command-line arguments as the initial URLs.

```
func main() {
    // Crawl the web breadth-first,
    // starting from the command-line arguments.
    breadthFirst(crawl, os.Args[1:])
}
```

Let's crawl the web starting from `https://golang.org`. Here are some of the resulting links:

```
$ go build gopl.io/ch5/findlinks3
$ ./findlinks3 https://golang.org
https://golang.org/
https://golang.org/doc/
https://golang.org/pkg/
https://golang.org/project/
https://code.google.com/p/go-tour/
https://golang.org/doc/code.html
https://www.youtube.com/watch?v=XCsL89YtqCs
http://research.swtch.com/gotour
https://vimeo.com/53221560
...
```

The process ends when all reachable web pages have been crawled or the memory of the computer is exhausted.

Exercise 5.10: Rewrite `topoSort` to use maps instead of slices and eliminate the initial sort. Verify that the results, though nondeterministic, are valid topological orderings.

Exercise 5.11: The instructor of the linear algebra course decides that calculus is now a prerequisite. Extend the `topoSort` function to report cycles.

Exercise 5.12: The `startElement` and `endElement` functions in `gopl.io/ch5/outline2` (§5.5) share a global variable, `depth`. Turn them into anonymous functions that share a variable local to the `outline` function.

Exercise 5.13: Modify `crawl` to make local copies of the pages it finds, creating directories as necessary. Don't make copies of pages that come from a different domain. For example, if the original page comes from `golang.org`, save all files from there, but exclude ones from `vimeo.com`.

Exercise 5.14: Use the `breadthFirst` function to explore a different structure. For example, you could use the course dependencies from the `topoSort` example (a directed graph), the file system hierarchy on your computer (a tree), or a list of bus or subway routes downloaded from your city government's web site (an undirected graph).

5.6.1. Caveat: Capturing Iteration Variables

In this section, we'll look at a pitfall of Go's lexical scope rules that can cause surprising results. We urge you to understand the problem before proceeding, because the trap can ensnare even experienced programmers.

Consider a program that must create a set of directories and later remove them. We can use a slice of function values to hold the clean-up operations. (For brevity, we have omitted all error handling in this example.)

```
var rmdirs []func()
for _, d := range tempDirs() {
    dir := d                   // NOTE: necessary!
    os.MkdirAll(dir, 0755) // creates parent directories too
    rmdirs = append(rmdirs, func() {
        os.RemoveAll(dir)
    })
}

// ...do some work...

for _, rmdir := range rmdirs {
    rmdir() // clean up
}
```

You may be wondering why we assigned the loop variable d to a new local variable dir within the loop body, instead of just naming the loop variable dir as in this subtly incorrect variant:

```
var rmdirs []func()
for _, dir := range tempDirs() {
    os.MkdirAll(dir, 0755)
    rmdirs = append(rmdirs, func() {
        os.RemoveAll(dir) // NOTE: incorrect!
    })
}
```

The reason is a consequence of the scope rules for loop variables. In the program immediately above, the for loop introduces a new lexical block in which the variable dir is declared. All function values created by this loop "capture" and share the same variable—an addressable storage location, not its value at that particular moment. The value of dir is updated in successive iterations, so by the time the cleanup functions are called, the dir variable has been updated several times by the now-completed for loop. Thus dir holds the value from the final iteration, and consequently all calls to os.RemoveAll will attempt to remove the same directory.

Frequently, the inner variable introduced to work around this problem—dir in our example—is given the exact same name as the outer variable of which it is a copy, leading to odd-looking but crucial variable declarations like this:

```
for _, dir := range tempDirs() {
    dir := dir // declares inner dir, initialized to outer dir
    // ...
}
```

The risk is not unique to range-based for loops. The loop in the example below suffers from the same problem due to unintended capture of the index variable i.

```
var rmdirs []func()
dirs := tempDirs()
for i := 0; i < len(dirs); i++ {
    os.MkdirAll(dirs[i], 0755) // OK
    rmdirs = append(rmdirs, func() {
        os.RemoveAll(dirs[i]) // NOTE: incorrect!
    })
}
```

The problem of iteration variable capture is most often encountered when using the go statement (Chapter 8) or with defer (which we will see in a moment) since both may delay the execution of a function value until after the loop has finished. But the problem is not inherent to go or defer.

5.7. Variadic Functions

A *variadic function* is one that can be called with varying numbers of arguments. The most familiar examples are fmt.Printf and its variants. Printf requires one fixed argument at the beginning, then accepts any number of subsequent arguments.

To declare a variadic function, the type of the final parameter is preceded by an ellipsis, "...", which indicates that the function may be called with any number of arguments of this type.

gopl.io/ch5/sum
```
func sum(vals ...int) int {
    total := 0
    for _, val := range vals {
        total += val
    }
    return total
}
```

The sum function above returns the sum of zero or more int arguments. Within the body of the function, the type of vals is an []int slice. When sum is called, any number of values may be provided for its vals parameter.

```
fmt.Println(sum())          //   "0"
fmt.Println(sum(3))         //   "3"
fmt.Println(sum(1, 2, 3, 4)) //   "10"
```

Implicitly, the caller allocates an array, copies the arguments into it, and passes a slice of the entire array to the function. The last call above thus behaves the same as the call below, which shows how to invoke a variadic function when the arguments are already in a slice: place an ellipsis after the final argument.

```
values := []int{1, 2, 3, 4}
fmt.Println(sum(values...)) // "10"
```

Although the ...int parameter behaves like a slice within the function body, the type of a variadic function is distinct from the type of a function with an ordinary slice parameter.

```
func f(...int) {}
func g([]int)  {}

fmt.Printf("%T\n", f) // "func(...int)"
fmt.Printf("%T\n", g) // "func([]int)"
```

Variadic functions are often used for string formatting. The errorf function below constructs a formatted error message with a line number at the beginning. The suffix f is a widely followed naming convention for variadic functions that accept a Printf-style format string.

```
func errorf(linenum int, format string, args ...interface{}) {
    fmt.Fprintf(os.Stderr, "Line %d: ", linenum)
    fmt.Fprintf(os.Stderr, format, args...)
    fmt.Fprintln(os.Stderr)
}

linenum, name := 12, "count"
errorf(linenum, "undefined: %s", name) // "Line 12: undefined: count"
```

The interface{} type means that this function can accept any values at all for its final arguments, as we'll explain in Chapter 7.

Exercise 5.15: Write variadic functions max and min, analogous to sum. What should these functions do when called with no arguments? Write variants that require at least one argument.

Exercise 5.16: Write a variadic version of strings.Join.

Exercise 5.17: Write a variadic function ElementsByTagName that, given an HTML node tree and zero or more names, returns all the elements that match one of those names. Here are two example calls:

```
func ElementsByTagName(doc *html.Node, name ...string) []*html.Node

images := ElementsByTagName(doc, "img")
headings := ElementsByTagName(doc, "h1", "h2", "h3", "h4")
```

5.8. Deferred Function Calls

Our findLinks examples used the output of http.Get as the input to html.Parse. This works well if the content of the requested URL is indeed HTML, but many pages contain images, plain text, and other file formats. Feeding such files into an HTML parser could have undesirable effects.

The program below fetches an HTML document and prints its title. The title function inspects the Content-Type header of the server's response and returns an error if the document is not HTML.

gopl.io/ch5/title1

```
func title(url string) error {
    resp, err := http.Get(url)
    if err != nil {
        return err
    }

    // Check Content-Type is HTML (e.g., "text/html; charset=utf-8").
    ct := resp.Header.Get("Content-Type")
    if ct != "text/html" && !strings.HasPrefix(ct, "text/html;") {
        resp.Body.Close()
        return fmt.Errorf("%s has type %s, not text/html", url, ct)
    }

    doc, err := html.Parse(resp.Body)
    resp.Body.Close()
    if err != nil {
        return fmt.Errorf("parsing %s as HTML: %v", url, err)
    }

    visitNode := func(n *html.Node) {
        if n.Type == html.ElementNode && n.Data == "title" &&
            n.FirstChild != nil {
            fmt.Println(n.FirstChild.Data)
        }
    }
    forEachNode(doc, visitNode, nil)
    return nil
}
```

Here's a typical session, slightly edited to fit:

```
$ go build gopl.io/ch5/title1
$ ./title1 http://gopl.io
The Go Programming Language
$ ./title1 https://golang.org/doc/effective_go.html
Effective Go - The Go Programming Language
$ ./title1 https://golang.org/doc/gopher/frontpage.png
title: https://golang.org/doc/gopher/frontpage.png
    has type image/png, not text/html
```

Observe the duplicated resp.Body.Close() call, which ensures that title closes the network connection on all execution paths, including failures. As functions grow more complex and have to handle more errors, such duplication of clean-up logic may become a maintenance problem. Let's see how Go's novel defer mechanism makes things simpler.

Syntactically, a defer statement is an ordinary function or method call prefixed by the keyword defer. The function and argument expressions are evaluated when the statement is executed, but the actual call is _deferred_ until the function that contains the defer statement has finished, whether normally, by executing a return statement or falling off the end, or abnormally, by panicking. Any number of calls may be deferred; they are executed in the reverse of the order in which they were deferred.

A defer statement is often used with paired operations like open and close, connect and disconnect, or lock and unlock to ensure that resources are released in all cases, no matter how complex the control flow. The right place for a defer statement that releases a resource is immediately after the resource has been successfully acquired. In the title function below, a single deferred call replaces both previous calls to resp.Body.Close():

gopl.io/ch5/title2

```go
func title(url string) error {
    resp, err := http.Get(url)
    if err != nil {
        return err
    }
    defer resp.Body.Close()

    ct := resp.Header.Get("Content-Type")
    if ct != "text/html" && !strings.HasPrefix(ct, "text/html;") {
        return fmt.Errorf("%s has type %s, not text/html", url, ct)
    }

    doc, err := html.Parse(resp.Body)
    if err != nil {
        return fmt.Errorf("parsing %s as HTML: %v", url, err)
    }

    // ...print doc's title element...

    return nil
}
```

The same pattern can be used for other resources beside network connections, for instance to close an open file:

io/ioutil

```go
package ioutil

func ReadFile(filename string) ([]byte, error) {
    f, err := os.Open(filename)
    if err != nil {
        return nil, err
    }
    defer f.Close()
    return ReadAll(f)
}
```

or to unlock a mutex (§9.2):

```go
var mu sync.Mutex
var m = make(map[string]int)
```

```
func lookup(key string) int {
    mu.Lock()
    defer mu.Unlock()
    return m[key]
}
```

The defer statement can also be used to pair "on entry" and "on exit" actions when debugging a complex function. The bigSlowOperation function below calls trace immediately, which does the "on entry" action then returns a function value that, when called, does the corresponding "on exit" action. By deferring a call to the returned function in this way, we can instrument the entry point and all exit points of a function in a single statement and even pass values, like the start time, between the two actions. But don't forget the final parentheses in the defer statement, or the "on entry" action will happen on exit and the on-exit action won't happen at all!

gopl.io/ch5/trace
```
func bigSlowOperation() {
    defer trace("bigSlowOperation")() // don't forget the extra parentheses
    // ...lots of work...
    time.Sleep(10 * time.Second) // simulate slow operation by sleeping
}

func trace(msg string) func() {
    start := time.Now()
    log.Printf("enter %s", msg)
    return func() { log.Printf("exit %s (%s)", msg, time.Since(start)) }
}
```

Each time bigSlowOperation is called, it logs its entry and exit and the elapsed time between them. (We used time.Sleep to simulate a slow operation.)

```
$ go build gopl.io/ch5/trace
$ ./trace
2015/11/18 09:53:26 enter bigSlowOperation
2015/11/18 09:53:36 exit bigSlowOperation (10.000589217s)
```

Deferred functions run *after* return statements have updated the function's result variables. Because an anonymous function can access its enclosing function's variables, including named results, a deferred anonymous function can observe the function's results.

Consider the function double:

```
func double(x int) int {
    return x + x
}
```

By naming its result variable and adding a defer statement, we can make the function print its arguments and results each time it is called.

```go
func double(x int) (result int) {
    defer func() { fmt.Printf("double(%d) = %d\n", x, result) }()
    return x + x
}

_ = double(4)
// Output:
// "double(4) = 8"
```

This trick is overkill for a function as simple as double but may be useful in functions with many return statements.

A deferred anonymous function can even change the values that the enclosing function returns to its caller:

```go
func triple(x int) (result int) {
    defer func() { result += x }()
    return double(x)
}

fmt.Println(triple(4)) // "12"
```

Because deferred functions aren't executed until the very end of a function's execution, a defer statement in a loop deserves extra scrutiny. The code below could run out of file descriptors since no file will be closed until all files have been processed:

```go
for _, filename := range filenames {
    f, err := os.Open(filename)
    if err != nil {
        return err
    }
    defer f.Close() // NOTE: risky; could run out of file descriptors
    // ...process f...
}
```

One solution is to move the loop body, including the defer statement, into another function that is called on each iteration.

```go
for _, filename := range filenames {
    if err := doFile(filename); err != nil {
        return err
    }
}

func doFile(filename string) error {
    f, err := os.Open(filename)
    if err != nil {
        return err
    }
    defer f.Close()
    // ...process f...
}
```

The example below is an improved `fetch` program (§1.5) that writes the HTTP response to a local file instead of to the standard output. It derives the file name from the last component of the URL path, which it obtains using the `path.Base` function.

gopl.io/ch5/fetch

```go
// Fetch downloads the URL and returns the
// name and length of the local file.
func fetch(url string) (filename string, n int64, err error) {
    resp, err := http.Get(url)
    if err != nil {
        return "", 0, err
    }
    defer resp.Body.Close()

    local := path.Base(resp.Request.URL.Path)
    if local == "/" {
        local = "index.html"
    }
    f, err := os.Create(local)
    if err != nil {
        return "", 0, err
    }
    n, err = io.Copy(f, resp.Body)
    // Close file, but prefer error from Copy, if any.
    if closeErr := f.Close(); err == nil {
        err = closeErr
    }
    return local, n, err
}
```

The deferred call to `resp.Body.Close` should be familiar by now. It's tempting to use a second deferred call, to `f.Close`, to close the local file, but this would be subtly wrong because `os.Create` opens a file for writing, creating it as needed. On many file systems, notably NFS, write errors are not reported immediately but may be postponed until the file is closed. Failure to check the result of the close operation could cause serious data loss to go unnoticed. However, if both `io.Copy` and `f.Close` fail, we should prefer to report the error from `io.Copy` since it occurred first and is more likely to tell us the root cause.

Exercise 5.18: Without changing its behavior, rewrite the `fetch` function to use `defer` to close the writable file.

5.9. Panic

Go's type system catches many mistakes at compile time, but others, like an out-of-bounds array access or nil pointer dereference, require checks at run time. When the Go runtime detects these mistakes, it *panics*.

During a typical panic, normal execution stops, all deferred function calls in that goroutine are executed, and the program crashes with a log message. This log message includes the *panic value*, which is usually an error message of some sort, and, for each goroutine, a *stack trace* showing the stack of function calls that were active at the time of the panic. This log message often has enough information to diagnose the root cause of the problem without running the program again, so it should always be included in a bug report about a panicking program.

Not all panics come from the runtime. The built-in panic function may be called directly; it accepts any value as an argument. A panic is often the best thing to do when some "impossible" situation happens, for instance, execution reaches a case that logically can't happen:

```go
switch s := suit(drawCard()); s {
case "Spades":   // ...
case "Hearts":   // ...
case "Diamonds": // ...
case "Clubs":    // ...
default:
    panic(fmt.Sprintf("invalid suit %q", s)) // Joker?
}
```

It's good practice to assert that the preconditions of a function hold, but this can easily be done to excess. Unless you can provide a more informative error message or detect an error sooner, there is no point asserting a condition that the runtime will check for you.

```go
func Reset(x *Buffer) {
    if x == nil {
        panic("x is nil") // unnecessary!
    }
    x.elements = nil
}
```

Although Go's panic mechanism resembles exceptions in other languages, the situations in which panic is used are quite different. Since a panic causes the program to crash, it is generally used for grave errors, such as a logical inconsistency in the program; diligent programmers consider any crash to be proof of a bug in their code. In a robust program, "expected" errors, the kind that arise from incorrect input, misconfiguration, or failing I/O, should be handled gracefully; they are best dealt with using error values.

Consider the function regexp.Compile, which compiles a regular expression into an efficient form for matching. It returns an error if called with an ill-formed pattern, but checking this error is unnecessary and burdensome if the caller knows that a particular call cannot fail. In such cases, it's reasonable for the caller to handle an error by panicking, since it is believed to be impossible.

Since most regular expressions are literals in the program source code, the regexp package provides a wrapper function regexp.MustCompile that does this check:

```go
package regexp

func Compile(expr string) (*Regexp, error) { /* ... */ }
```

```
func MustCompile(expr string) *Regexp {
    re, err := Compile(expr)
    if err != nil {
        panic(err)
    }
    return re
}
```

The wrapper function makes it convenient for clients to initialize a package-level variable with a compiled regular expression, like this:

```
var httpSchemeRE = regexp.MustCompile(`^https?:`) // "http:" or "https:"
```

Of course, MustCompile should not be called with untrusted input values. The Must prefix is a common naming convention for functions of this kind, like template.Must in Section 4.6.

When a panic occurs, all deferred functions are run in reverse order, starting with those of the topmost function on the stack and proceeding up to main, as the program below demonstrates:

gopl.io/ch5/defer1
```
func main() {
    f(3)
}

func f(x int) {
    fmt.Printf("f(%d)\n", x+0/x) // panics if x == 0
    defer fmt.Printf("defer %d\n", x)
    f(x - 1)
}
```

When run, the program prints the following to the standard output:

```
f(3)
f(2)
f(1)
defer 1
defer 2
defer 3
```

A panic occurs during the call to f(0), causing the three deferred calls to fmt.Printf to run. Then the runtime terminates the program, printing the panic message and a stack dump to the standard error stream (simplified for clarity):

```
panic: runtime error: integer divide by zero
main.f(0)
        src/gopl.io/ch5/defer1/defer.go:14
main.f(1)
        src/gopl.io/ch5/defer1/defer.go:16
main.f(2)
        src/gopl.io/ch5/defer1/defer.go:16
```

```
main.f(3)
        src/gopl.io/ch5/defer1/defer.go:16
main.main()
        src/gopl.io/ch5/defer1/defer.go:10
```

As we will see soon, it is possible for a function to recover from a panic so that it does not terminate the program.

For diagnostic purposes, the runtime package lets the programmer dump the stack using the same machinery. By deferring a call to printStack in main,

gopl.io/ch5/defer2

```
func main() {
    defer printStack()
    f(3)
}

func printStack() {
    var buf [4096]byte
    n := runtime.Stack(buf[:], false)
    os.Stdout.Write(buf[:n])
}
```

the following additional text (again simplified for clarity) is printed to the standard output:

```
goroutine 1 [running]:
main.printStack()
        src/gopl.io/ch5/defer2/defer.go:20
main.f(0)
        src/gopl.io/ch5/defer2/defer.go:27
main.f(1)
        src/gopl.io/ch5/defer2/defer.go:29
main.f(2)
        src/gopl.io/ch5/defer2/defer.go:29
main.f(3)
        src/gopl.io/ch5/defer2/defer.go:29
main.main()
        src/gopl.io/ch5/defer2/defer.go:15
```

Readers familiar with exceptions in other languages may be surprised that runtime.Stack can print information about functions that seem to have already been "unwound." Go's panic mechanism runs the deferred functions *before* it unwinds the stack.

5.10. Recover

Giving up is usually the right response to a panic, but not always. It might be possible to recover in some way, or at least clean up the mess before quitting. For example, a web server that encounters an unexpected problem could close the connection rather than leave the client hanging, and during development, it might report the error to the client too.

If the built-in recover function is called within a deferred function and the function contain-ing the defer statement is panicking, recover ends the current state of panic and returns the panic value. The function that was panicking does not continue where it left off but returns normally. If recover is called at any other time, it has no effect and returns nil.

To illustrate, consider the development of a parser for a language. Even when it appears to be working well, given the complexity of its job, bugs may still lurk in obscure corner cases. We might prefer that, instead of crashing, the parser turns these panics into ordinary parse errors, perhaps with an extra message exhorting the user to file a bug report.

```
func Parse(input string) (s *Syntax, err error) {
    defer func() {
        if p := recover(); p != nil {
            err = fmt.Errorf("internal error: %v", p)
        }
    }()
    // ...parser...
}
```

The deferred function in Parse recovers from a panic, using the panic value to construct an error message; a fancier version might include the entire call stack using runtime.Stack. The deferred function then assigns to the err result, which is returned to the caller.

Recovering indiscriminately from panics is a dubious practice because the state of a package's variables after a panic is rarely well defined or documented. Perhaps a critical update to a data structure was incomplete, a file or network connection was opened but not closed, or a lock was acquired but not released. Furthermore, by replacing a crash with, say, a line in a log file, indiscriminate recovery may cause bugs to go unnoticed.

Recovering from a panic within the same package can help simplify the handling of complex or unexpected errors, but as a general rule, you should not attempt to recover from another package's panic. Public APIs should report failures as errors. Similarly, you should not recover from a panic that may pass through a function you do not maintain, such as a caller-provided callback, since you cannot reason about its safety.

For example, the net/http package provides a web server that dispatches incoming requests to user-provided handler functions. Rather than let a panic in one of these handlers kill the process, the server calls recover, prints a stack trace, and continues serving. This is con-venient in practice, but it does risk leaking resources or leaving the failed handler in an unspecified state that could lead to other problems.

For all the above reasons, it's safest to recover selectively if at all. In other words, recover only from panics that were intended to be recovered from, which should be rare. This intention can be encoded by using a distinct, unexported type for the panic value and testing whether the value returned by recover has that type. (We'll see one way to do this in the next exam-ple.) If so, we report the panic as an ordinary error; if not, we call panic with the same value to resume the state of panic.

The example below is a variation on the `title` program that reports an error if the HTML document contains multiple `<title>` elements. If so, it aborts the recursion by calling `panic` with a value of the special type `bailout`.

gopl.io/ch5/title3

```go
// soleTitle returns the text of the first non-empty title element
// in doc, and an error if there was not exactly one.
func soleTitle(doc *html.Node) (title string, err error) {
    type bailout struct{}

    defer func() {
        switch p := recover(); p {
        case nil:
            // no panic
        case bailout{}:
            // "expected" panic
            err = fmt.Errorf("multiple title elements")
        default:
            panic(p) // unexpected panic; carry on panicking
        }
    }()

    // Bail out of recursion if we find more than one non-empty title.
    forEachNode(doc, func(n *html.Node) {
        if n.Type == html.ElementNode && n.Data == "title" &&
            n.FirstChild != nil {
            if title != "" {
                panic(bailout{}) // multiple title elements
            }
            title = n.FirstChild.Data
        }
    }, nil)
    if title == "" {
        return "", fmt.Errorf("no title element")
    }
    return title, nil
}
```

The deferred handler function calls `recover`, checks the panic value, and reports an ordinary error if the value was `bailout{}`. All other non-nil values indicate an unexpected panic, in which case the handler calls `panic` with that value, undoing the effect of `recover` and resuming the original state of panic. (This example does somewhat violate our advice about not using panics for "expected" errors, but it provides a compact illustration of the mechanics.)

From some conditions there is no recovery. Running out of memory, for example, causes the Go runtime to terminate the program with a fatal error.

Exercise 5.19: Use `panic` and `recover` to write a function that contains no `return` statement yet returns a non-zero value.

6

Methods

Since the early 1990s, object-oriented programming (OOP) has been the dominant programming paradigm in industry and education, and nearly all widely used languages developed since then have included support for it. Go is no exception.

Although there is no universally accepted definition of object-oriented programming, for our purposes, an *object* is simply a value or variable that has methods, and a *method* is a function associated with a particular type. An object-oriented program is one that uses methods to express the properties and operations of each data structure so that clients need not access the object's representation directly.

In earlier chapters, we have made regular use of methods from the standard library, like the Seconds method of type time.Duration:

```
const day = 24 * time.Hour
fmt.Println(day.Seconds()) // "86400"
```

and we defined a method of our own in Section 2.5, a String method for the Celsius type:

```
func (c Celsius) String() string { return fmt.Sprintf("%g°C", c) }
```

In this chapter, the first of two on object-oriented programming, we'll show how to define and use methods effectively. We'll also cover two key principles of object-oriented programming, *encapsulation* and *composition*.

6.1. Method Declarations

A method is declared with a variant of the ordinary function declaration in which an extra parameter appears before the function name. The parameter attaches the function to the type of that parameter.

Let's write our first method in a simple package for plane geometry:

gopl.io/ch6/geometry

```
package geometry

import "math"

type Point struct{ X, Y float64 }

// traditional function
func Distance(p, q Point) float64 {
    return math.Hypot(q.X-p.X, q.Y-p.Y)
}

// same thing, but as a method of the Point type
func (p Point) Distance(q Point) float64 {
    return math.Hypot(q.X-p.X, q.Y-p.Y)
}
```

The extra parameter p is called the method's *receiver*, a legacy from early object-oriented languages that described calling a method as "sending a message to an object."

In Go, we don't use a special name like this or self for the receiver; we choose receiver names just as we would for any other parameter. Since the receiver name will be frequently used, it's a good idea to choose something short and to be consistent across methods. A common choice is the first letter of the type name, like p for Point.

In a method call, the receiver argument appears before the method name. This parallels the declaration, in which the receiver parameter appears before the method name.

```
p := Point{1, 2}
q := Point{4, 6}
fmt.Println(Distance(p, q)) // "5", function call
fmt.Println(p.Distance(q))  // "5", method call
```

There's no conflict between the two declarations of functions called Distance above. The first declares a package-level function called geometry.Distance. The second declares a method of the type Point, so its name is Point.Distance.

The expression p.Distance is called a *selector*, because it selects the appropriate Distance method for the receiver p of type Point. Selectors are also used to select fields of struct types, as in p.X. Since methods and fields inhabit the same name space, declaring a method X on the struct type Point would be ambiguous and the compiler will reject it.

Since each type has its own name space for methods, we can use the name Distance for other methods so long as they belong to different types. Let's define a type Path that represents a sequence of line segments and give it a Distance method too.

```
// A Path is a journey connecting the points with straight lines.
type Path []Point
```

```go
// Distance returns the distance traveled along the path.
func (path Path) Distance() float64 {
    sum := 0.0
    for i := range path {
        if i > 0 {
            sum += path[i-1].Distance(path[i])
        }
    }
    return sum
}
```

Path is a named slice type, not a struct type like Point, yet we can still define methods for it. In allowing methods to be associated with any type, Go is unlike many other object-oriented languages. It is often convenient to define additional behaviors for simple types such as numbers, strings, slices, maps, and sometimes even functions. Methods may be declared on any named type defined in the same package, so long as its underlying type is neither a pointer nor an interface.

The two Distance methods have different types. They're not related to each other at all, though Path.Distance uses Point.Distance internally to compute the length of each segment that connects adjacent points.

Let's call the new method to compute the perimeter of a right triangle:

```go
perim := Path{
    {1, 1},
    {5, 1},
    {5, 4},
    {1, 1},
}
fmt.Println(perim.Distance()) // "12"
```

In the two calls above to methods named Distance, the compiler determines which function to call based on both the method name and the type of the receiver. In the first, path[i-1] has type Point so Point.Distance is called; in the second, perim has type Path, so Path.Distance is called.

All methods of a given type must have unique names, but different types can use the same name for a method, like the Distance methods for Point and Path; there's no need to qualify function names (for example, PathDistance) to disambiguate. Here we see the first benefit to using methods over ordinary functions: method names can be shorter. The benefit is magnified for calls originating outside the package, since they can use the shorter name *and* omit the package name:

```go
import "gopl.io/ch6/geometry"

perim := geometry.Path{{1, 1}, {5, 1}, {5, 4}, {1, 1}}
fmt.Println(geometry.PathDistance(perim)) // "12", standalone function
fmt.Println(perim.Distance())             // "12", method of geometry.Path
```

6.2. Methods with a Pointer Receiver

Because calling a function makes a copy of each argument value, if a function needs to update a variable, or if an argument is so large that we wish to avoid copying it, we must pass the address of the variable using a pointer. The same goes for methods that need to update the receiver variable: we attach them to the pointer type, such as *Point.

```
func (p *Point) ScaleBy(factor float64) {
    p.X *= factor
    p.Y *= factor
}
```

The name of this method is (*Point).ScaleBy. The parentheses are necessary; without them, the expression would be parsed as *(Point.ScaleBy).

In a realistic program, convention dictates that if any method of Point has a pointer receiver, then *all* methods of Point should have a pointer receiver, even ones that don't strictly need it. We've broken this rule for Point so that we can show both kinds of method.

Named types (Point) and pointers to them (*Point) are the only types that may appear in a receiver declaration. Furthermore, to avoid ambiguities, method declarations are not permitted on named types that are themselves pointer types:

```
type P *int
func (P) f() { /* ... */ } // compile error: invalid receiver type
```

The (*Point).ScaleBy method can be called by providing a *Point receiver, like this:

```
r := &Point{1, 2}
r.ScaleBy(2)
fmt.Println(*r) // "{2, 4}"
```

or this:

```
p := Point{1, 2}
pptr := &p
pptr.ScaleBy(2)
fmt.Println(p) // "{2, 4}"
```

or this:

```
p := Point{1, 2}
(&p).ScaleBy(2)
fmt.Println(p) // "{2, 4}"
```

But the last two cases are ungainly. Fortunately, the language helps us here. If the receiver p is a *variable* of type Point but the method requires a *Point receiver, we can use this shorthand:

```
p.ScaleBy(2)
```

and the compiler will perform an implicit &p on the variable. This works only for variables, including struct fields like p.X and array or slice elements like perim[0]. We cannot call a *Point method on a non-addressable Point receiver, because there's no way to obtain the address of a temporary value.

```
Point{1, 2}.ScaleBy(2) // compile error: can't take address of Point literal
```

But we *can* call a Point method like Point.Distance with a *Point receiver, because there is a way to obtain the value from the address: just load the value pointed to by the receiver. The compiler inserts an implicit * operation for us. These two function calls are equivalent:

```
pptr.Distance(q)
(*pptr).Distance(q)
```

Let's summarize these three cases again, since they are a frequent point of confusion. In every valid method call expression, exactly one of these three statements is true.

Either the receiver argument has the same type as the receiver parameter, for example both have type T or both have type *T:

```
Point{1, 2}.Distance(q) //  Point
pptr.ScaleBy(2)         // *Point
```

Or the receiver argument is a *variable* of type T and the receiver parameter has type *T. The compiler implicitly takes the address of the variable:

```
p.ScaleBy(2) // implicit (&p)
```

Or the receiver argument has type *T and the receiver parameter has type T. The compiler implicitly dereferences the receiver, in other words, loads the value:

```
pptr.Distance(q) // implicit (*pptr)
```

If all the methods of a named type T have a receiver type of T itself (not *T), it is safe to copy instances of that type; calling any of its methods necessarily makes a copy. For example, time.Duration values are liberally copied, including as arguments to functions. But if any method has a pointer receiver, you should avoid copying instances of T because doing so may violate internal invariants. For example, copying an instance of bytes.Buffer would cause the original and the copy to alias (§2.3.2) the same underlying array of bytes. Subsequent method calls would have unpredictable effects.

6.2.1. Nil Is a Valid Receiver Value

Just as some functions allow nil pointers as arguments, so do some methods for their receiver, especially if nil is a meaningful zero value of the type, as with maps and slices. In this simple linked list of integers, nil represents the empty list:

```
// An IntList is a linked list of integers.
// A nil *IntList represents the empty list.
type IntList struct {
    Value int
    Tail  *IntList
}
```

```
// Sum returns the sum of the list elements.
func (list *IntList) Sum() int {
    if list == nil {
        return 0
    }
    return list.Value + list.Tail.Sum()
}
```

When you define a type whose methods allow nil as a receiver value, it's worth pointing this out explicitly in its documentation comment, as we did above.

Here's part of the definition of the Values type from the net/url package:

net/url

```
package url

// Values maps a string key to a list of values.
type Values map[string][]string

// Get returns the first value associated with the given key,
// or "" if there are none.
func (v Values) Get(key string) string {
    if vs := v[key]; len(vs) > 0 {
        return vs[0]
    }
    return ""
}

// Add adds the value to key.
// It appends to any existing values associated with key.
func (v Values) Add(key, value string) {
    v[key] = append(v[key], value)
}
```

It exposes its representation as a map but also provides methods to simplify access to the map, whose values are slices of strings—it's a *multimap*. Its clients can use its intrinsic operators (make, slice literals, m[key], and so on), or its methods, or both, as they prefer:

gopl.io/ch6/urlvalues

```
m := url.Values{"lang": {"en"}} // direct construction
m.Add("item", "1")
m.Add("item", "2")

fmt.Println(m.Get("lang")) // "en"
fmt.Println(m.Get("q"))    // ""
fmt.Println(m.Get("item")) // "1"      (first value)
fmt.Println(m["item"])     // "[1 2]"  (direct map access)

m = nil
fmt.Println(m.Get("item")) // ""
m.Add("item", "3")         // panic: assignment to entry in nil map
```

In the final call to Get, the nil receiver behaves like an empty map. We could equivalently have written it as Values(nil).Get("item")), but nil.Get("item") will not compile because the type of nil has not been determined. By contrast, the final call to Add panics as it tries to update a nil map.

Because url.Values is a map type and a map refers to its key/value pairs indirectly, any updates and deletions that url.Values.Add makes to the map elements are visible to the caller. However, as with ordinary functions, any changes a method makes to the reference itself, like setting it to nil or making it refer to a different map data structure, will not be reflected in the caller.

6.3. Composing Types by Struct Embedding

Consider the type ColoredPoint:

gopl.io/ch6/coloredpoint

```
import "image/color"

type Point struct{ X, Y float64 }

type ColoredPoint struct {
    Point
    Color color.RGBA
}
```

We could have defined ColoredPoint as a struct of three fields, but instead we *embedded* a Point to provide the X and Y fields. As we saw in Section 4.4.3, embedding lets us take a syntactic shortcut to defining a ColoredPoint that contains all the fields of Point, plus some more. If we want, we can select the fields of ColoredPoint that were contributed by the embedded Point without mentioning Point:

```
var cp ColoredPoint
cp.X = 1
fmt.Println(cp.Point.X) // "1"
cp.Point.Y = 2
fmt.Println(cp.Y) // "2"
```

A similar mechanism applies to the *methods* of Point. We can call methods of the embedded Point field using a receiver of type ColoredPoint, even though ColoredPoint has no declared methods:

```
red := color.RGBA{255, 0, 0, 255}
blue := color.RGBA{0, 0, 255, 255}
var p = ColoredPoint{Point{1, 1}, red}
var q = ColoredPoint{Point{5, 4}, blue}
fmt.Println(p.Distance(q.Point)) // "5"
p.ScaleBy(2)
q.ScaleBy(2)
fmt.Println(p.Distance(q.Point)) // "10"
```

The methods of Point have been *promoted* to ColoredPoint. In this way, embedding allows complex types with many methods to be built up by the *composition* of several fields, each providing a few methods.

Readers familiar with class-based object-oriented languages may be tempted to view Point as
a base class and ColoredPoint as a subclass or derived class, or to interpret the relationship
between these types as if a ColoredPoint "is a" Point. But that would be a mistake. Notice
the calls to Distance above. Distance has a parameter of type Point, and q is not a Point, so
although q does have an embedded field of that type, we must explicitly select it. Attempting
to pass q would be an error:

```
p.Distance(q) // compile error: cannot use q (ColoredPoint) as Point
```

A ColoredPoint is not a Point, but it "has a" Point, and it has two additional methods Distance and ScaleBy promoted from Point. If you prefer to think in terms of implementation,
the embedded field instructs the compiler to generate additional wrapper methods that dele-
gate to the declared methods, equivalent to these:

```
func (p ColoredPoint) Distance(q Point) float64 {
    return p.Point.Distance(q)
}

func (p *ColoredPoint) ScaleBy(factor float64) {
    p.Point.ScaleBy(factor)
}
```

When Point.Distance is called by the first of these wrapper methods, its receiver value is
p.Point, not p, and there is no way for the method to access the ColoredPoint in which the
Point is embedded.

The type of an anonymous field may be a *pointer* to a named type, in which case fields and
methods are promoted indirectly from the pointed-to object. Adding another level of indirection lets us share common structures and vary the relationships between objects dynamically. The declaration of ColoredPoint below embeds a *Point:

```
type ColoredPoint struct {
    *Point
    Color color.RGBA
}

p := ColoredPoint{&Point{1, 1}, red}
q := ColoredPoint{&Point{5, 4}, blue}
fmt.Println(p.Distance(*q.Point)) // "5"
q.Point = p.Point                 // p and q now share the same Point
p.ScaleBy(2)
fmt.Println(*p.Point, *q.Point) // "{2 2} {2 2}"
```

A struct type may have more than one anonymous field. Had we declared ColoredPoint as

```
type ColoredPoint struct {
    Point
    color.RGBA
}
```

then a value of this type would have all the methods of `Point`, all the methods of `RGBA`, and any additional methods declared on `ColoredPoint` directly. When the compiler resolves a selector such as `p.ScaleBy` to a method, it first looks for a directly declared method named `ScaleBy`, then for methods promoted once from `ColoredPoint`'s embedded fields, then for methods promoted twice from embedded fields within `Point` and `RGBA`, and so on. The compiler reports an error if the selector was ambiguous because two methods were promoted from the same rank.

Methods can be declared only on named types (like `Point`) and pointers to them (*`Point`), but thanks to embedding, it's possible and sometimes useful for *unnamed* struct types to have methods too.

Here's a nice trick to illustrate. This example shows part of a simple cache implemented using two package-level variables, a mutex (§9.2) and the map that it guards:

```
var (
    mu sync.Mutex // guards mapping
    mapping = make(map[string]string)
)

func Lookup(key string) string {
    mu.Lock()
    v := mapping[key]
    mu.Unlock()
    return v
}
```

The version below is functionally equivalent but groups together the two related variables in a single package-level variable, `cache`:

```
var cache = struct {
    sync.Mutex
    mapping map[string]string
} {
    mapping: make(map[string]string),
}

func Lookup(key string) string {
    cache.Lock()
    v := cache.mapping[key]
    cache.Unlock()
    return v
}
```

The new variable gives more expressive names to the variables related to the cache, and because the `sync.Mutex` field is embedded within it, its `Lock` and `Unlock` methods are promoted to the unnamed struct type, allowing us to lock the `cache` with a self-explanatory syntax.

6.4. Method Values and Expressions

Usually we select and call a method in the same expression, as in `p.Distance()`, but it's possible to separate these two operations. The selector `p.Distance` yields a *method value*, a function that binds a method (`Point.Distance`) to a specific receiver value p. This function can then be invoked without a receiver value; it needs only the non-receiver arguments.

```
p := Point{1, 2}
q := Point{4, 6}

distanceFromP := p.Distance         // method value
fmt.Println(distanceFromP(q))       // "5"
var origin Point                    // {0, 0}
fmt.Println(distanceFromP(origin)) // "2.23606797749979", √5

scaleP := p.ScaleBy // method value
scaleP(2)              // p becomes (2, 4)
scaleP(3)              //       then (6, 12)
scaleP(10)             //       then (60, 120)
```

Method values are useful when a package's API calls for a function value, and the client's desired behavior for that function is to call a method on a specific receiver. For example, the function `time.AfterFunc` calls a function value after a specified delay. This program uses it to launch the rocket r after 10 seconds:

```
type Rocket struct { /* ... */ }
func (r *Rocket) Launch() { /* ... */ }

r := new(Rocket)
time.AfterFunc(10 * time.Second, func() { r.Launch() })
```

The method value syntax is shorter:

```
time.AfterFunc(10 * time.Second, r.Launch)
```

Related to the method value is the *method expression*. When calling a method, as opposed to an ordinary function, we must supply the receiver in a special way using the selector syntax. A method expression, written `T.f` or `(*T).f` where T is a type, yields a function value with a regular first parameter taking the place of the receiver, so it can be called in the usual way.

```
p := Point{1, 2}
q := Point{4, 6}

distance := Point.Distance      // method expression
fmt.Println(distance(p, q)) // "5"
fmt.Printf("%T\n", distance) // "func(Point, Point) float64"

scale := (*Point).ScaleBy
scale(&p, 2)
fmt.Println(p)               // "{2 4}"
fmt.Printf("%T\n", scale) // "func(*Point, float64)"
```

Method expressions can be helpful when you need a value to represent a choice among several methods belonging to the same type so that you can call the chosen method with many different receivers. In the following example, the variable op represents either the addition or the subtraction method of type `Point`, and `Path.TranslateBy` calls it for each point in the Path:

```
type Point struct{ X, Y float64 }

func (p Point) Add(q Point) Point { return Point{p.X + q.X, p.Y + q.Y} }
func (p Point) Sub(q Point) Point { return Point{p.X - q.X, p.Y - q.Y} }

type Path []Point

func (path Path) TranslateBy(offset Point, add bool) {
    var op func(p, q Point) Point
    if add {
        op = Point.Add
    } else {
        op = Point.Sub
    }
    for i := range path {
        // Call either path[i].Add(offset) or path[i].Sub(offset).
        path[i] = op(path[i], offset)
    }
}
```

6.5. Example: Bit Vector Type

Sets in Go are usually implemented as a `map[T]bool`, where `T` is the element type. A set represented by a map is very flexible but, for certain problems, a specialized representation may outperform it. For example, in domains such as dataflow analysis where set elements are small non-negative integers, sets have many elements, and set operations like union and intersection are common, a *bit vector* is ideal.

A bit vector uses a slice of unsigned integer values or "words," each bit of which represents a possible element of the set. The set contains i if the i-th bit is set. The following program demonstrates a simple bit vector type with three methods:

gopl.io/ch6/intset
```
// An IntSet is a set of small non-negative integers.
// Its zero value represents the empty set.
type IntSet struct {
    words []uint64
}

// Has reports whether the set contains the non-negative value x.
func (s *IntSet) Has(x int) bool {
    word, bit := x/64, uint(x%64)
    return word < len(s.words) && s.words[word]&(1<<bit) != 0
}
```

```go
// Add adds the non-negative value x to the set.
func (s *IntSet) Add(x int) {
    word, bit := x/64, uint(x%64)
    for word >= len(s.words) {
        s.words = append(s.words, 0)
    }
    s.words[word] |= 1 << bit
}

// UnionWith sets s to the union of s and t.
func (s *IntSet) UnionWith(t *IntSet) {
    for i, tword := range t.words {
        if i < len(s.words) {
            s.words[i] |= tword
        } else {
            s.words = append(s.words, tword)
        }
    }
}
```

Since each word has 64 bits, to locate the bit for x, we use the quotient x/64 as the word index and the remainder x%64 as the bit index within that word. The UnionWith operation uses the bitwise OR operator | to compute the union 64 elements at a time. (We'll revisit the choice of 64-bit words in Exercise 6.5.)

This implementation lacks many desirable features, some of which are posed as exercises below, but one is hard to live without: a way to print an IntSet as a string. Let's give it a String method as we did with Celsius in Section 2.5:

```go
// String returns the set as a string of the form "{1 2 3}".
func (s *IntSet) String() string {
    var buf bytes.Buffer
    buf.WriteByte('{')
    for i, word := range s.words {
        if word == 0 {
            continue
        }
        for j := 0; j < 64; j++ {
            if word&(1<<uint(j)) != 0 {
                if buf.Len() > len("{") {
                    buf.WriteByte(' ')
                }
                fmt.Fprintf(&buf, "%d", 64*i+j)
            }
        }
    }
    buf.WriteByte('}')
    return buf.String()
}
```

Notice the similarity of the `String` method above with `intsToString` in Section 3.5.4; `bytes.Buffer` is often used this way in `String` methods. The `fmt` package treats types with a `String` method specially so that values of complicated types can display themselves in a user-friendly manner. Instead of printing the raw representation of the value (a struct in this case), `fmt` calls the `String` method. The mechanism relies on interfaces and type assertions, which we'll explain in Chapter 7.

We can now demonstrate `IntSet` in action:

```
var x, y IntSet
x.Add(1)
x.Add(144)
x.Add(9)
fmt.Println(x.String()) // "{1 9 144}"

y.Add(9)
y.Add(42)
fmt.Println(y.String()) // "{9 42}"

x.UnionWith(&y)
fmt.Println(x.String()) // "{1 9 42 144}"

fmt.Println(x.Has(9), x.Has(123)) // "true false"
```

A word of caution: we declared `String` and `Has` as methods of the pointer type `*IntSet` not out of necessity, but for consistency with the other two methods, which need a pointer receiver because they assign to `s.words`. Consequently, an `IntSet` *value* does not have a `String` method, occasionally leading to surprises like this:

```
fmt.Println(&x)         // "{1 9 42 144}"
fmt.Println(x.String()) // "{1 9 42 144}"
fmt.Println(x)          // "{[4398046511618 0 65536]}"
```

In the first case, we print an `*IntSet` pointer, which does have a `String` method. In the second case, we call `String()` on an `IntSet` variable; the compiler inserts the implicit & operation, giving us a pointer, which has the `String` method. But in the third case, because the `IntSet` value does not have a `String` method, `fmt.Println` prints the representation of the struct instead. It's important not to forget the & operator. Making `String` a method of `IntSet`, not `*IntSet`, might be a good idea, but this is a case-by-case judgment.

Exercise 6.1: Implement these additional methods:

```
func (*IntSet) Len() int      // return the number of elements
func (*IntSet) Remove(x int)  // remove x from the set
func (*IntSet) Clear()        // remove all elements from the set
func (*IntSet) Copy() *IntSet // return a copy of the set
```

Exercise 6.2: Define a variadic `(*IntSet).AddAll(...int)` method that allows a list of values to be added, such as `s.AddAll(1, 2, 3)`.

Exercise 6.3: `(*IntSet).UnionWith` computes the union of two sets using |, the word-parallel bitwise OR operator. Implement methods for `IntersectWith`, `DifferenceWith`, and `SymmetricDifference` for the corresponding set operations. (The symmetric difference of two sets contains the elements present in one set or the other but not both.)

Exercise 6.4: Add a method Elems that returns a slice containing the elements of the set, suitable for iterating over with a range loop.

Exercise 6.5: The type of each word used by IntSet is uint64, but 64-bit arithmetic may be inefficient on a 32-bit platform. Modify the program to use the uint type, which is the most efficient unsigned integer type for the platform. Instead of dividing by 64, define a constant holding the effective size of uint in bits, 32 or 64. You can use the perhaps too-clever expression 32 << (^uint(0) >> 63) for this purpose.

6.6. Encapsulation

A variable or method of an object is said to be *encapsulated* if it is inaccessible to clients of the object. Encapsulation, sometimes called *information hiding*, is a key aspect of object-oriented programming.

Go has only one mechanism to control the visibility of names: capitalized identifiers are exported from the package in which they are defined, and uncapitalized names are not. The same mechanism that limits access to members of a package also limits access to the fields of a struct or the methods of a type. As a consequence, to encapsulate an object, we must make it a struct.

That's the reason the IntSet type from the previous section was declared as a struct type even though it has only a single field:

```
type IntSet struct {
    words []uint64
}
```

We could instead define IntSet as a slice type as follows, though of course we'd have to replace each occurrence of s.words by *s in its methods:

```
type IntSet []uint64
```

Although this version of IntSet would be essentially equivalent, it would allow clients from other packages to read and modify the slice directly. Put another way, whereas the expression *s could be used in any package, s.words may appear only in the package that defines IntSet.

Another consequence of this name-based mechanism is that the unit of encapsulation is the package, not the type as in many other languages. The fields of a struct type are visible to all code within the same package. Whether the code appears in a function or a method makes no difference.

Encapsulation provides three benefits. First, because clients cannot directly modify the object's variables, one need inspect fewer statements to understand the possible values of those variables.

Second, hiding implementation details prevents clients from depending on things that might change, which gives the designer greater freedom to evolve the implementation without breaking API compatibility.

As an example, consider the bytes.Buffer type. It is frequently used to accumulate very short strings, so it is a profitable optimization to reserve a little extra space in the object to avoid memory allocation in this common case. Since Buffer is a struct type, this space takes the form of an extra field of type [64]byte with an uncapitalized name. When this field was added, because it was not exported, clients of Buffer outside the bytes package were unaware of any change except improved performance. Buffer and its Grow method are shown below, simplified for clarity:

```
type Buffer struct {
    buf     []byte
    initial [64]byte
    /* ... */
}

// Grow expands the buffer's capacity, if necessary,
// to guarantee space for another n bytes. [...]
func (b *Buffer) Grow(n int) {
    if b.buf == nil {
        b.buf = b.initial[:0] // use preallocated space initially
    }
    if len(b.buf)+n > cap(b.buf) {
        buf := make([]byte, b.Len(), 2*cap(b.buf) + n)
        copy(buf, b.buf)
        b.buf = buf
    }
}
```

The third benefit of encapsulation, and in many cases the most important, is that it prevents clients from setting an object's variables arbitrarily. Because the object's variables can be set only by functions in the same package, the author of that package can ensure that all those functions maintain the object's internal invariants. For example, the Counter type below permits clients to increment the counter or to reset it to zero, but not to set it to some arbitrary value:

```
type Counter struct { n int }

func (c *Counter) N() int      { return c.n }
func (c *Counter) Increment() { c.n++ }
func (c *Counter) Reset()      { c.n = 0 }
```

Functions that merely access or modify internal values of a type, such as the methods of the Logger type from log package, below, are called *getters* and *setters*. However, when naming a getter method, we usually omit the Get prefix. This preference for brevity extends to all methods, not just field accessors, and to other redundant prefixes as well, such as Fetch, Find, and Lookup.

```go
package log

type Logger struct {
    flags  int
    prefix string
    // ...
}

func (l *Logger) Flags() int
func (l *Logger) SetFlags(flag int)
func (l *Logger) Prefix() string
func (l *Logger) SetPrefix(prefix string)
```

Go style does not forbid exported fields. Of course, once exported, a field cannot be unexported without an incompatible change to the API, so the initial choice should be deliberate and should consider the complexity of the invariants that must be maintained, the likelihood of future changes, and the quantity of client code that would be affected by a change.

Encapsulation is not always desirable. By revealing its representation as an int64 number of nanoseconds, time.Duration lets us use all the usual arithmetic and comparison operations with durations, and even to define constants of this type:

```go
const day = 24 * time.Hour
fmt.Println(day.Seconds()) // "86400"
```

As another example, contrast IntSet with the geometry.Path type from the beginning of this chapter. Path was defined as a slice type, allowing its clients to construct instances using the slice literal syntax, to iterate over its points using a range loop, and so on, whereas these operations are denied to clients of IntSet.

Here's the crucial difference: geometry.Path is intrinsically a sequence of points, no more and no less, and we don't foresee adding new fields to it, so it makes sense for the geometry package to reveal that Path is a slice. In contrast, an IntSet merely happens to be represented as a []uint64 slice. It could have been represented using []uint, or something completely different for sets that are sparse or very small, and it might perhaps benefit from additional features like an extra field to record the number of elements in the set. For these reasons, it makes sense for IntSet to be opaque.

In this chapter, we learned how to associate methods with named types, and how to call those methods. Although methods are crucial to object-oriented programming, they're only half the picture. To complete it, we need *interfaces*, the subject of the next chapter.

7

Interfaces

Interface types express generalizations or abstractions about the behaviors of other types. By generalizing, interfaces let us write functions that are more flexible and adaptable because they are not tied to the details of one particular implementation.

Many object-oriented languages have some notion of interfaces, but what makes Go's interfaces so distinctive is that they are *satisfied implicitly*. In other words, there's no need to declare all the interfaces that a given concrete type satisfies; simply possessing the necessary methods is enough. This design lets you create new interfaces that are satisfied by existing concrete types without changing the existing types, which is particularly useful for types defined in packages that you don't control.

In this chapter, we'll start by looking at the basic mechanics of interface types and their values. Along the way, we'll study several important interfaces from the standard library. Many Go programs make as much use of standard interfaces as they do of their own ones. Finally, we'll look at *type assertions* (§7.10) and *type switches* (§7.13) and see how they enable a different kind of generality.

7.1. Interfaces as Contracts

All the types we've looked at so far have been *concrete types*. A concrete type specifies the exact representation of its values and exposes the intrinsic operations of that representation, such as arithmetic for numbers, or indexing, append, and range for slices. A concrete type may also provide additional behaviors through its methods. When you have a value of a concrete type, you know exactly what it *is* and what you can *do* with it.

There is another kind of type in Go called an *interface type*. An interface is an *abstract type*. It doesn't expose the representation or internal structure of its values, or the set of basic operations they support; it reveals only some of their methods. When you have a value of an interface type, you know nothing about what it *is*; you know only what it can *do*, or more precisely, what behaviors are provided by its methods.

Throughout the book, we've been using two similar functions for string formatting: `fmt.Printf`, which writes the result to the standard output (a file), and `fmt.Sprintf`, which returns the result as a `string`. It would be unfortunate if the hard part, formatting the result, had to be duplicated because of these superficial differences in how the result is used. Thanks to interfaces, it does not. Both of these functions are, in effect, wrappers around a third function, `fmt.Fprintf`, that is agnostic about what happens to the result it computes:

```
package fmt

func Fprintf(w io.Writer, format string, args ...interface{}) (int, error)

func Printf(format string, args ...interface{}) (int, error) {
    return Fprintf(os.Stdout, format, args...)
}

func Sprintf(format string, args ...interface{}) string {
    var buf bytes.Buffer
    Fprintf(&buf, format, args...)
    return buf.String()
}
```

The `F` prefix of `Fprintf` stands for *file* and indicates that the formatted output should be written to the file provided as the first argument. In the `Printf` case, the argument, `os.Stdout`, is an `*os.File`. In the `Sprintf` case, however, the argument is not a file, though it superficially resembles one: `&buf` is a pointer to a memory buffer to which bytes can be written.

The first parameter of `Fprintf` is not a file either. It's an `io.Writer`, which is an interface type with the following declaration:

```
package io

// Writer is the interface that wraps the basic Write method.
type Writer interface {
    // Write writes len(p) bytes from p to the underlying data stream.
    // It returns the number of bytes written from p (0 <= n <= len(p))
    // and any error encountered that caused the write to stop early.
    // Write must return a non-nil error if it returns n < len(p).
    // Write must not modify the slice data, even temporarily.
    //
    // Implementations must not retain p.
    Write(p []byte) (n int, err error)
}
```

The `io.Writer` interface defines the contract between `Fprintf` and its callers. On the one hand, the contract requires that the caller provide a value of a concrete type like `*os.File` or `*bytes.Buffer` that has a method called `Write` with the appropriate signature and behavior. On the other hand, the contract guarantees that `Fprintf` will do its job given any value that satisfies the `io.Writer` interface. `Fprintf` may not assume that it is writing to a file or to memory, only that it can call Write.

Because fmt.Fprintf assumes nothing about the representation of the value and relies only on the behaviors guaranteed by the io.Writer contract, we can safely pass a value of any concrete type that satisfies io.Writer as the first argument to fmt.Fprintf. This freedom to substitute one type for another that satisfies the same interface is called *substitutability*, and is a hallmark of object-oriented programming.

Let's test this out using a new type. The Write method of the *ByteCounter type below merely counts the bytes written to it before discarding them. (The conversion is required to make the types of len(p) and *c match in the += assignment statement.)

gopl.io/ch7/bytecounter

```
type ByteCounter int

func (c *ByteCounter) Write(p []byte) (int, error) {
    *c += ByteCounter(len(p)) // convert int to ByteCounter
    return len(p), nil
}
```

Since *ByteCounter satisfies the io.Writer contract, we can pass it to Fprintf, which does its string formatting oblivious to this change; the ByteCounter correctly accumulates the length of the result.

```
var c ByteCounter
c.Write([]byte("hello"))
fmt.Println(c) // "5", = len("hello")

c = 0 // reset the counter
var name = "Dolly"
fmt.Fprintf(&c, "hello, %s", name)
fmt.Println(c) // "12", = len("hello, Dolly")
```

Besides io.Writer, there is another interface of great importance to the fmt package. Fprintf and Fprintln provide a way for types to control how their values are printed. In Section 2.5, we defined a String method for the Celsius type so that temperatures would print as "100°C", and in Section 6.5 we equipped *IntSet with a String method so that sets would be rendered using traditional set notation like "{1 2 3}". Declaring a String method makes a type satisfy one of the most widely used interfaces of all, fmt.Stringer:

```
package fmt

// The String method is used to print values passed
// as an operand to any format that accepts a string
// or to an unformatted printer such as Print.
type Stringer interface {
    String() string
}
```

We'll explain how the fmt package discovers which values satisfy this interface in Section 7.10.

Exercise 7.1: Using the ideas from ByteCounter, implement counters for words and for lines. You will find bufio.ScanWords useful.

Exercise 7.2: Write a function `CountingWriter` with the signature below that, given an `io.Writer`, returns a new `Writer` that wraps the original, and a pointer to an `int64` variable that at any moment contains the number of bytes written to the new `Writer`.

```
func CountingWriter(w io.Writer) (io.Writer, *int64)
```

Exercise 7.3: Write a `String` method for the *tree type in gopl.io/ch4/treesort (§4.4) that reveals the sequence of values in the tree.

7.2. Interface Types

An interface type specifies a set of methods that a concrete type must possess to be considered an instance of that interface.

The `io.Writer` type is one of the most widely used interfaces because it provides an abstraction of all the types to which bytes can be written, which includes files, memory buffers, network connections, HTTP clients, archivers, hashers, and so on. The `io` package defines many other useful interfaces. A `Reader` represents any type from which you can read bytes, and a `Closer` is any value that you can close, such as a file or a network connection. (By now you've probably noticed the naming convention for many of Go's single-method interfaces.)

```
package io

type Reader interface {
    Read(p []byte) (n int, err error)
}

type Closer interface {
    Close() error
}
```

Looking farther, we find declarations of new interface types as combinations of existing ones. Here are two examples:

```
type ReadWriter interface {
    Reader
    Writer
}

type ReadWriteCloser interface {
    Reader
    Writer
    Closer
}
```

The syntax used above, which resembles struct embedding, lets us name another interface as a shorthand for writing out all of its methods. This is called *embedding* an interface. We could have written io.ReadWriter without embedding, albeit less succinctly, like this:

```
type ReadWriter interface {
    Read(p []byte) (n int, err error)
    Write(p []byte) (n int, err error)
}
```

or even using a mixture of the two styles:

```
type ReadWriter interface {
    Read(p []byte) (n int, err error)
    Writer
}
```

All three declarations have the same effect. The order in which the methods appear is immaterial. All that matters is the set of methods.

Exercise 7.4: The strings.NewReader function returns a value that satisfies the io.Reader interface (and others) by reading from its argument, a string. Implement a simple version of NewReader yourself, and use it to make the HTML parser (§5.2) take input from a string.

Exercise 7.5: The LimitReader function in the io package accepts an io.Reader r and a number of bytes n, and returns another Reader that reads from r but reports an end-of-file condition after n bytes. Implement it.

```
func LimitReader(r io.Reader, n int64) io.Reader
```

7.3. Interface Satisfaction

A type *satisfies* an interface if it possesses all the methods the interface requires. For example, an *os.File satisfies io.Reader, Writer, Closer, and ReadWriter. A *bytes.Buffer satisfies Reader, Writer, and ReadWriter, but does not satisfy Closer because it does not have a Close method. As a shorthand, Go programmers often say that a concrete type "is a" particular interface type, meaning that it satisfies the interface. For example, a *bytes.Buffer is an io.Writer; an *os.File is an io.ReadWriter.

The assignability rule (§2.4.2) for interfaces is very simple: an expression may be assigned to an interface only if its type satisfies the interface. So:

```
var w io.Writer
w = os.Stdout           // OK: *os.File has Write method
w = new(bytes.Buffer)   // OK: *bytes.Buffer has Write method
w = time.Second         // compile error: time.Duration lacks Write method

var rwc io.ReadWriteCloser
rwc = os.Stdout         // OK: *os.File has Read, Write, Close methods
rwc = new(bytes.Buffer) // compile error: *bytes.Buffer lacks Close method
```

This rule applies even when the right-hand side is itself an interface:

```
w = rwc                 // OK: io.ReadWriteCloser has Write method
rwc = w                 // compile error: io.Writer lacks Close method
```

Because `ReadWriter` and `ReadWriteCloser` include all the methods of `Writer`, any type that satisfies `ReadWriter` or `ReadWriteCloser` necessarily satisfies `Writer`.

Before we go further, we should explain one subtlety in what it means for a type to have a method. Recall from Section 6.2 that for each named concrete type `T`, some of its methods have a receiver of type `T` itself whereas others require a `*T` pointer. Recall also that it is legal to call a `*T` method on an argument of type `T` so long as the argument is a *variable*; the compiler implicitly takes its address. But this is mere syntactic sugar: a value of type `T` does not possess all the methods that a `*T` pointer does, and as a result it might satisfy fewer interfaces.

An example will make this clear. The `String` method of the `IntSet` type from Section 6.5 requires a pointer receiver, so we cannot call that method on a non-addressable `IntSet` value:

```
type IntSet struct { /* ... */ }
func (*IntSet) String() string

var _ = IntSet{}.String() // compile error: String requires *IntSet receiver
```

but we can call it on an `IntSet` variable:

```
var s IntSet
var _ = s.String() // OK: s is a variable and &s has a String method
```

However, since only `*IntSet` has a `String` method, only `*IntSet` satisfies the `fmt.Stringer` interface:

```
var _ fmt.Stringer = &s // OK
var _ fmt.Stringer = s  // compile error: IntSet lacks String method
```

Section 12.8 includes a program that prints the methods of an arbitrary value, and the `godoc -analysis=type` tool (§10.7.4) displays the methods of each type and the relationship between interfaces and concrete types.

Like an envelope that wraps and conceals the letter it holds, an interface wraps and conceals the concrete type and value that it holds. Only the methods revealed by the interface type may be called, even if the concrete type has others:

```
os.Stdout.Write([]byte("hello")) // OK: *os.File has Write method
os.Stdout.Close()                // OK: *os.File has Close method

var w io.Writer
w = os.Stdout
w.Write([]byte("hello")) // OK: io.Writer has Write method
w.Close()                // compile error: io.Writer lacks Close method
```

An interface with more methods, such as `io.ReadWriter`, tells us more about the values it contains, and places greater demands on the types that implement it, than does an interface with fewer methods such as `io.Reader`. So what does the type `interface{}`, which has no methods at all, tell us about the concrete types that satisfy it?

That's right: nothing. This may seem useless, but in fact the type `interface{}`, which is called the *empty interface* type, is indispensable. Because the empty interface type places no demands on the types that satisfy it, we can assign *any* value to the empty interface.

```
var any interface{}
any = true
any = 12.34
any = "hello"
any = map[string]int{"one": 1}
any = new(bytes.Buffer)
```

Although it wasn't obvious, we've been using the empty interface type since the very first example in this book, because it is what allows functions like fmt.Println, or errorf in Section 5.7, to accept arguments of any type.

Of course, having created an interface{} value containing a boolean, float, string, map, pointer, or any other type, we can do nothing directly to the value it holds since the interface has no methods. We need a way to get the value back out again. We'll see how to do that using a *type assertion* in Section 7.10.

Since interface satisfaction depends only on the methods of the two types involved, there is no need to declare the relationship between a concrete type and the interfaces it satisfies. That said, it is occasionally useful to document and assert the relationship when it is intended but not otherwise enforced by the program. The declaration below asserts at compile time that a value of type *bytes.Buffer satisfies io.Writer:

```
// *bytes.Buffer must satisfy io.Writer
var w io.Writer = new(bytes.Buffer)
```

We needn't allocate a new variable since any value of type *bytes.Buffer will do, even nil, which we write as (*bytes.Buffer)(nil) using an explicit conversion. And since we never intend to refer to w, we can replace it with the blank identifier. Together, these changes give us this more frugal variant:

```
// *bytes.Buffer must satisfy io.Writer
var _ io.Writer = (*bytes.Buffer)(nil)
```

Non-empty interface types such as io.Writer are most often satisfied by a pointer type, particularly when one or more of the interface methods implies some kind of mutation to the receiver, as the Write method does. A pointer to a struct is an especially common method-bearing type.

But pointer types are by no means the only types that satisfy interfaces, and even interfaces with mutator methods may be satisfied by one of Go's other reference types. We've seen examples of slice types with methods (geometry.Path, §6.1) and map types with methods (url.Values, §6.2.1), and later we'll see a function type with methods (http.HandlerFunc, §7.7). Even basic types may satisfy interfaces; as we saw in Section 7.4, time.Duration satisfies fmt.Stringer.

A concrete type may satisfy many unrelated interfaces. Consider a program that organizes or sells digitized cultural artifacts like music, films, and books. It might define the following set of concrete types:

```
Album
Book
Movie
Magazine
Podcast
TVEpisode
Track
```

We can express each abstraction of interest as an interface. Some properties are common to all artifacts, such as a title, a creation date, and a list of creators (authors or artists).

```
type Artifact interface {
    Title() string
    Creators() []string
    Created() time.Time
}
```

Other properties are restricted to certain types of artifacts. Properties of the printed word are relevant only to books and magazines, whereas only movies and TV episodes have a screen resolution.

```
type Text interface {
    Pages() int
    Words() int
    PageSize() int
}

type Audio interface {
    Stream() (io.ReadCloser, error)
    RunningTime() time.Duration
    Format() string // e.g., "MP3", "WAV"
}

type Video interface {
    Stream() (io.ReadCloser, error)
    RunningTime() time.Duration
    Format() string // e.g., "MP4", "WMV"
    Resolution() (x, y int)
}
```

These interfaces are but one useful way to group related concrete types together and express the facets they share in common. We may discover other groupings later. For example, if we find we need to handle Audio and Video items in the same way, we can define a Streamer interface to represent their common aspects without changing any existing type declarations.

```
type Streamer interface {
    Stream() (io.ReadCloser, error)
    RunningTime() time.Duration
    Format() string
}
```

Each grouping of concrete types based on their shared behaviors can be expressed as an interface type. Unlike class-based languages, in which the set of interfaces satisfied by a class is explicit, in Go we can define new abstractions or groupings of interest when we need them, without modifying the declaration of the concrete type. This is particularly useful when the concrete type comes from a package written by a different author. Of course, there do need to be underlying commonalities in the concrete types.

7.4. Parsing Flags with `flag.Value`

In this section, we'll see how another standard interface, `flag.Value`, helps us define new notations for command-line flags. Consider the program below, which sleeps for a specified period of time.

gopl.io/ch7/sleep
```go
var period = flag.Duration("period", 1*time.Second, "sleep period")

func main() {
    flag.Parse()
    fmt.Printf("Sleeping for %v...", *period)
    time.Sleep(*period)
    fmt.Println()
}
```

Before it goes to sleep it prints the time period. The `fmt` package calls the `time.Duration`'s `String` method to print the period not as a number of nanoseconds, but in a user-friendly notation:

```
$ go build gopl.io/ch7/sleep
$ ./sleep
Sleeping for 1s...
```

By default, the sleep period is one second, but it can be controlled through the -period command-line flag. The `flag.Duration` function creates a flag variable of type `time.Duration` and allows the user to specify the duration in a variety of user-friendly formats, including the same notation printed by the `String` method. This symmetry of design leads to a nice user interface.

```
$ ./sleep -period 50ms
Sleeping for 50ms...
$ ./sleep -period 2m30s
Sleeping for 2m30s...
$ ./sleep -period 1.5h
Sleeping for 1h30m0s...
$ ./sleep -period "1 day"
invalid value "1 day" for flag -period: time: invalid duration 1 day
```

Because duration-valued flags are so useful, this feature is built into the `flag` package, but it's easy to define new flag notations for our own data types. We need only define a type that satisfies the `flag.Value` interface, whose declaration is below:

```
package flag

// Value is the interface to the value stored in a flag.
type Value interface {
    String() string
    Set(string) error
}
```

The String method formats the flag's value for use in command-line help messages; thus every flag.Value is also a fmt.Stringer. The Set method parses its string argument and updates the flag value. In effect, the Set method is the inverse of the String method, and it is good practice for them to use the same notation.

Let's define a celsiusFlag type that allows a temperature to be specified in Celsius, or in Fahrenheit with an appropriate conversion. Notice that celsiusFlag embeds a Celsius (§2.5), thereby getting a String method for free. To satisfy flag.Value, we need only declare the Set method:

gopl.io/ch7/tempconv
```
// *celsiusFlag satisfies the flag.Value interface.
type celsiusFlag struct{ Celsius }

func (f *celsiusFlag) Set(s string) error {
    var unit string
    var value float64
    fmt.Sscanf(s, "%f%s", &value, &unit) // no error check needed
    switch unit {
    case "C", "°C":
        f.Celsius = Celsius(value)
        return nil
    case "F", "°F":
        f.Celsius = FToC(Fahrenheit(value))
        return nil
    }
    return fmt.Errorf("invalid temperature %q", s)
}
```

The call to fmt.Sscanf parses a floating-point number (value) and a string (unit) from the input s. Although one must usually check Sscanf's error result, in this case we don't need to because if there was a problem, no switch case will match.

The CelsiusFlag function below wraps it all up. To the caller, it returns a pointer to the Celsius field embedded within the celsiusFlag variable f. The Celsius field is the variable that will be updated by the Set method during flags processing. The call to Var adds the flag to the application's set of command-line flags, the global variable flag.CommandLine. Programs with unusually complex command-line interfaces may have several variables of this type. The call to Var assigns a *celsiusFlag argument to a flag.Value parameter, causing the compiler to check that *celsiusFlag has the necessary methods.

```
// CelsiusFlag defines a Celsius flag with the specified name,
// default value, and usage, and returns the address of the flag variable.
// The flag argument must have a quantity and a unit, e.g., "100C".
func CelsiusFlag(name string, value Celsius, usage string) *Celsius {
    f := celsiusFlag{value}
    flag.CommandLine.Var(&f, name, usage)
    return &f.Celsius
}
```

Now we can start using the new flag in our programs:

gopl.io/ch7/tempflag

```
var temp = tempconv.CelsiusFlag("temp", 20.0, "the temperature")

func main() {
    flag.Parse()
    fmt.Println(*temp)
}
```

Here's a typical session:

```
$ go build gopl.io/ch7/tempflag
$ ./tempflag
20°C
$ ./tempflag -temp -18C
-18°C
$ ./tempflag -temp 212°F
100°C
$ ./tempflag -temp 273.15K
invalid value "273.15K" for flag -temp: invalid temperature "273.15K"
Usage of ./tempflag:
  -temp value
        the temperature (default 20°C)
$ ./tempflag -help
Usage of ./tempflag:
  -temp value
        the temperature (default 20°C)
```

Exercise 7.6: Add support for Kelvin temperatures to `tempflag`.

Exercise 7.7: Explain why the help message contains °C when the default value of `20.0` does not.

7.5. Interface Values

Conceptually, a value of an interface type, or *interface value*, has two components, a concrete type and a value of that type. These are called the interface's *dynamic type* and *dynamic value*.

For a statically typed language like Go, types are a compile-time concept, so a type is not a value. In our conceptual model, a set of values called *type descriptors* provide information about each type, such as its name and methods. In an interface value, the type component is represented by the appropriate type descriptor.

In the four statements below, the variable w takes on three different values. (The initial and final values are the same.)

```
var w io.Writer
w = os.Stdout
w = new(bytes.Buffer)
w = nil
```

Let's take a closer look at the value and dynamic behavior of w after each statement. The first statement declares w:

```
var w io.Writer
```

In Go, variables are always initialized to a well-defined value, and interfaces are no exception. The zero value for an interface has both its type and value components set to nil (Figure 7.1).

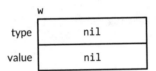

Figure 7.1. A nil interface value.

An interface value is described as nil or non-nil based on its dynamic type, so this is a nil interface value. You can test whether an interface value is nil using w == nil or w != nil. Calling any method of a nil interface value causes a panic:

```
w.Write([]byte("hello")) // panic: nil pointer dereference
```

The second statement assigns a value of type *os.File to w:

```
w = os.Stdout
```

This assignment involves an implicit conversion from a concrete type to an interface type, and is equivalent to the explicit conversion io.Writer(os.Stdout). A conversion of this kind, whether explicit or implicit, captures the type and the value of its operand. The interface value's dynamic type is set to the type descriptor for the pointer type *os.File, and its dynamic value holds a copy of os.Stdout, which is a pointer to the os.File variable representing the standard output of the process (Figure 7.2).

Figure 7.2. An interface value containing an *os.File pointer.

Calling the `Write` method on an interface value containing an `*os.File` pointer causes the `(*os.File).Write` method to be called. The call prints `"hello"`.

```
w.Write([]byte("hello")) // "hello"
```

In general, we cannot know at compile time what the dynamic type of an interface value will be, so a call through an interface must use *dynamic dispatch*. Instead of a direct call, the compiler must generate code to obtain the address of the method named `Write` from the type descriptor, then make an indirect call to that address. The receiver argument for the call is a copy of the interface's dynamic value, `os.Stdout`. The effect is as if we had made this call directly:

```
os.Stdout.Write([]byte("hello")) // "hello"
```

The third statement assigns a value of type `*bytes.Buffer` to the interface value:

```
w = new(bytes.Buffer)
```

The dynamic type is now `*bytes.Buffer` and the dynamic value is a pointer to the newly allocated buffer (Figure 7.3).

Figure 7.3. An interface value containing a `*bytes.Buffer` pointer.

A call to the `Write` method uses the same mechanism as before:

```
w.Write([]byte("hello")) // writes "hello" to the bytes.Buffer
```

This time, the type descriptor is `*bytes.Buffer`, so the `(*bytes.Buffer).Write` method is called, with the address of the buffer as the value of the receiver parameter. The call appends `"hello"` to the buffer.

Finally, the fourth statement assigns `nil` to the interface value:

```
w = nil
```

This resets both its components to `nil`, restoring `w` to the same state as when it was declared, which was shown in Figure 7.1.

An interface value can hold arbitrarily large dynamic values. For example, the `time.Time` type, which represents an instant in time, is a struct type with several unexported fields. If we create an interface value from it,

```
var x interface{} = time.Now()
```

the result might look like Figure 7.4. Conceptually, the dynamic value always fits inside the interface value, no matter how large its type. (This is only a conceptual model; a realistic implementation is quite different.)

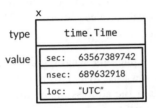

Figure 7.4. An interface value holding a `time.Time` struct.

Interface values may be compared using `==` and `!=`. Two interface values are equal if both are nil, or if their dynamic types are identical and their dynamic values are equal according to the usual behavior of `==` for that type. Because interface values are comparable, they may be used as the keys of a map or as the operand of a switch statement.

However, if two interface values are compared and have the same dynamic type, but that type is not comparable (a slice, for instance), then the comparison fails with a panic:

```
var x interface{} = []int{1, 2, 3}
fmt.Println(x == x) // panic: comparing uncomparable type []int
```

In this respect, interface types are unusual. Other types are either safely comparable (like basic types and pointers) or not comparable at all (like slices, maps, and functions), but when comparing interface values or aggregate types that contain interface values, we must be aware of the potential for a panic. A similar risk exists when using interfaces as map keys or switch operands. Only compare interface values if you are certain that they contain dynamic values of comparable types.

When handling errors, or during debugging, it is often helpful to report the dynamic type of an interface value. For that, we use the `fmt` package's `%T` verb:

```
var w io.Writer
fmt.Printf("%T\n", w) // "<nil>"

w = os.Stdout
fmt.Printf("%T\n", w) // "*os.File"

w = new(bytes.Buffer)
fmt.Printf("%T\n", w) // "*bytes.Buffer"
```

Internally, `fmt` uses reflection to obtain the name of the interface's dynamic type. We'll look at reflection in Chapter 12.

7.5.1. Caveat: An Interface Containing a Nil Pointer Is Non-Nil

A nil interface value, which contains no value at all, is not the same as an interface value containing a pointer that happens to be nil. This subtle distinction creates a trap into which every Go programmer has stumbled.

Consider the program below. With debug set to true, the main function collects the output of the function f in a bytes.Buffer.

```
const debug = true

func main() {
    var buf *bytes.Buffer
    if debug {
        buf = new(bytes.Buffer) // enable collection of output
    }
    f(buf) // NOTE: subtly incorrect!
    if debug {
        // ...use buf...
    }
}

// If out is non-nil, output will be written to it.
func f(out io.Writer) {
    // ...do something...
    if out != nil {
        out.Write([]byte("done!\n"))
    }
}
```

We might expect that changing debug to false would disable the collection of the output, but in fact it causes the program to panic during the out.Write call:

```
if out != nil {
    out.Write([]byte("done!\n")) // panic: nil pointer dereference
}
```

When main calls f, it assigns a nil pointer of type *bytes.Buffer to the out parameter, so the dynamic value of out is nil. However, its dynamic type is *bytes.Buffer, meaning that out is a non-nil interface containing a nil pointer value (Figure 7.5), so the defensive check out != nil is still true.

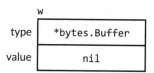

Figure 7.5. A non-nil interface containing a nil pointer.

As before, the dynamic dispatch mechanism determines that (*bytes.Buffer).Write must be called but this time with a receiver value that is nil. For some types, such as *os.File, nil is a valid receiver (§6.2.1), but *bytes.Buffer is not among them. The method is called, but it panics as it tries to access the buffer.

The problem is that although a nil *bytes.Buffer pointer has the methods needed to satisfy the interface, it doesn't satisfy the *behavioral* requirements of the interface. In particular, the call violates the implicit precondition of (*bytes.Buffer).Write that its receiver is not nil, so assigning the nil pointer to the interface was a mistake. The solution is to change the type of buf in main to io.Writer, thereby avoiding the assignment of the dysfunctional value to the interface in the first place:

```
var buf io.Writer
if debug {
    buf = new(bytes.Buffer) // enable collection of output
}
f(buf) // OK
```

Now that we've covered the mechanics of interface values, let's take a look at some more important interfaces from Go's standard library. In the next three sections, we'll see how interfaces are used for sorting, web serving, and error handling.

7.6. Sorting with sort.Interface

Like string formatting, sorting is a frequently used operation in many programs. Although a minimal Quicksort can be written in about 15 lines, a robust implementation is much longer, and it is not the kind of code we should wish to write anew or copy each time we need it.

Fortunately, the sort package provides in-place sorting of any sequence according to any ordering function. Its design is rather unusual. In many languages, the sorting algorithm is associated with the sequence data type, while the ordering function is associated with the type of the elements. By contrast, Go's sort.Sort function assumes nothing about the representation of either the sequence or its elements. Instead, it uses an interface, sort.Interface, to specify the contract between the generic sort algorithm and each sequence type that may be sorted. An implementation of this interface determines both the concrete representation of the sequence, which is often a slice, and the desired ordering of its elements.

An in-place sort algorithm needs three things—the length of the sequence, a means of comparing two elements, and a way to swap two elements—so they are the three methods of sort.Interface:

```
package sort

type Interface interface {
    Len() int
    Less(i, j int) bool // i, j are indices of sequence elements
    Swap(i, j int)
}
```

To sort any sequence, we need to define a type that implements these three methods, then apply sort.Sort to an instance of that type. As perhaps the simplest example, consider sorting a slice of strings. The new type StringSlice and its Len, Less, and Swap methods are shown below.

```go
type StringSlice []string
func (p StringSlice) Len() int            { return len(p) }
func (p StringSlice) Less(i, j int) bool  { return p[i] < p[j] }
func (p StringSlice) Swap(i, j int)       { p[i], p[j] = p[j], p[i] }
```

Now we can sort a slice of strings, names, by converting the slice to a `StringSlice` like this:

```go
sort.Sort(StringSlice(names))
```

The conversion yields a slice value with the same length, capacity, and underlying array as names but with a type that has the three methods required for sorting.

Sorting a slice of strings is so common that the `sort` package provides the `StringSlice` type, as well as a function called `Strings` so that the call above can be simplified to `sort.Strings(names)`.

The technique here is easily adapted to other sort orders, for instance, to ignore capitalization or special characters. (The Go program that sorts index terms and page numbers for this book does this, with extra logic for Roman numerals.) For more complicated sorting, we use the same idea, but with more complicated data structures or more complicated implementations of the `sort.Interface` methods.

Our running example for sorting will be a music playlist, displayed as a table. Each track is a single row, and each column is an attribute of that track, like artist, title, and running time. Imagine that a graphical user interface presents the table, and that clicking the head of a column causes the playlist to be sorted by that attribute; clicking the same column head again reverses the order. Let's look at what might happen in response to each click.

The variable `tracks` below contains a playlist. (One of the authors apologizes for the other author's musical tastes.) Each element is indirect, a pointer to a `Track`. Although the code below would work if we stored the `Tracks` directly, the sort function will swap many pairs of elements, so it will run faster if each element is a pointer, which is a single machine word, instead of an entire `Track`, which might be eight words or more.

gopl.io/ch7/sorting

```go
type Track struct {
    Title  string
    Artist string
    Album  string
    Year   int
    Length time.Duration
}

var tracks = []*Track{
    {"Go", "Delilah", "From the Roots Up", 2012, length("3m38s")},
    {"Go", "Moby", "Moby", 1992, length("3m37s")},
    {"Go Ahead", "Alicia Keys", "As I Am", 2007, length("4m36s")},
    {"Ready 2 Go", "Martin Solveig", "Smash", 2011, length("4m24s")},
}
```

```
func length(s string) time.Duration {
    d, err := time.ParseDuration(s)
    if err != nil {
        panic(s)
    }
    return d
}
```

The printTracks function prints the playlist as a table. A graphical display would be nicer, but this little routine uses the text/tabwriter package to produce a table whose columns are neatly aligned and padded as shown below. Observe that *tabwriter.Writer satisfies io.Writer. It collects each piece of data written to it; its Flush method formats the entire table and writes it to os.Stdout.

```
func printTracks(tracks []*Track) {
    const format = "%v\t%v\t%v\t%v\t%v\t\n"
    tw := new(tabwriter.Writer).Init(os.Stdout, 0, 8, 2, ' ', 0)
    fmt.Fprintf(tw, format, "Title", "Artist", "Album", "Year", "Length")
    fmt.Fprintf(tw, format, "-----", "------", "-----", "----", "------")
    for _, t := range tracks {
        fmt.Fprintf(tw, format, t.Title, t.Artist, t.Album, t.Year, t.Length)
    }
    tw.Flush() // calculate column widths and print table
}
```

To sort the playlist by the Artist field, we define a new slice type with the necessary Len, Less, and Swap methods, analogous to what we did for StringSlice.

```
type byArtist []*Track

func (x byArtist) Len() int           { return len(x) }
func (x byArtist) Less(i, j int) bool { return x[i].Artist < x[j].Artist }
func (x byArtist) Swap(i, j int)      { x[i], x[j] = x[j], x[i] }
```

To call the generic sort routine, we must first convert tracks to the new type, byArtist, that defines the order:

```
sort.Sort(byArtist(tracks))
```

After sorting the slice by artist, the output from printTracks is

```
Title       Artist          Album             Year  Length
-----       ------          -----             ----  ------
Go Ahead    Alicia Keys     As I Am           2007  4m36s
Go          Delilah         From the Roots Up 2012  3m38s
Ready 2 Go  Martin Solveig  Smash             2011  4m24s
Go          Moby            Moby              1992  3m37s
```

If the user requests "sort by artist" a second time, we'll sort the tracks in reverse. We needn't define a new type byReverseArtist with an inverted Less method, however, since the sort package provides a Reverse function that transforms any sort order to its inverse.

```
sort.Sort(sort.Reverse(byArtist(tracks)))
```

After reverse-sorting the slice by artist, the output from printTracks is

```
Title      Artist          Album              Year  Length
-----      ------          -----              ----  ------
Go         Moby            Moby               1992  3m37s
Ready 2 Go Martin Solveig  Smash              2011  4m24s
Go         Delilah         From the Roots Up  2012  3m38s
Go Ahead   Alicia Keys     As I Am            2007  4m36s
```

The sort.Reverse function deserves a closer look since it uses composition (§6.3), which is an important idea. The sort package defines an unexported type reverse, which is a struct that embeds a sort.Interface. The Less method for reverse calls the Less method of the embedded sort.Interface value, but with the indices flipped, reversing the order of the sort results.

```
package sort

type reverse struct{ Interface } // that is, sort.Interface

func (r reverse) Less(i, j int) bool { return r.Interface.Less(j, i) }

func Reverse(data Interface) Interface { return reverse{data} }
```

Len and Swap, the other two methods of reverse, are implicitly provided by the original sort.Interface value because it is an embedded field. The exported function Reverse returns an instance of the reverse type that contains the original sort.Interface value.

To sort by a different column, we must define a new type, such as byYear:

```
type byYear []*Track

func (x byYear) Len() int           { return len(x) }
func (x byYear) Less(i, j int) bool { return x[i].Year < x[j].Year }
func (x byYear) Swap(i, j int)      { x[i], x[j] = x[j], x[i] }
```

After sorting tracks by year using sort.Sort(byYear(tracks)), printTracks shows a chronological listing:

```
Title      Artist          Album              Year  Length
-----      ------          -----              ----  ------
Go         Moby            Moby               1992  3m37s
Go Ahead   Alicia Keys     As I Am            2007  4m36s
Ready 2 Go Martin Solveig  Smash              2011  4m24s
Go         Delilah         From the Roots Up  2012  3m38s
```

For every slice element type and every ordering function we need, we declare a new implementation of sort.Interface. As you can see, the Len and Swap methods have identical definitions for all slice types. In the next example, the concrete type customSort combines a slice with a function, letting us define a new sort order by writing only the comparison function. Incidentally, the concrete types that implement sort.Interface are not always slices; customSort is a struct type.

```
type customSort struct {
    t    []*Track
    less func(x, y *Track) bool
}

func (x customSort) Len() int          { return len(x.t) }
func (x customSort) Less(i, j int) bool { return x.less(x.t[i], x.t[j]) }
func (x customSort) Swap(i, j int)      { x.t[i], x.t[j] = x.t[j], x.t[i] }
```

Let's define a multi-tier ordering function whose primary sort key is the Title, whose secondary key is the Year, and whose tertiary key is the running time, Length. Here's the call to Sort using an anonymous ordering function:

```
sort.Sort(customSort{tracks, func(x, y *Track) bool {
    if x.Title != y.Title {
        return x.Title < y.Title
    }
    if x.Year != y.Year {
        return x.Year < y.Year
    }
    if x.Length != y.Length {
        return x.Length < y.Length
    }
    return false
}})
```

And here's the result. Notice that the tie between the two tracks titled "Go" is broken in favor of the older one.

Title	Artist	Album	Year	Length
Go	Moby	Moby	1992	3m37s
Go	Delilah	From the Roots Up	2012	3m38s
Go Ahead	Alicia Keys	As I Am	2007	4m36s
Ready 2 Go	Martin Solveig	Smash	2011	4m24s

Although sorting a sequence of length n requires $O(n \log n)$ comparison operations, testing whether a sequence is already sorted requires at most $n-1$ comparisons. The IsSorted function from the sort package checks this for us. Like sort.Sort, it abstracts both the sequence and its ordering function using sort.Interface, but it never calls the Swap method: This code demonstrates the IntsAreSorted and Ints functions and the IntSlice type:

```
values := []int{3, 1, 4, 1}
fmt.Println(sort.IntsAreSorted(values)) // "false"
sort.Ints(values)
fmt.Println(values)                      // "[1 1 3 4]"
fmt.Println(sort.IntsAreSorted(values)) // "true"
sort.Sort(sort.Reverse(sort.IntSlice(values)))
fmt.Println(values)                      // "[4 3 1 1]"
fmt.Println(sort.IntsAreSorted(values)) // "false"
```

For convenience, the sort package provides versions of its functions and types specialized for
[]int, []string, and []float64 using their natural orderings. For other types, such as
[]int64 or []uint, we're on our own, though the path is short.

Exercise 7.8: Many GUIs provide a table widget with a stateful multi-tier sort: the primary
sort key is the most recently clicked column head, the secondary sort key is the second-most
recently clicked column head, and so on. Define an implementation of sort.Interface for
use by such a table. Compare that approach with repeated sorting using sort.Stable.

Exercise 7.9: Use the html/template package (§4.6) to replace printTracks with a function
that displays the tracks as an HTML table. Use the solution to the previous exercise to arrange
that each click on a column head makes an HTTP request to sort the table.

Exercise 7.10: The sort.Interface type can be adapted to other uses. Write a function
IsPalindrome(s sort.Interface) bool that reports whether the sequence s is a palindrome, in other words, reversing the sequence would not change it. Assume that the elements
at indices i and j are equal if !s.Less(i, j) && !s.Less(j, i).

7.7. The http.Handler Interface

In Chapter 1, we saw a glimpse of how to use the net/http package to implement web clients
(§1.5) and servers (§1.7). In this section, we'll look more closely at the server API, whose
foundation is the http.Handler interface:

net/http
```
package http

type Handler interface {
    ServeHTTP(w ResponseWriter, r *Request)
}

func ListenAndServe(address string, h Handler) error
```

The ListenAndServe function requires a server address, such as "localhost:8000", and an
instance of the Handler interface to which all requests should be dispatched. It runs forever,
or until the server fails (or fails to start) with an error, always non-nil, which it returns.

Imagine an e-commerce site with a database mapping the items for sale to their prices in dol-
lars. The program below shows the simplest imaginable implementation. It models the inventory as a map type, database, to which we've attached a ServeHTTP method so that it satisfies
the http.Handler interface. The handler ranges over the map and prints the items.

gopl.io/ch7/http1
```
func main() {
    db := database{"shoes": 50, "socks": 5}
    log.Fatal(http.ListenAndServe("localhost:8000", db))
}
```

```
type dollars float32

func (d dollars) String() string { return fmt.Sprintf("$%.2f", d) }

type database map[string]dollars

func (db database) ServeHTTP(w http.ResponseWriter, req *http.Request) {
    for item, price := range db {
        fmt.Fprintf(w, "%s: %s\n", item, price)
    }
}
```

If we start the server,

```
$ go build gopl.io/ch7/http1
$ ./http1 &
```

then connect to it with the `fetch` program from Section 1.5 (or a web browser if you prefer), we get the following output:

```
$ go build gopl.io/ch1/fetch
$ ./fetch http://localhost:8000
shoes: $50.00
socks: $5.00
```

So far, the server can only list its entire inventory and will do this for every request, regardless of URL. A more realistic server defines multiple different URLs, each triggering a different behavior. Let's call the existing one `/list` and add another one called `/price` that reports the price of a single item, specified as a request parameter like `/price?item=socks`.

gopl.io/ch7/http2

```
func (db database) ServeHTTP(w http.ResponseWriter, req *http.Request) {
    switch req.URL.Path {
    case "/list":
        for item, price := range db {
            fmt.Fprintf(w, "%s: %s\n", item, price)
        }
    case "/price":
        item := req.URL.Query().Get("item")
        price, ok := db[item]
        if !ok {
            w.WriteHeader(http.StatusNotFound) // 404
            fmt.Fprintf(w, "no such item: %q\n", item)
            return
        }
        fmt.Fprintf(w, "%s\n", price)
    default:
        w.WriteHeader(http.StatusNotFound) // 404
        fmt.Fprintf(w, "no such page: %s\n", req.URL)
    }
}
```

Now the handler decides what logic to execute based on the path component of the URL, req.URL.Path. If the handler doesn't recognize the path, it reports an HTTP error to the client by calling w.WriteHeader(http.StatusNotFound); this must be done before writing any text to w. (Incidentally, http.ResponseWriter is another interface. It augments io.Writer with methods for sending HTTP response headers.) Equivalently, we could use the http.Error utility function:

```
msg := fmt.Sprintf("no such page: %s\n", req.URL)
http.Error(w, msg, http.StatusNotFound) // 404
```

The case for /price calls the URL's Query method to parse the HTTP request parameters as a map, or more precisely, a multimap of type url.Values (§6.2.1) from the net/url package. It then finds the first item parameter and looks up its price. If the item wasn't found, it reports an error.

Here's an example session with the new server:

```
$ go build gopl.io/ch7/http2
$ go build gopl.io/ch1/fetch
$ ./http2 &
$ ./fetch http://localhost:8000/list
shoes: $50.00
socks: $5.00
$ ./fetch http://localhost:8000/price?item=socks
$5.00
$ ./fetch http://localhost:8000/price?item=shoes
$50.00
$ ./fetch http://localhost:8000/price?item=hat
no such item: "hat"
$ ./fetch http://localhost:8000/help
no such page: /help
```

Obviously we could keep adding cases to ServeHTTP, but in a realistic application, it's convenient to define the logic for each case in a separate function or method. Furthermore, related URLs may need similar logic; several image files may have URLs of the form /images/*.png, for instance. For these reasons, net/http provides ServeMux, a *request multiplexer*, to simplify the association between URLs and handlers. A ServeMux aggregates a collection of http.Handlers into a single http.Handler. Again, we see that different types satisfying the same interface are *substitutable*: the web server can dispatch requests to any http.Handler, regardless of which concrete type is behind it.

For a more complex application, several ServeMuxes may be composed to handle more intricate dispatching requirements. Go doesn't have a canonical web framework analogous to Ruby's Rails or Python's Django. This is not to say that such frameworks don't exist, but the building blocks in Go's standard library are flexible enough that frameworks are often unnecessary. Furthermore, although frameworks are convenient in the early phases of a project, their additional complexity can make longer-term maintenance harder.

In the program below, we create a ServeMux and use it to associate the URLs with the corresponding handlers for the /list and /price operations, which have been split into separate methods. We then use the ServeMux as the main handler in the call to ListenAndServe.

gopl.io/ch7/http3

```go
func main() {
    db := database{"shoes": 50, "socks": 5}
    mux := http.NewServeMux()
    mux.Handle("/list", http.HandlerFunc(db.list))
    mux.Handle("/price", http.HandlerFunc(db.price))
    log.Fatal(http.ListenAndServe("localhost:8000", mux))
}

type database map[string]dollars

func (db database) list(w http.ResponseWriter, req *http.Request) {
    for item, price := range db {
        fmt.Fprintf(w, "%s: %s\n", item, price)
    }
}

func (db database) price(w http.ResponseWriter, req *http.Request) {
    item := req.URL.Query().Get("item")
    price, ok := db[item]
    if !ok {
        w.WriteHeader(http.StatusNotFound) // 404
        fmt.Fprintf(w, "no such item: %q\n", item)
        return
    }
    fmt.Fprintf(w, "%s\n", price)
}
```

Let's focus on the two calls to mux.Handle that register the handlers. In the first one, db.list is a method value (§6.4), that is, a value of type

```go
func(w http.ResponseWriter, req *http.Request)
```

that, when called, invokes the database.list method with the receiver value db. So db.list is a function that implements handler-like behavior, but since it has no methods, it doesn't satisfy the http.Handler interface and can't be passed directly to mux.Handle.

The expression http.HandlerFunc(db.list) is a conversion, not a function call, since http.HandlerFunc is a type. It has the following definition:

net/http

```go
package http

type HandlerFunc func(w ResponseWriter, r *Request)

func (f HandlerFunc) ServeHTTP(w ResponseWriter, r *Request) {
    f(w, r)
}
```

HandlerFunc demonstrates some unusual features of Go's interface mechanism. It is a function type that has methods and satisfies an interface, http.Handler. The behavior of its ServeHTTP method is to call the underlying function. HandlerFunc is thus an adapter that lets a function value satisfy an interface, where the function and the interface's sole method have the same signature. In effect, this trick lets a single type such as database satisfy the http.Handler interface several different ways: once through its list method, once through its price method, and so on.

Because registering a handler this way is so common, ServeMux has a convenience method called HandleFunc that does it for us, so we can simplify the handler registration code to this:

gopl.io/ch7/http3a

```
mux.HandleFunc("/list", db.list)
mux.HandleFunc("/price", db.price)
```

It's easy to see from the code above how one would construct a program in which there are two different web servers, listening on different ports, defining different URLs, and dispatching to different handlers. We would just construct another ServeMux and make another call to ListenAndServe, perhaps concurrently. But in most programs, one web server is plenty. Also, it's typical to define HTTP handlers across many files of an application, and it would be a nuisance if they all had to be explicitly registered with the application's ServeMux instance.

So, for convenience, net/http provides a global ServeMux instance called DefaultServeMux and package-level functions called http.Handle and http.HandleFunc. To use Default-ServeMux as the server's main handler, we needn't pass it to ListenAndServe; nil will do.

The server's main function can then be simplified to

gopl.io/ch7/http4

```
func main() {
    db := database{"shoes": 50, "socks": 5}
    http.HandleFunc("/list", db.list)
    http.HandleFunc("/price", db.price)
    log.Fatal(http.ListenAndServe("localhost:8000", nil))
}
```

Finally, an important reminder: as we mentioned in Section 1.7, the web server invokes each handler in a new goroutine, so handlers must take precautions such as *locking* when accessing variables that other goroutines, including other requests to the same handler, may be accessing. We'll talk about concurrency in the next two chapters.

Exercise 7.11: Add additional handlers so that clients can create, read, update, and delete database entries. For example, a request of the form /update?item=socks&price=6 will update the price of an item in the inventory and report an error if the item does not exist or if the price is invalid. (Warning: this change introduces concurrent variable updates.)

Exercise 7.12: Change the handler for /list to print its output as an HTML table, not text. You may find the html/template package (§4.6) useful.

7.8. The error Interface

Since the beginning of this book, we've been using and creating values of the mysterious predeclared error type without explaining what it really is. In fact, it's just an interface type with a single method that returns an error message:

```
type error interface {
    Error() string
}
```

The simplest way to create an error is by calling errors.New, which returns a new error for a given error message. The entire errors package is only four lines long:

```
package errors

func New(text string) error { return &errorString{text} }

type errorString struct { text string }

func (e *errorString) Error() string { return e.text }
```

The underlying type of errorString is a struct, not a string, to protect its representation from inadvertent (or premeditated) updates. And the reason that the pointer type *errorString, not errorString alone, satisfies the error interface is so that every call to New allocates a distinct error instance that is equal to no other. We would not want a distinguished error such as io.EOF to compare equal to one that merely happened to have the same message.

```
fmt.Println(errors.New("EOF") == errors.New("EOF")) // "false"
```

Calls to errors.New are relatively infrequent because there's a convenient wrapper function, fmt.Errorf, that does string formatting too. We used it several times in Chapter 5.

```
package fmt

import "errors"

func Errorf(format string, args ...interface{}) error {
    return errors.New(Sprintf(format, args...))
}
```

Although *errorString may be the simplest type of error, it is far from the only one. For example, the syscall package provides Go's low-level system-call API. On many platforms, it defines a numeric type Errno that satisfies error, and on Unix platforms, Errno's Error method does a lookup in a table of strings, as shown below:

```
package syscall

type Errno uintptr // operating system error code
```

```go
var errors = [...]string{
    1:   "operation not permitted",    // EPERM
    2:   "no such file or directory",  // ENOENT
    3:   "no such process",            // ESRCH
    // ...
}

func (e Errno) Error() string {
    if 0 <= int(e) && int(e) < len(errors) {
        return errors[e]
    }
    return fmt.Sprintf("errno %d", e)
}
```

The following statement creates an interface value holding the Errno value 2, signifying the POSIX ENOENT condition:

```go
var err error = syscall.Errno(2)
fmt.Println(err.Error()) // "no such file or directory"
fmt.Println(err)         // "no such file or directory"
```

The value of err is shown graphically in Figure 7.6.

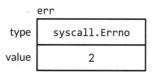

Figure 7.6. An interface value holding a syscall.Errno integer.

Errno is an efficient representation of system-call errors drawn from a finite set, and it satisfies the standard error interface. We'll see other types that satisfy this interface in Section 7.11.

7.9. Example: Expression Evaluator

In this section, we'll build an evaluator for simple arithmetic expressions. We'll use an interface, Expr, to represent any expression in this language. For now, this interface needs no methods, but we'll add some later.

```go
// An Expr is an arithmetic expression.
type Expr interface{}
```

Our expression language consists of floating-point literals; the binary operators +, -, *, and /; the unary operators -x and +x; function calls pow(x,y), sin(x), and sqrt(x); variables such as x and pi; and of course parentheses and standard operator precedence. All values are of type float64. Here are some example expressions:

```
sqrt(A / pi)
pow(x, 3) + pow(y, 3)
(F - 32) * 5 / 9
```

The five concrete types below represent particular kinds of expression. A `Var` represents a reference to a variable. (We'll soon see why it is exported.) A `literal` represents a floating-point constant. The `unary` and `binary` types represent operator expressions with one or two operands, which can be any kind of `Expr`. A `call` represents a function call; we'll restrict its fn field to pow, sin, or sqrt.

gopl.io/ch7/eval
```go
// A Var identifies a variable, e.g., x.
type Var string

// A literal is a numeric constant, e.g., 3.141.
type literal float64

// A unary represents a unary operator expression, e.g., -x.
type unary struct {
    op rune // one of '+', '-'
    x  Expr
}

// A binary represents a binary operator expression, e.g., x+y.
type binary struct {
    op   rune // one of '+', '-', '*', '/'
    x, y Expr
}

// A call represents a function call expression, e.g., sin(x).
type call struct {
    fn   string // one of "pow", "sin", "sqrt"
    args []Expr
}
```

To evaluate an expression containing variables, we'll need an *environment* that maps variable names to values:

```go
type Env map[Var]float64
```

We'll also need each kind of expression to define an `Eval` method that returns the expression's value in a given environment. Since every expression must provide this method, we add it to the `Expr` interface. The package exports only the types `Expr`, `Env`, and `Var`; clients can use the evaluator without access to the other expression types.

```go
type Expr interface {
    // Eval returns the value of this Expr in the environment env.
    Eval(env Env) float64
}
```

The concrete `Eval` methods are shown below. The method for `Var` performs an environment lookup, which returns zero if the variable is not defined, and the method for `literal` simply returns the literal value.

```
func (v Var) Eval(env Env) float64 {
    return env[v]
}
func (l literal) Eval(_ Env) float64 {
    return float64(l)
}
```

The Eval methods for unary and binary recursively evaluate their operands, then apply the operation op to them. We don't consider divisions by zero or infinity to be errors, since they produce a result, albeit non-finite. Finally, the method for call evaluates the arguments to the pow, sin, or sqrt function, then calls the corresponding function in the math package.

```
func (u unary) Eval(env Env) float64 {
    switch u.op {
    case '+':
        return +u.x.Eval(env)
    case '-':
        return -u.x.Eval(env)
    }
    panic(fmt.Sprintf("unsupported unary operator: %q", u.op))
}
func (b binary) Eval(env Env) float64 {
    switch b.op {
    case '+':
        return b.x.Eval(env) + b.y.Eval(env)
    case '-':
        return b.x.Eval(env) - b.y.Eval(env)
    case '*':
        return b.x.Eval(env) * b.y.Eval(env)
    case '/':
        return b.x.Eval(env) / b.y.Eval(env)
    }
    panic(fmt.Sprintf("unsupported binary operator: %q", b.op))
}
func (c call) Eval(env Env) float64 {
    switch c.fn {
    case "pow":
        return math.Pow(c.args[0].Eval(env), c.args[1].Eval(env))
    case "sin":
        return math.Sin(c.args[0].Eval(env))
    case "sqrt":
        return math.Sqrt(c.args[0].Eval(env))
    }
    panic(fmt.Sprintf("unsupported function call: %s", c.fn))
}
```

Several of these methods can fail. For example, a call expression could have an unknown function or the wrong number of arguments. It's also possible to construct a unary or binary expression with an invalid operator such as ! or < (although the Parse function mentioned

below will never do this). These errors cause Eval to panic. Other errors, like evaluating a
Var not present in the environment, merely cause Eval to return the wrong result. All of these
errors could be detected by inspecting the Expr before evaluating it. That will be the job of the
Check method, which we will show soon, but first let's test Eval.

The TestEval function below is a test of the evaluator. It uses the testing package, which
we'll explain in Chapter 11, but for now it's enough to know that calling t.Errorf reports an
error. The function loops over a table of inputs that defines three expressions and different
environments for each one. The first expression computes the radius of a circle given its area
A, the second computes the sum of the cubes of two variables x and y, and the third converts a
Fahrenheit temperature F to Celsius.

```
func TestEval(t *testing.T) {
    tests := []struct {
        expr string
        env  Env
        want string
    }{
        {"sqrt(A / pi)", Env{"A": 87616, "pi": math.Pi}, "167"},
        {"pow(x, 3) + pow(y, 3)", Env{"x": 12, "y": 1}, "1729"},
        {"pow(x, 3) + pow(y, 3)", Env{"x": 9, "y": 10}, "1729"},
        {"5 / 9 * (F - 32)", Env{"F": -40}, "-40"},
        {"5 / 9 * (F - 32)", Env{"F": 32}, "0"},
        {"5 / 9 * (F - 32)", Env{"F": 212}, "100"},
    }
    var prevExpr string
    for _, test := range tests {
        // Print expr only when it changes.
        if test.expr != prevExpr {
            fmt.Printf("\n%s\n", test.expr)
            prevExpr = test.expr
        }
        expr, err := Parse(test.expr)
        if err != nil {
            t.Error(err) // parse error
            continue
        }
        got := fmt.Sprintf("%.6g", expr.Eval(test.env))
        fmt.Printf("\t%v => %s\n", test.env, got)
        if got != test.want {
            t.Errorf("%s.Eval() in %v = %q, want %q\n",
                test.expr, test.env, got, test.want)
        }
    }
}
```

For each entry in the table, the test parses the expression, evaluates it in the environment, and
prints the result. We don't have space to show the Parse function here, but you'll find it if you
download the package using go get.

The go `test` command (§11.1) runs a package's tests:

```
$ go test -v gopl.io/ch7/eval
```

The -v flag lets us see the printed output of the test, which is normally suppressed for a successful test like this one. Here is the output of the test's `fmt.Printf` statements:

```
sqrt(A / pi)
    map[A:87616 pi:3.141592653589793] => 167

pow(x, 3) + pow(y, 3)
    map[x:12 y:1] => 1729
    map[x:9 y:10] => 1729

5 / 9 * (F - 32)
    map[F:-40] => -40
    map[F:32] => 0
    map[F:212] => 100
```

Fortunately the inputs so far have all been well formed, but our luck is unlikely to last. Even in
interpreted languages, it is common to check the syntax for *static* errors, that is, mistakes that
can be detected without running the program. By separating the static checks from the
dynamic ones, we can detect errors sooner and perform many checks only once instead of
each time an expression is evaluated.

Let's add another method to the Expr interface. The Check method checks for static errors in
an expression syntax tree. We'll explain its vars parameter in a moment.

```
type Expr interface {
    Eval(env Env) float64
    // Check reports errors in this Expr and adds its Vars to the set.
    Check(vars map[Var]bool) error
}
```

The concrete Check methods are shown below. Evaluation of `literal` and Var cannot fail, so
the Check methods for these types return nil. The methods for unary and binary first check
that the operator is valid, then recursively check the operands. Similarly, the method for call
first checks that the function is known and has the right number of arguments, then recursively checks each argument.

```
func (v Var) Check(vars map[Var]bool) error {
    vars[v] = true
    return nil
}

func (literal) Check(vars map[Var]bool) error {
    return nil
}
```

```go
func (u unary) Check(vars map[Var]bool) error {
    if !strings.ContainsRune("+-", u.op) {
        return fmt.Errorf("unexpected unary op %q", u.op)
    }
    return u.x.Check(vars)
}

func (b binary) Check(vars map[Var]bool) error {
    if !strings.ContainsRune("+-*/", b.op) {
        return fmt.Errorf("unexpected binary op %q", b.op)
    }
    if err := b.x.Check(vars); err != nil {
        return err
    }
    return b.y.Check(vars)
}

func (c call) Check(vars map[Var]bool) error {
    arity, ok := numParams[c.fn]
    if !ok {
        return fmt.Errorf("unknown function %q", c.fn)
    }
    if len(c.args) != arity {
        return fmt.Errorf("call to %s has %d args, want %d",
            c.fn, len(c.args), arity)
    }
    for _, arg := range c.args {
        if err := arg.Check(vars); err != nil {
            return err
        }
    }
    return nil
}

var numParams = map[string]int{"pow": 2, "sin": 1, "sqrt": 1}
```

We've listed a selection of flawed inputs and the errors they elicit, in two groups. The Parse function (not shown) reports syntax errors and the Check function reports semantic errors.

```
x % 2                   unexpected '%'
math.Pi                 unexpected '.'
!true                   unexpected '!'
"hello"                 unexpected '"'

log(10)                 unknown function "log"
sqrt(1, 2)              call to sqrt has 2 args, want 1
```

Check's argument, a set of Vars, accumulates the set of variable names found within the expression. Each of these variables must be present in the environment for evaluation to succeed. This set is logically the *result* of the call to Check, but because the method is recursive, it is more convenient for Check to populate a set passed as a parameter. The client must provide an empty set in the initial call.

In Section 3.2, we plotted a function f(x,y) that was fixed at compile time. Now that we can parse, check, and evaluate expressions in strings, we can build a web application that receives an expression at run time from the client and plots the surface of that function. We can use the vars set to check that the expression is a function of only two variables, x and y—three, actually, since we'll provide r, the radius, as a convenience. And we'll use the Check method to reject ill-formed expressions before evaluation begins so that we don't repeat those checks during the 40,000 evaluations (100×100 cells, each with four corners) of the function that follow.

The parseAndCheck function combines these parsing and checking steps:

gopl.io/ch7/surface

```go
import "gopl.io/ch7/eval"

func parseAndCheck(s string) (eval.Expr, error) {
    if s == "" {
        return nil, fmt.Errorf("empty expression")
    }
    expr, err := eval.Parse(s)
    if err != nil {
        return nil, err
    }
    vars := make(map[eval.Var]bool)
    if err := expr.Check(vars); err != nil {
        return nil, err
    }
    for v := range vars {
        if v != "x" && v != "y" && v != "r" {
            return nil, fmt.Errorf("undefined variable: %s", v)
        }
    }
    return expr, nil
}
```

To make this a web application, all we need is the plot function below, which has the familiar signature of an http.HandlerFunc:

```go
func plot(w http.ResponseWriter, r *http.Request) {
    r.ParseForm()
    expr, err := parseAndCheck(r.Form.Get("expr"))
    if err != nil {
        http.Error(w, "bad expr: "+err.Error(), http.StatusBadRequest)
        return
    }
    w.Header().Set("Content-Type", "image/svg+xml")
    surface(w, func(x, y float64) float64 {
        r := math.Hypot(x, y) // distance from (0,0)
        return expr.Eval(eval.Env{"x": x, "y": y, "r": r})
    })
}
```

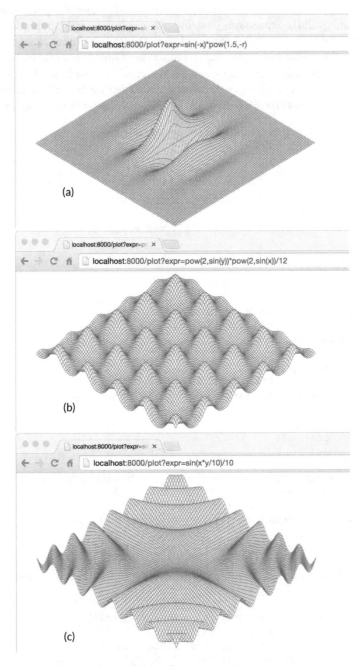

Figure 7.7. The surfaces of three functions: (a) `sin(-x)*pow(1.5,-r)`;
(b) `pow(2,sin(y))*pow(2,sin(x))/12`; (c) `sin(x*y/10)/10`.

The plot function parses and checks the expression specified in the HTTP request and uses it to create an anonymous function of two variables. The anonymous function has the same signature as the fixed function f from the original surface-plotting program, but it evaluates the user-supplied expression. The environment defines x, y, and the radius r. Finally, plot calls surface, which is just the main function from gopl.io/ch3/surface, modified to take the function to plot and the output io.Writer as parameters, instead of using the fixed function f and os.Stdout. Figure 7.7 shows three surfaces produced by the program.

Exercise 7.13: Add a String method to Expr to pretty-print the syntax tree. Check that the results, when parsed again, yield an equivalent tree.

Exercise 7.14: Define a new concrete type that satisfies the Expr interface and provides a new operation such as computing the minimum value of its operands. Since the Parse function does not create instances of this new type, to use it you will need to construct a syntax tree directly (or extend the parser).

Exercise 7.15: Write a program that reads a single expression from the standard input, prompts the user to provide values for any variables, then evaluates the expression in the resulting environment. Handle all errors gracefully.

Exercise 7.16: Write a web-based calculator program.

7.10. Type Assertions

A *type assertion* is an operation applied to an interface value. Syntactically, it looks like x.(T), where x is an expression of an interface type and T is a type, called the "asserted" type. A type assertion checks that the dynamic type of its operand matches the asserted type.

There are two possibilities. First, if the asserted type T is a concrete type, then the type assertion checks whether x's dynamic type is *identical to* T. If this check succeeds, the result of the type assertion is x's dynamic value, whose type is of course T. In other words, a type assertion to a concrete type extracts the concrete value from its operand. If the check fails, then the operation panics. For example:

```
var w io.Writer
w = os.Stdout
f := w.(*os.File)      // success: f == os.Stdout
c := w.(*bytes.Buffer) // panic: interface holds *os.File, not *bytes.Buffer
```

Second, if instead the asserted type T is an interface type, then the type assertion checks whether x's dynamic type *satisfies* T. If this check succeeds, the dynamic value is not extracted; the result is still an interface value with the same type and value components, but the result has the interface type T. In other words, a type assertion to an interface type changes the type of the expression, making a different (and usually larger) set of methods accessible, but it preserves the dynamic type and value components inside the interface value.

After the first type assertion below, both w and rw hold os.Stdout so each has a dynamic type of *os.File, but w, an io.Writer, exposes only the file's Write method, whereas rw exposes its Read method too.

```
var w io.Writer
w = os.Stdout
rw := w.(io.ReadWriter) // success: *os.File has both Read and Write

w = new(ByteCounter)
rw = w.(io.ReadWriter) // panic: *ByteCounter has no Read method
```

No matter what type was asserted, if the operand is a nil interface value, the type assertion fails. A type assertion to a less restrictive interface type (one with fewer methods) is rarely needed, as it behaves just like an assignment, except in the nil case.

```
w = rw              // io.ReadWriter is assignable to io.Writer
w = rw.(io.Writer) // fails only if rw == nil
```

Often we're not sure of the dynamic type of an interface value, and we'd like to test whether it is some particular type. If the type assertion appears in an assignment in which two results are expected, such as the following declarations, the operation does not panic on failure but instead returns an additional second result, a boolean indicating success:

```
var w io.Writer = os.Stdout
f, ok := w.(*os.File)      // success:  ok, f == os.Stdout
b, ok := w.(*bytes.Buffer) // failure: !ok, b == nil
```

The second result is conventionally assigned to a variable named ok. If the operation failed, ok is false, and the first result is equal to the zero value of the asserted type, which in this example is a nil *bytes.Buffer.

The ok result is often immediately used to decide what to do next. The extended form of the if statement makes this quite compact:

```
if f, ok := w.(*os.File); ok {
    // ...use f...
}
```

When the operand of a type assertion is a variable, rather than invent another name for the new local variable, you'll sometimes see the original name reused, shadowing the original, like this:

```
if w, ok := w.(*os.File); ok {
    // ...use w...
}
```

7.11. Discriminating Errors with Type Assertions

Consider the set of errors returned by file operations in the os package. I/O can fail for any number of reasons, but three kinds of failure often must be handled differently: file already exists (for create operations), file not found (for read operations), and permission denied. The os package provides these three helper functions to classify the failure indicated by a given error value:

```
package os

func IsExist(err error) bool
func IsNotExist(err error) bool
func IsPermission(err error) bool
```

A naïve implementation of one of these predicates might check that the error message contains a certain substring,

```
func IsNotExist(err error) bool {
    // NOTE: not robust!
    return strings.Contains(err.Error(), "file does not exist")
}
```

but because the logic for handling I/O errors can vary from one platform to another, this approach is not robust and the same failure may be reported with a variety of different error messages. Checking for substrings of error messages may be useful during testing to ensure that functions fail in the expected manner, but it's inadequate for production code.

A more reliable approach is to represent structured error values using a dedicated type. The os package defines a type called PathError to describe failures involving an operation on a file path, like Open or Delete, and a variant called LinkError to describe failures of operations involving two file paths, like Symlink and Rename. Here's os.PathError:

```
package os

// PathError records an error and the operation and file path that caused it.
type PathError struct {
    Op   string
    Path string
    Err  error
}

func (e *PathError) Error() string {
    return e.Op + " " + e.Path + ": " + e.Err.Error()
}
```

Most clients are oblivious to PathError and deal with all errors in a uniform way by calling their Error methods. Although PathError's Error method forms a message by simply concatenating the fields, PathError's structure preserves the underlying components of the error. Clients that need to distinguish one kind of failure from another can use a type assertion to detect the specific type of the error; the specific type provides more detail than a simple string.

```
_, err := os.Open("/no/such/file")
fmt.Println(err) // "open /no/such/file: No such file or directory"
fmt.Printf("%#v\n", err)
// Output:
// &os.PathError{Op:"open", Path:"/no/such/file", Err:0x2}
```

That's how the three helper functions work. For example, IsNotExist, shown below, reports whether an error is equal to syscall.ENOENT (§7.8) or to the distinguished error os.ErrNotExist (see io.EOF in §5.4.2), or is a *PathError whose underlying error is one of those two.

```
import (
    "errors"
    "syscall"
)

var ErrNotExist = errors.New("file does not exist")

// IsNotExist returns a boolean indicating whether the error is known to
// report that a file or directory does not exist. It is satisfied by
// ErrNotExist as well as some syscall errors.
func IsNotExist(err error) bool {
    if pe, ok := err.(*PathError); ok {
        err = pe.Err
    }
    return err == syscall.ENOENT || err == ErrNotExist
}
```

And here it is in action:

```
_, err := os.Open("/no/such/file")
fmt.Println(os.IsNotExist(err)) // "true"
```

Of course, PathError's structure is lost if the error message is combined into a larger string, for instance by a call to fmt.Errorf. Error discrimination must usually be done immediately after the failing operation, before an error is propagated to the caller.

7.12. Querying Behaviors with Interface Type Assertions

The logic below is similar to the part of the net/http web server responsible for writing HTTP header fields such as "Content-type: text/html". The io.Writer w represents the HTTP response; the bytes written to it are ultimately sent to someone's web browser.

```
func writeHeader(w io.Writer, contentType string) error {
    if _, err := w.Write([]byte("Content-Type: ")); err != nil {
        return err
    }
    if _, err := w.Write([]byte(contentType)); err != nil {
        return err
    }
    // ...
}
```

Because the Write method requires a byte slice, and the value we wish to write is a string, a []byte(...) conversion is required. This conversion allocates memory and makes a copy, but the copy is thrown away almost immediately after. Let's pretend that this is a core part of the web server and that our profiling has revealed that this memory allocation is slowing it down. Can we avoid allocating memory here?

The io.Writer interface tells us only one fact about the concrete type that w holds: that bytes may be written to it. If we look behind the curtains of the net/http package, we see that the dynamic type that w holds in this program also has a WriteString method that allows strings to be efficiently written to it, avoiding the need to allocate a temporary copy. (This may seem like a shot in the dark, but a number of important types that satisfy io.Writer also have a WriteString method, including *bytes.Buffer, *os.File and *bufio.Writer.)

We cannot assume that an arbitrary io.Writer w also has the WriteString method. But we can define a new interface that has just this method and use a type assertion to test whether the dynamic type of w satisfies this new interface.

```go
// writeString writes s to w.
// If w has a WriteString method, it is invoked instead of w.Write.
func writeString(w io.Writer, s string) (n int, err error) {
    type stringWriter interface {
        WriteString(string) (n int, err error)
    }
    if sw, ok := w.(stringWriter); ok {
        return sw.WriteString(s) // avoid a copy
    }
    return w.Write([]byte(s)) // allocate temporary copy
}

func writeHeader(w io.Writer, contentType string) error {
    if _, err := writeString(w, "Content-Type: "); err != nil {
        return err
    }
    if _, err := writeString(w, contentType); err != nil {
        return err
    }
    // ...
}
```

To avoid repeating ourselves, we've moved the check into the utility function writeString, but it is so useful that the standard library provides it as io.WriteString. It is the recommended way to write a string to an io.Writer.

What's curious in this example is that there is no standard interface that defines the WriteString method and specifies its required behavior. Furthermore, whether or not a concrete type satisfies the stringWriter interface is determined only by its methods, not by any declared relationship between it and the interface type. What this means is that the technique above relies on the assumption that *if* a type satisfies the interface below, *then* WriteString(s) must have the same effect as Write([]byte(s)).

```
interface {
    io.Writer
    WriteString(s string) (n int, err error)
}
```

Although `io.WriteString` documents its assumption, few functions that call it are likely to document that they too make the same assumption. Defining a method of a particular type is taken as an implicit assent for a certain behavioral contract. Newcomers to Go, especially those from a background in strongly typed languages, may find this lack of explicit intention unsettling, but it is rarely a problem in practice. With the exception of the empty interface `interface{}`, interface types are seldom satisfied by unintended coincidence.

The `writeString` function above uses a type assertion to see whether a value of a general interface type also satisfies a more specific interface type, and if so, it uses the behaviors of the specific interface. This technique can be put to good use whether or not the queried interface is standard like `io.ReadWriter` or user-defined like `stringWriter`.

It's also how `fmt.Fprintf` distinguishes values that satisfy `error` or `fmt.Stringer` from all other values. Within `fmt.Fprintf`, there is a step that converts a single operand to a string, something like this:

```
package fmt

func formatOneValue(x interface{}) string {
    if err, ok := x.(error); ok {
        return err.Error()
    }
    if str, ok := x.(Stringer); ok {
        return str.String()
    }
    // ...all other types...
}
```

If x satisfies either of the two interfaces, that determines the formatting of the value. If not, the default case handles all other types more or less uniformly using reflection; we'll find out how in Chapter 12.

Again, this makes the assumption that any type with a `String` method satisfies the behavioral contract of `fmt.Stringer`, which is to return a string suitable for printing.

7.13. Type Switches

Interfaces are used in two distinct styles. In the first style, exemplified by `io.Reader`, `io.Writer`, `fmt.Stringer`, `sort.Interface`, `http.Handler`, and `error`, an interface's methods express the similarities of the concrete types that satisfy the interface but hide the representation details and intrinsic operations of those concrete types. The emphasis is on the methods, not on the concrete types.

The second style exploits the ability of an interface value to hold values of a variety of concrete types and considers the interface to be the *union* of those types. Type assertions are used to discriminate among these types dynamically and treat each case differently. In this style, the emphasis is on the concrete types that satisfy the interface, not on the interface's methods (if indeed it has any), and there is no hiding of information. We'll describe interfaces used this way as *discriminated unions*.

If you're familiar with object-oriented programming, you may recognize these two styles as *subtype polymorphism* and *ad hoc polymorphism*, but you needn't remember those terms. For the remainder of this chapter, we'll present examples of the second style.

Go's API for querying an SQL database, like those of other languages, lets us cleanly separate the fixed part of a query from the variable parts. An example client might look like this:

```
import "database/sql"

func listTracks(db sql.DB, artist string, minYear, maxYear int) {
    result, err := db.Exec(
        "SELECT * FROM tracks WHERE artist = ? AND ? <= year AND year <= ?",
        artist, minYear, maxYear)
    // ...
}
```

The Exec method replaces each '?' in the query string with an SQL literal denoting the corresponding argument value, which may be a boolean, a number, a string, or nil. Constructing queries this way helps avoid SQL injection attacks, in which an adversary takes control of the query by exploiting improper quotation of input data. Within Exec, we might find a function like the one below, which converts each argument value to its literal SQL notation.

```
func sqlQuote(x interface{}) string {
    if x == nil {
        return "NULL"
    } else if _, ok := x.(int); ok {
        return fmt.Sprintf("%d", x)
    } else if _, ok := x.(uint); ok {
        return fmt.Sprintf("%d", x)
    } else if b, ok := x.(bool); ok {
        if b {
            return "TRUE"
        }
        return "FALSE"
    } else if s, ok := x.(string); ok {
        return sqlQuoteString(s) // (not shown)
    } else {
        panic(fmt.Sprintf("unexpected type %T: %v", x, x))
    }
}
```

A switch statement simplifies an if-else chain that performs a series of value equality tests. An analogous *type switch* statement simplifies an if-else chain of type assertions.

In its simplest form, a type switch looks like an ordinary switch statement in which the oper-
and is x.(type)—that's literally the keyword type—and each case has one or more types. A
type switch enables a multi-way branch based on the interface value's dynamic type. The nil
case matches if x == nil, and the default case matches if no other case does. A type switch
for sqlQuote would have these cases:

```
switch x.(type) {
case nil:       // ...
case int, uint: // ...
case bool:      // ...
case string:    // ...
default:        // ...
}
```

As with an ordinary switch statement (§1.8), cases are considered in order and, when a match
is found, the case's body is executed. Case order becomes significant when one or more case
types are interfaces, since then there is a possibility of two cases matching. The position of the
default case relative to the others is immaterial. No fallthrough is allowed.

Notice that in the original function, the logic for the bool and string cases needs access to
the value extracted by the type assertion. Since this is typical, the type switch statement has an
extended form that binds the extracted value to a new variable within each case:

```
switch x := x.(type) { /* ... */ }
```

Here we've called the new variables x too; as with type assertions, reuse of variable names is
common. Like a switch statement, a type switch implicitly creates a lexical block, so the declaration of the new variable called x does not conflict with a variable x in an outer block. Each
case also implicitly creates a separate lexical block.

Rewriting sqlQuote to use the extended form of type switch makes it significantly clearer:

```
func sqlQuote(x interface{}) string {
    switch x := x.(type) {
    case nil:
        return "NULL"
    case int, uint:
        return fmt.Sprintf("%d", x) // x has type interface{} here.
    case bool:
        if x {
            return "TRUE"
        }
        return "FALSE"
    case string:
        return sqlQuoteString(x) // (not shown)
    default:
        panic(fmt.Sprintf("unexpected type %T: %v", x, x))
    }
}
```

In this version, within the block of each single-type case, the variable x has the same type as the case. For instance, x has type bool within the bool case and string within the string case. In all other cases, x has the (interface) type of the switch operand, which is interface{} in this example. When the same action is required for multiple cases, like int and uint, the type switch makes it easy to combine them.

Although sqlQuote accepts an argument of any type, the function runs to completion only if the argument's type matches one of the cases in the type switch; otherwise it panics with an "unexpected type" message. Although the type of x is interface{}, we consider it a *discriminated union* of int, uint, bool, string, and nil.

7.14. Example: Token-Based XML Decoding

Section 4.5 showed how to decode JSON documents into Go data structures with the Marshal and Unmarshal functions from the encoding/json package. The encoding/xml package provides a similar API. This approach is convenient when we want to construct a representation of the document tree, but that's unnecessary for many programs. The encoding/xml package also provides a lower-level *token-based* API for decoding XML. In the token-based style, the parser consumes the input and produces a stream of tokens, primarily of four kinds—StartElement, EndElement, CharData, and Comment—each being a concrete type in the encoding/xml package. Each call to (*xml.Decoder).Token returns a token.

The relevant parts of the API are shown here:

encoding/xml
```
package xml

type Name struct {
    Local string // e.g., "Title" or "id"
}

type Attr struct { // e.g., name="value"
    Name  Name
    Value string
}

// A Token includes StartElement, EndElement, CharData,
// and Comment, plus a few esoteric types (not shown).
type Token interface{}
type StartElement struct { // e.g., <name>
    Name Name
    Attr []Attr
}
type EndElement struct { Name Name } // e.g., </name>
type CharData []byte                 // e.g., <p>CharData</p>
type Comment []byte                  // e.g., <!-- Comment -->

type Decoder struct{ /* ... */ }
```

```
func NewDecoder(io.Reader) *Decoder
func (*Decoder) Token() (Token, error) // returns next Token in sequence
```

The Token interface, which has no methods, is also an example of a discriminated union. The purpose of a traditional interface like io.Reader is to hide details of the concrete types that satisfy it so that new implementations can be created; each concrete type is treated uniformly. By contrast, the set of concrete types that satisfy a discriminated union is fixed by the design and exposed, not hidden. Discriminated union types have few methods; functions that operate on them are expressed as a set of cases using a type switch, with different logic in each case.

The xmlselect program below extracts and prints the text found beneath certain elements in an XML document tree. Using the API above, it can do its job in a single pass over the input without ever materializing the tree.

gopl.io/ch7/xmlselect

```
// Xmlselect prints the text of selected elements of an XML document.
package main

import (
    "encoding/xml"
    "fmt"
    "io"
    "os"
    "strings"
)

func main() {
    dec := xml.NewDecoder(os.Stdin)
    var stack []string // stack of element names
    for {
        tok, err := dec.Token()
        if err == io.EOF {
            break
        } else if err != nil {
            fmt.Fprintf(os.Stderr, "xmlselect: %v\n", err)
            os.Exit(1)
        }
        switch tok := tok.(type) {
        case xml.StartElement:
            stack = append(stack, tok.Name.Local) // push
        case xml.EndElement:
            stack = stack[:len(stack)-1] // pop
        case xml.CharData:
            if containsAll(stack, os.Args[1:]) {
                fmt.Printf("%s: %s\n", strings.Join(stack, " "), tok)
            }
        }
    }
}
```

```
// containsAll reports whether x contains the elements of y, in order.
func containsAll(x, y []string) bool {
    for len(y) <= len(x) {
        if len(y) == 0 {
            return true
        }
        if x[0] == y[0] {
            y = y[1:]
        }
        x = x[1:]
    }
    return false
}
```

Each time the loop in main encounters a StartElement, it pushes the element's name onto a stack, and for each EndElement it pops the name from the stack. The API guarantees that the sequence of StartElement and EndElement tokens will be properly matched, even in ill-formed documents. Comments are ignored. When xmlselect encounters a CharData, it prints the text only if the stack contains all the elements named by the command-line arguments, in order.

The command below prints the text of any h2 elements appearing beneath two levels of div elements. Its input is the XML specification, itself an XML document.

```
$ go build gopl.io/ch1/fetch
$ ./fetch http://www.w3.org/TR/2006/REC-xml11-20060816 |
    ./xmlselect div div h2
html body div div h2: 1 Introduction
html body div div h2: 2 Documents
html body div div h2: 3 Logical Structures
html body div div h2: 4 Physical Structures
html body div div h2: 5 Conformance
html body div div h2: 6 Notation
html body div div h2: A References
html body div div h2: B Definitions for Character Normalization
...
```

Exercise 7.17: Extend xmlselect so that elements may be selected not just by name, but by their attributes too, in the manner of CSS, so that, for instance, an element like <div id="page" class="wide"> could be selected by a matching id or class as well as its name.

Exercise 7.18: Using the token-based decoder API, write a program that will read an arbitrary XML document and construct a tree of generic nodes that represents it. Nodes are of two kinds: CharData nodes represent text strings, and Element nodes represent named elements and their attributes. Each element node has a slice of child nodes.

You may find the following declarations helpful.

```
import "encoding/xml"
```

```
type Node interface{} // CharData or *Element

type CharData string

type Element struct {
    Type     xml.Name
    Attr     []xml.Attr
    Children []Node
}
```

7.15. A Few Words of Advice

When designing a new package, novice Go programmers often start by creating a set of inter-faces and only later define the concrete types that satisfy them. This approach results in many interfaces, each of which has only a single implementation. Don't do that. Such interfaces are unnecessary abstractions; they also have a run-time cost. You can restrict which methods of a type or fields of a struct are visible outside a package using the export mechanism (§6.6). Interfaces are only needed when there are two or more concrete types that must be dealt with in a uniform way.

We make an exception to this rule when an interface is satisfied by a single concrete type but that type cannot live in the same package as the interface because of its dependencies. In that case, an interface is a good way to decouple two packages.

Because interfaces are used in Go only when they are satisfied by two or more types, they necessarily abstract away from the details of any particular implementation. The result is smaller interfaces with fewer, simpler methods, often just one as with `io.Writer` or `fmt.Stringer`. Small interfaces are easier to satisfy when new types come along. A good rule of thumb for interface design is *ask only for what you need.*

This concludes our tour of methods and interfaces. Go has great support for the object-oriented style of programming, but this does not mean you need to use it exclusively. Not everything need be an object; standalone functions have their place, as do unencapsulated data types. Observe that together, the examples in the first five chapters of this book call no more than two dozen methods, like `input.Scan`, as opposed to ordinary function calls like `fmt.Printf`.

8

Goroutines and Channels

Concurrent programming, the expression of a program as a composition of several autonomous activities, has never been more important than it is today. Web servers handle requests for thousands of clients at once. Tablet and phone apps render animations in the user interface while simultaneously performing computation and network requests in the background. Even traditional batch problems—read some data, compute, write some output—use concurrency to hide the latency of I/O operations and to exploit a modern computer's many processors, which every year grow in number but not in speed.

Go enables two styles of concurrent programming. This chapter presents goroutines and channels, which support *communicating sequential processes* or *CSP*, a model of concurrency in which values are passed between independent activities (goroutines) but variables are for the most part confined to a single activity. Chapter 9 covers some aspects of the more traditional model of *shared memory multithreading*, which will be familiar if you've used threads in other mainstream languages. Chapter 9 also points out some important hazards and pitfalls of concurrent programming that we won't delve into in this chapter.

Even though Go's support for concurrency is one of its great strengths, reasoning about concurrent programs is inherently harder than about sequential ones, and intuitions acquired from sequential programming may at times lead us astray. If this is your first encounter with concurrency, we recommend spending a little extra time thinking about the examples in these two chapters.

8.1. Goroutines

In Go, each concurrently executing activity is called a *goroutine*. Consider a program that has two functions, one that does some computation and one that writes some output, and assume that neither function calls the other. A sequential program may call one function and then call the other, but in a *concurrent* program with two or more goroutines, calls to *both* functions can be active at the same time. We'll see such a program in a moment.

If you have used operating system threads or threads in other languages, then you can assume for now that a goroutine is similar to a thread, and you'll be able to write correct programs. The differences between threads and goroutines are essentially quantitative, not qualitative, and will be described in Section 9.8.

When a program starts, its only goroutine is the one that calls the main function, so we call it the *main goroutine*. New goroutines are created by the go statement. Syntactically, a go statement is an ordinary function or method call prefixed by the keyword go. A go statement causes the function to be called in a newly created goroutine. The go statement itself completes immediately:

```
f()    // call f(); wait for it to return
go f() // create a new goroutine that calls f(); don't wait
```

In the example below, the main goroutine computes the 45th Fibonacci number. Since it uses the terribly inefficient recursive algorithm, it runs for an appreciable time, during which we'd like to provide the user with a visual indication that the program is still running, by displaying an animated textual "spinner."

gopl.io/ch8/spinner
```
func main() {
    go spinner(100 * time.Millisecond)
    const n = 45
    fibN := fib(n) // slow
    fmt.Printf("\rFibonacci(%d) = %d\n", n, fibN)
}

func spinner(delay time.Duration) {
    for {
        for _, r := range `-\|/` {
            fmt.Printf("\r%c", r)
            time.Sleep(delay)
        }
    }
}

func fib(x int) int {
    if x < 2 {
        return x
    }
    return fib(x-1) + fib(x-2)
}
```

After several seconds of animation, the `fib(45)` call returns and the main function prints its result:

```
Fibonacci(45) = 1134903170
```

The `main` function then returns. When this happens, all goroutines are abruptly terminated and the program exits. Other than by returning from `main` or exiting the program, there is no programmatic way for one goroutine to stop another, but as we will see later, there are ways to communicate with a goroutine to request that it stop itself.

Notice how the program is expressed as the composition of two autonomous activities, spinning and Fibonacci computation. Each is written as a separate function but both make progress concurrently.

8.2. Example: Concurrent Clock Server

Networking is a natural domain in which to use concurrency since servers typically handle many connections from their clients at once, each client being essentially independent of the others. In this section, we'll introduce the `net` package, which provides the components for building networked client and server programs that communicate over TCP, UDP, or Unix domain sockets. The `net/http` package we've been using since Chapter 1 is built on top of functions from the `net` package.

Our first example is a sequential clock server that writes the current time to the client once per second:

gopl.io/ch8/clock1

```
// Clock1 is a TCP server that periodically writes the time.
package main

import (
    "io"
    "log"
    "net"
    "time"
)

func main() {
    listener, err := net.Listen("tcp", "localhost:8000")
    if err != nil {
        log.Fatal(err)
    }
    for {
        conn, err := listener.Accept()
        if err != nil {
            log.Print(err) // e.g., connection aborted
            continue
        }
        handleConn(conn) // handle one connection at a time
    }
}
```

```go
func handleConn(c net.Conn) {
    defer c.Close()
    for {
        _, err := io.WriteString(c, time.Now().Format("15:04:05\n"))
        if err != nil {
            return // e.g., client disconnected
        }
        time.Sleep(1 * time.Second)
    }
}
```

The Listen function creates a net.Listener, an object that listens for incoming connections on a network port, in this case TCP port localhost:8000. The listener's Accept method blocks until an incoming connection request is made, then returns a net.Conn object representing the connection.

The handleConn function handles one complete client connection. In a loop, it writes the current time, time.Now(), to the client. Since net.Conn satisfies the io.Writer interface, we can write directly to it. The loop ends when the write fails, most likely because the client has disconnected, at which point handleConn closes its side of the connection using a deferred call to Close and goes back to waiting for another connection request.

The time.Time.Format method provides a way to format date and time information by example. Its argument is a template indicating how to format a reference time, specifically Mon Jan 2 03:04:05PM 2006 UTC-0700. The reference time has eight components (day of the week, month, day of the month, and so on). Any collection of them can appear in the Format string in any order and in a number of formats; the selected components of the date and time will be displayed in the selected formats. Here we are just using the hour, minute, and second of the time. The time package defines templates for many standard time formats, such as time.RFC1123. The same mechanism is used in reverse when parsing a time using time.Parse.

To connect to the server, we'll need a client program such as nc ("netcat"), a standard utility program for manipulating network connections:

```
$ go build gopl.io/ch8/clock1
$ ./clock1 &
$ nc localhost 8000
13:58:54
13:58:55
13:58:56
13:58:57
^C
```

The client displays the time sent by the server each second until we interrupt the client with Control-C, which on Unix systems is echoed as ^C by the shell. If nc or netcat is not installed on your system, you can use telnet or this simple Go version of netcat that uses net.Dial to connect to a TCP server:

gopl.io/ch8/netcat1

```go
// Netcat1 is a read-only TCP client.
package main

import (
    "io"
    "log"
    "net"
    "os"
)

func main() {
    conn, err := net.Dial("tcp", "localhost:8000")
    if err != nil {
        log.Fatal(err)
    }
    defer conn.Close()
    mustCopy(os.Stdout, conn)
}

func mustCopy(dst io.Writer, src io.Reader) {
    if _, err := io.Copy(dst, src); err != nil {
        log.Fatal(err)
    }
}
```

This program reads data from the connection and writes it to the standard output until an end-of-file condition or an error occurs. The mustCopy function is a utility used in several examples in this section. Let's run two clients at the same time on different terminals, one shown to the left and one to the right:

```
$ go build gopl.io/ch8/netcat1
$ ./netcat1
13:58:54                                  $ ./netcat1
13:58:55
13:58:56
^C
                                          13:58:57
                                          13:58:58
                                          13:58:59
                                          ^C
$ killall clock1
```

The killall command is a Unix utility that kills all processes with the given name.

The second client must wait until the first client is finished because the server is *sequential*; it deals with only one client at a time. Just one small change is needed to make the server concurrent: adding the go keyword to the call to handleConn causes each call to run in its own goroutine.

gopl.io/ch8/clock2

```
    for {
        conn, err := listener.Accept()
        if err != nil {
            log.Print(err) // e.g., connection aborted
            continue
        }
        go handleConn(conn) // handle connections concurrently
    }
```

Now, multiple clients can receive the time at once:

```
$ go build gopl.io/ch8/clock2
$ ./clock2 &
$ go build gopl.io/ch8/netcat1
$ ./netcat1
14:02:54                              $ ./netcat1
14:02:55                              14:02:55
14:02:56                              14:02:56
14:02:57                              ^C
14:02:58
14:02:59                              $ ./netcat1
14:03:00                              14:03:00
14:03:01                              14:03:01
^C                                    14:03:02
                                      ^C
$ killall clock2
```

Exercise 8.1: Modify `clock2` to accept a port number, and write a program, `clockwall`, that acts as a client of several clock servers at once, reading the times from each one and displaying the results in a table, akin to the wall of clocks seen in some business offices. If you have access to geographically distributed computers, run instances remotely; otherwise run local instances on different ports with fake time zones.

```
$ TZ=US/Eastern    ./clock2 -port 8010 &
$ TZ=Asia/Tokyo    ./clock2 -port 8020 &
$ TZ=Europe/London ./clock2 -port 8030 &
$ clockwall NewYork=localhost:8010 London=localhost:8020 Tokyo=localhost:8030
```

Exercise 8.2: Implement a concurrent File Transfer Protocol (FTP) server. The server should interpret commands from each client such as `cd` to change directory, `ls` to list a directory, `get` to send the contents of a file, and `close` to close the connection. You can use the standard `ftp` command as the client, or write your own.

8.3. Example: Concurrent Echo Server

The clock server used one goroutine per connection. In this section, we'll build an echo server that uses multiple goroutines per connection. Most echo servers merely write whatever they read, which can be done with this trivial version of handleConn:

```go
func handleConn(c net.Conn) {
    io.Copy(c, c) // NOTE: ignoring errors
    c.Close()
}
```

A more interesting echo server might simulate the reverberations of a real echo, with the response loud at first ("HELLO!"), then moderate ("Hello!") after a delay, then quiet ("hello!") before fading to nothing, as in this version of handleConn:

gopl.io/ch8/reverb1

```go
func echo(c net.Conn, shout string, delay time.Duration) {
    fmt.Fprintln(c, "\t", strings.ToUpper(shout))
    time.Sleep(delay)
    fmt.Fprintln(c, "\t", shout)
    time.Sleep(delay)
    fmt.Fprintln(c, "\t", strings.ToLower(shout))
}

func handleConn(c net.Conn) {
    input := bufio.NewScanner(c)
    for input.Scan() {
        echo(c, input.Text(), 1*time.Second)
    }
    // NOTE: ignoring potential errors from input.Err()
    c.Close()
}
```

We'll need to upgrade our client program so that it sends terminal input to the server while also copying the server response to the output, which presents another opportunity to use concurrency:

gopl.io/ch8/netcat2

```go
func main() {
    conn, err := net.Dial("tcp", "localhost:8000")
    if err != nil {
        log.Fatal(err)
    }
    defer conn.Close()
    go mustCopy(os.Stdout, conn)
    mustCopy(conn, os.Stdin)
}
```

While the main goroutine reads the standard input and sends it to the server, a second goroutine reads and prints the server's response. When the main goroutine encounters the end of the input, for example, after the user types Control-D (^D) at the terminal (or the equivalent Control-Z on Microsoft Windows), the program stops, even if the other goroutine still has work to do. (We'll see how to make the program wait for both sides to finish once we've introduced channels in Section 8.4.1.)

In the session below, the client's input is left-aligned and the server's responses are indented. The client shouts at the echo server three times:

```
$ go build gopl.io/ch8/reverb1
$ ./reverb1 &
$ go build gopl.io/ch8/netcat2
$ ./netcat2
Hello?
    HELLO?
    Hello?
    hello?
Is there anybody there?
    IS THERE ANYBODY THERE?
Yooo-hooo!
    Is there anybody there?
    is there anybody there?
    YOOO-HOOO!
    Yooo-hooo!
    yooo-hooo!
^D
$ killall reverb1
```

Notice that the third shout from the client is not dealt with until the second shout has petered out, which is not very realistic. A real echo would consist of the *composition* of the three independent shouts. To simulate it, we'll need more goroutines. Again, all we need to do is add the go keyword, this time to the call to echo:

gopl.io/ch8/reverb2

```
func handleConn(c net.Conn) {
    input := bufio.NewScanner(c)
    for input.Scan() {
        go echo(c, input.Text(), 1*time.Second)
    }
    // NOTE: ignoring potential errors from input.Err()
    c.Close()
}
```

The arguments to the function started by go are evaluated when the go statement itself is executed; thus input.Text() is evaluated in the main goroutine.

Now the echoes are concurrent and overlap in time:

```
$ go build gopl.io/ch8/reverb2
$ ./reverb2 &
$ ./netcat2
Is there anybody there?
    IS THERE ANYBODY THERE?
```

```
Yooo-hooo!
    Is there anybody there?
    YOOO-HOOO!
    is there anybody there?
    Yooo-hooo!
    yooo-hooo!
^D
$ killall reverb2
```

All that was required to make the server use concurrency, not just to handle connections from multiple clients but even within a single connection, was the insertion of two go keywords.

However in adding these keywords, we had to consider carefully that it is safe to call methods of net.Conn concurrently, which is not true for most types. We'll discuss the crucial concept of *concurrency safety* in the next chapter.

8.4. Channels

If goroutines are the activities of a concurrent Go program, *channels* are the connections between them. A channel is a communication mechanism that lets one goroutine send values to another goroutine. Each channel is a conduit for values of a particular type, called the channel's *element type*. The type of a channel whose elements have type int is written chan int.

To create a channel, we use the built-in make function:

```
ch := make(chan int) // ch has type 'chan int'
```

As with maps, a channel is a *reference* to the data structure created by make. When we copy a channel or pass one as an argument to a function, we are copying a reference, so caller and callee refer to the same data structure. As with other reference types, the zero value of a channel is nil.

Two channels of the same type may be compared using ==. The comparison is true if both are references to the same channel data structure. A channel may also be compared to nil.

A channel has two principal operations, *send* and *receive*, collectively known as *communications*. A send statement transmits a value from one goroutine, through the channel, to another goroutine executing a corresponding receive expression. Both operations are written using the <- operator. In a send statement, the <- separates the channel and value operands. In a receive expression, <- precedes the channel operand. A receive expression whose result is not used is a valid statement.

```
ch <- x  // a send statement

x = <-ch // a receive expression in an assignment statement
<-ch     // a receive statement; result is discarded
```

Channels support a third operation, *close*, which sets a flag indicating that no more values will ever be sent on this channel; subsequent attempts to send will panic. Receive operations on a closed channel yield the values that have been sent until no more values are left; any receive operations thereafter complete immediately and yield the zero value of the channel's element type.

To close a channel, we call the built-in `close` function:

```
close(ch)
```

A channel created with a simple call to make is called an *unbuffered* channel, but make accepts an optional second argument, an integer called the channel's *capacity*. If the capacity is non-zero, make creates a *buffered* channel.

```
ch = make(chan int)    // unbuffered channel
ch = make(chan int, 0) // unbuffered channel
ch = make(chan int, 3) // buffered channel with capacity 3
```

We'll look at unbuffered channels first and buffered channels in Section 8.4.4.

8.4.1. Unbuffered Channels

A send operation on an unbuffered channel blocks the sending goroutine until another goroutine executes a corresponding receive on the same channel, at which point the value is transmitted and both goroutines may continue. Conversely, if the receive operation was attempted first, the receiving goroutine is blocked until another goroutine performs a send on the same channel.

Communication over an unbuffered channel causes the sending and receiving goroutines to *synchronize*. Because of this, unbuffered channels are sometimes called *synchronous* channels. When a value is sent on an unbuffered channel, the receipt of the value *happens before* the reawakening of the sending goroutine.

In discussions of concurrency, when we say *x happens before y*, we don't mean merely that *x* occurs earlier in time than *y*; we mean that it is guaranteed to do so and that all its prior effects, such as updates to variables, are complete and that you may rely on them.

When *x* neither happens before *y* nor after *y*, we say that *x is concurrent with y*. This doesn't mean that *x* and *y* are necessarily simultaneous, merely that we cannot assume anything about their ordering. As we'll see in the next chapter, it's necessary to order certain events during the program's execution to avoid the problems that arise when two goroutines access the same variable concurrently.

The client program in Section 8.3 copies input to the server in its main goroutine, so the client program terminates as soon as the input stream closes, even if the background goroutine is still working. To make the program wait for the background goroutine to complete before exiting, we use a channel to synchronize the two goroutines:

gopl.io/ch8/netcat3

```
func main() {
    conn, err := net.Dial("tcp", "localhost:8000")
    if err != nil {
        log.Fatal(err)
    }
    done := make(chan struct{})
    go func() {
        io.Copy(os.Stdout, conn) // NOTE: ignoring errors
        log.Println("done")
        done <- struct{}{} // signal the main goroutine
    }()
    mustCopy(conn, os.Stdin)
    conn.Close()
    <-done // wait for background goroutine to finish
}
```

When the user closes the standard input stream, mustCopy returns and the main goroutine calls conn.Close(), closing both halves of the network connection. Closing the write half of the connection causes the server to see an end-of-file condition. Closing the read half causes the background goroutine's call to io.Copy to return a "read from closed connection" error, which is why we've removed the error logging; Exercise 8.3 suggests a better solution. (Notice that the go statement calls a literal function, a common construction.)

Before it returns, the background goroutine logs a message, then sends a value on the done channel. The main goroutine waits until it has received this value before returning. As a result, the program always logs the "done" message before exiting.

Messages sent over channels have two important aspects. Each message has a value, but sometimes the fact of communication and the moment at which it occurs are just as important. We call messages *events* when we wish to stress this aspect. When the event carries no additional information, that is, its sole purpose is synchronization, we'll emphasize this by using a channel whose element type is struct{}, though it's common to use a channel of bool or int for the same purpose since done <- 1 is shorter than done <- struct{}{}.

Exercise 8.3: In netcat3, the interface value conn has the concrete type *net.TCPConn, which represents a TCP connection. A TCP connection consists of two halves that may be closed independently using its CloseRead and CloseWrite methods. Modify the main goroutine of netcat3 to close only the write half of the connection so that the program will continue to print the final echoes from the reverb1 server even after the standard input has been closed. (Doing this for the reverb2 server is harder; see Exercise 8.4.)

8.4.2. Pipelines

Channels can be used to connect goroutines together so that the output of one is the input to another. This is called a *pipeline*. The program below consists of three goroutines connected by two channels, as shown schematically in Figure 8.1.

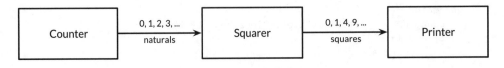

Figure 8.1. A three-stage pipeline.

The first goroutine, *counter*, generates the integers 0, 1, 2, ..., and sends them over a channel to
the second goroutine, *squarer*, which receives each value, squares it, and sends the result over
another channel to the third goroutine, *printer*, which receives the squared values and prints
them. For clarity of this example, we have intentionally chosen very simple functions, though
of course they are too computationally trivial to warrant their own goroutines in a realistic
program.

gopl.io/ch8/pipeline1

```go
func main() {
    naturals := make(chan int)
    squares := make(chan int)

    // Counter
    go func() {
        for x := 0; ; x++ {
            naturals <- x
        }
    }()

    // Squarer
    go func() {
        for {
            x := <-naturals
            squares <- x * x
        }
    }()

    // Printer (in main goroutine)
    for {
        fmt.Println(<-squares)
    }
}
```

As you might expect, the program prints the infinite series of squares 0, 1, 4, 9, and so on.
Pipelines like this may be found in long-running server programs where channels are used for
lifelong communication between goroutines containing infinite loops. But what if we want to
send only a finite number of values through the pipeline?

If the sender knows that no further values will ever be sent on a channel, it is useful to communicate this fact to the receiver goroutines so that they can stop waiting. This is accom-
plished by *closing* the channel using the built-in close function:

```
    close(naturals)
```

After a channel has been closed, any further send operations on it will panic. After the closed channel has been *drained*, that is, after the last sent element has been received, all subsequent receive operations will proceed without blocking but will yield a zero value. Closing the naturals channel above would cause the squarer's loop to spin as it receives a never-ending stream of zero values, and to send these zeros to the printer.

There is no way to test directly whether a channel has been closed, but there is a variant of the receive operation that produces two results: the received channel element, plus a boolean value, conventionally called ok, which is true for a successful receive and false for a receive on a closed and drained channel. Using this feature, we can modify the squarer's loop to stop when the naturals channel is drained and close the squares channel in turn.

```go
// Squarer
go func() {
    for {
        x, ok := <-naturals
        if !ok {
            break // channel was closed and drained
        }
        squares <- x * x
    }
    close(squares)
}()
```

Because the syntax above is clumsy and this pattern is common, the language lets us use a range loop to iterate over channels too. This is a more convenient syntax for receiving all the values sent on a channel and terminating the loop after the last one.

In the pipeline below, when the counter goroutine finishes its loop after 100 elements, it closes the naturals channel, causing the squarer to finish its loop and close the squares channel. (In a more complex program, it might make sense for the counter and squarer functions to defer the calls to close at the outset.) Finally, the main goroutine finishes its loop and the program exits.

gopl.io/ch8/pipeline2
```go
func main() {
    naturals := make(chan int)
    squares := make(chan int)

    // Counter
    go func() {
        for x := 0; x < 100; x++ {
            naturals <- x
        }
        close(naturals)
    }()
```

```go
    // Squarer
    go func() {
        for x := range naturals {
            squares <- x * x
        }
        close(squares)
    }()
    // Printer (in main goroutine)
    for x := range squares {
        fmt.Println(x)
    }
}
```

You needn't close every channel when you've finished with it. It's only necessary to close a channel when it is important to tell the receiving goroutines that all data have been sent. A channel that the garbage collector determines to be unreachable will have its resources reclaimed whether or not it is closed. (Don't confuse this with the close operation for open files. It *is* important to call the Close method on every file when you've finished with it.)

Attempting to close an already-closed channel causes a panic, as does closing a nil channel. Closing channels has another use as a broadcast mechanism, which we'll cover in Section 8.9.

8.4.3. Unidirectional Channel Types

As programs grow, it is natural to break up large functions into smaller pieces. Our previous example used three goroutines, communicating over two channels, which were local variables of main. The program naturally divides into three functions:

```go
func counter(out chan int)
func squarer(out, in chan int)
func printer(in chan int)
```

The squarer function, sitting in the middle of the pipeline, takes two parameters, the input channel and the output channel. Both have the same type, but their intended uses are opposite: in is only to be received from, and out is only to be sent to. The names in and out convey this intention, but still, nothing prevents squarer from sending to in or receiving from out.

This arrangement is typical. When a channel is supplied as a function parameter, it is nearly always with the intent that it be used exclusively for sending or exclusively for receiving.

To document this intent and prevent misuse, the Go type system provides *unidirectional* channel types that expose only one or the other of the send and receive operations. The type chan<- int, a *send-only* channel of int, allows sends but not receives. Conversely, the type <-chan int, a *receive-only* channel of int, allows receives but not sends. (The position of the <- arrow relative to the chan keyword is a mnemonic.) Violations of this discipline are detected at compile time.

Since the close operation asserts that no more sends will occur on a channel, only the sending goroutine is in a position to call it, and for this reason it is a compile-time error to attempt to close a receive-only channel.

Here's the squaring pipeline once more, this time with unidirectional channel types:

gopl.io/ch8/pipeline3

```go
func counter(out chan<- int) {
    for x := 0; x < 100; x++ {
        out <- x
    }
    close(out)
}

func squarer(out chan<- int, in <-chan int) {
    for v := range in {
        out <- v * v
    }
    close(out)
}

func printer(in <-chan int) {
    for v := range in {
        fmt.Println(v)
    }
}

func main() {
    naturals := make(chan int)
    squares := make(chan int)

    go counter(naturals)
    go squarer(squares, naturals)
    printer(squares)
}
```

The call counter(naturals) implicitly converts naturals, a value of type chan int, to the type of the parameter, chan<- int. The printer(squares) call does a similar implicit conversion to <-chan int. Conversions from bidirectional to unidirectional channel types are permitted in any assignment. There is no going back, however: once you have a value of a unidirectional type such as chan<- int, there is no way to obtain from it a value of type chan int that refers to the same channel data structure.

8.4.4. Buffered Channels

A buffered channel has a queue of elements. The queue's maximum size is determined when it is created, by the capacity argument to make. The statement below creates a buffered channel capable of holding three string values. Figure 8.2 is a graphical representation of ch and the channel to which it refers.

```
ch = make(chan string, 3)
```

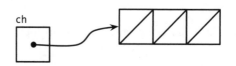

Figure 8.2. An empty buffered channel.

A send operation on a buffered channel inserts an element at the back of the queue, and a receive operation removes an element from the front. If the channel is full, the send operation blocks its goroutine until space is made available by another goroutine's receive. Conversely, if the channel is empty, a receive operation blocks until a value is sent by another goroutine.

We can send up to three values on this channel without the goroutine blocking:

```
ch <- "A"
ch <- "B"
ch <- "C"
```

At this point, the channel is full (Figure 8.3), and a fourth send statement would block.

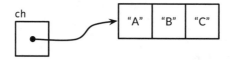

Figure 8.3. A full buffered channel.

If we receive one value,

```
fmt.Println(<-ch) // "A"
```

the channel is neither full nor empty (Figure 8.4), so either a send operation or a receive operation could proceed without blocking. In this way, the channel's buffer decouples the sending and receiving goroutines.

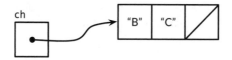

Figure 8.4. A partially full buffered channel.

In the unlikely event that a program needs to know the channel's buffer capacity, it can be obtained by calling the built-in cap function:

```
fmt.Println(cap(ch)) // "3"
```

When applied to a channel, the built-in `len` function returns the number of elements currently buffered. Since in a concurrent program this information is likely to be stale as soon as it is retrieved, its value is limited, but it could conceivably be useful during fault diagnosis or performance optimization.

```
fmt.Println(len(ch)) // "2"
```

After two more receive operations the channel is empty again, and a fourth would block:

```
fmt.Println(<-ch) // "B"
fmt.Println(<-ch) // "C"
```

In this example, the send and receive operations were all performed by the same goroutine, but in real programs they are usually executed by different goroutines. Novices are sometimes tempted to use buffered channels within a single goroutine as a queue, lured by their pleasingly simple syntax, but this is a mistake. Channels are deeply connected to goroutine scheduling, and without another goroutine receiving from the channel, a sender—and perhaps the whole program—risks becoming blocked forever. If all you need is a simple queue, make one using a slice.

The example below shows an application of a buffered channel. It makes parallel requests to three *mirrors*, that is, equivalent but geographically distributed servers. It sends their responses over a buffered channel, then receives and returns only the first response, which is the quickest one to arrive. Thus mirroredQuery returns a result even before the two slower servers have responded. (Incidentally, it's quite normal for several goroutines to send values to the same channel concurrently, as in this example, or to receive from the same channel.)

```
func mirroredQuery() string {
    responses := make(chan string, 3)
    go func() { responses <- request("asia.gopl.io") }()
    go func() { responses <- request("europe.gopl.io") }()
    go func() { responses <- request("americas.gopl.io") }()
    return <-responses // return the quickest response
}

func request(hostname string) (response string) { /* ... */ }
```

Had we used an unbuffered channel, the two slower goroutines would have gotten stuck trying to send their responses on a channel from which no goroutine will ever receive. This situation, called a *goroutine leak*, would be a bug. Unlike garbage variables, leaked goroutines are not automatically collected, so it is important to make sure that goroutines terminate themselves when no longer needed.

The choice between unbuffered and buffered channels, and the choice of a buffered channel's capacity, may both affect the correctness of a program. Unbuffered channels give stronger synchronization guarantees because every send operation is synchronized with its corresponding receive; with buffered channels, these operations are decoupled. Also, when we know an upper bound on the number of values that will be sent on a channel, it's not unusual to create a buffered channel of that size and perform all the sends before the first value is received. Failure to allocate sufficient buffer capacity would cause the program to deadlock.

Channel buffering may also affect program performance. Imagine three cooks in a cake shop, one baking, one icing, and one inscribing each cake before passing it on to the next cook in the assembly line. In a kitchen with little space, each cook that has finished a cake must wait for the next cook to become ready to accept it; this rendezvous is analogous to communication over an unbuffered channel.

If there is space for one cake between each cook, a cook may place a finished cake there and immediately start work on the next; this is analogous to a buffered channel with capacity 1. So long as the cooks work at about the same rate on average, most of these handovers proceed quickly, smoothing out transient differences in their respective rates. More space between cooks—larger buffers—can smooth out bigger transient variations in their rates without stalling the assembly line, such as happens when one cook takes a short break, then later rushes to catch up.

On the other hand, if an earlier stage of the assembly line is consistently faster than the following stage, the buffer between them will spend most of its time full. Conversely, if the later stage is faster, the buffer will usually be empty. A buffer provides no benefit in this case.

The assembly line metaphor is a useful one for channels and goroutines. For example, if the second stage is more elaborate, a single cook may not be able to keep up with the supply from the first cook or meet the demand from the third. To solve the problem, we could hire another cook to help the second, performing the same task but working independently. This is analogous to creating another goroutine communicating over the same channels.

We don't have space to show it here, but the `gopl.io/ch8/cake` package simulates this cake shop, with several parameters you can vary. It includes benchmarks (§11.4) for a few of the scenarios described above.

8.5. Looping in Parallel

In this section, we'll explore some common concurrency patterns for executing all the iterations of a loop in parallel. We'll consider the problem of producing thumbnail-size images from a set of full-size ones. The `gopl.io/ch8/thumbnail` package provides an `ImageFile` function that can scale a single image. We won't show its implementation but it can be downloaded from `gopl.io`.

gopl.io/ch8/thumbnail
```
package thumbnail

// ImageFile reads an image from infile and writes
// a thumbnail-size version of it in the same directory.
// It returns the generated file name, e.g., "foo.thumb.jpg".
func ImageFile(infile string) (string, error)
```

The program below loops over a list of image file names and produces a thumbnail for each one:

gopl.io/ch8/thumbnail

```
// makeThumbnails makes thumbnails of the specified files.
func makeThumbnails(filenames []string) {
    for _, f := range filenames {
        if _, err := thumbnail.ImageFile(f); err != nil {
            log.Println(err)
        }
    }
}
```

Obviously the order in which we process the files doesn't matter, since each scaling operation is independent of all the others. Problems like this that consist entirely of subproblems that are completely independent of each other are described as *embarrassingly parallel*. Embarrassingly parallel problems are the easiest kind to implement concurrently and enjoy performance that scales linearly with the amount of parallelism.

Let's execute all these operations in parallel, thereby hiding the latency of the file I/O and using multiple CPUs for the image-scaling computations. Our first attempt at a concurrent version just adds a go keyword. We'll ignore errors for now and address them later.

```
// NOTE: incorrect!
func makeThumbnails2(filenames []string) {
    for _, f := range filenames {
        go thumbnail.ImageFile(f) // NOTE: ignoring errors
    }
}
```

This version runs really fast—too fast, in fact, since it takes less time than the original, even when the slice of file names contains only a single element. If there's no parallelism, how can the concurrent version possibly run faster? The answer is that makeThumbnails returns before it has finished doing what it was supposed to do. It starts all the goroutines, one per file name, but doesn't wait for them to finish.

There is no direct way to wait until a goroutine has finished, but we can change the inner goroutine to report its completion to the outer goroutine by sending an event on a shared channel. Since we know that there are exactly len(filenames) inner goroutines, the outer goroutine need only count that many events before it returns:

```
// makeThumbnails3 makes thumbnails of the specified files in parallel.
func makeThumbnails3(filenames []string) {
    ch := make(chan struct{})
    for _, f := range filenames {
        go func(f string) {
            thumbnail.ImageFile(f) // NOTE: ignoring errors
            ch <- struct{}{}
        }(f)
    }
```

```
    // Wait for goroutines to complete.
    for range filenames {
        <-ch
    }
}
```

Notice that we passed the value of f as an explicit argument to the literal function instead of using the declaration of f from the enclosing for loop:

```
for _, f := range filenames {
    go func() {
        thumbnail.ImageFile(f) // NOTE: incorrect!
        // ...
    }()
}
```

Recall the problem of loop variable capture inside an anonymous function, described in Section 5.6.1. Above, the single variable f is shared by all the anonymous function values and updated by successive loop iterations. By the time the new goroutines start executing the literal function, the for loop may have updated f and started another iteration or (more likely) finished entirely, so when these goroutines read the value of f, they all observe it to have the value of the final element of the slice. By adding an explicit parameter, we ensure that we use the value of f that is current when the go statement is executed.

What if we want to return values from each worker goroutine to the main one? If the call to thumbnail.ImageFile fails to create a file, it returns an error. The next version of makeThumbnails returns the first error it receives from any of the scaling operations:

```
// makeThumbnails4 makes thumbnails for the specified files in parallel.
// It returns an error if any step failed.
func makeThumbnails4(filenames []string) error {
    errors := make(chan error)

    for _, f := range filenames {
        go func(f string) {
            _, err := thumbnail.ImageFile(f)
            errors <- err
        }(f)
    }

    for range filenames {
        if err := <-errors; err != nil {
            return err // NOTE: incorrect: goroutine leak!
        }
    }

    return nil
}
```

This function has a subtle bug. When it encounters the first non-nil error, it returns the error to the caller, leaving no goroutine draining the errors channel. Each remaining worker goroutine will block forever when it tries to send a value on that channel, and will never terminate. This situation, a goroutine leak (§8.4.4), may cause the whole program to get stuck or to run out of memory.

The simplest solution is to use a buffered channel with sufficient capacity that no worker goroutine will block when it sends a message. (An alternative solution is to create another goroutine to drain the channel while the main goroutine returns the first error without delay.)

The next version of makeThumbnails uses a buffered channel to return the names of the generated image files along with any errors.

```
// makeThumbnails5 makes thumbnails for the specified files in parallel.
// It returns the generated file names in an arbitrary order,
// or an error if any step failed.
func makeThumbnails5(filenames []string) (thumbfiles []string, err error) {
    type item struct {
        thumbfile string
        err       error
    }

    ch := make(chan item, len(filenames))
    for _, f := range filenames {
        go func(f string) {
            var it item
            it.thumbfile, it.err = thumbnail.ImageFile(f)
            ch <- it
        }(f)
    }

    for range filenames {
        it := <-ch
        if it.err != nil {
            return nil, it.err
        }
        thumbfiles = append(thumbfiles, it.thumbfile)
    }

    return thumbfiles, nil
}
```

Our final version of makeThumbnails, below, returns the total number of bytes occupied by the new files. Unlike the previous versions, however, it receives the file names not as a slice but over a channel of strings, so we cannot predict the number of loop iterations.

To know when the last goroutine has finished (which may not be the last one to start), we need to increment a counter before each goroutine starts and decrement it as each goroutine finishes. This demands a special kind of counter, one that can be safely manipulated from multiple goroutines and that provides a way to wait until it becomes zero. This counter type is known as sync.WaitGroup, and the code below shows how to use it:

```go
// makeThumbnails6 makes thumbnails for each file received from the channel.
// It returns the number of bytes occupied by the files it creates.
func makeThumbnails6(filenames <-chan string) int64 {
    sizes := make(chan int64)
    var wg sync.WaitGroup // number of working goroutines
    for f := range filenames {
        wg.Add(1)
        // worker
        go func(f string) {
            defer wg.Done()
            thumb, err := thumbnail.ImageFile(f)
            if err != nil {
                log.Println(err)
                return
            }
            info, _ := os.Stat(thumb) // OK to ignore error
            sizes <- info.Size()
        }(f)
    }

    // closer
    go func() {
        wg.Wait()
        close(sizes)
    }()

    var total int64
    for size := range sizes {
        total += size
    }
    return total
}
```

Note the asymmetry in the Add and Done methods. Add, which increments the counter, must be called before the worker goroutine starts, not within it; otherwise we would not be sure that the Add *happens before* the "closer" goroutine calls Wait. Also, Add takes a parameter, but Done does not; it's equivalent to Add(-1). We use defer to ensure that the counter is decremented even in the error case. The structure of the code above is a common and idiomatic pattern for looping in parallel when we don't know the number of iterations.

The sizes channel carries each file size back to the main goroutine, which receives them using a range loop and computes the sum. Observe how we create a closer goroutine that waits for the workers to finish before closing the sizes channel. These two operations, wait and close, must be concurrent with the loop over sizes. Consider the alternatives: if the wait operation were placed in the main goroutine before the loop, it would never end, and if placed after the loop, it would be unreachable since with nothing closing the channel, the loop would never terminate.

Figure 8.5 illustrates the sequence of events in the makeThumbnails6 function. The vertical lines represent goroutines. The thin segments indicate sleep, the thick segments activity. The

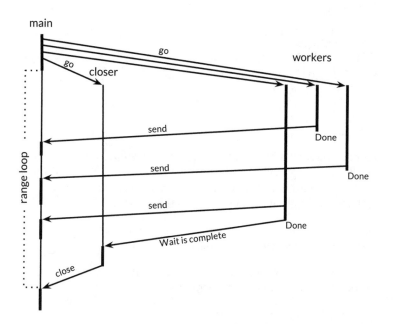

Figure 8.5. The sequence of events in makeThumbnails6.

diagonal arrows indicate events that synchronize one goroutine with another. Time flows down. Notice how the main goroutine spends most of its time in the range loop asleep, waiting for a worker to send a value or the closer to close the channel.

Exercise 8.4: Modify the reverb2 server to use a sync.WaitGroup per connection to count the number of active echo goroutines. When it falls to zero, close the write half of the TCP connection as described in Exercise 8.3. Verify that your modified netcat3 client from that exercise waits for the final echoes of multiple concurrent shouts, even after the standard input has been closed.

Exercise 8.5: Take an existing CPU-bound sequential program, such as the Mandelbrot program of Section 3.3 or the 3-D surface computation of Section 3.2, and execute its main loop in parallel using channels for communication. How much faster does it run on a multiprocessor machine? What is the optimal number of goroutines to use?

8.6. Example: Concurrent Web Crawler

In Section 5.6, we made a simple web crawler that explored the link graph of the web in breadth-first order. In this section, we'll make it concurrent so that independent calls to crawl can exploit the I/O parallelism available in the web. The crawl function remains exactly as it was in gopl.io/ch5/findlinks3:

gopl.io/ch8/crawl1

```go
func crawl(url string) []string {
    fmt.Println(url)
    list, err := links.Extract(url)
    if err != nil {
        log.Print(err)
    }
    return list
}
```

The main function resembles breadthFirst (§5.6). As before, a worklist records the queue of items that need processing, each item being a list of URLs to crawl, but this time, instead of representing the queue using a slice, we use a channel. Each call to crawl occurs in its own goroutine and sends the links it discovers back to the worklist.

```go
func main() {
    worklist := make(chan []string)

    // Start with the command-line arguments.
    go func() { worklist <- os.Args[1:] }()

    // Crawl the web concurrently.
    seen := make(map[string]bool)
    for list := range worklist {
        for _, link := range list {
            if !seen[link] {
                seen[link] = true
                go func(link string) {
                    worklist <- crawl(link)
                }(link)
            }
        }
    }
}
```

Notice that the crawl goroutine takes link as an explicit parameter to avoid the problem of loop variable capture we first saw in Section 5.6.1. Also notice that the initial send of the command-line arguments to the worklist must run in its own goroutine to avoid *deadlock*, a stuck situation in which both the main goroutine and a crawler goroutine attempt to send to each other while neither is receiving. An alternative solution would be to use a buffered channel.

The crawler is now highly concurrent and prints a storm of URLs, but it has two problems. The first problem manifests itself as error messages in the log after a few seconds of operation:

```
$ go build gopl.io/ch8/crawl1
$ ./crawl1 http://gopl.io/
http://gopl.io/
https://golang.org/help/
```

```
https://golang.org/doc/
https://golang.org/blog/
...
2015/07/15 18:22:12 Get ...: dial tcp: lookup blog.golang.org: no such host
2015/07/15 18:22:12 Get ...: dial tcp 23.21.222.120:443: socket:
                                                 too many open files
...
```

The initial error message is a surprising report of a DNS lookup failure for a reliable domain. The subsequent error message reveals the cause: the program created so many network connections at once that it exceeded the per-process limit on the number of open files, causing operations such as DNS lookups and calls to net.Dial to start failing.

The program is *too* parallel. Unbounded parallelism is rarely a good idea since there is always a limiting factor in the system, such as the number of CPU cores for compute-bound workloads, the number of spindles and heads for local disk I/O operations, the bandwidth of the network for streaming downloads, or the serving capacity of a web service. The solution is to limit the number of parallel uses of the resource to match the level of parallelism that is available. A simple way to do that in our example is to ensure that no more than *n* calls to links.Extract are active at once, where *n* is comfortably less than the file descriptor limit—20, say. This is analogous to the way a doorman at a crowded nightclub admits a guest only when some other guest leaves.

We can limit parallelism using a buffered channel of capacity *n* to model a concurrency primitive called a *counting semaphore*. Conceptually, each of the *n* vacant slots in the channel buffer represents a token entitling the holder to proceed. Sending a value into the channel acquires a token, and receiving a value from the channel releases a token, creating a new vacant slot. This ensures that at most *n* sends can occur without an intervening receive. (Although it might be more intuitive to treat *filled* slots in the channel buffer as tokens, using vacant slots avoids the need to fill the channel buffer after creating it.) Since the channel element type is not important, we'll use struct{}, which has size zero.

Let's rewrite the crawl function so that the call to links.Extract is bracketed by operations to acquire and release a token, thus ensuring that at most 20 calls to it are active at one time. It's good practice to keep the semaphore operations as close as possible to the I/O operation they regulate.

gopl.io/ch8/crawl2

```go
// tokens is a counting semaphore used to
// enforce a limit of 20 concurrent requests.
var tokens = make(chan struct{}, 20)

func crawl(url string) []string {
    fmt.Println(url)
    tokens <- struct{}{} // acquire a token
    list, err := links.Extract(url)
    <-tokens // release the token
```

```
        if err != nil {
            log.Print(err)
        }
        return list
    }
```

The second problem is that the program never terminates, even when it has discovered all the links reachable from the initial URLs. (Of course, you're unlikely to notice this problem unless you choose the initial URLs carefully or implement the depth-limiting feature of Exercise 8.6.) For the program to terminate, we need to break out of the main loop when the worklist is empty *and* no crawl goroutines are active.

```
    func main() {
        worklist := make(chan []string)
        var n int // number of pending sends to worklist

        // Start with the command-line arguments.
        n++
        go func() { worklist <- os.Args[1:] }()

        // Crawl the web concurrently.
        seen := make(map[string]bool)
        for ; n > 0; n-- {
            list := <-worklist
            for _, link := range list {
                if !seen[link] {
                    seen[link] = true
                    n++
                    go func(link string) {
                        worklist <- crawl(link)
                    }(link)
                }
            }
        }
    }
```

In this version, the counter n keeps track of the number of sends to the worklist that are yet to occur. Each time we know that an item needs to be sent to the worklist, we increment n, once before we send the initial command-line arguments, and again each time we start a crawler goroutine. The main loop terminates when n falls to zero, since there is no more work to be done.

Now the concurrent crawler runs about 20 times faster than the breadth-first crawler from Section 5.6, without errors, and terminates correctly if it should complete its task.

The program below shows an alternative solution to the problem of excessive concurrency. This version uses the original crawl function that has no counting semaphore, but calls it from one of 20 long-lived crawler goroutines, thus ensuring that at most 20 HTTP requests are active concurrently.

gopl.io/ch8/crawl3

```go
func main() {
    worklist := make(chan []string)  // lists of URLs, may have duplicates
    unseenLinks := make(chan string) // de-duplicated URLs

    // Add command-line arguments to worklist.
    go func() { worklist <- os.Args[1:] }()

    // Create 20 crawler goroutines to fetch each unseen link.
    for i := 0; i < 20; i++ {
        go func() {
            for link := range unseenLinks {
                foundLinks := crawl(link)
                go func() { worklist <- foundLinks }()
            }
        }()
    }

    // The main goroutine de-duplicates worklist items
    // and sends the unseen ones to the crawlers.
    seen := make(map[string]bool)
    for list := range worklist {
        for _, link := range list {
            if !seen[link] {
                seen[link] = true
                unseenLinks <- link
            }
        }
    }
}
```

The crawler goroutines are all fed by the same channel, unseenLinks. The main goroutine is responsible for de-duplicating items it receives from the worklist, and then sending each unseen one over the unseenLinks channel to a crawler goroutine.

The seen map is *confined* within the main goroutine; that is, it can be accessed only by that goroutine. Like other forms of information hiding, confinement helps us reason about the correctness of a program. For example, local variables cannot be mentioned by name from outside the function in which they are declared; variables that do not escape (§2.3.4) from a function cannot be accessed from outside that function; and encapsulated fields of an object cannot be accessed except by the methods of that object. In all cases, information hiding helps to limit unintended interactions between parts of the program.

Links found by crawl are sent to the worklist from a dedicated goroutine to avoid deadlock.

To save space, we have not addressed the problem of termination in this example.

Exercise 8.6: Add depth-limiting to the concurrent crawler. That is, if the user sets -depth=3, then only URLs reachable by at most three links will be fetched.

Exercise 8.7: Write a concurrent program that creates a local mirror of a web site, fetching each reachable page and writing it to a directory on the local disk. Only pages within the original domain (for instance, golang.org) should be fetched. URLs within mirrored pages should be altered as needed so that they refer to the mirrored page, not the original.

8.7. Multiplexing with select

The program below does the countdown for a rocket launch. The time.Tick function returns a channel on which it sends events periodically, acting like a metronome. The value of each event is a timestamp, but it is rarely as interesting as the fact of its delivery.

gopl.io/ch8/countdown1
```go
func main() {
    fmt.Println("Commencing countdown.")
    tick := time.Tick(1 * time.Second)
    for countdown := 10; countdown > 0; countdown-- {
        fmt.Println(countdown)
        <-tick
    }
    launch()
}
```

Now let's add the ability to abort the launch sequence by pressing the return key during the countdown. First, we start a goroutine that tries to read a single byte from the standard input and, if it succeeds, sends a value on a channel called abort.

gopl.io/ch8/countdown2
```go
abort := make(chan struct{})
go func() {
    os.Stdin.Read(make([]byte, 1)) // read a single byte
    abort <- struct{}{}
}()
```

Now each iteration of the countdown loop needs to wait for an event to arrive on one of the two channels: the ticker channel if everything is fine ("nominal" in NASA jargon) or an abort event if there was an "anomaly." We can't just receive from each channel because whichever operation we try first will block until completion. We need to *multiplex* these operations, and to do that, we need a *select statement*.

```go
select {
case <-ch1:
    // ...
case x := <-ch2:
    // ...use x...
case ch3 <- y:
    // ...
default:
    // ...
}
```

The general form of a select statement is shown above. Like a switch statement, it has a number of cases and an optional default. Each case specifies a *communication* (a send or receive operation on some channel) and an associated block of statements. A receive expression may appear on its own, as in the first case, or within a short variable declaration, as in the second case; the second form lets you refer to the received value.

A select waits until a communication for some case is ready to proceed. It then performs that communication and executes the case's associated statements; the other communications do not happen. A select with no cases, select{}, waits forever.

Let's return to our rocket launch program. The time.After function immediately returns a channel, and starts a new goroutine that sends a single value on that channel after the specified time. The select statement below waits until the first of two events arrives, either an abort event or the event indicating that 10 seconds have elapsed. If 10 seconds go by with no abort, the launch proceeds.

```go
func main() {
    // ...create abort channel...

    fmt.Println("Commencing countdown.  Press return to abort.")
    select {
    case <-time.After(10 * time.Second):
        // Do nothing.
    case <-abort:
        fmt.Println("Launch aborted!")
        return
    }
    launch()
}
```

The example below is more subtle. The channel ch, whose buffer size is 1, is alternately empty then full, so only one of the cases can proceed, either the send when i is even, or the receive when i is odd. It always prints 0 2 4 6 8.

```go
ch := make(chan int, 1)
for i := 0; i < 10; i++ {
    select {
    case x := <-ch:
        fmt.Println(x) // "0" "2" "4" "6" "8"
    case ch <- i:
    }
}
```

If multiple cases are ready, select picks one at random, which ensures that every channel has an equal chance of being selected. Increasing the buffer size of the previous example makes its output nondeterministic, because when the buffer is neither full nor empty, the select statement figuratively tosses a coin.

Let's make our launch program print the countdown. The select statement below causes each iteration of the loop to wait up to 1 second for an abort, but no longer.

gopl.io/ch8/countdown3

```go
func main() {
    // ...create abort channel...

    fmt.Println("Commencing countdown.  Press return to abort.")
    tick := time.Tick(1 * time.Second)
    for countdown := 10; countdown > 0; countdown-- {
        fmt.Println(countdown)
        select {
        case <-tick:
            // Do nothing.
        case <-abort:
            fmt.Println("Launch aborted!")
            return
        }
    }
    launch()
}
```

The `time.Tick` function behaves as if it creates a goroutine that calls `time.Sleep` in a loop, sending an event each time it wakes up. When the countdown function above returns, it stops receiving events from `tick`, but the ticker goroutine is still there, trying in vain to send on a channel from which no goroutine is receiving—a *goroutine leak* (§8.4.4).

The `Tick` function is convenient, but it's appropriate only when the ticks will be needed throughout the lifetime of the application. Otherwise, we should use this pattern:

```go
ticker := time.NewTicker(1 * time.Second)

<-ticker.C // receive from the ticker's channel

ticker.Stop() // cause the ticker's goroutine to terminate
```

Sometimes we want to try to send or receive on a channel but avoid blocking if the channel is not ready—a *non-blocking* communication. A select statement can do that too. A `select` may have a `default`, which specifies what to do when none of the other communications can proceed immediately.

The select statement below receives a value from the abort channel if there is one to receive; otherwise it does nothing. This is a non-blocking receive operation; doing it repeatedly is called *polling* a channel.

```go
select {
case <-abort:
    fmt.Printf("Launch aborted!\n")
    return
default:
    // do nothing
}
```

The zero value for a channel is `nil`. Perhaps surprisingly, nil channels are sometimes useful. Because send and receive operations on a nil channel block forever, a case in a select statement whose channel is nil is never selected. This lets us use `nil` to enable or disable cases that correspond to features like handling timeouts or cancellation, responding to other input events, or emitting output. We'll see an example in the next section.

Exercise 8.8: Using a select statement, add a timeout to the echo server from Section 8.3 so that it disconnects any client that shouts nothing within 10 seconds.

8.8. Example: Concurrent Directory Traversal

In this section, we'll build a program that reports the disk usage of one or more directories specified on the command line, like the Unix du command. Most of its work is done by the `walkDir` function below, which enumerates the entries of the directory `dir` using the `dirents` helper function.

gopl.io/ch8/du1

```
// walkDir recursively walks the file tree rooted at dir
// and sends the size of each found file on fileSizes.
func walkDir(dir string, fileSizes chan<- int64) {
    for _, entry := range dirents(dir) {
        if entry.IsDir() {
            subdir := filepath.Join(dir, entry.Name())
            walkDir(subdir, fileSizes)
        } else {
            fileSizes <- entry.Size()
        }
    }
}

// dirents returns the entries of directory dir.
func dirents(dir string) []os.FileInfo {
    entries, err := ioutil.ReadDir(dir)
    if err != nil {
        fmt.Fprintf(os.Stderr, "du1: %v\n", err)
        return nil
    }
    return entries
}
```

The `ioutil.ReadDir` function returns a slice of `os.FileInfo`—the same information that a call to `os.Stat` returns for a single file. For each subdirectory, `walkDir` recursively calls itself, and for each file, `walkDir` sends a message on the `fileSizes` channel. The message is the size of the file in bytes.

The main function, shown below, uses two goroutines. The background goroutine calls `walkDir` for each directory specified on the command line and finally closes the `fileSizes` channel. The main goroutine computes the sum of the file sizes it receives from the channel and finally prints the total.

```go
// The du1 command computes the disk usage of the files in a directory.
package main

import (
    "flag"
    "fmt"
    "io/ioutil"
    "os"
    "path/filepath"
)

func main() {
    // Determine the initial directories.
    flag.Parse()
    roots := flag.Args()
    if len(roots) == 0 {
        roots = []string{"."}
    }

    // Traverse the file tree.
    fileSizes := make(chan int64)
    go func() {
        for _, root := range roots {
            walkDir(root, fileSizes)
        }
        close(fileSizes)
    }()

    // Print the results.
    var nfiles, nbytes int64
    for size := range fileSizes {
        nfiles++
        nbytes += size
    }
    printDiskUsage(nfiles, nbytes)
}

func printDiskUsage(nfiles, nbytes int64) {
    fmt.Printf("%d files  %.1f GB\n", nfiles, float64(nbytes)/1e9)
}
```

This program pauses for a long while before printing its result:

```
$ go build gopl.io/ch8/du1
$ ./du1 $HOME /usr /bin /etc
213201 files  62.7 GB
```

The program would be nicer if it kept us informed of its progress. However, simply moving the printDiskUsage call into the loop would cause it to print thousands of lines of output.

The variant of du below prints the totals periodically, but only if the -v flag is specified since not all users will want to see progress messages. The background goroutine that loops over roots remains unchanged. The main goroutine now uses a ticker to generate events every

500ms, and a select statement to wait for either a file size message, in which case it updates the totals, or a tick event, in which case it prints the current totals. If the -v flag is not specified, the tick channel remains nil, and its case in the select is effectively disabled.

gopl.io/ch8/du2

```
var verbose = flag.Bool("v", false, "show verbose progress messages")

func main() {
    // ...start background goroutine...

    // Print the results periodically.
    var tick <-chan time.Time
    if *verbose {
        tick = time.Tick(500 * time.Millisecond)
    }
    var nfiles, nbytes int64
loop:
    for {
        select {
        case size, ok := <-fileSizes:
            if !ok {
                break loop // fileSizes was closed
            }
            nfiles++
            nbytes += size
        case <-tick:
            printDiskUsage(nfiles, nbytes)
        }
    }
    printDiskUsage(nfiles, nbytes) // final totals
}
```

Since the program no longer uses a range loop, the first select case must explicitly test whether the fileSizes channel has been closed, using the two-result form of receive operation. If the channel has been closed, the program breaks out of the loop. The labeled break statement breaks out of both the select and the for loop; an unlabeled break would break out of only the select, causing the loop to begin the next iteration.

The program now gives us a leisurely stream of updates:

```
$ go build gopl.io/ch8/du2
$ ./du2 -v $HOME /usr /bin /etc
28608 files   8.3 GB
54147 files   10.3 GB
93591 files   15.1 GB
127169 files   52.9 GB
175931 files   62.2 GB
213201 files   62.7 GB
```

However, it still takes too long to finish. There's no reason why all the calls to walkDir can't be done concurrently, thereby exploiting parallelism in the disk system. The third version of du, below, creates a new goroutine for each call to walkDir. It uses a sync.WaitGroup (§8.5) to count the number of calls to walkDir that are still active, and a closer goroutine to close the fileSizes channel when the counter drops to zero.

gopl.io/ch8/du3

```
func main() {
    // ...determine roots...

    // Traverse each root of the file tree in parallel.
    fileSizes := make(chan int64)
    var n sync.WaitGroup
    for _, root := range roots {
        n.Add(1)
        go walkDir(root, &n, fileSizes)
    }
    go func() {
        n.Wait()
        close(fileSizes)
    }()
    // ...select loop...
}

func walkDir(dir string, n *sync.WaitGroup, fileSizes chan<- int64) {
    defer n.Done()
    for _, entry := range dirents(dir) {
        if entry.IsDir() {
            n.Add(1)
            subdir := filepath.Join(dir, entry.Name())
            go walkDir(subdir, n, fileSizes)
        } else {
            fileSizes <- entry.Size()
        }
    }
}
```

Since this program creates many thousands of goroutines at its peak, we have to change dirents to use a counting semaphore to prevent it from opening too many files at once, just as we did for the web crawler in Section 8.6:

```
// sema is a counting semaphore for limiting concurrency in dirents.
var sema = make(chan struct{}, 20)

// dirents returns the entries of directory dir.
func dirents(dir string) []os.FileInfo {
    sema <- struct{}{}        // acquire token
    defer func() { <-sema }() // release token
    // ...
```

This version runs several times faster than the previous one, though there is a lot of variability from system to system.

Exercise 8.9: Write a version of du that computes and periodically displays separate totals for each of the root directories.

8.9. Cancellation

Sometimes we need to instruct a goroutine to stop what it is doing, for example, in a web server performing a computation on behalf of a client that has disconnected.

There is no way for one goroutine to terminate another directly, since that would leave all its shared variables in undefined states. In the rocket launch program (§8.7) we sent a single value on a channel named abort, which the countdown goroutine interpreted as a request to stop itself. But what if we need to cancel two goroutines, or an arbitrary number?

One possibility might be to send as many events on the abort channel as there are goroutines to cancel. If some of the goroutines have already terminated themselves, however, our count will be too large, and our sends will get stuck. On the other hand, if those goroutines have spawned other goroutines, our count will be too small, and some goroutines will remain unaware of the cancellation. In general, it's hard to know how many goroutines are working on our behalf at any given moment. Moreover, when a goroutine receives a value from the abort channel, it consumes that value so that other goroutines won't see it. For cancellation, what we need is a reliable mechanism to *broadcast* an event over a channel so that many goroutines can see it *as* it occurs and can later see that it *has* occurred.

Recall that after a channel has been closed and drained of all sent values, subsequent receive operations proceed immediately, yielding zero values. We can exploit this to create a broadcast mechanism: don't send a value on the channel, *close* it.

We can add cancellation to the du program from the previous section with a few simple changes. First, we create a cancellation channel on which no values are ever sent, but whose closure indicates that it is time for the program to stop what it is doing. We also define a utility function, cancelled, that checks or *polls* the cancellation state at the instant it is called.

gopl.io/ch8/du4
```go
var done = make(chan struct{})

func cancelled() bool {
    select {
    case <-done:
        return true
    default:
        return false
    }
}
```

Next, we create a goroutine that will read from the standard input, which is typically connected to the terminal. As soon as any input is read (for instance, the user presses the return key), this goroutine broadcasts the cancellation by closing the done channel.

```
// Cancel traversal when input is detected.
go func() {
    os.Stdin.Read(make([]byte, 1)) // read a single byte
    close(done)
}()
```

Now we need to make our goroutines respond to the cancellation. In the main goroutine, we add a third case to the select statement that tries to receive from the done channel. The function returns if this case is ever selected, but before it returns it must first drain the fileSizes channel, discarding all values until the channel is closed. It does this to ensure that any active calls to walkDir can run to completion without getting stuck sending to fileSizes.

```
for {
    select {
    case <-done:
        // Drain fileSizes to allow existing goroutines to finish.
        for range fileSizes {
            // Do nothing.
        }
        return
    case size, ok := <-fileSizes:
        // ...

    }
}
```

The walkDir goroutine polls the cancellation status when it begins, and returns without doing anything if the status is set. This turns all goroutines created after cancellation into no-ops:

```
func walkDir(dir string, n *sync.WaitGroup, fileSizes chan<- int64) {
    defer n.Done()
    if cancelled() {
        return
    }
    for _, entry := range dirents(dir) {
        // ...
    }
}
```

It might be profitable to poll the cancellation status again within walkDir's loop, to avoid creating goroutines after the cancellation event. Cancellation involves a trade-off; a quicker response often requires more intrusive changes to program logic. Ensuring that no expensive operations ever occur after the cancellation event may require updating many places in your code, but often most of the benefit can be obtained by checking for cancellation in a few important places.

A little profiling of this program revealed that the bottleneck was the acquisition of a semaphore token in dirents. The select below makes this operation cancellable and reduces the typical cancellation latency of the program from hundreds of milliseconds to tens:

```
func dirents(dir string) []os.FileInfo {
    select {
    case sema <- struct{}{}: // acquire token
    case <-done:
        return nil // cancelled
    }
    defer func() { <-sema }() // release token

    // ...read directory...

}
```

Now, when cancellation occurs, all the background goroutines quickly stop and the main function returns. Of course, when main returns, a program exits, so it can be hard to tell a main function that cleans up after itself from one that does not. There's a handy trick we can use during testing: if instead of returning from main in the event of cancellation, we execute a call to panic, then the runtime will dump the stack of every goroutine in the program. If the main goroutine is the only one left, then it has cleaned up after itself. But if other goroutines remain, they may not have been properly cancelled, or perhaps they have been cancelled but the cancellation takes time; a little investigation may be worthwhile. The panic dump often contains sufficient information to distinguish these cases.

Exercise 8.10: HTTP requests may be cancelled by closing the optional Cancel channel in the http.Request struct. Modify the web crawler of Section 8.6 to support cancellation.

Hint: the http.Get convenience function does not give you an opportunity to customize a Request. Instead, create the request using http.NewRequest, set its Cancel field, then perform the request by calling http.DefaultClient.Do(req).

Exercise 8.11: Following the approach of mirroredQuery in Section 8.4.4, implement a variant of fetch that requests several URLs concurrently. As soon as the first response arrives, cancel the other requests.

8.10. Example: Chat Server

We'll finish this chapter with a chat server that lets several users broadcast textual messages to each other. There are four kinds of goroutine in this program. There is one instance apiece of the main and broadcaster goroutines, and for each client connection there is one handle-Conn and one clientWriter goroutine. The broadcaster is a good illustration of how select is used, since it has to respond to three different kinds of messages.

The job of the main goroutine, shown below, is to listen for and accept incoming network connections from clients. For each one, it creates a new handleConn goroutine, just as in the concurrent echo server we saw at the start of this chapter.

gopl.io/ch8/chat

```go
func main() {
    listener, err := net.Listen("tcp", "localhost:8000")
    if err != nil {
        log.Fatal(err)
    }
    go broadcaster()
    for {
        conn, err := listener.Accept()
        if err != nil {
            log.Print(err)
            continue
        }
        go handleConn(conn)
    }
}
```

Next is the broadcaster. Its local variable clients records the current set of connected clients.
The only information recorded about each client is the identity of its outgoing message channel, about which more later.

```go
type client chan<- string // an outgoing message channel

var (
    entering = make(chan client)
    leaving  = make(chan client)
    messages = make(chan string) // all incoming client messages
)

func broadcaster() {
    clients := make(map[client]bool) // all connected clients
    for {
        select {
        case msg := <-messages:
            // Broadcast incoming message to all
            // clients' outgoing message channels.
            for cli := range clients {
                cli <- msg
            }

        case cli := <-entering:
            clients[cli] = true

        case cli := <-leaving:
            delete(clients, cli)
            close(cli)
        }
    }
}
```

The broadcaster listens on the global entering and leaving channels for announcements of
arriving and departing clients. When it receives one of these events, it updates the clients

set, and if the event was a departure, it closes the client's outgoing message channel. The broadcaster also listens for events on the global messages channel, to which each client sends all its incoming messages. When the broadcaster receives one of these events, it broadcasts the message to every connected client.

Now let's look at the per-client goroutines. The handleConn function creates a new outgoing message channel for its client and announces the arrival of this client to the broadcaster over the entering channel. Then it reads every line of text from the client, sending each line to the broadcaster over the global incoming message channel, prefixing each message with the identity of its sender. Once there is nothing more to read from the client, handleConn announces the departure of the client over the leaving channel and closes the connection.

```go
func handleConn(conn net.Conn) {
    ch := make(chan string) // outgoing client messages
    go clientWriter(conn, ch)

    who := conn.RemoteAddr().String()
    ch <- "You are " + who
    messages <- who + " has arrived"
    entering <- ch

    input := bufio.NewScanner(conn)
    for input.Scan() {
        messages <- who + ": " + input.Text()
    }
    // NOTE: ignoring potential errors from input.Err()

    leaving <- ch
    messages <- who + " has left"
    conn.Close()
}

func clientWriter(conn net.Conn, ch <-chan string) {
    for msg := range ch {
        fmt.Fprintln(conn, msg) // NOTE: ignoring network errors
    }
}
```

In addition, handleConn creates a clientWriter goroutine for each client that receives messages broadcast to the client's outgoing message channel and writes them to the client's network connection. The client writer's loop terminates when the broadcaster closes the channel after receiving a leaving notification.

The display below shows the server in action with two clients in separate windows on the same computer, using netcat to chat:

```
$ go build gopl.io/ch8/chat
$ go build gopl.io/ch8/netcat3
```

```
$ ./chat &
$ ./netcat3
You are 127.0.0.1:64208                $ ./netcat3
127.0.0.1:64211 has arrived            You are 127.0.0.1:64211
Hi!
127.0.0.1:64208: Hi!                      127.0.0.1:64208: Hi!
                                          Hi yourself.
127.0.0.1:64211: Hi yourself.             127.0.0.1:64211: Hi yourself.
^C

                                          127.0.0.1:64208 has left
$ ./netcat3
You are 127.0.0.1:64216                   127.0.0.1:64216 has arrived
                                          Welcome.
127.0.0.1:64211: Welcome.                 127.0.0.1:64211: Welcome.
                                          ^C
127.0.0.1:64211 has left
```

While hosting a chat session for n clients, this program runs $2n+2$ concurrently communicating goroutines, yet it needs no explicit locking operations (§9.2). The clients map is confined to a single goroutine, the broadcaster, so it cannot be accessed concurrently. The only variables that are shared by multiple goroutines are channels and instances of net.Conn, both of which are *concurrency safe*. We'll talk more about confinement, concurrency safety, and the implications of sharing variables across goroutines in the next chapter.

Exercise 8.12: Make the broadcaster announce the current set of clients to each new arrival. This requires that the clients set and the entering and leaving channels record the client name too.

Exercise 8.13: Make the chat server disconnect idle clients, such as those that have sent no messages in the last five minutes. Hint: calling conn.Close() in another goroutine unblocks active Read calls such as the one done by input.Scan().

Exercise 8.14: Change the chat server's network protocol so that each client provides its name on entering. Use that name instead of the network address when prefixing each message with its sender's identity.

Exercise 8.15: Failure of any client program to read data in a timely manner ultimately causes all clients to get stuck. Modify the broadcaster to skip a message rather than wait if a client writer is not ready to accept it. Alternatively, add buffering to each client's outgoing message channel so that most messages are not dropped; the broadcaster should use a non-blocking send to this channel.

9

Concurrency with Shared Variables

In the previous chapter, we presented several programs that use goroutines and channels to express concurrency in a direct and natural way. However, in doing so, we glossed over a number of important and subtle issues that programmers must bear in mind when writing concurrent code.

In this chapter, we'll take a closer look at the mechanics of concurrency. In particular, we'll point out some of the problems associated with sharing variables among multiple goroutines, the analytical techniques for recognizing those problems, and the patterns for solving them. Finally, we'll explain some of the technical differences between goroutines and operating system threads.

9.1. Race Conditions

In a sequential program, that is, a program with only one goroutine, the steps of the program happen in the familiar execution order determined by the program logic. For instance, in a sequence of statements, the first one happens before the second one, and so on. In a program with two or more goroutines, the steps within each goroutine happen in the familiar order, but in general we don't know whether an event x in one goroutine happens before an event y in another goroutine, or happens after it, or is simultaneous with it. When we cannot confidently say that one event *happens before* the other, then the events x and y are *concurrent*.

Consider a function that works correctly in a sequential program. That function is *concurrency-safe* if it continues to work correctly even when called concurrently, that is, from two or more goroutines with no additional synchronization. We can generalize this notion to a set of collaborating functions, such as the methods and operations of a particular type. A type is concurrency-safe if all its accessible methods and operations are concurrency-safe.

We can make a program concurrency-safe without making every concrete type in that program concurrency-safe. Indeed, concurrency-safe types are the exception rather than the rule, so you should access a variable concurrently only if the documentation for its type says that this is safe. We avoid concurrent access to most variables either by *confining* them to a single goroutine or by maintaining a higher-level invariant of *mutual exclusion*. We'll explain these terms in this chapter.

In contrast, exported package-level functions *are* generally expected to be concurrency-safe. Since package-level variables cannot be confined to a single goroutine, functions that modify them must enforce mutual exclusion.

There are many reasons a function might not work when called concurrently, including deadlock, livelock, and resource starvation. We don't have space to discuss all of them, so we'll focus on the most important one, the *race condition*.

A race condition is a situation in which the program does not give the correct result for some interleavings of the operations of multiple goroutines. Race conditions are pernicious because they may remain latent in a program and appear infrequently, perhaps only under heavy load or when using certain compilers, platforms, or architectures. This makes them hard to reproduce and diagnose.

It is traditional to explain the seriousness of race conditions through the metaphor of financial loss, so we'll consider a simple bank account program.

```
// Package bank implements a bank with only one account.
package bank

var balance int

func Deposit(amount int) { balance = balance + amount }

func Balance() int { return balance }
```

(We could have written the body of the Deposit function as balance += amount, which is equivalent, but the longer form will simplify the explanation.)

For a program this trivial, we can see at a glance that any sequence of calls to Deposit and Balance will give the right answer, that is, Balance will report the sum of all amounts previously deposited. However, if we call these functions not in a sequence but concurrently, Balance is no longer guaranteed to give the right answer. Consider the following two goroutines, which represent two transactions on a joint bank account:

```
// Alice:
go func() {
    bank.Deposit(200)                      // A1
    fmt.Println("=", bank.Balance()) // A2
}()
```

```
// Bob:
go bank.Deposit(100)                    // B
```

Alice deposits $200, then checks her balance, while Bob deposits $100. Since the steps A1 and A2 occur concurrently with B, we cannot predict the order in which they happen. Intuitively, it might seem that there are only three possible orderings, which we'll call "Alice first," "Bob first," and "Alice/Bob/Alice." The following table shows the value of the balance variable after each step. The quoted strings represent the printed balance slips.

```
Alice first             Bob first           Alice/Bob/Alice
        0                       0                       0
A1      200             B       100         A1      200
A2 "= 200"              A1      300         B       300
B       300             A2 "= 300"          A2 "= 300"
```

In all cases the final balance is $300. The only variation is whether Alice's balance slip includes Bob's transaction or not, but the customers are satisfied either way.

But this intuition is wrong. There is a fourth possible outcome, in which Bob's deposit occurs in the middle of Alice's deposit, after the balance has been read (balance + amount) but before it has been updated (balance = ...), causing Bob's transaction to disappear. This is because Alice's deposit operation A1 is really a sequence of two operations, a read and a write; call them A1r and A1w. Here's the problematic interleaving:

```
Data race
        0
A1r     0               ... = balance + amount
B       100
A1w     200             balance = ...
A2   "= 200"
```

After A1r, the expression balance + amount evaluates to 200, so this is the value written during A1w, despite the intervening deposit. The final balance is only $200. The bank is $100 richer at Bob's expense.

This program contains a particular kind of race condition called a *data race*. A data race occurs whenever two goroutines access the same variable concurrently and at least one of the accesses is a write.

Things get even messier if the data race involves a variable of a type that is larger than a single machine word, such as an interface, a string, or a slice. This code updates x concurrently to two slices of different lengths:

```
var x []int
go func() { x = make([]int, 10) }()
go func() { x = make([]int, 1000000) }()
x[999999] = 1 // NOTE: undefined behavior; memory corruption possible!
```

The value of x in the final statement is not defined; it could be nil, or a slice of length 10, or a slice of length 1,000,000. But recall that there are three parts to a slice: the pointer, the length, and the capacity. If the pointer comes from the first call to make and the length comes from the second, x would be a chimera, a slice whose nominal length is 1,000,000 but whose under-lying array has only 10 elements. In this eventuality, storing to element 999,999 would clobber an arbitrary faraway memory location, with consequences that are impossible to predict and hard to debug and localize. This semantic minefield is called *undefined behavior* and is well known to C programmers; fortunately it is rarely as troublesome in Go as in C.

Even the notion that a concurrent program is an interleaving of several sequential programs is a false intuition. As we'll see in Section 9.4, data races may have even stranger outcomes. Many programmers—even some very clever ones—will occasionally offer justifications for known data races in their programs: "the cost of mutual exclusion is too high," "this logic is only for logging," "I don't mind if I drop some messages," and so on. The absence of problems on a given compiler and platform may give them false confidence. A good rule of thumb is that *there is no such thing as a benign data race*. So how do we avoid data races in our programs?

We'll repeat the definition, since it is so important: A data race occurs whenever two goroutines access the same variable concurrently and at least one of the accesses is a write. It follows from this definition that there are three ways to avoid a data race.

The first way is not to write the variable. Consider the map below, which is lazily populated as each key is requested for the first time. If Icon is called sequentially, the program works fine, but if Icon is called concurrently, there is a data race accessing the map.

```
var icons = make(map[string]image.Image)

func loadIcon(name string) image.Image

// NOTE: not concurrency-safe!
func Icon(name string) image.Image {
    icon, ok := icons[name]
    if !ok {
        icon = loadIcon(name)
        icons[name] = icon
    }
    return icon
}
```

If instead we initialize the map with all necessary entries before creating additional goroutines and never modify it again, then any number of goroutines may safely call Icon concurrently since each only reads the map.

```
var icons = map[string]image.Image{
    "spades.png":   loadIcon("spades.png"),
    "hearts.png":   loadIcon("hearts.png"),
    "diamonds.png": loadIcon("diamonds.png"),
    "clubs.png":    loadIcon("clubs.png"),
}

// Concurrency-safe.
func Icon(name string) image.Image { return icons[name] }
```

In the example above, the `icons` variable is assigned during package initialization, which *happens before* the program's `main` function starts running. Once initialized, `icons` is never modified. Data structures that are never modified or are immutable are inherently concurrency-safe and need no synchronization. But obviously we can't use this approach if updates are essential, as with a bank account.

The second way to avoid a data race is to avoid accessing the variable from multiple goroutines. This is the approach taken by many of the programs in the previous chapter. For example, the main goroutine in the concurrent web crawler (§8.6) is the sole goroutine that accesses the `seen` map, and the `broadcaster` goroutine in the chat server (§8.10) is the only goroutine that accesses the `clients` map. These variables are *confined* to a single goroutine.

Since other goroutines cannot access the variable directly, they must use a channel to send the confining goroutine a request to query or update the variable. This is what is meant by the Go mantra "Do not communicate by sharing memory; instead, share memory by communicating." A goroutine that brokers access to a confined variable using channel requests is called a *monitor goroutine* for that variable. For example, the `broadcaster` goroutine monitors access to the `clients` map.

Here's the bank example rewritten with the `balance` variable confined to a monitor goroutine called `teller`:

gopl.io/ch9/bank1

```
// Package bank provides a concurrency-safe bank with one account.
package bank

var deposits = make(chan int) // send amount to deposit
var balances = make(chan int) // receive balance

func Deposit(amount int) { deposits <- amount }
func Balance() int       { return <-balances }

func teller() {
    var balance int // balance is confined to teller goroutine
    for {
        select {
        case amount := <-deposits:
            balance += amount
        case balances <- balance:
        }
    }
}

func init() {
    go teller() // start the monitor goroutine
}
```

Even when a variable cannot be confined to a single goroutine for its entire lifetime, confinement may still be a solution to the problem of concurrent access. For example, it's common to share a variable between goroutines in a pipeline by passing its address from one stage to the next over a channel. If each stage of the pipeline refrains from accessing the variable after sending it to the next stage, then all accesses to the variable are sequential. In effect, the variable is confined to one stage of the pipeline, then confined to the next, and so on. This discipline is sometimes called *serial confinement*.

In the example below, Cakes are serially confined, first to the baker goroutine, then to the icer goroutine:

```
type Cake struct{ state string }

func baker(cooked chan<- *Cake) {
    for {
        cake := new(Cake)
        cake.state = "cooked"
        cooked <- cake // baker never touches this cake again
    }
}

func icer(iced chan<- *Cake, cooked <-chan *Cake) {
    for cake := range cooked {
        cake.state = "iced"
        iced <- cake // icer never touches this cake again
    }
}
```

The third way to avoid a data race is to allow many goroutines to access the variable, but only one at a time. This approach is known as *mutual exclusion* and is the subject of the next section.

Exercise 9.1: Add a function `Withdraw(amount int) bool` to the `gopl.io/ch9/bank1` program. The result should indicate whether the transaction succeeded or failed due to insufficient funds. The message sent to the monitor goroutine must contain both the amount to withdraw and a new channel over which the monitor goroutine can send the boolean result back to `Withdraw`.

9.2. Mutual Exclusion: `sync.Mutex`

In Section 8.6, we used a buffered channel as a *counting semaphore* to ensure that no more than 20 goroutines made simultaneous HTTP requests. With the same idea, we can use a channel of capacity 1 to ensure that at most one goroutine accesses a shared variable at a time. A semaphore that counts only to 1 is called a *binary semaphore*.

gopl.io/ch9/bank2
```
var (
    sema    = make(chan struct{}, 1) // a binary semaphore guarding balance
    balance int
)
```

```go
func Deposit(amount int) {
    sema <- struct{}{} // acquire token
    balance = balance + amount
    <-sema // release token
}
func Balance() int {
    sema <- struct{}{} // acquire token
    b := balance
    <-sema // release token
    return b
}
```

This pattern of *mutual exclusion* is so useful that it is supported directly by the Mutex type from the sync package. Its Lock method acquires the token (called a *lock*) and its Unlock method releases it:

gopl.io/ch9/bank3

```go
import "sync"

var (
    mu      sync.Mutex // guards balance
    balance int
)

func Deposit(amount int) {
    mu.Lock()
    balance = balance + amount
    mu.Unlock()
}

func Balance() int {
    mu.Lock()
    b := balance
    mu.Unlock()
    return b
}
```

Each time a goroutine accesses the variables of the bank (just balance here), it must call the mutex's Lock method to acquire an exclusive lock. If some other goroutine has acquired the lock, this operation will block until the other goroutine calls Unlock and the lock becomes available again. The mutex *guards* the shared variables. By convention, the variables guarded by a mutex are declared immediately after the declaration of the mutex itself. If you deviate from this, be sure to document it.

The region of code between Lock and Unlock in which a goroutine is free to read and modify the shared variables is called a *critical section*. The lock holder's call to Unlock *happens before* any other goroutine can acquire the lock for itself. It is essential that the goroutine release the lock once it is finished, on all paths through the function, including error paths.

The bank program above exemplifies a common concurrency pattern. A set of exported functions encapsulates one or more variables so that the only way to access the variables is through these functions (or methods, for the variables of an object). Each function acquires a mutex lock at the beginning and releases it at the end, thereby ensuring that the shared variables are not accessed concurrently. This arrangement of functions, mutex lock, and variables is called a *monitor*. (This older use of the word "monitor" inspired the term "monitor goroutine." Both uses share the meaning of a broker that ensures variables are accessed sequentially.)

Since the critical sections in the `Deposit` and `Balance` functions are so short—a single line, no branching—calling `Unlock` at the end is straightforward. In more complex critical sections, especially those in which errors must be dealt with by returning early, it can be hard to tell that calls to `Lock` and `Unlock` are strictly paired on all paths. Go's `defer` statement comes to the rescue: by deferring a call to `Unlock`, the critical section implicitly extends to the end of the current function, freeing us from having to remember to insert `Unlock` calls in one or more places far from the call to `Lock`.

```
func Balance() int {
    mu.Lock()
    defer mu.Unlock()
    return balance
}
```

In the example above, the `Unlock` executes *after* the return statement has read the value of balance, so the `Balance` function is concurrency-safe. As a bonus, we no longer need the local variable b.

Furthermore, a deferred `Unlock` will run even if the critical section panics, which may be important in programs that make use of `recover` (§5.10). A `defer` is marginally more expensive than an explicit call to `Unlock`, but not enough to justify less clear code. As always with concurrent programs, favor clarity and resist premature optimization. Where possible, use `defer` and let critical sections extend to the end of a function.

Consider the `Withdraw` function below. On success, it reduces the balance by the specified amount and returns `true`. But if the account holds insufficient funds for the transaction, `Withdraw` restores the balance and returns `false`.

```
// NOTE: not atomic!
func Withdraw(amount int) bool {
    Deposit(-amount)
    if Balance() < 0 {
        Deposit(amount)
        return false // insufficient funds
    }
    return true
}
```

This function eventually gives the correct result, but it has a nasty side effect. When an excessive withdrawal is attempted, the balance transiently dips below zero. This may cause a concurrent withdrawal for a modest sum to be spuriously rejected. So if Bob tries to buy a sports car, Alice can't pay for her morning coffee. The problem is that `Withdraw` is not *atomic*: it consists of a sequence of three separate operations, each of which acquires and then releases the mutex lock, but nothing locks the whole sequence.

Ideally, `Withdraw` should acquire the mutex lock once around the whole operation. However, this attempt won't work:

```
// NOTE: incorrect!
func Withdraw(amount int) bool {
    mu.Lock()
    defer mu.Unlock()
    Deposit(-amount)
    if Balance() < 0 {
        Deposit(amount)
        return false // insufficient funds
    }
    return true
}
```

`Deposit` tries to acquire the mutex lock a second time by calling `mu.Lock()`, but because mutex locks are not *re-entrant*—it's not possible to lock a mutex that's already locked—this leads to a deadlock where nothing can proceed, and `Withdraw` blocks forever.

There is a good reason Go's mutexes are not re-entrant. The purpose of a mutex is to ensure that certain invariants of the shared variables are maintained at critical points during program execution. One of the invariants is "no goroutine is accessing the shared variables," but there may be additional invariants specific to the data structures that the mutex guards. When a goroutine acquires a mutex lock, it may assume that the invariants hold. While it holds the lock, it may update the shared variables so that the invariants are temporarily violated. However, when it releases the lock, it must guarantee that order has been restored and the invariants hold once again. Although a re-entrant mutex would ensure that no other goroutines are accessing the shared variables, it cannot protect the additional invariants of those variables.

A common solution is to divide a function such as `Deposit` into two: an unexported function, `deposit`, that assumes the lock is already held and does the real work, and an exported function `Deposit` that acquires the lock before calling `deposit`. We can then express `Withdraw` in terms of `deposit` like this:

```
func Withdraw(amount int) bool {
    mu.Lock()
    defer mu.Unlock()
    deposit(-amount)
    if balance < 0 {
        deposit(amount)
        return false // insufficient funds
    }
    return true
}
```

```go
func Deposit(amount int) {
    mu.Lock()
    defer mu.Unlock()
    deposit(amount)
}

func Balance() int {
    mu.Lock()
    defer mu.Unlock()
    return balance
}

// This function requires that the lock be held.
func deposit(amount int) { balance += amount }
```

Of course, the deposit function shown here is so trivial that a realistic Withdraw function wouldn't bother calling it, but nonetheless it illustrates the principle.

Encapsulation (§6.6), by reducing unexpected interactions in a program, helps us maintain data structure invariants. For the same reason, encapsulation also helps us maintain concurrency invariants. When you use a mutex, make sure that both it and the variables it guards are not exported, whether they are package-level variables or the fields of a struct.

9.3. Read/Write Mutexes: sync.RWMutex

In a fit of anxiety after seeing his $100 deposit vanish without a trace, Bob writes a program to check his bank balance hundreds of times a second. He runs it at home, at work, and on his phone. The bank notices that the increased traffic is delaying deposits and withdrawals, because all the Balance requests run sequentially, holding the lock exclusively and temporarily preventing other goroutines from running.

Since the Balance function only needs to *read* the state of the variable, it would in fact be safe for multiple Balance calls to run concurrently, so long as no Deposit or Withdraw call is running. In this scenario we need a special kind of lock that allows read-only operations to proceed in parallel with each other, but write operations to have fully exclusive access. This lock is called a *multiple readers, single writer* lock, and in Go it's provided by sync.RWMutex:

```go
var mu sync.RWMutex
var balance int

func Balance() int {
    mu.RLock() // readers lock
    defer mu.RUnlock()
    return balance
}
```

The Balance function now calls the RLock and RUnlock methods to acquire and release a *readers* or *shared* lock. The Deposit function, which is unchanged, calls the mu.Lock and mu.Unlock methods to acquire and release a *writer* or *exclusive* lock.

After this change, most of Bob's `Balance` requests run in parallel with each other and finish more quickly. The lock is available for more of the time, and `Deposit` requests can proceed in a timely manner.

`RLock` can be used only if there are no writes to shared variables in the critical section. In general, we should not assume that *logically* read-only functions or methods don't also update some variables. For example, a method that appears to be a simple accessor might also increment an internal usage counter, or update a cache so that repeat calls are faster. If in doubt, use an exclusive `Lock`.

It's only profitable to use an `RWMutex` when most of the goroutines that acquire the lock are readers, and the lock is under *contention*, that is, goroutines routinely have to wait to acquire it. An `RWMutex` requires more complex internal bookkeeping, making it slower than a regular mutex for uncontended locks.

9.4. Memory Synchronization

You may wonder why the `Balance` method needs mutual exclusion, either channel-based or mutex-based. After all, unlike `Deposit`, it consists only of a single operation, so there is no danger of another goroutine executing "in the middle" of it. There are two reasons we need a mutex. The first is that it's equally important that `Balance` not execute in the middle of some other operation like `Withdraw`. The second (and more subtle) reason is that synchronization is about more than just the order of execution of multiple goroutines; synchronization also affects memory.

In a modern computer there may be dozens of processors, each with its own local cache of the main memory. For efficiency, writes to memory are buffered within each processor and flushed out to main memory only when necessary. They may even be committed to main memory in a different order than they were written by the writing goroutine. Synchronization primitives like channel communications and mutex operations cause the processor to flush out and commit all its accumulated writes so that the effects of goroutine execution up to that point are guaranteed to be visible to goroutines running on other processors.

Consider the possible outputs of the following snippet of code:

```
var x, y int
go func() {
    x = 1                    // A1
    fmt.Print("y:", y, " ") // A2
}()
go func() {
    y = 1                    // B1
    fmt.Print("x:", x, " ") // B2
}()
```

Since these two goroutines are concurrent and access shared variables without mutual exclusion, there is a data race, so we should not be surprised that the program is not deterministic. We might expect it to print any one of these four results, which correspond to intuitive interleavings of the labeled statements of the program:

```
y:0 x:1
x:0 y:1
x:1 y:1
y:1 x:1
```

The fourth line could be explained by the sequence A1,B1,A2,B2 or by B1,A1,A2,B2, for example. However, these two outcomes might come as a surprise:

```
x:0 y:0
y:0 x:0
```

but depending on the compiler, CPU, and many other factors, they can happen too. What possible interleaving of the four statements could explain them?

Within a single goroutine, the effects of each statement are guaranteed to occur in the order of execution; goroutines are *sequentially consistent*. But in the absence of explicit synchronization using a channel or mutex, there is no guarantee that events are seen in the same order by all goroutines. Although goroutine *A* must observe the effect of the write x = 1 before it reads the value of y, it does not necessarily observe the write to y done by goroutine *B*, so *A* may print a *stale* value of y.

It is tempting to try to understand concurrency as if it corresponds to *some* interleaving of the statements of each goroutine, but as the example above shows, this is not how a modern compiler or CPU works. Because the assignment and the Print refer to different variables, a compiler may conclude that the order of the two statements cannot affect the result, and swap them. If the two goroutines execute on different CPUs, each with its own cache, writes by one goroutine are not visible to the other goroutine's Print until the caches are synchronized with main memory.

All these concurrency problems can be avoided by the consistent use of simple, established patterns. Where possible, confine variables to a single goroutine; for all other variables, use mutual exclusion.

9.5. Lazy Initialization: sync.Once

It is good practice to defer an expensive initialization step until the moment it is needed. Initializing a variable up front increases the start-up latency of a program and is unnecessary if execution doesn't always reach the part of the program that uses that variable. Let's return to the icons variable we saw earlier in the chapter:

```
var icons map[string]image.Image
```

This version of Icon uses *lazy initialization*:

```go
func loadIcons() {
    icons = map[string]image.Image{
        "spades.png":   loadIcon("spades.png"),
        "hearts.png":   loadIcon("hearts.png"),
        "diamonds.png": loadIcon("diamonds.png"),
        "clubs.png":    loadIcon("clubs.png"),
    }
}

// NOTE: not concurrency-safe!
func Icon(name string) image.Image {
    if icons == nil {
        loadIcons() // one-time initialization
    }
    return icons[name]
}
```

For a variable accessed by only a single goroutine, we can use the pattern above, but this pattern is not safe if Icon is called concurrently. Like the bank's original Deposit function, Icon consists of multiple steps: it tests whether icons is nil, then it loads the icons, then it updates icons to a non-nil value. Intuition might suggest that the worst possible outcome of the race condition above is that the loadIcons function is called several times. While the first goroutine is busy loading the icons, another goroutine entering Icon would find the variable still equal to nil, and would also call loadIcons.

But this intuition is also wrong. (We hope that by now you are developing a new intuition about concurrency, that intuitions about concurrency are not to be trusted!) Recall the discussion of memory from Section 9.4. In the absence of explicit synchronization, the compiler and CPU are free to reorder accesses to memory in any number of ways, so long as the behavior of each goroutine is sequentially consistent. One possible reordering of the statements of loadIcons is shown below. It stores the empty map in the icons variable before populating it:

```go
func loadIcons() {
    icons = make(map[string]image.Image)
    icons["spades.png"] = loadIcon("spades.png")
    icons["hearts.png"] = loadIcon("hearts.png")
    icons["diamonds.png"] = loadIcon("diamonds.png")
    icons["clubs.png"] = loadIcon("clubs.png")
}
```

Consequently, a goroutine finding icons to be non-nil may not assume that the initialization of the variable is complete.

The simplest correct way to ensure that all goroutines observe the effects of loadIcons is to synchronize them using a mutex:

```go
var mu sync.Mutex // guards icons
var icons map[string]image.Image
```

```
// Concurrency-safe.
func Icon(name string) image.Image {
    mu.Lock()
    defer mu.Unlock()
    if icons == nil {
        loadIcons()
    }
    return icons[name]
}
```

However, the cost of enforcing mutually exclusive access to icons is that two goroutines cannot access the variable concurrently, even once the variable has been safely initialized and will
never be modified again. This suggests a multiple-readers lock:

```
var mu sync.RWMutex // guards icons
var icons map[string]image.Image

// Concurrency-safe.
func Icon(name string) image.Image {
    mu.RLock()
    if icons != nil {
        icon := icons[name]
        mu.RUnlock()
        return icon
    }
    mu.RUnlock()

    // acquire an exclusive lock
    mu.Lock()
    if icons == nil { // NOTE: must recheck for nil
        loadIcons()
    }
    icon := icons[name]
    mu.Unlock()
    return icon
}
```

There are now two critical sections. The goroutine first acquires a reader lock, consults the
map, then releases the lock. If an entry was found (the common case), it is returned. If no
entry was found, the goroutine acquires a writer lock. There is no way to upgrade a shared
lock to an exclusive one without first releasing the shared lock, so we must recheck the icons
variable in case another goroutine already initialized it in the interim.

The pattern above gives us greater concurrency but is complex and thus error-prone.
Fortunately, the sync package provides a specialized solution to the problem of one-time initialization: sync.Once. Conceptually, a Once consists of a mutex and a boolean variable that
records whether initialization has taken place; the mutex guards both the boolean and the
client's data structures. The sole method, Do, accepts the initialization function as its argument. Let's use Once to simplify the Icon function:

```
var loadIconsOnce sync.Once
var icons map[string]image.Image

// Concurrency-safe.
func Icon(name string) image.Image {
    loadIconsOnce.Do(loadIcons)
    return icons[name]
}
```

Each call to `Do(loadIcons)` locks the mutex and checks the boolean variable. In the first call, in which the variable is false, `Do` calls `loadIcons` and sets the variable to true. Subsequent calls do nothing, but the mutex synchronization ensures that the effects of `loadIcons` on memory (specifically, `icons`) become visible to all goroutines. Using `sync.Once` in this way, we can avoid sharing variables with other goroutines until they have been properly constructed.

Exercise 9.2: Rewrite the `PopCount` example from Section 2.6.2 so that it initializes the lookup table using `sync.Once` the first time it is needed. (Realistically, the cost of synchronization would be prohibitive for a small and highly optimized function like `PopCount`.)

9.6. The Race Detector

Even with the greatest of care, it's all too easy to make concurrency mistakes. Fortunately, the Go runtime and toolchain are equipped with a sophisticated and easy-to-use dynamic analysis tool, the *race detector*.

Just add the `-race` flag to your go `build`, go `run`, or go `test` command. This causes the compiler to build a modified version of your application or test with additional instrumentation that effectively records all accesses to shared variables that occurred during execution, along with the identity of the goroutine that read or wrote the variable. In addition, the modified program records all synchronization events, such as go statements, channel operations, and calls to `(*sync.Mutex).Lock`, `(*sync.WaitGroup).Wait`, and so on. (The complete set of synchronization events is specified by the *The Go Memory Model* document that accompanies the language specification.)

The race detector studies this stream of events, looking for cases in which one goroutine reads or writes a shared variable that was most recently written by a different goroutine without an intervening synchronization operation. This indicates a concurrent access to the shared variable, and thus a data race. The tool prints a report that includes the identity of the variable, and the stacks of active function calls in the reading goroutine and the writing goroutine. This is usually sufficient to pinpoint the problem. Section 9.7 contains an example of the race detector in action.

The race detector reports all data races that were actually executed. However, it can only detect race conditions that occur during a run; it cannot prove that none will ever occur. For best results, make sure that your tests exercise your packages using concurrency.

Due to extra bookkeeping, a program built with race detection needs more time and memory to run, but the overhead is tolerable even for many production jobs. For infrequently occurring race conditions, letting the race detector do its job can save hours or days of debugging.

9.7. Example: Concurrent Non-Blocking Cache

In this section, we'll build a *concurrent non-blocking cache*, an abstraction that solves a problem that arises often in real-world concurrent programs but is not well addressed by existing libraries. This is the problem of *memoizing* a function, that is, caching the result of a function so that it need be computed only once. Our solution will be concurrency-safe and will avoid the contention associated with designs based on a single lock for the whole cache.

We'll use the `httpGetBody` function below as an example of the type of function we might want to memoize. It makes an HTTP GET request and reads the request body. Calls to this function are relatively expensive, so we'd like to avoid repeating them unnecessarily.

```
func httpGetBody(url string) (interface{}, error) {
    resp, err := http.Get(url)
    if err != nil {
        return nil, err
    }
    defer resp.Body.Close()
    return ioutil.ReadAll(resp.Body)
}
```

The final line hides a minor subtlety. `ReadAll` returns two results, a `[]byte` and an `error`, but since these are assignable to the declared result types of `httpGetBody`—`interface{}` and `error`, respectively—we can return the result of the call without further ado. We chose this return type for `httpGetBody` so that it conforms to the type of functions that our cache is designed to memoize.

Here's the first draft of the cache:

gopl.io/ch9/memo1
```
// Package memo provides a concurrency-unsafe
// memoization of a function of type Func.
package memo

// A Memo caches the results of calling a Func.
type Memo struct {
    f     Func
    cache map[string]result
}

// Func is the type of the function to memoize.
type Func func(key string) (interface{}, error)
```

```
type result struct {
    value interface{}
    err    error
}

func New(f Func) *Memo {
    return &Memo{f: f, cache: make(map[string]result)}
}

// NOTE: not concurrency-safe!
func (memo *Memo) Get(key string) (interface{}, error) {
    res, ok := memo.cache[key]
    if !ok {
        res.value, res.err = memo.f(key)
        memo.cache[key] = res
    }
    return res.value, res.err
}
```

A `Memo` instance holds the function `f` to memoize, of type `Func`, and the cache, which is a mapping from strings to `result`s. Each `result` is simply the pair of results returned by a call to `f`—a value and an error. We'll show several variations of `Memo` as the design progresses, but all will share these basic aspects.

An example of how to use `Memo` appears below. For each element in a stream of incoming URLs, we call `Get`, logging the latency of the call and the amount of data it returns:

```
m := memo.New(httpGetBody)
for url := range incomingURLs() {
    start := time.Now()
    value, err := m.Get(url)
    if err != nil {
        log.Print(err)
    }
    fmt.Printf("%s, %s, %d bytes\n",
        url, time.Since(start), len(value.([]byte)))
}
```

We can use the `testing` package (the topic of Chapter 11) to systematically investigate the effect of memoization. From the test output below, we see that the URL stream contains duplicates, and that although the first call to `(*Memo).Get` for each URL takes hundreds of milliseconds, the second request returns the same amount of data in under a millisecond.

```
$ go test -v gopl.io/ch9/memo1
=== RUN   Test
https://golang.org, 175.026418ms, 7537 bytes
https://godoc.org, 172.686825ms, 6878 bytes
https://play.golang.org, 115.762377ms, 5767 bytes
http://gopl.io, 749.887242ms, 2856 bytes
```

```
https://golang.org, 721ns, 7537 bytes
https://godoc.org, 152ns, 6878 bytes
https://play.golang.org, 205ns, 5767 bytes
http://gopl.io, 326ns, 2856 bytes
--- PASS: Test (1.21s)
PASS
ok  gopl.io/ch9/memo1   1.257s
```

This test executes all calls to Get sequentially.

Since HTTP requests are a great opportunity for parallelism, let's change the test so that it makes all requests concurrently. The test uses a sync.WaitGroup to wait until the last request is complete before returning.

```
m := memo.New(httpGetBody)
var n sync.WaitGroup
for url := range incomingURLs() {
    n.Add(1)
    go func(url string) {
        start := time.Now()
        value, err := m.Get(url)
        if err != nil {
            log.Print(err)
        }
        fmt.Printf("%s, %s, %d bytes\n",
            url, time.Since(start), len(value.([]byte)))
        n.Done()
    }(url)
}
n.Wait()
```

The test runs much faster, but unfortunately it is unlikely to work correctly all the time. We may notice unexpected cache misses, or cache hits that return incorrect values, or even crashes.

Worse, it is likely to work correctly *some* of the time, so we may not even notice that it has a problem. But if we run it with the -race flag, the race detector (§9.6) often prints a report such as this one:

```
$ go test -run=TestConcurrent -race -v gopl.io/ch9/memo1
=== RUN   TestConcurrent
...
WARNING: DATA RACE
Write by goroutine 36:
  runtime.mapassign1()
      ~/go/src/runtime/hashmap.go:411 +0x0
  gopl.io/ch9/memo1.(*Memo).Get()
      ~/gobook2/src/gopl.io/ch9/memo1/memo.go:32 +0x205
  ...
```

```
Previous write by goroutine 35:
  runtime.mapassign1()
      ~/go/src/runtime/hashmap.go:411 +0x0
  gopl.io/ch9/memo1.(*Memo).Get()
      ~/gobook2/src/gopl.io/ch9/memo1/memo.go:32 +0x205
...
Found 1 data race(s)
FAIL    gopl.io/ch9/memo1    2.393s
```

The reference to `memo.go:32` tells us that two goroutines have updated the `cache` map without any intervening synchronization. `Get` is not concurrency-safe: it has a data race.

```
28  func (memo *Memo) Get(key string) (interface{}, error) {
29      res, ok := memo.cache[key]
30      if !ok {
31          res.value, res.err = memo.f(key)
32          memo.cache[key] = res
33      }
34      return res.value, res.err
35  }
```

The simplest way to make the cache concurrency-safe is to use monitor-based synchronization. All we need to do is add a mutex to the `Memo`, acquire the mutex lock at the start of `Get`, and release it before `Get` returns, so that the two `cache` operations occur within the critical section:

gopl.io/ch9/memo2

```
type Memo struct {
    f     Func
    mu    sync.Mutex // guards cache
    cache map[string]result
}

// Get is concurrency-safe.
func (memo *Memo) Get(key string) (value interface{}, err error) {
    memo.mu.Lock()
    res, ok := memo.cache[key]
    if !ok {
        res.value, res.err = memo.f(key)
        memo.cache[key] = res
    }
    memo.mu.Unlock()
    return res.value, res.err
}
```

Now the race detector is silent, even when running the tests concurrently. Unfortunately this change to `Memo` reverses our earlier performance gains. By holding the lock for the duration of each call to `f`, `Get` serializes all the I/O operations we intended to parallelize. What we need is a *non-blocking* cache, one that does not serialize calls to the function it memoizes.

In the next implementation of Get, below, the calling goroutine acquires the lock twice: once for the lookup, and then a second time for the update if the lookup returned nothing. In between, other goroutines are free to use the cache.

gopl.io/ch9/memo3

```go
func (memo *Memo) Get(key string) (value interface{}, err error) {
    memo.mu.Lock()
    res, ok := memo.cache[key]
    memo.mu.Unlock()
    if !ok {
        res.value, res.err = memo.f(key)

        // Between the two critical sections, several goroutines
        // may race to compute f(key) and update the map.
        memo.mu.Lock()
        memo.cache[key] = res
        memo.mu.Unlock()
    }
    return res.value, res.err
}
```

The performance improves again, but now we notice that some URLs are being fetched twice. This happens when two or more goroutines call Get for the same URL at about the same time. Both consult the cache, find no value there, and then call the slow function f. Then both of them update the map with the result they obtained. One of the results is overwritten by the other.

Ideally we'd like to avoid this redundant work. This feature is sometimes called *duplicate suppression*. In the version of Memo below, each map element is a pointer to an entry struct. Each entry contains the memoized result of a call to the function f, as before, but it additionally contains a channel called ready. Just after the entry's result has been set, this channel will be closed, to *broadcast* (§8.9) to any other goroutines that it is now safe for them to read the result from the entry.

gopl.io/ch9/memo4

```go
type entry struct {
    res   result
    ready chan struct{} // closed when res is ready
}

func New(f Func) *Memo {
    return &Memo{f: f, cache: make(map[string]*entry)}
}

type Memo struct {
    f     Func
    mu    sync.Mutex // guards cache
    cache map[string]*entry
}
```

```
func (memo *Memo) Get(key string) (value interface{}, err error) {
    memo.mu.Lock()
    e := memo.cache[key]
    if e == nil {
        // This is the first request for this key.
        // This goroutine becomes responsible for computing
        // the value and broadcasting the ready condition.
        e = &entry{ready: make(chan struct{})}
        memo.cache[key] = e
        memo.mu.Unlock()

        e.res.value, e.res.err = memo.f(key)

        close(e.ready) // broadcast ready condition
    } else {
        // This is a repeat request for this key.
        memo.mu.Unlock()

        <-e.ready // wait for ready condition
    }
    return e.res.value, e.res.err
}
```

A call to Get now involves acquiring the mutex lock that guards the cache map, looking in the map for a pointer to an existing entry, allocating and inserting a new entry if none was found, then releasing the lock. If there was an existing entry, its value is not necessarily ready yet—another goroutine could still be calling the slow function f—so the calling goroutine must wait for the entry's "ready" condition before it reads the entry's result. It does this by reading a value from the ready channel, since this operation blocks until the channel is closed.

If there was no existing entry, then by inserting a new "not ready" entry into the map, the current goroutine becomes responsible for invoking the slow function, updating the entry, and broadcasting the readiness of the new entry to any other goroutines that might (by then) be waiting for it.

Notice that the variables e.res.value and e.res.err in the entry are shared among multiple goroutines. The goroutine that creates the entry sets their values, and other goroutines read their values once the "ready" condition has been broadcast. Despite being accessed by multiple goroutines, no mutex lock is necessary. The closing of the ready channel *happens before* any other goroutine receives the broadcast event, so the write to those variables in the first goroutine *happens before* they are read by subsequent goroutines. There is no data race.

Our concurrent, duplicate-suppressing, non-blocking cache is complete.

The implementation of Memo above uses a mutex to guard a map variable that is shared by each goroutine that calls Get. It's interesting to contrast this design with an alternative one in which the map variable is confined to a *monitor goroutine* to which callers of Get must send a message.

The declarations of Func, result, and entry remain as before:

```
// Func is the type of the function to memoize.
type Func func(key string) (interface{}, error)

// A result is the result of calling a Func.
type result struct {
    value interface{}
    err   error
}

type entry struct {
    res   result
    ready chan struct{} // closed when res is ready
}
```

However, the Memo type now consists of a channel, requests, through which the caller of Get communicates with the monitor goroutine. The element type of the channel is a request. Using this structure, the caller of Get sends the monitor goroutine both the key, that is, the argument to the memoized function, and another channel, response, over which the result should be sent back when it becomes available. This channel will carry only a single value.

gopl.io/ch9/memo5

```
// A request is a message requesting that the Func be applied to key.
type request struct {
    key      string
    response chan<- result // the client wants a single result
}

type Memo struct{ requests chan request }

// New returns a memoization of f.  Clients must subsequently call Close.
func New(f Func) *Memo {
    memo := &Memo{requests: make(chan request)}
    go memo.server(f)
    return memo
}

func (memo *Memo) Get(key string) (interface{}, error) {
    response := make(chan result)
    memo.requests <- request{key, response}
    res := <-response
    return res.value, res.err
}

func (memo *Memo) Close() { close(memo.requests) }
```

The Get method, above, creates a response channel, puts it in the request, sends it to the monitor goroutine, then immediately receives from it.

The cache variable is confined to the monitor goroutine (*Memo).server, shown below. The monitor reads requests in a loop until the request channel is closed by the Close method. For each request, it consults the cache, creating and inserting a new entry if none was found.

```go
func (memo *Memo) server(f Func) {
    cache := make(map[string]*entry)
    for req := range memo.requests {
        e := cache[req.key]
        if e == nil {
            // This is the first request for this key.
            e = &entry{ready: make(chan struct{})}
            cache[req.key] = e
            go e.call(f, req.key) // call f(key)
        }
        go e.deliver(req.response)
    }
}

func (e *entry) call(f Func, key string) {
    // Evaluate the function.
    e.res.value, e.res.err = f(key)
    // Broadcast the ready condition.
    close(e.ready)
}

func (e *entry) deliver(response chan<- result) {
    // Wait for the ready condition.
    <-e.ready
    // Send the result to the client.
    response <- e.res
}
```

In a similar manner to the mutex-based version, the first request for a given key becomes responsible for calling the function f on that key, storing the result in the entry, and broadcasting the readiness of the entry by closing the ready channel. This is done by (*entry).call.

A subsequent request for the same key finds the existing entry in the map, waits for the result to become ready, and sends the result through the response channel to the client goroutine that called Get. This is done by (*entry).deliver. The call and deliver methods must be called in their own goroutines to ensure that the monitor goroutine does not stop processing new requests.

This example shows that it's possible to build many concurrent structures using either of the two approaches—shared variables and locks, or communicating sequential processes—without excessive complexity.

It's not always obvious which approach is preferable in a given situation, but it's worth knowing how they correspond. Sometimes switching from one approach to the other can make your code simpler.

Exercise 9.3: Extend the Func type and the (*Memo).Get method so that callers may provide an optional done channel through which they can cancel the operation (§8.9). The results of a cancelled Func call should not be cached.

9.8. Goroutines and Threads

In the previous chapter we said that the difference between goroutines and operating system (OS) threads could be ignored until later. Although the differences between them are essentially quantitative, a big enough quantitative difference becomes a qualitative one, and so it is with goroutines and threads. The time has now come to distinguish them.

9.8.1. Growable Stacks

Each OS thread has a fixed-size block of memory (often as large as 2MB) for its *stack*, the work area where it saves the local variables of function calls that are in progress or temporarily suspended while another function is called. This fixed-size stack is simultaneously too much and too little. A 2MB stack would be a huge waste of memory for a little goroutine, such as one that merely waits for a `WaitGroup` then closes a channel. It's not uncommon for a Go program to create hundreds of thousands of goroutines at one time, which would be impossible with stacks this large. Yet despite their size, fixed-size stacks are not always big enough for the most complex and deeply recursive of functions. Changing the fixed size can improve space efficiency and allow more threads to be created, or it can enable more deeply recursive functions, but it cannot do both.

In contrast, a goroutine starts life with a small stack, typically 2KB. A goroutine's stack, like the stack of an OS thread, holds the local variables of active and suspended function calls, but unlike an OS thread, a goroutine's stack is not fixed; it grows and shrinks as needed. The size limit for a goroutine stack may be as much as 1GB, orders of magnitude larger than a typical fixed-size thread stack, though of course few goroutines use that much.

Exercise 9.4: Construct a pipeline that connects an arbitrary number of goroutines with channels. What is the maximum number of pipeline stages you can create without running out of memory? How long does a value take to transit the entire pipeline?

9.8.2. Goroutine Scheduling

OS threads are scheduled by the OS kernel. Every few milliseconds, a hardware timer interrupts the processor, which causes a kernel function called the *scheduler* to be invoked. This function suspends the currently executing thread and saves its registers in memory, looks over the list of threads and decides which one should run next, restores that thread's registers from memory, then resumes the execution of that thread. Because OS threads are scheduled by the kernel, passing control from one thread to another requires a full *context switch*, that is, saving the state of one user thread to memory, restoring the state of another, and updating the scheduler's data structures. This operation is slow, due to its poor locality and the number of memory accesses required, and has historically only gotten worse as the number of CPU cycles required to access memory has increased.

The Go runtime contains its own scheduler that uses a technique known as *m:n scheduling*, because it multiplexes (or schedules) *m* goroutines on *n* OS threads. The job of the Go scheduler is analogous to that of the kernel scheduler, but it is concerned only with the goroutines of a single Go program.

Unlike the operating system's thread scheduler, the Go scheduler is not invoked periodically by a hardware timer, but implicitly by certain Go language constructs. For example, when a goroutine calls `time.Sleep` or blocks in a channel or mutex operation, the scheduler puts it to sleep and runs another goroutine until it is time to wake the first one up. Because it doesn't need a switch to kernel context, rescheduling a goroutine is much cheaper than rescheduling a thread.

Exercise 9.5: Write a program with two goroutines that send messages back and forth over two unbuffered channels in ping-pong fashion. How many communications per second can the program sustain?

9.8.3. GOMAXPROCS

The Go scheduler uses a parameter called GOMAXPROCS to determine how many OS threads may be actively executing Go code simultaneously. Its default value is the number of CPUs on the machine, so on a machine with 8 CPUs, the scheduler will schedule Go code on up to 8 OS threads at once. (GOMAXPROCS is the *n* in *m:n* scheduling.) Goroutines that are sleeping or blocked in a communication do not need a thread at all. Goroutines that are blocked in I/O or other system calls or are calling non-Go functions, do need an OS thread, but GOMAXPROCS need not account for them.

You can explicitly control this parameter using the GOMAXPROCS environment variable or the `runtime.GOMAXPROCS` function. We can see the effect of GOMAXPROCS on this little program, which prints an endless stream of zeros and ones:

```
for {
    go fmt.Print(0)
    fmt.Print(1)
}

$ GOMAXPROCS=1 go run hacker-cliché.go
111111111111111111111000000000000000000000011111...

$ GOMAXPROCS=2 go run hacker-cliché.go
010101010101010101011001100101011010010100110...
```

In the first run, at most one goroutine was executed at a time. Initially, it was the main goroutine, which prints ones. After a period of time, the Go scheduler put it to sleep and woke up the goroutine that prints zeros, giving it a turn to run on the OS thread. In the second run, there were two OS threads available, so both goroutines ran simultaneously, printing digits at about the same rate. We must stress that many factors are involved in goroutine scheduling, and the runtime is constantly evolving, so your results may differ from the ones above.

Exercise 9.6: Measure how the performance of a compute-bound parallel program (see Exercise 8.5) varies with GOMAXPROCS. What is the optimal value on your computer? How many CPUs does your computer have?

9.8.4. Goroutines Have No Identity

In most operating systems and programming languages that support multithreading, the current thread has a distinct identity that can be easily obtained as an ordinary value, typically an integer or pointer. This makes it easy to build an abstraction called *thread-local storage*, which is essentially a global map keyed by thread identity, so that each thread can store and retrieve values independent of other threads.

Goroutines have no notion of identity that is accessible to the programmer. This is by design, since thread-local storage tends to be abused. For example, in a web server implemented in a language with thread-local storage, it's common for many functions to find information about the HTTP request on whose behalf they are currently working by looking in that storage. However, just as with programs that rely excessively on global variables, this can lead to an unhealthy "action at a distance" in which the behavior of a function is not determined by its arguments alone, but by the identity of the thread in which it runs. Consequently, if the identity of the thread should change—some worker threads are enlisted to help, say—the function misbehaves mysteriously.

Go encourages a simpler style of programming in which parameters that affect the behavior of a function are explicit. Not only does this make programs easier to read, but it lets us freely assign subtasks of a given function to many different goroutines without worrying about their identity.

You've now learned about all the language features you need for writing Go programs. In the next two chapters, we'll step back to look at some of the practices and tools that support programming in the large: how to structure a project as a set of packages, and how to obtain, build, test, benchmark, profile, document, and share those packages.

10

Packages and the Go Tool

A modest-size program today might contain 10,000 functions. Yet its author need think about only a few of them and design even fewer, because the vast majority were written by others and made available for reuse through *packages*.

Go comes with over 100 standard packages that provide the foundations for most applications. The Go community, a thriving ecosystem of package design, sharing, reuse, and improvement, has published many more, and you can find a searchable index of them at http://godoc.org. In this chapter, we'll show how to use existing packages and create new ones.

Go also comes with the go tool, a sophisticated but simple-to-use command for managing workspaces of Go packages. Since the beginning of the book, we've been showing how to use the go tool to download, build, and run example programs. In this chapter, we'll look at the tool's underlying concepts and tour more of its capabilities, which include printing documentation and querying metadata about the packages in the workspace. In the next chapter we'll explore its testing features.

10.1. Introduction

The purpose of any package system is to make the design and maintenance of large programs practical by grouping related features together into units that can be easily understood and changed, independent of the other packages of the program. This *modularity* allows packages to be shared and reused by different projects, distributed within an organization, or made available to the wider world.

Each package defines a distinct name space that encloses its identifiers. Each name is associated with a particular package, letting us choose short, clear names for the types, functions, and so on that we use most often, without creating conflicts with other parts of the program.

Packages also provide *encapsulation* by controlling which names are visible or exported outside the package. Restricting the visibility of package members hides the helper functions and types behind the package's API, allowing the package maintainer to change the implementation with confidence that no code outside the package will be affected. Restricting visibility also hides variables so that clients can access and update them only through exported functions that preserve internal invariants or enforce mutual exclusion in a concurrent program.

When we change a file, we must recompile the file's package and potentially all the packages that depend on it. Go compilation is notably faster than most other compiled languages, even when building from scratch. There are three main reasons for the compiler's speed. First, all imports must be explicitly listed at the beginning of each source file, so the compiler does not have to read and process an entire file to determine its dependencies. Second, the dependencies of a package form a directed acyclic graph, and because there are no cycles, packages can be compiled separately and perhaps in parallel. Finally, the object file for a compiled Go package records export information not just for the package itself, but for its dependencies too. When compiling a package, the compiler must read one object file for each import but need not look beyond these files.

10.2. Import Paths

Each package is identified by a unique string called its *import path*. Import paths are the strings that appear in `import` declarations.

```
import (
    "fmt"
    "math/rand"
    "encoding/json"

    "golang.org/x/net/html"

    "github.com/go-sql-driver/mysql"
)
```

As we mentioned in Section 2.6.1, the Go language specification doesn't define the meaning of these strings or how to determine a package's import path, but leaves these issues to the tools. In this chapter, we'll take a detailed look at how the go tool interprets them, since that's what the majority of Go programmers use for building, testing, and so on. Other tools do exist, though. For example, Go programmers using Google's internal multi-language build system follow different rules for naming and locating packages, specifying tests, and so on, that more closely match the conventions of that system.

For packages you intend to share or publish, import paths should be globally unique. To avoid conflicts, the import paths of all packages other than those from the standard library should start with the Internet domain name of the organization that owns or hosts the package; this also makes it possible to find packages. For example, the declaration above imports an HTML parser maintained by the Go team and a popular third-party MySQL database driver.

10.3. The Package Declaration

A `package` declaration is required at the start of every Go source file. Its main purpose is to
determine the default identifier for that package (called the *package name*) when it is imported
by another package.

For example, every file of the `math/rand` package starts with `package rand`, so when you
import this package, you can access its members as `rand.Int`, `rand.Float64`, and so on.

```
package main

import (
    "fmt"
    "math/rand"
)

func main() {
    fmt.Println(rand.Int())
}
```

Conventionally, the package name is the last segment of the import path, and as a result, two
packages may have the same name even though their import paths necessarily differ. For
example, the packages whose import paths are `math/rand` and `crypto/rand` both have the
name `rand`. We'll see how to use both in the same program in a moment.

There are three major exceptions to the "last segment" convention. The first is that a package
defining a command (an executable Go program) always has the name `main`, regardless of the
package's import path. This is a signal to `go build` (§10.7.3) that it must invoke the linker to
make an executable file.

The second exception is that some files in the directory may have the suffix `_test` on their
package name if the file name ends with `_test.go`. Such a directory may define *two* packages:
the usual one, plus another one called an *external test package*. The `_test` suffix signals to
`go test` that it must build both packages, and it indicates which files belong to each package.
External test packages are used to avoid cycles in the import graph arising from dependencies
of the test; they are covered in more detail in Section 11.2.4.

The third exception is that some tools for dependency management append version number
suffixes to package import paths, such as `"gopkg.in/yaml.v2"`. The package name excludes
the suffix, so in this case it would be just `yaml`.

10.4. Import Declarations

A Go source file may contain zero or more `import` declarations immediately after the `package`
declaration and before the first non-import declaration. Each import declaration may specify
the import path of a single package, or multiple packages in a parenthesized list. The two
forms below are equivalent but the second form is more common.

```
import "fmt"
import "os"

import (
    "fmt"
    "os"
)
```

Imported packages may be grouped by introducing blank lines; such groupings usually indicate different domains. The order is not significant, but by convention the lines of each group are sorted alphabetically. (Both gofmt and goimports will group and sort for you.)

```
import (
    "fmt"
    "html/template"
    "os"

    "golang.org/x/net/html"
    "golang.org/x/net/ipv4"
)
```

If we need to import two packages whose names are the same, like math/rand and crypto/rand, into a third package, the import declaration must specify an alternative name for at least one of them to avoid a conflict. This is called a *renaming import*.

```
import (
    "crypto/rand"
    mrand "math/rand" // alternative name mrand avoids conflict
)
```

The alternative name affects only the importing file. Other files, even ones in the same package, may import the package using its default name, or a different name.

A renaming import may be useful even when there is no conflict. If the name of the imported package is unwieldy, as is sometimes the case for automatically generated code, an abbreviated name may be more convenient. The same short name should be used consistently to avoid confusion. Choosing an alternative name can help avoid conflicts with common local variable names. For example, in a file with many local variables named path, we might import the standard "path" package as pathpkg.

Each import declaration establishes a dependency from the current package to the imported package. The go build tool reports an error if these dependencies form a cycle.

10.5. Blank Imports

It is an error to import a package into a file but not refer to the name it defines within that file. However, on occasion we must import a package merely for the side effects of doing so: evaluation of the initializer expressions of its package-level variables and execution of its init functions (§2.6.2). To suppress the "unused import" error we would otherwise encounter, we must use a renaming import in which the alternative name is _, the blank identifier. As usual, the blank identifier can never be referenced.

```
import _ "image/png" // register PNG decoder
```

This is known as a *blank import*. It is most often used to implement a compile-time mechanism whereby the main program can enable optional features by blank-importing additional packages. First we'll see how to use it, then we'll see how it works.

The standard library's `image` package exports a `Decode` function that reads bytes from an `io.Reader`, figures out which image format was used to encode the data, invokes the appropriate decoder, then returns the resulting `image.Image`. Using `image.Decode`, it's easy to build a simple image converter that reads an image in one format and writes it out in another:

gopl.io/ch10/jpeg

```
// The jpeg command reads a PNG image from the standard input
// and writes it as a JPEG image to the standard output.
package main

import (
    "fmt"
    "image"
    "image/jpeg"
    _ "image/png" // register PNG decoder
    "io"
    "os"
)

func main() {
    if err := toJPEG(os.Stdin, os.Stdout); err != nil {
        fmt.Fprintf(os.Stderr, "jpeg: %v\n", err)
        os.Exit(1)
    }
}

func toJPEG(in io.Reader, out io.Writer) error {
    img, kind, err := image.Decode(in)
    if err != nil {
        return err
    }
    fmt.Fprintln(os.Stderr, "Input format =", kind)
    return jpeg.Encode(out, img, &jpeg.Options{Quality: 95})
}
```

If we feed the output of `gopl.io/ch3/mandelbrot` (§3.3) to the converter program, it detects the PNG input format and writes a JPEG version of Figure 3.3.

```
$ go build gopl.io/ch3/mandelbrot
$ go build gopl.io/ch10/jpeg
$ ./mandelbrot | ./jpeg >mandelbrot.jpg
Input format = png
```

Notice the blank import of image/png. Without that line, the program compiles and links as usual but can no longer recognize or decode input in PNG format:

```
$ go build gopl.io/ch10/jpeg
$ ./mandelbrot | ./jpeg >mandelbrot.jpg
jpeg: image: unknown format
```

Here's how it works. The standard library provides decoders for GIF, PNG, and JPEG, and users may provide others, but to keep executables small, decoders are not included in an application unless explicitly requested. The image.Decode function consults a table of supported formats. Each entry in the table specifies four things: the name of the format; a string that is a prefix of all images encoded this way, used to detect the encoding; a function Decode that decodes an encoded image; and another function DecodeConfig that decodes only the image metadata, such as its size and color space. An entry is added to the table by calling image.RegisterFormat, typically from within the package initializer of the supporting package for each format, like this one in image/png:

```
package png // image/png

func Decode(r io.Reader) (image.Image, error)
func DecodeConfig(r io.Reader) (image.Config, error)

func init() {
    const pngHeader = "\x89PNG\r\n\x1a\n"
    image.RegisterFormat("png", pngHeader, Decode, DecodeConfig)
}
```

The effect is that an application need only blank-import the package for the format it needs to make the image.Decode function able to decode it.

The database/sql package uses a similar mechanism to let users install just the database drivers they need. For example:

```
import (
    "database/mysql"
    _ "github.com/lib/pq"              // enable support for Postgres
    _ "github.com/go-sql-driver/mysql" // enable support for MySQL
)

db, err = sql.Open("postgres", dbname) // OK
db, err = sql.Open("mysql", dbname)    // OK
db, err = sql.Open("sqlite3", dbname)  // returns error:
                                       //     unknown driver "sqlite3"
```

Exercise 10.1: Extend the jpeg program so that it converts any supported input format to any output format, using image.Decode to detect the input format and a flag to select the output format.

Exercise 10.2: Define a generic archive file-reading function capable of reading ZIP files (archive/zip) and POSIX tar files (archive/tar). Use a registration mechanism similar to the one described above so that support for each file format can be plugged in using blank imports.

10.6. Packages and Naming

In this section, we'll offer some advice on how to follow Go's distinctive conventions for naming packages and their members.

When creating a package, keep its name short, but not so short as to be cryptic. The most frequently used packages in the standard library are named bufio, bytes, flag, fmt, http, io, json, os, sort, sync, and time.

Be descriptive and unambiguous where possible. For example, don't name a utility package util when a name such as imageutil or ioutil is specific yet still concise. Avoid choosing package names that are commonly used for related local variables, or you may compel the package's clients to use renaming imports, as with the path package.

Package names usually take the singular form. The standard packages bytes, errors, and strings use the plural to avoid hiding the corresponding predeclared types and, in the case of go/types, to avoid conflict with a keyword.

Avoid package names that already have other connotations. For example, we originally used the name temp for the temperature conversion package in Section 2.5, but that didn't last long. It was a terrible idea because "temp" is an almost universal synonym for "temporary." We went through a brief period with the name temperature, but that was too long and didn't say what the package did. In the end, it became tempconv, which is shorter and parallel with strconv.

Now let's turn to the naming of package members. Since each reference to a member of another package uses a qualified identifier such as fmt.Println, the burden of describing the package member is borne equally by the package name and the member name. We need not mention the concept of formatting in Println because the package name fmt does that already. When designing a package, consider how the two parts of a qualified identifier work together, not the member name alone. Here are some characteristic examples:

```
    bytes.Equal        flag.Int        http.Get        json.Marshal
```

We can identify some common naming patterns. The strings package provides a number of independent functions for manipulating strings:

```
    package strings

    func Index(needle, haystack string) int

    type Replacer struct{ /* ... */ }
    func NewReplacer(oldnew ...string) *Replacer

    type Reader struct{ /* ... */ }
    func NewReader(s string) *Reader
```

The word string does not appear in any of their names. Clients refer to them as strings.Index, strings.Replacer, and so on.

Other packages that we might describe as *single-type packages*, such as html/template and math/rand, expose one principal data type plus its methods, and often a New function to create instances.

```
package rand // "math/rand"

type Rand struct{ /* ... */ }
func New(source Source) *Rand
```

This can lead to repetition, as in `template.Template` or `rand.Rand`, which is why the names of these kinds of packages are often especially short.

At the other extreme, there are packages like `net/http` that have a lot of names without a lot of structure, because they perform a complicated task. Despite having over twenty types and many more functions, the package's most important members have the simplest names: `Get`, `Post`, `Handle`, `Error`, `Client`, `Server`.

10.7. The Go Tool

The rest of this chapter concerns the go tool, which is used for downloading, querying, formatting, building, testing, and installing packages of Go code.

The go tool combines the features of a diverse set of tools into one command set. It is a package manager (analogous to `apt` or `rpm`) that answers queries about its inventory of packages, computes their dependencies, and downloads them from remote version-control systems. It is a build system that computes file dependencies and invokes compilers, assemblers, and linkers, although it is intentionally less complete than the standard Unix `make`. And it is a test driver, as we will see in Chapter 11.

Its command-line interface uses the "Swiss army knife" style, with over a dozen subcommands, some of which we have already seen, like `get`, `run`, `build`, and `fmt`. You can run `go help` to see the index of its built-in documentation, but for reference, we've listed the most commonly used commands below:

```
$ go
...
    build       compile packages and dependencies
    clean       remove object files
    doc         show documentation for package or symbol
    env         print Go environment information
    fmt         run gofmt on package sources
    get         download and install packages and dependencies
    install     compile and install packages and dependencies
    list        list packages
    run         compile and run Go program
    test        test packages
    version     print Go version
    vet         run go tool vet on packages

Use "go help [command]" for more information about a command.
...
```

To keep the need for configuration to a minimum, the go tool relies heavily on conventions. For example, given the name of a Go source file, the tool can find its enclosing package, because each directory contains a single package and the import path of a package corresponds to the directory hierarchy in the workspace. Given the import path of a package, the tool can find the corresponding directory in which it stores object files. It can also find the URL of the server that hosts the source code repository.

10.7.1. Workspace Organization

The only configuration most users ever need is the GOPATH environment variable, which specifies the root of the workspace. When switching to a different workspace, users update the value of GOPATH. For instance, we set GOPATH to $HOME/gobook while working on this book:

```
$ export GOPATH=$HOME/gobook
$ go get gopl.io/...
```

After you download all the programs for this book using the command above, your workspace will contain a hierarchy like this one:

```
GOPATH/
    src/
        gopl.io/
            .git/
            ch1/
                helloworld/
                    main.go
                dup/
                    main.go
                ...
        golang.org/x/net/
            .git/
            html/
                parse.go
                node.go
                ...
    bin/
        helloworld
        dup
    pkg/
        darwin_amd64/
            ...
```

GOPATH has three subdirectories. The src subdirectory holds source code. Each package resides in a directory whose name relative to $GOPATH/src is the package's import path, such as gopl.io/ch1/helloworld. Observe that a single GOPATH workspace contains multiple version-control repositories beneath src, such as gopl.io or golang.org. The pkg subdirectory is where the build tools store compiled packages, and the bin subdirectory holds executable programs like helloworld.

A second environment variable, GOROOT, specifies the root directory of the Go distribution, which provides all the packages of the standard library. The directory structure beneath GOROOT resembles that of GOPATH, so, for example, the source files of the fmt package reside in the $GOROOT/src/fmt directory. Users never need to set GOROOT since, by default, the go tool will use the location where it was installed.

The go env command prints the effective values of the environment variables relevant to the toolchain, including the default values for the missing ones. GOOS specifies the target operating system (for example, android, linux, darwin, or windows) and GOARCH specifies the target processor architecture, such as amd64, 386, or arm. Although GOPATH is the only variable you must set, the others occasionally appear in our explanations.

```
$ go env
GOPATH="/home/gopher/gobook"
GOROOT="/usr/local/go"
GOARCH="amd64"
GOOS="darwin"
...
```

10.7.2. Downloading Packages

When using the go tool, a package's import path indicates not only where to find it in the local workspace, but where to find it on the Internet so that go get can retrieve and update it.

The go get command can download a single package or an entire subtree or repository using the ... notation, as in the previous section. The tool also computes and downloads all the dependencies of the initial packages, which is why the golang.org/x/net/html package appeared in the workspace in the previous example.

Once go get has downloaded the packages, it builds them and then *installs* the libraries and commands. We'll look at the details in the next section, but an example will show how straightforward the process is. The first command below gets the golint tool, which checks for common style problems in Go source code. The second command runs golint on gopl.io/ch2/popcount from Section 2.6.2. It helpfully reports that we have forgotten to write a doc comment for the package:

```
$ go get github.com/golang/lint/golint
$ $GOPATH/bin/golint gopl.io/ch2/popcount
src/gopl.io/ch2/popcount/main.go:1:1:
   package comment should be of the form "Package popcount ..."
```

The go get command has support for popular code-hosting sites like GitHub, Bitbucket, and Launchpad and can make the appropriate requests to their version-control systems. For less well-known sites, you may have to indicate which version-control protocol to use in the import path, such as Git or Mercurial. Run go help importpath for the details.

The directories that go get creates are true clients of the remote repository, not just copies of the files, so you can use version-control commands to see a diff of local edits you've made or to update to a different revision. For example, the `golang.org/x/net` directory is a Git client:

```
$ cd $GOPATH/src/golang.org/x/net
$ git remote -v
origin  https://go.googlesource.com/net (fetch)
origin  https://go.googlesource.com/net (push)
```

Notice that the apparent domain name in the package's import path, `golang.org`, differs from the actual domain name of the Git server, `go.googlesource.com`. This is a feature of the go tool that lets packages use a custom domain name in their import path while being hosted by a generic service such as `googlesource.com` or `github.com`. HTML pages beneath `https://golang.org/x/net/html` include the metadata shown below, which redirects the go tool to the Git repository at the actual hosting site:

```
$ go build gopl.io/ch1/fetch
$ ./fetch https://golang.org/x/net/html | grep go-import
<meta name="go-import"
      content="golang.org/x/net git https://go.googlesource.com/net">
```

If you specify the -u flag, go get will ensure that all packages it visits, including dependencies, are updated to their latest version before being built and installed. Without that flag, packages that already exist locally will not be updated.

The go get -u command generally retrieves the latest version of each package, which is convenient when you're getting started but may be inappropriate for deployed projects, where precise control of dependencies is critical for release hygiene. The usual solution to this problem is to *vendor* the code, that is, to make a persistent local copy of all the necessary dependencies, and to update this copy carefully and deliberately. Prior to Go 1.5, this required changing those packages' import paths, so our copy of `golang.org/x/net/html` would become `gopl.io/vendor/golang.org/x/net/html`. More recent versions of the go tool support vendoring directly, though we don't have space to show the details here. See *Vendor Directories* in the output of the go help gopath command.

Exercise 10.3: Using `fetch http://gopl.io/ch1/helloworld?go-get=1`, find out which service hosts the code samples for this book. (HTTP requests from go get include the go-get parameter so that servers can distinguish them from ordinary browser requests.)

10.7.3. Building Packages

The go build command compiles each argument package. If the package is a library, the result is discarded; this merely checks that the package is free of compile errors. If the package is named main, go build invokes the linker to create an executable in the current directory; the name of the executable is taken from the last segment of the package's import path.

Since each directory contains one package, each executable program, or *command* in Unix terminology, requires its own directory. These directories are sometimes children of a directory named cmd, such as the `golang.org/x/tools/cmd/godoc` command which serves Go package documentation through a web interface (§10.7.4).

Packages may be specified by their import paths, as we saw above, or by a relative directory name, which must start with a . or .. segment even if this would not ordinarily be required. If no argument is provided, the current directory is assumed. Thus the following commands build the same package, though each writes the executable to the directory in which go build is run:

```
$ cd $GOPATH/src/gopl.io/ch1/helloworld
$ go build
```

and:

```
$ cd anywhere
$ go build gopl.io/ch1/helloworld
```

and:

```
$ cd $GOPATH
$ go build ./src/gopl.io/ch1/helloworld
```

but not:

```
$ cd $GOPATH
$ go build src/gopl.io/ch1/helloworld
Error: cannot find package "src/gopl.io/ch1/helloworld".
```

Packages may also be specified as a list of file names, though this tends to be used only for small programs and one-off experiments. If the package name is main, the executable name comes from the basename of the first .go file.

```
$ cat quoteargs.go
package main

import (
    "fmt"
    "os"
)

func main() {
    fmt.Printf("%q\n", os.Args[1:])
}
$ go build quoteargs.go
$ ./quoteargs one "two three" four\ five
["one" "two three" "four five"]
```

Particularly for throwaway programs like this one, we want to run the executable as soon as we've built it. The go run command combines these two steps:

```
$ go run quoteargs.go one "two three" four\ five
["one" "two three" "four five"]
```

The first argument that doesn't end in .go is assumed to be the beginning of the list of arguments to the Go executable.

By default, the go build command builds the requested package and all its dependencies, then throws away all the compiled code except the final executable, if any. Both the dependency analysis and the compilation are surprisingly fast, but as projects grow to dozens of packages and hundreds of thousands of lines of code, the time to recompile dependencies can become noticeable, potentially several seconds, even when those dependencies haven't changed at all.

The go install command is very similar to go build, except that it saves the compiled code for each package and command instead of throwing it away. Compiled packages are saved beneath the $GOPATH/pkg directory corresponding to the src directory in which the source resides, and command executables are saved in the $GOPATH/bin directory. (Many users put $GOPATH/bin on their executable search path.) Thereafter, go build and go install do not run the compiler for those packages and commands if they have not changed, making subsequent builds much faster. For convenience, go build -i installs the packages that are dependencies of the build target.

Since compiled packages vary by platform and architecture, go install saves them beneath a subdirectory whose name incorporates the values of the GOOS and GOARCH environment variables. For example, on a Mac the golang.org/x/net/html package is compiled and installed in the file golang.org/x/net/html.a under $GOPATH/pkg/darwin_amd64.

It is straightforward to *cross-compile* a Go program, that is, to build an executable intended for a different operating system or CPU. Just set the GOOS or GOARCH variables during the build. The cross program prints the operating system and architecture for which it was built:

gopl.io/ch10/cross
```
func main() {
    fmt.Println(runtime.GOOS, runtime.GOARCH)
}
```

The following commands produce 64-bit and 32-bit executables respectively:

```
$ go build gopl.io/ch10/cross
$ ./cross
darwin amd64
$ GOARCH=386 go build gopl.io/ch10/cross
$ ./cross
darwin 386
```

Some packages may need to compile different versions of the code for certain platforms or processors, to deal with low-level portability issues or to provide optimized versions of important routines, for instance. If a file name includes an operating system or processor architecture name like net_linux.go or asm_amd64.s, then the go tool will compile the file only when building for that target. Special comments called *build tags* give more fine-grained control. For example, if a file contains this comment:

```
// +build linux darwin
```

before the package declaration (and its doc comment), go build will compile it only when building for Linux or Mac OS X, and this comment says never to compile the file:

```
// +build ignore
```

For more details, see the *Build Constraints* section of the go/build package's documentation:

```
$ go doc go/build
```

10.7.4. Documenting Packages

Go style strongly encourages good documentation of package APIs. Each declaration of an exported package member and the package declaration itself should be immediately preceded by a comment explaining its purpose and usage.

Go *doc comments* are always complete sentences, and the first sentence is usually a summary that starts with the name being declared. Function parameters and other identifiers are mentioned without quotation or markup. For example, here's the doc comment for fmt.Fprintf:

```
// Fprintf formats according to a format specifier and writes to w.
// It returns the number of bytes written and any write error encountered.
func Fprintf(w io.Writer, format string, a ...interface{}) (int, error)
```

The details of Fprintf's formatting are explained in a doc comment associated with the fmt package itself. A comment immediately preceding a package declaration is considered the doc comment for the package as a whole. There must be only one, though it may appear in any file. Longer package comments may warrant a file of their own; fmt's is over 300 lines. This file is usually called doc.go.

Good documentation need not be extensive, and documentation is no substitute for simplicity. Indeed, Go's conventions favor brevity and simplicity in documentation as in all things, since documentation, like code, requires maintenance too. Many declarations can be explained in one well-worded sentence, and if the behavior is truly obvious, no comment is needed.

Throughout the book, as space permits, we've preceded many declarations by doc comments, but you will find better examples as you browse the standard library. Two tools can help you do that.

The go doc tool prints the declaration and doc comment of the entity specified on the command line, which may be a package:

```
$ go doc time
package time // import "time"

Package time provides functionality for measuring and displaying time.

const Nanosecond Duration = 1 ...
func After(d Duration) <-chan Time
func Sleep(d Duration)
func Since(t Time) Duration
func Now() Time
type Duration int64
type Time struct { ... }
...many more...
```

or a package member:

```
$ go doc time.Since
func Since(t Time) Duration

    Since returns the time elapsed since t.
    It is shorthand for time.Now().Sub(t).
```

or a method:

```
$ go doc time.Duration.Seconds
func (d Duration) Seconds() float64

    Seconds returns the duration as a floating-point number of seconds.
```

The tool does not need complete import paths or correct identifier case. This command prints the documentation of (*json.Decoder).Decode from the encoding/json package:

```
$ go doc json.decode
func (dec *Decoder) Decode(v interface{}) error

    Decode reads the next JSON-encoded value from its input and stores
    it in the value pointed to by v.
```

The second tool, confusingly named godoc, serves cross-linked HTML pages that provide the same information as go doc and much more. The godoc server at https://golang.org/pkg covers the standard library. Figure 10.1 shows the documentation for the time package, and in Section 11.6 we'll see godoc's interactive display of example programs. The godoc server at https://godoc.org has a searchable index of thousands of open-source packages.

You can also run an instance of godoc in your workspace if you want to browse your own packages. Visit http://localhost:8000/pkg in your browser while running this command:

```
$ godoc -http :8000
```

Its -analysis=type and -analysis=pointer flags augment the documentation and the source code with the results of advanced static analysis.

10.7.5. Internal Packages

The package is the most important mechanism for encapsulation in Go programs. Unexported identifiers are visible only within the same package, and exported identifiers are visible to the world.

Sometimes, though, a middle ground would be helpful, a way to define identifiers that are visible to a small set of trusted packages, but not to everyone. For example, when we're breaking up a large package into more manageable parts, we may not want to reveal the interfaces between those parts to other packages. Or we may want to share utility functions across several packages of a project without exposing them more widely. Or perhaps we just want to experiment with a new package without prematurely committing to its API, by putting it "on probation" with a limited set of clients.

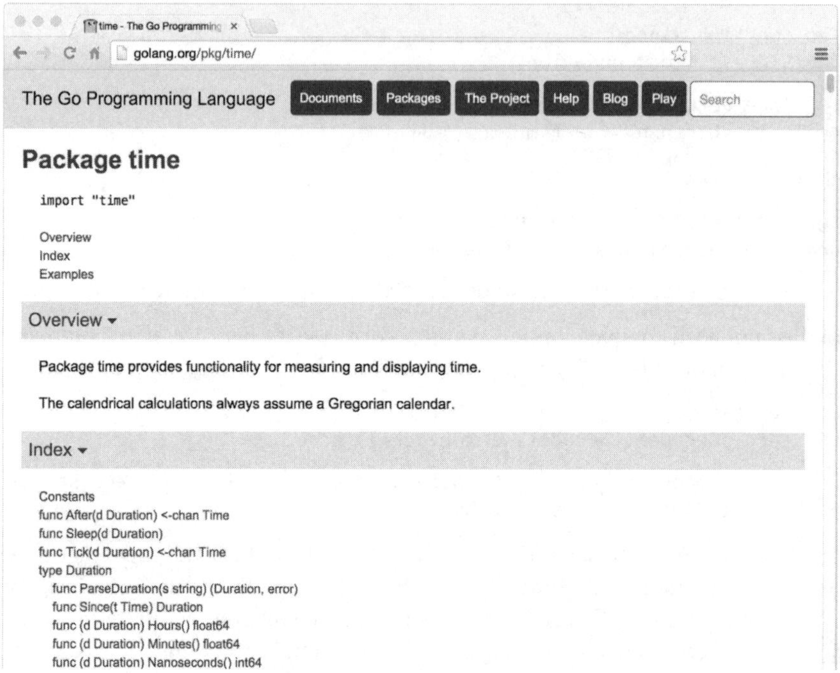

Figure 10.1. The `time` package in `godoc`.

To address these needs, the `go build` tool treats a package specially if its import path contains a path segment named `internal`. Such packages are called *internal packages*. An internal package may be imported only by another package that is inside the tree rooted at the parent of the `internal` directory. For example, given the packages below, `net/http/internal/chunked` can be imported from `net/http/httputil` or `net/http`, but not from `net/url`. However, `net/url` may import `net/http/httputil`.

```
net/http
net/http/internal/chunked
net/http/httputil
net/url
```

10.7.6. Querying Packages

The `go list` tool reports information about available packages. In its simplest form, `go list` tests whether a package is present in the workspace and prints its import path if so:

```
$ go list github.com/go-sql-driver/mysql
github.com/go-sql-driver/mysql
```

An argument to go list may contain the "..." wildcard, which matches any substring of a
package's import path. We can use it to enumerate all the packages within a Go workspace:

```
$ go list ...
archive/tar
archive/zip
bufio
bytes
cmd/addr2line
cmd/api
...many more...
```

or within a specific subtree:

```
$ go list gopl.io/ch3/...
gopl.io/ch3/basename1
gopl.io/ch3/basename2
gopl.io/ch3/comma
gopl.io/ch3/mandelbrot
gopl.io/ch3/netflag
gopl.io/ch3/printints
gopl.io/ch3/surface
```

or related to a particular topic:

```
$ go list ...xml...
encoding/xml
gopl.io/ch7/xmlselect
```

The go list command obtains the complete metadata for each package, not just the import
path, and makes this information available to users or other tools in a variety of formats. The
-json flag causes go list to print the entire record of each package in JSON format:

```
$ go list -json hash
{
    "Dir": "/home/gopher/go/src/hash",
    "ImportPath": "hash",
    "Name": "hash",
    "Doc": "Package hash provides interfaces for hash functions.",
    "Target": "/home/gopher/go/pkg/darwin_amd64/hash.a",
    "Goroot": true,
    "Standard": true,
    "Root": "/home/gopher/go",
    "GoFiles": [
            "hash.go"
    ],
    "Imports": [
        "io"
    ],
```

```
    "Deps": [
        "errors",
        "io",
        "runtime",
        "sync",
        "sync/atomic",
        "unsafe"
    ]
}
```

The -f flag lets users customize the output format using the template language of package text/template (§4.6). This command prints the transitive dependencies of the strconv package, separated by spaces:

```
$ go list -f '{{join .Deps " "}}' strconv
errors math runtime unicode/utf8 unsafe
```

and this command prints the direct imports of each package in the compress subtree of the standard library:

```
$ go list -f '{{.ImportPath}} -> {{join .Imports " "}}' compress/...
compress/bzip2 -> bufio io sort
compress/flate -> bufio fmt io math sort strconv
compress/gzip -> bufio compress/flate errors fmt hash hash/crc32 io time
compress/lzw -> bufio errors fmt io
compress/zlib -> bufio compress/flate errors fmt hash hash/adler32 io
```

The go list command is useful for both one-off interactive queries and for build and test automation scripts. We'll use it again in Section 11.2.4. For more information, including the set of available fields and their meaning, see the output of go help list.

In this chapter, we've explained all the important subcommands of the go tool—except one. In the next chapter, we'll see how the go test command is used for testing Go programs.

Exercise 10.4: Construct a tool that reports the set of all packages in the workspace that transitively depend on the packages specified by the arguments. Hint: you will need to run go list twice, once for the initial packages and once for all packages. You may want to parse its JSON output using the encoding/json package (§4.5).

11

Testing

Maurice Wilkes, the developer of EDSAC, the first stored-program computer, had a startling insight while climbing the stairs of his laboratory in 1949. In *Memoirs of a Computer Pioneer*, he recalled, "The realization came over me with full force that a good part of the remainder of my life was going to be spent in finding errors in my own programs." Surely every programmer of a stored-program computer since then can sympathize with Wilkes, though perhaps not without some bemusement at his naïveté about the difficulties of software construction.

Programs today are far larger and more complex than in Wilkes's time, of course, and a great deal of effort has been spent on techniques to make this complexity manageable. Two techniques in particular stand out for their effectiveness. The first is routine peer review of programs before they are deployed. The second, the subject of this chapter, is testing.

Testing, by which we implicitly mean *automated* testing, is the practice of writing small programs that check that the code under test (the *production* code) behaves as expected for certain inputs, which are usually either carefully chosen to exercise certain features or randomized to ensure broad coverage.

The field of software testing is enormous. The task of testing occupies all programmers some of the time and some programmers all of the time. The literature on testing includes thousands of printed books and millions of words of blog posts. In every mainstream programming language, there are dozens of software packages intended for test construction, some with a great deal of theory, and the field seems to attract more than a few prophets with cult-like followings. It is almost enough to convince programmers that to write effective tests they must acquire a whole new set of skills.

Go's approach to testing can seem rather low-tech in comparison. It relies on one command, `go test`, and a set of conventions for writing test functions that `go test` can run. The comparatively lightweight mechanism is effective for pure testing, and it extends naturally to benchmarks and systematic examples for documentation.

In practice, writing test code is not much different from writing the original program itself. We write short functions that focus on one part of the task. We have to be careful of boundary conditions, think about data structures, and reason about what results a computation should produce from suitable inputs. But this is the same process as writing ordinary Go code; it needn't require new notations, conventions, and tools.

11.1. The go test Tool

The go test subcommand is a test driver for Go packages that are organized according to certain conventions. In a package directory, files whose names end with _test.go are not part of the package ordinarily built by go build but are a part of it when built by go test.

Within *_test.go files, three kinds of functions are treated specially: tests, benchmarks, and examples. A *test function*, which is a function whose name begins with Test, exercises some program logic for correct behavior; go test calls the test function and reports the result, which is either PASS or FAIL. A *benchmark function* has a name beginning with Benchmark and measures the performance of some operation; go test reports the mean execution time of the operation. And an *example function*, whose name starts with Example, provides machine-checked documentation. We will cover tests in detail in Section 11.2, benchmarks in Section 11.4, and examples in Section 11.6.

The go test tool scans the *_test.go files for these special functions, generates a temporary main package that calls them all in the proper way, builds and runs it, reports the results, and then cleans up.

11.2. Test Functions

Each test file must import the testing package. Test functions have the following signature:

```
func TestName(t *testing.T) {
    // ...
}
```

Test function names must begin with Test; the optional suffix *Name* must begin with a capital letter:

```
func TestSin(t *testing.T) { /* ... */ }
func TestCos(t *testing.T) { /* ... */ }
func TestLog(t *testing.T) { /* ... */ }
```

The t parameter provides methods for reporting test failures and logging additional information. Let's define an example package gopl.io/ch11/word1, containing a single function IsPalindrome that reports whether a string reads the same forward and backward. (This implementation tests every byte twice if the string is a palindrome; we'll come back to that shortly.)

gopl.io/ch11/word1

```
// Package word provides utilities for word games.
package word

// IsPalindrome reports whether s reads the same forward and backward.
// (Our first attempt.)
func IsPalindrome(s string) bool {
    for i := range s {
        if s[i] != s[len(s)-1-i] {
            return false
        }
    }
    return true
}
```

In the same directory, the file word_test.go contains two test functions named TestPalin-
drome and TestNonPalindrome. Each checks that IsPalindrome gives the right answer for a
single input and reports failures using t.Error:

```
package word

import "testing"

func TestPalindrome(t *testing.T) {
    if !IsPalindrome("detartrated") {
        t.Error(`IsPalindrome("detartrated") = false`)
    }
    if !IsPalindrome("kayak") {
        t.Error(`IsPalindrome("kayak") = false`)
    }
}

func TestNonPalindrome(t *testing.T) {
    if IsPalindrome("palindrome") {
        t.Error(`IsPalindrome("palindrome") = true`)
    }
}
```

A go test (or go build) command with no package arguments operates on the package in
the current directory. We can build and run the tests with the following command.

```
$ cd $GOPATH/src/gopl.io/ch11/word1
$ go test
ok    gopl.io/ch11/word1    0.008s
```

Satisfied, we ship the program, but no sooner have the launch party guests departed than the
bug reports start to arrive. A French user named Noelle Eve Elleon complains that IsPalindrome doesn't recognize "été." Another, from Central America, is disappointed that it rejects
"A man, a plan, a canal: Panama." These specific and small bug reports naturally lend themselves to new test cases.

```
func TestFrenchPalindrome(t *testing.T) {
    if !IsPalindrome("été") {
        t.Error(`IsPalindrome("été") = false`)
    }
}

func TestCanalPalindrome(t *testing.T) {
    input := "A man, a plan, a canal: Panama"
    if !IsPalindrome(input) {
        t.Errorf(`IsPalindrome(%q) = false`, input)
    }
}
```

To avoid writing the long input string twice, we use Errorf, which provides formatting like Printf.

When the two new tests have been added, the go test command fails with informative error messages.

```
$ go test
--- FAIL: TestFrenchPalindrome (0.00s)
    word_test.go:28: IsPalindrome("été") = false
--- FAIL: TestCanalPalindrome (0.00s)
    word_test.go:35: IsPalindrome("A man, a plan, a canal: Panama") = false
FAIL
FAIL    gopl.io/ch11/word1  0.014s
```

It's good practice to write the test first and observe that it triggers the same failure described by the user's bug report. Only then can we be confident that whatever fix we come up with addresses the right problem.

As a bonus, running go test is usually quicker than manually going through the steps described in the bug report, allowing us to iterate more rapidly. If the test suite contains many slow tests, we may make even faster progress if we're selective about which ones we run.

The -v flag prints the name and execution time of each test in the package:

```
$ go test -v
=== RUN TestPalindrome
--- PASS: TestPalindrome (0.00s)
=== RUN TestNonPalindrome
--- PASS: TestNonPalindrome (0.00s)
=== RUN TestFrenchPalindrome
--- FAIL: TestFrenchPalindrome (0.00s)
    word_test.go:28: IsPalindrome("été") = false
=== RUN TestCanalPalindrome
--- FAIL: TestCanalPalindrome (0.00s)
    word_test.go:35: IsPalindrome("A man, a plan, a canal: Panama") = false
FAIL
exit status 1
FAIL    gopl.io/ch11/word1  0.017s
```

and the -run flag, whose argument is a regular expression, causes go test to run only those tests whose function name matches the pattern:

```
$ go test -v -run="French|Canal"
=== RUN TestFrenchPalindrome
--- FAIL: TestFrenchPalindrome (0.00s)
    word_test.go:28: IsPalindrome("été") = false
=== RUN TestCanalPalindrome
--- FAIL: TestCanalPalindrome (0.00s)
    word_test.go:35: IsPalindrome("A man, a plan, a canal: Panama") = false
FAIL
exit status 1
FAIL    gopl.io/ch11/word1  0.014s
```

Of course, once we've gotten the selected tests to pass, we should invoke go test with no flags to run the entire test suite one last time before we commit the change.

Now our task is to fix the bugs. A quick investigation reveals the cause of the first bug to be IsPalindrome's use of byte sequences, not rune sequences, so that non-ASCII characters such as the é in "été" confuse it. The second bug arises from not ignoring spaces, punctuation, and letter case.

Chastened, we rewrite the function more carefully:

gopl.io/ch11/word2

```
// Package word provides utilities for word games.
package word

import "unicode"

// IsPalindrome reports whether s reads the same forward and backward.
// Letter case is ignored, as are non-letters.
func IsPalindrome(s string) bool {
    var letters []rune
    for _, r := range s {
        if unicode.IsLetter(r) {
            letters = append(letters, unicode.ToLower(r))
        }
    }
    for i := range letters {
        if letters[i] != letters[len(letters)-1-i] {
            return false
        }
    }
    return true
}
```

We also write a more comprehensive set of test cases that combines all the previous ones and a number of new ones into a table.

```go
func TestIsPalindrome(t *testing.T) {
    var tests = []struct {
        input string
        want  bool
    }{
        {"", true},
        {"a", true},
        {"aa", true},
        {"ab", false},
        {"kayak", true},
        {"detartrated", true},
        {"A man, a plan, a canal: Panama", true},
        {"Evil I did dwell; lewd did I live.", true},
        {"Able was I ere I saw Elba", true},
        {"été", true},
        {"Et se resservir, ivresse reste.", true},
        {"palindrome", false}, // non-palindrome
        {"desserts", false},   // semi-palindrome
    }
    for _, test := range tests {
        if got := IsPalindrome(test.input); got != test.want {
            t.Errorf("IsPalindrome(%q) = %v", test.input, got)
        }
    }
}
```

Our new tests pass:

```
$ go test gopl.io/ch11/word2
ok      gopl.io/ch11/word2       0.015s
```

This style of *table-driven* testing is very common in Go. It is straightforward to add new table entries as needed, and since the assertion logic is not duplicated, we can invest more effort in producing a good error message.

The output of a failing test does *not* include the entire stack trace at the moment of the call to t.Errorf. Nor does t.Errorf cause a panic or stop the execution of the test, unlike assertion failures in many test frameworks for other languages. Tests are independent of each other. If an early entry in the table causes the test to fail, later table entries will still be checked, and thus we may learn about multiple failures during a single run.

When we really must stop a test function, perhaps because some initialization code failed or to prevent a failure already reported from causing a confusing cascade of others, we use t.Fatal or t.Fatalf. These must be called from the same goroutine as the Test function, not from another one created during the test.

Test failure messages are usually of the form "f(x) = y, want z", where f(x) explains the attempted operation and its input, y is the actual result, and z the expected result. Where convenient, as in our palindrome example, actual Go syntax is used for the f(x) part. Displaying x is particularly important in a table-driven test, since a given assertion is executed many times with different values. Avoid boilerplate and redundant information. When testing a boolean function such as IsPalindrome, omit the want z part since it adds no information. If x, y, or z is lengthy, print a concise summary of the relevant parts instead. The author of a test should strive to help the programmer who must diagnose a test failure.

Exercise 11.1: Write tests for the charcount program in Section 4.3.

Exercise 11.2: Write a set of tests for IntSet (§6.5) that checks that its behavior after each operation is equivalent to a set based on built-in maps. Save your implementation for benchmarking in Exercise 11.7.

11.2.1. Randomized Testing

Table-driven tests are convenient for checking that a function works on inputs carefully selected to exercise interesting cases in the logic. Another approach, *randomized testing*, explores a broader range of inputs by constructing inputs at random.

How do we know what output to expect from our function, given a random input? There are two strategies. The first is to write an alternative implementation of the function that uses a less efficient but simpler and clearer algorithm, and check that both implementations give the same result. The second is to create input values according to a pattern so that we know what output to expect.

The example below uses the second approach: the randomPalindrome function generates words that are known to be palindromes by construction.

```go
import "math/rand"

// randomPalindrome returns a palindrome whose length and contents
// are derived from the pseudo-random number generator rng.
func randomPalindrome(rng *rand.Rand) string {
    n := rng.Intn(25) // random length up to 24
    runes := make([]rune, n)
    for i := 0; i < (n+1)/2; i++ {
        r := rune(rng.Intn(0x1000)) // random rune up to '\u0999'
        runes[i] = r
        runes[n-1-i] = r
    }
    return string(runes)
}

func TestRandomPalindromes(t *testing.T) {
    // Initialize a pseudo-random number generator.
    seed := time.Now().UTC().UnixNano()
    t.Logf("Random seed: %d", seed)
    rng := rand.New(rand.NewSource(seed))
```

```
    for i := 0; i < 1000; i++ {
        p := randomPalindrome(rng)
        if !IsPalindrome(p) {
            t.Errorf("IsPalindrome(%q) = false", p)
        }
    }
}
```

Since randomized tests are nondeterministic, it is critical that the log of the failing test record sufficient information to reproduce the failure. In our example, the input p to IsPalindrome tells us all we need to know, but for functions that accept more complex inputs, it may be simpler to log the seed of the pseudo-random number generator (as we do above) than to dump the entire input data structure. Armed with that seed value, we can easily modify the test to replay the failure deterministically.

By using the current time as a source of randomness, the test will explore novel inputs each time it is run, over the entire course of its lifetime. This is especially valuable if your project uses an automated system to run all its tests periodically.

Exercise 11.3: TestRandomPalindromes only tests palindromes. Write a randomized test that generates and verifies *non*-palindromes.

Exercise 11.4: Modify randomPalindrome to exercise IsPalindrome's handling of punctuation and spaces.

11.2.2. Testing a Command

The go test tool is useful for testing library packages, but with a little effort we can use it to test commands as well. A package named main ordinarily produces an executable program, but it can be imported as a library too.

Let's write a test for the echo program of Section 2.3.2. We've split the program into two functions: echo does the real work, while main parses and reads the flag values and reports any errors returned by echo.

gopl.io/ch11/echo
```
// Echo prints its command-line arguments.
package main

import (
    "flag"
    "fmt"
    "io"
    "os"
    "strings"
)
```

```go
var (
    n = flag.Bool("n", false, "omit trailing newline")
    s = flag.String("s", " ", "separator")
)

var out io.Writer = os.Stdout // modified during testing

func main() {
    flag.Parse()
    if err := echo(!*n, *s, flag.Args()); err != nil {
        fmt.Fprintf(os.Stderr, "echo: %v\n", err)
        os.Exit(1)
    }
}

func echo(newline bool, sep string, args []string) error {
    fmt.Fprint(out, strings.Join(args, sep))
    if newline {
        fmt.Fprintln(out)
    }
    return nil
}
```

From the test, we will call echo with a variety of arguments and flag settings and check that it prints the correct output in each case, so we've added parameters to echo to reduce its dependence on global variables. That said, we've also introduced another global variable, out, the io.Writer to which the result will be written. By having echo write through this variable, not directly to os.Stdout, the tests can substitute a different Writer implementation that records what was written for later inspection. Here's the test, in file echo_test.go:

```go
package main

import (
    "bytes"
    "fmt"
    "testing"
)

func TestEcho(t *testing.T) {
    var tests = []struct {
        newline bool
        sep     string
        args    []string
        want    string
    }{
        {true, "", []string{}, "\n"},
        {false, "", []string{}, ""},
        {true, "\t", []string{"one", "two", "three"}, "one\ttwo\tthree\n"},
        {true, ",", []string{"a", "b", "c"}, "a,b,c\n"},
        {false, ":", []string{"1", "2", "3"}, "1:2:3"},
    }
```

```
    for _, test := range tests {
        descr := fmt.Sprintf("echo(%v, %q, %q)",
            test.newline, test.sep, test.args)

        out = new(bytes.Buffer) // captured output
        if err := echo(test.newline, test.sep, test.args); err != nil {
            t.Errorf("%s failed: %v", descr, err)
            continue
        }
        got := out.(*bytes.Buffer).String()
        if got != test.want {
            t.Errorf("%s = %q, want %q", descr, got, test.want)
        }
    }
}
```

Notice that the test code is in the same package as the production code. Although the package name is main and it defines a main function, during testing this package acts as a library that exposes the function TestEcho to the test driver; its main function is ignored.

By organizing the test as a table, we can easily add new test cases. Let's see what happens when the test fails, by adding this line to the table:

```
    {true, ",", []string{"a", "b", "c"}, "a b c\n"}, // NOTE: wrong expectation!
```

go test prints

```
$ go test gopl.io/ch11/echo
--- FAIL: TestEcho (0.00s)
    echo_test.go:31: echo(true, ",", ["a" "b" "c"]) = "a,b,c", want "a b c\n"
FAIL
FAIL    gopl.io/ch11/echo    0.006s
```

The error message describes the attempted operation (using Go-like syntax), the actual behavior, and the expected behavior, in that order. With an informative error message such as this, you may have a pretty good idea about the root cause before you've even located the source code of the test.

It's important that code being tested not call log.Fatal or os.Exit, since these will stop the process in its tracks; calling these functions should be regarded as the exclusive right of main. If something totally unexpected happens and a function panics, the test driver will recover, though the test will of course be considered a failure. Expected errors such as those resulting from bad user input, missing files, or improper configuration should be reported by returning a non-nil error value. Fortunately (though unfortunate as an illustration), our echo example is so simple that it will never return a non-nil error.

11.2.3. White-Box Testing

One way of categorizing tests is by the level of knowledge they require of the internal workings of the package under test. A *black-box* test assumes nothing about the package other than what is exposed by its API and specified by its documentation; the package's internals are opaque. In contrast, a *white-box* test has privileged access to the internal functions and data structures of the package and can make observations and changes that an ordinary client cannot. For example, a white-box test can check that the invariants of the package's data types are maintained after every operation. (The name *white box* is traditional, but *clear box* would be more accurate.)

The two approaches are complementary. Black-box tests are usually more robust, needing fewer updates as the software evolves. They also help the test author empathize with the client of the package and can reveal flaws in the API design. In contrast, white-box tests can provide more detailed coverage of the trickier parts of the implementation.

We've already seen examples of both kinds. `TestIsPalindrome` calls only the exported function `IsPalindrome` and is thus a black-box test. `TestEcho` calls the `echo` function and updates the global variable `out`, both of which are unexported, making it a white-box test.

While developing `TestEcho`, we modified the `echo` function to use the package-level variable `out` when writing its output, so that the test could replace the standard output with an alternative implementation that records the data for later inspection. Using the same technique, we can replace other parts of the production code with easy-to-test "fake" implementations. The advantage of fake implementations is that they can be simpler to configure, more predictable, more reliable, and easier to observe. They can also avoid undesirable side effects such as updating a production database or charging a credit card.

The code below shows the quota-checking logic in a web service that provides networked storage to users. When users exceed 90% of their quota, the system sends them a warning email.

gopl.io/ch11/storage1

```
package storage

import (
    "fmt"
    "log"
    "net/smtp"
)

var usage = make(map[string]int64)

func bytesInUse(username string) int64 { return usage[username] }

// Email sender configuration.
// NOTE: never put passwords in source code!
const sender = "notifications@example.com"
const password = "correcthorsebatterystaple"
const hostname = "smtp.example.com"

const template = `Warning: you are using %d bytes of storage,
%d%% of your quota.`
```

```go
func CheckQuota(username string) {
    used := bytesInUse(username)
    const quota = 1000000000 // 1GB
    percent := 100 * used / quota
    if percent < 90 {
        return // OK
    }
    msg := fmt.Sprintf(template, used, percent)
    auth := smtp.PlainAuth("", sender, password, hostname)
    err := smtp.SendMail(hostname+":587", auth, sender,
        []string{username}, []byte(msg))
    if err != nil {
        log.Printf("smtp.SendMail(%s) failed: %s", username, err)
    }
}
```

We'd like to test it, but we don't want the test to send out real email. So we move the email logic into its own function and store that function in an unexported package-level variable, notifyUser.

gopl.io/ch11/storage2

```go
var notifyUser = func(username, msg string) {
    auth := smtp.PlainAuth("", sender, password, hostname)
    err := smtp.SendMail(hostname+":587", auth, sender,
        []string{username}, []byte(msg))
    if err != nil {
        log.Printf("smtp.SendEmail(%s) failed: %s", username, err)
    }
}

func CheckQuota(username string) {
    used := bytesInUse(username)
    const quota = 1000000000 // 1GB
    percent := 100 * used / quota
    if percent < 90 {
        return // OK
    }
    msg := fmt.Sprintf(template, used, percent)
    notifyUser(username, msg)
}
```

We can now write a test that substitutes a simple fake notification mechanism instead of sending real email. This one records the notified user and the contents of the message.

```go
package storage

import (
    "strings"
    "testing"
)
```

```
func TestCheckQuotaNotifiesUser(t *testing.T) {
    var notifiedUser, notifiedMsg string
    notifyUser = func(user, msg string) {
        notifiedUser, notifiedMsg = user, msg
    }

    const user = "joe@example.org"
    usage[user] = 980000000 // simulate a 980MB-used condition

    CheckQuota(user)
    if notifiedUser == "" && notifiedMsg == "" {
        t.Fatalf("notifyUser not called")
    }
    if notifiedUser != user {
        t.Errorf("wrong user (%s) notified, want %s",
            notifiedUser, user)
    }
    const wantSubstring = "98% of your quota"
    if !strings.Contains(notifiedMsg, wantSubstring) {
        t.Errorf("unexpected notification message <<%s>>, "+
            "want substring %q", notifiedMsg, wantSubstring)
    }
}
```

There's one problem: after this test function has returned, CheckQuota no longer works as it should because it's still using the test's fake implementation of notifyUsers. (There is always a risk of this kind when updating global variables.) We must modify the test to restore the previous value so that subsequent tests observe no effect, and we must do this on all execution paths, including test failures and panics. This naturally suggests defer.

```
func TestCheckQuotaNotifiesUser(t *testing.T) {
    // Save and restore original notifyUser.
    saved := notifyUser
    defer func() { notifyUser = saved }()

    // Install the test's fake notifyUser.
    var notifiedUser, notifiedMsg string
    notifyUser = func(user, msg string) {
        notifiedUser, notifiedMsg = user, msg
    }
    // ...rest of test...
}
```

This pattern can be used to temporarily save and restore all kinds of global variables, including command-line flags, debugging options, and performance parameters; to install and remove hooks that cause the production code to call some test code when something interesting happens; and to coax the production code into rare but important states, such as timeouts, errors, and even specific interleavings of concurrent activities.

Using global variables in this way is safe only because go test does not normally run multiple tests concurrently.

11.2.4. External Test Packages

Consider the packages net/url, which provides a URL parser, and net/http, which provides a web server and HTTP client library. As we might expect, the higher-level net/http depends on the lower-level net/url. However, one of the tests in net/url is an example demonstrating the interaction between URLs and the HTTP client library. In other words, a test of the lower-level package imports the higher-level package.

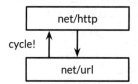

Figure 11.1. A test of net/url depends on net/http.

Declaring this test function in the net/url package would create a cycle in the package import graph, as depicted by the upwards arrow in Figure 11.1, but as we explained in Section 10.1, the Go specification forbids import cycles.

We resolve the problem by declaring the test function in an *external test package*, that is, in a file in the net/url directory whose package declaration reads package url_test. The extra suffix _test is a signal to go test that it should build an additional package containing just these files and run its tests. It may be helpful to think of this external test package as if it had the import path net/url_test, but it cannot be imported under this or any other name.

Because external tests live in a separate package, they may import helper packages that also depend on the package being tested; an in-package test cannot do this. In terms of the design layers, the external test package is logically higher up than both of the packages it depends upon, as shown in Figure 11.2.

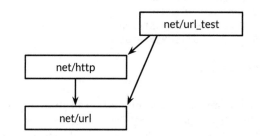

Figure 11.2. External test packages break dependency cycles.

By avoiding import cycles, external test packages allow tests, especially *integration tests* (which test the interaction of several components), to import other packages freely, exactly as an application would.

We can use the go list tool to summarize which Go source files in a package directory are production code, in-package tests, and external tests. We'll use the fmt package as an example. GoFiles is the list of files that contain the production code; these are the files that go build will include in your application:

```
$ go list -f={{.GoFiles}} fmt
[doc.go format.go print.go scan.go]
```

TestGoFiles is the list of files that also belong to the fmt package, but these files, whose names all end in _test.go, are included only when building tests:

```
$ go list -f={{.TestGoFiles}} fmt
[export_test.go]
```

The package's tests would usually reside in these files, though unusually fmt has none; we'll explain the purpose of export_test.go in a moment.

XTestGoFiles is the list of files that constitute the external test package, fmt_test, so these files must import the fmt package in order to use it. Again, they are included only during testing:

```
$ go list -f={{.XTestGoFiles}} fmt
[fmt_test.go scan_test.go stringer_test.go]
```

Sometimes an external test package may need privileged access to the internals of the package under test, if for example a white-box test must live in a separate package to avoid an import cycle. In such cases, we use a trick: we add declarations to an in-package _test.go file to expose the necessary internals to the external test. This file thus offers the test a "back door" to the package. If the source file exists only for this purpose and contains no tests itself, it is often called export_test.go.

For example, the implementation of the fmt package needs the functionality of unicode.IsSpace as part of fmt.Scanf. To avoid creating an undesirable dependency, fmt does not import the unicode package and its large tables of data; instead, it contains a simpler implementation, which it calls isSpace.

To ensure that the behaviors of fmt.isSpace and unicode.IsSpace do not drift apart, fmt prudently contains a test. It is an external test, and thus it cannot access isSpace directly, so fmt opens a back door to it by declaring an exported variable that holds the internal isSpace function. This is the entirety of the fmt package's export_test.go file.

```
package fmt

var IsSpace = isSpace
```

This test file defines no tests; it just declares the exported symbol fmt.IsSpace for use by the external test. This trick can also be used whenever an external test needs to use some of the techniques of white-box testing.

11.2.5. Writing Effective Tests

Many newcomers to Go are surprised by the minimalism of Go's testing framework. Other languages' frameworks provide mechanisms for identifying test functions (often using reflection or metadata), hooks for performing "setup" and "teardown" operations before and after the tests run, and libraries of utility functions for asserting common predicates, comparing values, formatting error messages, and aborting a failed test (often using exceptions). Although these mechanisms can make tests very concise, the resulting tests often seem like they are written in a foreign language. Furthermore, although they may report PASS or FAIL correctly, their manner may be unfriendly to the unfortunate maintainer, with cryptic failure messages like "assert: 0 == 1" or page after page of stack traces.

Go's attitude to testing stands in stark contrast. It expects test authors to do most of this work themselves, defining functions to avoid repetition, just as they would for ordinary programs. The process of testing is not one of rote form filling; a test has a user interface too, albeit one whose only users are also its maintainers. A good test does not explode on failure but prints a clear and succinct description of the symptom of the problem, and perhaps other relevant facts about the context. Ideally, the maintainer should not need to read the source code to decipher a test failure. A good test should not give up after one failure but should try to report several errors in a single run, since the pattern of failures may itself be revealing.

The assertion function below compares two values, constructs a generic error message, and stops the program. It's easy to use and it's correct, but when it fails, the error message is almost useless. It does not solve the hard problem of providing a good user interface.

```go
import (
    "fmt"
    "strings"
    "testing"
)
// A poor assertion function.
func assertEqual(x, y int) {
    if x != y {
        panic(fmt.Sprintf("%d != %d", x, y))
    }
}
func TestSplit(t *testing.T) {
    words := strings.Split("a:b:c", ":")
    assertEqual(len(words), 3)
    // ...
}
```

In this sense, assertion functions suffer from *premature abstraction*: by treating the failure of this particular test as a mere difference of two integers, we forfeit the opportunity to provide meaningful context. We can provide a better message by starting from the concrete details, as in the example below. Only once repetitive patterns emerge in a given test suite is it time to introduce abstractions.

```
func TestSplit(t *testing.T) {
    s, sep := "a:b:c", ":"
    words := strings.Split(s, sep)
    if got, want := len(words), 3; got != want {
        t.Errorf("Split(%q, %q) returned %d words, want %d",
            s, sep, got, want)
    }
    // ...
}
```

Now the test reports the function that was called, its inputs, and the significance of the result; it explicitly identifies the actual value and the expectation; and it continues to execute even if this assertion should fail. Once we've written a test like this, the natural next step is often not to define a function to replace the entire if statement, but to execute the test in a loop in which s, sep, and want vary, like the table-driven test of IsPalindrome.

The previous example didn't need any utility functions, but of course that shouldn't stop us from introducing functions when they help make the code simpler. (We'll look at one such utility function, reflect.DeepEqual, in Section 13.3.) The key to a good test is to start by implementing the concrete behavior that you want and only then use functions to simplify the code and eliminate repetition. Best results are rarely obtained by starting with a library of abstract, generic testing functions.

Exercise 11.5: Extend TestSplit to use a table of inputs and expected outputs.

11.2.6. Avoiding Brittle Tests

An application that often fails when it encounters new but valid inputs is called *buggy*; a test that spuriously fails when a sound change was made to the program is called *brittle*. Just as a buggy program frustrates its users, a brittle test exasperates its maintainers. The most brittle tests, which fail for almost any change to the production code, good or bad, are sometimes called *change detector* or *status quo* tests, and the time spent dealing with them can quickly deplete any benefit they once seemed to provide.

When a function under test produces a complex output such as a long string, an elaborate data structure, or a file, it's tempting to check that the output is exactly equal to some "golden" value that was expected when the test was written. But as the program evolves, parts of the output will likely change, probably in good ways, but change nonetheless. And it's not just the output; functions with complex inputs often break because the input used in a test is no longer valid.

The easiest way to avoid brittle tests is to check only the properties you care about. Test your program's simpler and more stable interfaces in preference to its internal functions. Be selective in your assertions. Don't check for exact string matches, for example, but look for relevant substrings that will remain unchanged as the program evolves. It's often worth writing a substantial function to distill a complex output down to its essence so that assertions will be reliable. Even though that may seem like a lot of up-front effort, it can pay for itself quickly in time that would otherwise be spent fixing spuriously failing tests.

11.3. Coverage

By its nature, testing is never complete. As the influential computer scientist Edsger Dijkstra put it, "Testing shows the presence, not the absence of bugs." No quantity of tests can ever prove a package free of bugs. At best, they increase our confidence that the package works well in a wide range of important scenarios.

The degree to which a test suite exercises the package under test is called the test's *coverage*. Coverage can't be quantified directly—the dynamics of all but the most trivial programs are beyond precise measurement—but there are heuristics that can help us direct our testing efforts to where they are more likely to be useful.

Statement coverage is the simplest and most widely used of these heuristics. The statement coverage of a test suite is the fraction of source statements that are executed at least once during the test. In this section, we'll use Go's cover tool, which is integrated into go test, to measure statement coverage and help identify obvious gaps in the tests.

The code below is a table-driven test for the expression evaluator we built back in Chapter 7:

gopl.io/ch7/eval
```go
func TestCoverage(t *testing.T) {
    var tests = []struct {
        input string
        env   Env
        want  string // expected error from Parse/Check or result from Eval
    }{
        {"x % 2", nil, "unexpected '%'"},
        {"!true", nil, "unexpected '!'"},
        {"log(10)", nil, `unknown function "log"`},
        {"sqrt(1, 2)", nil, "call to sqrt has 2 args, want 1"},
        {"sqrt(A / pi)", Env{"A": 87616, "pi": math.Pi}, "167"},
        {"pow(x, 3) + pow(y, 3)", Env{"x": 9, "y": 10}, "1729"},
        {"5 / 9 * (F - 32)", Env{"F": -40}, "-40"},
    }

    for _, test := range tests {
        expr, err := Parse(test.input)
        if err == nil {
            err = expr.Check(map[Var]bool{})
        }
        if err != nil {
            if err.Error() != test.want {
                t.Errorf("%s: got %q, want %q", test.input, err, test.want)
            }
            continue
        }
```

```
            got := fmt.Sprintf("%.6g", expr.Eval(test.env))
            if got != test.want {
                t.Errorf("%s: %v => %s, want %s",
                    test.input, test.env, got, test.want)
            }
        }
    }
```

First, let's check that the test passes:

```
$ go test -v -run=Coverage gopl.io/ch7/eval
=== RUN TestCoverage
--- PASS: TestCoverage (0.00s)
PASS
ok      gopl.io/ch7/eval     0.011s
```

This command displays the usage message of the coverage tool:

```
$ go tool cover
Usage of 'go tool cover':
Given a coverage profile produced by 'go test':
    go test -coverprofile=c.out

Open a web browser displaying annotated source code:
    go tool cover -html=c.out
...
```

The go tool command runs one of the executables from the Go toolchain. These programs live in the directory $GOROOT/pkg/tool/${GOOS}_${GOARCH}. Thanks to go build, we rarely need to invoke them directly.

Now we run the test with the -coverprofile flag:

```
$ go test -run=Coverage -coverprofile=c.out gopl.io/ch7/eval
ok      gopl.io/ch7/eval     0.032s  coverage: 68.5% of statements
```

This flag enables the collection of coverage data by *instrumenting* the production code. That is, it modifies a copy of the source code so that before each block of statements is executed, a boolean variable is set, with one variable per block. Just before the modified program exits, it writes the value of each variable to the specified log file c.out and prints a summary of the fraction of statements that were executed. (If all you need is the summary, use go test -cover.)

If go test is run with the -covermode=count flag, the instrumentation for each block increments a counter instead of setting a boolean. The resulting log of execution counts of each block enables quantitative comparisons between "hotter" blocks, which are more frequently executed, and "colder" ones.

Having gathered the data, we run the cover tool, which processes the log, generates an HTML report, and opens it in a new browser window (Figure 11.3).

```
$ go tool cover -html=c.out
```

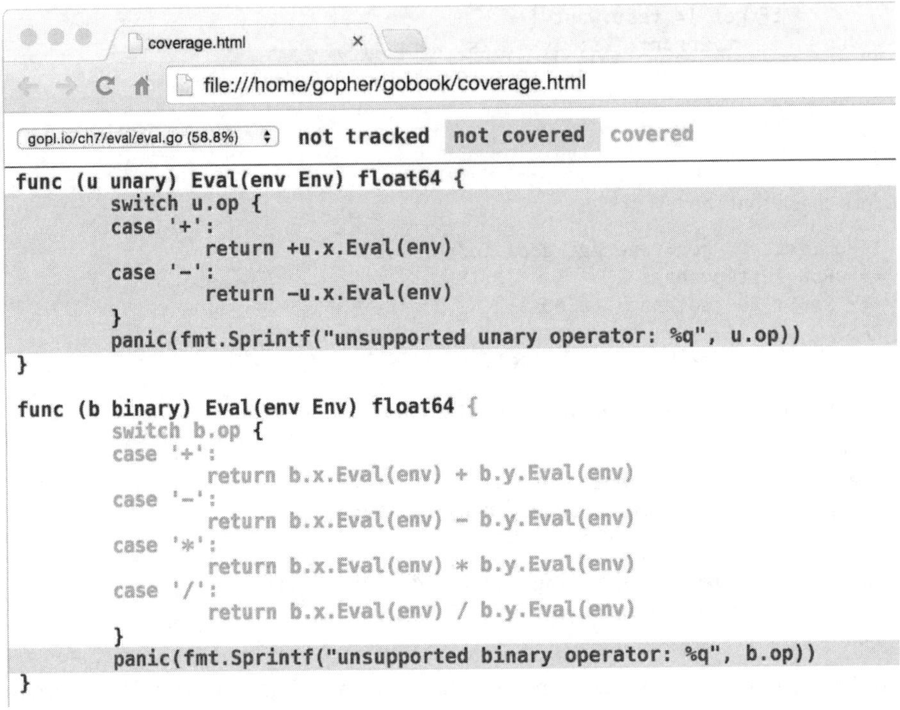

Figure 11.3. A coverage report.

Each statement is colored green if it was covered or red if it was not covered. For clarity, we've shaded the background of the red text. We can see immediately that none of our inputs exercised the unary operator `Eval` method. If we add this new test case to the table and re-run the previous two commands, the unary expression code becomes green:

```
{"-x * -x", eval.Env{"x": 2}, "4"}
```

The two `panic` statements remain red, however. This should not be surprising, because these statements are supposed to be unreachable.

Achieving 100% statement coverage sounds like a noble goal, but it is not usually feasible in practice, nor is it likely to be a good use of effort. Just because a statement is executed does not mean it is bug-free; statements containing complex expressions must be executed many times with different inputs to cover the interesting cases. Some statements, like the `panic` statements above, can never be reached. Others, such as those that handle esoteric errors, are hard to exercise but rarely reached in practice. Testing is fundamentally a pragmatic endeavor, a trade-off between the cost of writing tests and the cost of failures that could have been prevented by tests. Coverage tools can help identify the weakest spots, but devising good test cases demands the same rigorous thinking as programming in general.

11.4. Benchmark Functions

Benchmarking is the practice of measuring the performance of a program on a fixed workload. In Go, a benchmark function looks like a test function, but with the Benchmark prefix and a *testing.B parameter that provides most of the same methods as a *testing.T, plus a few extra related to performance measurement. It also exposes an integer field N, which specifies the number of times to perform the operation being measured.

Here's a benchmark for IsPalindrome that calls it N times in a loop.

```
import "testing"

func BenchmarkIsPalindrome(b *testing.B) {
    for i := 0; i < b.N; i++ {
        IsPalindrome("A man, a plan, a canal: Panama")
    }
}
```

We run it with the command below. Unlike tests, by default no benchmarks are run. The argument to the -bench flag selects which benchmarks to run. It is a regular expression matching the names of Benchmark functions, with a default value that matches none of them. The "." pattern causes it to match all benchmarks in the word package, but since there's only one, -bench=IsPalindrome would have been equivalent.

```
$ cd $GOPATH/src/gopl.io/ch11/word2
$ go test -bench=.
PASS
BenchmarkIsPalindrome-8 1000000                    1035 ns/op
ok      gopl.io/ch11/word2      2.179s
```

The benchmark name's numeric suffix, 8 here, indicates the value of GOMAXPROCS, which is important for concurrent benchmarks.

The report tells us that each call to IsPalindrome took about 1.035 microseconds, averaged over 1,000,000 runs. Since the benchmark runner initially has no idea how long the operation takes, it makes some initial measurements using small values of N and then extrapolates to a value large enough for a stable timing measurement to be made.

The reason the loop is implemented by the benchmark function, and not by the calling code in the test driver, is so that the benchmark function has the opportunity to execute any necessary one-time setup code outside the loop without this adding to the measured time of each iteration. If this setup code is still perturbing the results, the testing.B parameter provides methods to stop, resume, and reset the timer, but these are rarely needed.

Now that we have a benchmark and tests, it's easy to try out ideas for making the program faster. Perhaps the most obvious optimization is to make IsPalindrome's second loop stop checking at the midpoint, to avoid doing each comparison twice:

```
n := len(letters)/2
for i := 0; i < n; i++ {
    if letters[i] != letters[len(letters)-1-i] {
        return false
    }
}
return true
```

But as is often the case, an obvious optimization doesn't always yield the expected benefit. This one delivered a mere 4% improvement in one experiment.

```
$ go test -bench=.
PASS
BenchmarkIsPalindrome-8 1000000                    992 ns/op
ok       gopl.io/ch11/word2      2.093s
```

Another idea is to pre-allocate a sufficiently large array for use by letters, rather than expand it by successive calls to append. Declaring letters as an array of the right size, like this,

```
letters := make([]rune, 0, len(s))
for _, r := range s {
    if unicode.IsLetter(r) {
        letters = append(letters, unicode.ToLower(r))
    }
}
```

yields an improvement of nearly 35%, and the benchmark runner now reports the average over 2,000,000 iterations.

```
$ go test -bench=.
PASS
BenchmarkIsPalindrome-8 2000000                    697 ns/op
ok       gopl.io/ch11/word2      1.468s
```

As this example shows, the fastest program is often the one that makes the fewest memory allocations. The -benchmem command-line flag will include memory allocation statistics in its report. Here we compare the number of allocations before the optimization:

```
$ go test -bench=. -benchmem
PASS
BenchmarkIsPalindrome     1000000   1026 ns/op    304 B/op   4 allocs/op
```

and after it:

```
$ go test -bench=. -benchmem
PASS
BenchmarkIsPalindrome     2000000    807 ns/op    128 B/op   1 allocs/op
```

Consolidating the allocations in a single call to make eliminated 75% of the allocations and halved the quantity of allocated memory.

Benchmarks like this tell us the absolute time required for a given operation, but in many settings the interesting performance questions are about the *relative* timings of two different operations. For example, if a function takes 1ms to process 1,000 elements, how long will it take to process 10,000 or a million? Such comparisons reveal the asymptotic growth of the running time of the function. Another example: what is the best size for an I/O buffer? Benchmarks of application throughput over a range of sizes can help us choose the smallest buffer that delivers satisfactory performance. A third example: which algorithm performs best for a given job? Benchmarks that evaluate two different algorithms on the same input data can often show the strengths and weaknesses of each one on important or representative workloads.

Comparative benchmarks are just regular code. They typically take the form of a single parameterized function, called from several Benchmark functions with different values, like this:

```
func benchmark(b *testing.B, size int) { /* ... */ }
func Benchmark10(b *testing.B)   { benchmark(b, 10) }
func Benchmark100(b *testing.B)  { benchmark(b, 100) }
func Benchmark1000(b *testing.B) { benchmark(b, 1000) }
```

The parameter size, which specifies the size of the input, varies across benchmarks but is constant within each benchmark. Resist the temptation to use the parameter b.N as the input size. Unless you interpret it as an iteration count for a fixed-size input, the results of your benchmark will be meaningless.

Patterns revealed by comparative benchmarks are particularly useful during program design, but we don't throw the benchmarks away when the program is working. As the program evolves, or its input grows, or it is deployed on new operating systems or processors with different characteristics, we can reuse those benchmarks to revisit design decisions.

Exercise 11.6: Write benchmarks to compare the PopCount implementation in Section 2.6.2 with your solutions to Exercise 2.4 and Exercise 2.5. At what point does the table-based approach break even?

Exercise 11.7: Write benchmarks for Add, UnionWith, and other methods of *IntSet (§6.5) using large pseudo-random inputs. How fast can you make these methods run? How does the choice of word size affect performance? How fast is IntSet compared to a set implementation based on the built-in map type?

11.5. Profiling

Benchmarks are useful for measuring the performance of specific operations, but when we're trying to make a slow program faster, we often have no idea where to begin. Every programmer knows Donald Knuth's aphorism about premature optimization, which appeared in "Structured Programming with go to Statements" in 1974. Although often misinterpreted to mean performance doesn't matter, in its original context we can discern a different meaning:

> There is no doubt that the grail of efficiency leads to abuse. Programmers waste enormous amounts of time thinking about, or worrying about, the speed of noncritical

parts of their programs, and these attempts at efficiency actually have a strong negative impact when debugging and maintenance are considered. We *should* forget about small efficiencies, say about 97% of the time: premature optimization is the root of all evil.

Yet we should not pass up our opportunities in that critical 3%. A good programmer will not be lulled into complacency by such reasoning, he will be wise to look carefully at the critical code; but only *after* that code has been identified. It is often a mistake to make a priori judgments about what parts of a program are really critical, since the universal experience of programmers who have been using measurement tools has been that their intuitive guesses fail.

When we wish to look carefully at the speed of our programs, the best technique for identifying the critical code is *profiling*. Profiling is an automated approach to performance measurement based on sampling a number of profile *events* during execution, then extrapolating from them during a post-processing step; the resulting statistical summary is called a *profile*.

Go supports many kinds of profiling, each concerned with a different aspect of performance, but all of them involve recording a sequence of events of interest, each of which has an accompanying stack trace—the stack of function calls active at the moment of the event. The go test tool has built-in support for several kinds of profiling.

A *CPU profile* identifies the functions whose execution requires the most CPU time. The currently running thread on each CPU is interrupted periodically by the operating system every few milliseconds, with each interruption recording one profile event before normal execution resumes.

A *heap profile* identifies the statements responsible for allocating the most memory. The profiling library samples calls to the internal memory allocation routines so that on average, one profile event is recorded per 512KB of allocated memory.

A *blocking profile* identifies the operations responsible for blocking goroutines the longest, such as system calls, channel sends and receives, and acquisitions of locks. The profiling library records an event every time a goroutine is blocked by one of these operations.

Gathering a profile for code under test is as easy as enabling one of the flags below. Be careful when using more than one flag at a time, however: the machinery for gathering one kind of profile may skew the results of others.

```
$ go test -cpuprofile=cpu.out
$ go test -blockprofile=block.out
$ go test -memprofile=mem.out
```

It's easy to add profiling support to non-test programs too, though the details of how we do that vary between short-lived command-line tools and long-running server applications. Profiling is especially useful in long-running applications, so the Go runtime's profiling features can be enabled under programmer control using the runtime API.

Once we've gathered a profile, we need to analyze it using the pprof tool. This is a standard part of the Go distribution, but since it's not an everyday tool, it's accessed indirectly using go tool pprof. It has dozens of features and options, but basic use requires only two arguments, the executable that produced the profile and the profile log.

To make profiling efficient and to save space, the log does not include function names; instead, functions are identified by their addresses. This means that pprof needs the executable in order to make sense of the log. Although go test usually discards the test executable once the test is complete, when profiling is enabled it saves the executable as foo.test, where foo is the name of the tested package.

The commands below show how to gather and display a simple CPU profile. We've selected one of the benchmarks from the net/http package. It is usually better to profile specific benchmarks that have been constructed to be representative of workloads one cares about. Benchmarking test cases is almost never representative, which is why we disabled them by using the filter -run=NONE.

```
$ go test -run=NONE -bench=ClientServerParallelTLS64 \
    -cpuprofile=cpu.log net/http
PASS
BenchmarkClientServerParallelTLS64-8   1000
   3141325 ns/op   143010 B/op   1747 allocs/op
ok      net/http        3.395s

$ go tool pprof -text -nodecount=10 ./http.test cpu.log
2570ms of 3590ms total (71.59%)
Dropped 129 nodes (cum <= 17.95ms)
Showing top 10 nodes out of 166 (cum >= 60ms)
    flat  flat%   sum%      cum   cum%
  1730ms 48.19% 48.19%   1750ms 48.75%  crypto/elliptic.p256ReduceDegree
   230ms  6.41% 54.60%    250ms  6.96%  crypto/elliptic.p256Diff
   120ms  3.34% 57.94%    120ms  3.34%  math/big.addMulVVW
   110ms  3.06% 61.00%    110ms  3.06%  syscall.Syscall
    90ms  2.51% 63.51%   1130ms 31.48%  crypto/elliptic.p256Square
    70ms  1.95% 65.46%    120ms  3.34%  runtime.scanobject
    60ms  1.67% 67.13%    830ms 23.12%  crypto/elliptic.p256Mul
    60ms  1.67% 68.80%    190ms  5.29%  math/big.nat.montgomery
    50ms  1.39% 70.19%     50ms  1.39%  crypto/elliptic.p256ReduceCarry
    50ms  1.39% 71.59%     60ms  1.67%  crypto/elliptic.p256Sum
```

The -text flag specifies the output format, in this case, a textual table with one row per function, sorted so the "hottest" functions—those that consume the most CPU cycles—appear first. The -nodecount=10 flag limits the result to 10 rows. For gross performance problems, this textual format may be enough to pinpoint the cause.

This profile tells us that elliptic-curve cryptography is important to the performance of this particular HTTPS benchmark. By contrast, if a profile is dominated by memory allocation functions from the runtime package, reducing memory consumption may be a worthwhile optimization.

For more subtle problems, you may be better off using one of pprof's graphical displays. These require GraphViz, which can be downloaded from www.graphviz.org. The -web flag then renders a directed graph of the functions of the program, annotated by their CPU profile numbers and colored to indicate the hottest functions.

We've only scratched the surface of Go's profiling tools here. To find out more, read the "Profiling Go Programs" article on the Go Blog.

11.6. Example Functions

The third kind of function treated specially by go test is an example function, one whose name starts with Example. It has neither parameters nor results. Here's an example function for IsPalindrome:

```
func ExampleIsPalindrome() {
    fmt.Println(IsPalindrome("A man, a plan, a canal: Panama"))
    fmt.Println(IsPalindrome("palindrome"))
    // Output:
    // true
    // false
}
```

Example functions serve three purposes. The primary one is documentation: a good example can be a more succinct or intuitive way to convey the behavior of a library function than its prose description, especially when used as a reminder or quick reference. An example can also demonstrate the interaction between several types and functions belonging to one API, whereas prose documentation must always be attached to one place, like a type or function declaration or the package as a whole. And unlike examples within comments, example functions are real Go code, subject to compile-time checking, so they don't become stale as the code evolves.

Based on the suffix of the Example function, the web-based documentation server godoc associates example functions with the function or package they exemplify, so ExampleIs-Palindrome would be shown with the documentation for the IsPalindrome function, and an example function called just Example would be associated with the word package as a whole.

The second purpose is that examples are executable tests run by go test. If the example function contains a final // Output: comment like the one above, the test driver will execute the function and check that what it printed to its standard output matches the text within the comment.

The third purpose of an example is hands-on experimentation. The godoc server at golang.org uses the Go Playground to let the user edit and run each example function from within a web browser, as shown in Figure 11.4. This is often the fastest way to get a feel for a particular function or language feature.

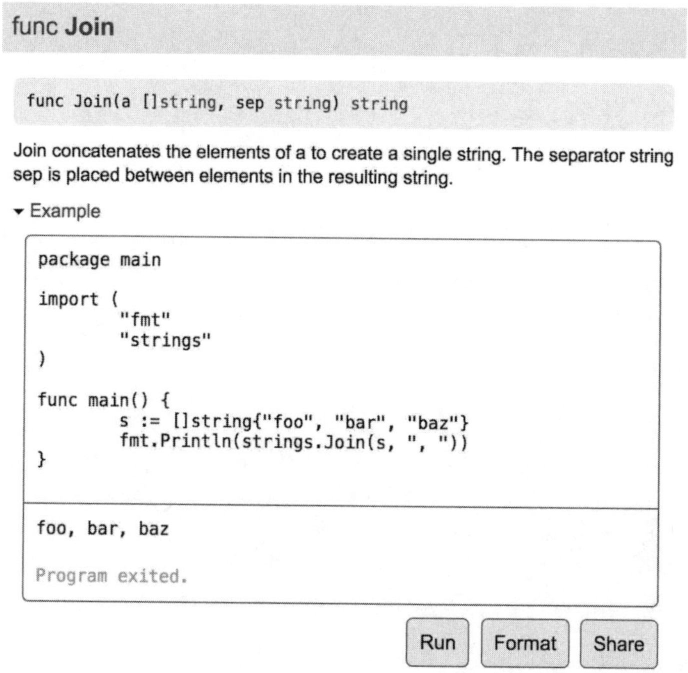

func **Join**

```
func Join(a []string, sep string) string
```

Join concatenates the elements of a to create a single string. The separator string sep is placed between elements in the resulting string.

▾ Example

```
package main

import (
        "fmt"
        "strings"
)

func main() {
        s := []string{"foo", "bar", "baz"}
        fmt.Println(strings.Join(s, ", "))
}
```

```
foo, bar, baz

Program exited.
```

[Run] [Format] [Share]

Figure 11.4. An interactive example of `strings.Join` in godoc.

The final two chapters of the book examine the `reflect` and `unsafe` packages, which few Go programmers regularly use—and even fewer *need* to use. If you haven't written any substantial Go programs yet, now would be a good time to do that.

12

Reflection

Go provides a mechanism to update variables and inspect their values at run time, to call their methods, and to apply the operations intrinsic to their representation, all without knowing their types at compile time. This mechanism is called *reflection*. Reflection also lets us treat types themselves as first-class values.

In this chapter, we'll explore Go's reflection features to see how they increase the expressiveness of the language, and in particular how they are crucial to the implementation of two important APIs: string formatting provided by `fmt`, and protocol encoding provided by packages like `encoding/json` and `encoding/xml`. Reflection is also essential to the template mechanism provided by the `text/template` and `html/template` packages we saw in Section 4.6. However, reflection is complex to reason about and not for casual use, so although these packages are implemented using reflection, they do not expose reflection in their own APIs.

12.1. Why Reflection?

Sometimes we need to write a function capable of dealing uniformly with values of types that don't satisfy a common interface, don't have a known representation, or don't exist at the time we design the function—or even all three.

A familiar example is the formatting logic within `fmt.Fprintf`, which can usefully print an arbitrary value of any type, even a user-defined one. Let's try to implement a function like it using what we know already. For simplicity, our function will accept one argument and will return the result as a string like `fmt.Sprint` does, so we'll call it `Sprint`.

We start with a type switch that tests whether the argument defines a `String` method, and call it if so. We then add switch cases that test the value's dynamic type against each of the basic types—string, int, bool, and so on—and perform the appropriate formatting operation in each case.

```
func Sprint(x interface{}) string {
    type stringer interface {
        String() string
    }
    switch x := x.(type) {
    case stringer:
        return x.String()
    case string:
        return x
    case int:
        return strconv.Itoa(x)
    // ...similar cases for int16, uint32, and so on...
    case bool:
        if x {
            return "true"
        }
        return "false"
    default:
        // array, chan, func, map, pointer, slice, struct
        return "???"
    }
}
```

But how do we deal with other types, like []float64, map[string][]string, and so on? We could add more cases, but the number of such types is infinite. And what about named types, like url.Values? Even if the type switch had a case for its underlying type map[string][]string, it wouldn't match url.Values because the two types are not identical, and the type switch cannot include a case for each type like url.Values because that would require this library to depend upon its clients.

Without a way to inspect the representation of values of unknown types, we quickly get stuck. What we need is reflection.

12.2. reflect.Type and reflect.Value

Reflection is provided by the reflect package. It defines two important types, Type and Value. A Type represents a Go type. It is an interface with many methods for discriminating among types and inspecting their components, like the fields of a struct or the parameters of a function. The sole implementation of reflect.Type is the type descriptor (§7.5), the same entity that identifies the dynamic type of an interface value.

The reflect.TypeOf function accepts any interface{} and returns its dynamic type as a reflect.Type:

```
t := reflect.TypeOf(3)  // a reflect.Type
fmt.Println(t.String()) // "int"
fmt.Println(t)          // "int"
```

The TypeOf(3) call above assigns the value 3 to the interface{} parameter. Recall from Section 7.5 that an assignment from a concrete value to an interface type performs an implicit interface conversion, which creates an interface value consisting of two components: its *dynamic type* is the operand's type (int) and its *dynamic value* is the operand's value (3).

Because reflect.TypeOf returns an interface value's dynamic type, it always returns a concrete type. So, for example, the code below prints "*os.File", not "io.Writer". Later, we will see that reflect.Type is capable of representing interface types too.

```
var w io.Writer = os.Stdout
fmt.Println(reflect.TypeOf(w)) // "*os.File"
```

Notice that reflect.Type satisfies fmt.Stringer. Because printing the dynamic type of an interface value is useful for debugging and logging, fmt.Printf provides a shorthand, %T, that uses reflect.TypeOf internally:

```
fmt.Printf("%T\n", 3) // "int"
```

The other important type in the reflect package is Value. A reflect.Value can hold a value of any type. The reflect.ValueOf function accepts any interface{} and returns a reflect.Value containing the interface's dynamic value. As with reflect.TypeOf, the results of reflect.ValueOf are always concrete, but a reflect.Value can hold interface values too.

```
v := reflect.ValueOf(3) // a reflect.Value
fmt.Println(v)          // "3"
fmt.Printf("%v\n", v)   // "3"
fmt.Println(v.String()) // NOTE: "<int Value>"
```

Like reflect.Type, reflect.Value also satisfies fmt.Stringer, but unless the Value holds a string, the result of the String method reveals only the type. Instead, use the fmt package's %v verb, which treats reflect.Values specially.

Calling the Type method on a Value returns its type as a reflect.Type:

```
t := v.Type()           // a reflect.Type
fmt.Println(t.String()) // "int"
```

The inverse operation to reflect.ValueOf is the reflect.Value.Interface method. It returns an interface{} holding the same concrete value as the reflect.Value:

```
v := reflect.ValueOf(3) // a reflect.Value
x := v.Interface()      // an interface{}
i := x.(int)            // an int
fmt.Printf("%d\n", i)   // "3"
```

A reflect.Value and an interface{} can both hold arbitrary values. The difference is that an empty interface hides the representation and intrinsic operations of the value it holds and exposes none of its methods, so unless we know its dynamic type and use a type assertion to

peer inside it (as we did above), there is little we can do to the value within. In contrast, a
Value has many methods for inspecting its contents, regardless of its type. Let's use them for
our second attempt at a general formatting function, which we'll call format.Any.

Instead of a type switch, we use reflect.Value's Kind method to discriminate the cases.
Although there are infinitely many types, there are only a finite number of *kinds* of type: the
basic types Bool, String, and all the numbers; the aggregate types Array and Struct; the reference types Chan, Func, Ptr, Slice, and Map; Interface types; and finally Invalid, meaning
no value at all. (The zero value of a reflect.Value has kind Invalid.)

gopl.io/ch12/format

```
package format

import (
    "reflect"
    "strconv"
)

// Any formats any value as a string.
func Any(value interface{}) string {
    return formatAtom(reflect.ValueOf(value))
}

// formatAtom formats a value without inspecting its internal structure.
func formatAtom(v reflect.Value) string {
    switch v.Kind() {
    case reflect.Invalid:
        return "invalid"
    case reflect.Int, reflect.Int8, reflect.Int16,
        reflect.Int32, reflect.Int64:
        return strconv.FormatInt(v.Int(), 10)
    case reflect.Uint, reflect.Uint8, reflect.Uint16,
        reflect.Uint32, reflect.Uint64, reflect.Uintptr:
        return strconv.FormatUint(v.Uint(), 10)
    // ...floating-point and complex cases omitted for brevity...
    case reflect.Bool:
        return strconv.FormatBool(v.Bool())
    case reflect.String:
        return strconv.Quote(v.String())
    case reflect.Chan, reflect.Func, reflect.Ptr, reflect.Slice, reflect.Map:
        return v.Type().String() + " 0x" +
            strconv.FormatUint(uint64(v.Pointer()), 16)
    default: // reflect.Array, reflect.Struct, reflect.Interface
        return v.Type().String() + " value"
    }
}
```

So far, our function treats each value as an indivisible thing with no internal structure—hence
formatAtom. For aggregate types (structs and arrays) and interfaces it prints only the *type* of
the value, and for reference types (channels, functions, pointers, slices, and maps), it prints the
type and the reference address in hexadecimal. This is less than ideal but still a major

improvement, and since Kind is concerned only with the underlying representation, format.Any works for named types too. For example:

```
var x int64 = 1
var d time.Duration = 1 * time.Nanosecond
fmt.Println(format.Any(x))                        // "1"
fmt.Println(format.Any(d))                        // "1"
fmt.Println(format.Any([]int64{x}))               // "[]int64 0x8202b87b0"
fmt.Println(format.Any([]time.Duration{d})) // "[]time.Duration 0x8202b87e0"
```

12.3. Display, a Recursive Value Printer

Next we'll take a look at how to improve the display of composite types. Rather than try to copy fmt.Sprint exactly, we'll build a debugging utility function called Display that, given an arbitrarily complex value x, prints the complete structure of that value, labeling each element with the path by which it was found. Let's start with an example.

```
e, _ := eval.Parse("sqrt(A / pi)")
Display("e", e)
```

In the call above, the argument to Display is a syntax tree from the expression evaluator in Section 7.9. The output of Display is shown below:

```
Display e (eval.call):
e.fn = "sqrt"
e.args[0].type = eval.binary
e.args[0].value.op = 47
e.args[0].value.x.type = eval.Var
e.args[0].value.x.value = "A"
e.args[0].value.y.type = eval.Var
e.args[0].value.y.value = "pi"
```

Where possible, you should avoid exposing reflection in the API of a package. We'll define an unexported function display to do the real work of the recursion, and export Display, a simple wrapper around it that accepts an interface{} parameter:

gopl.io/ch12/display
```
func Display(name string, x interface{}) {
    fmt.Printf("Display %s (%T):\n", name, x)
    display(name, reflect.ValueOf(x))
}
```

In display, we'll use the formatAtom function we defined earlier to print elementary values—basic types, functions, and channels—but we'll use the methods of reflect.Value to recursively display each component of a more complex type. As the recursion descends, the path string, which initially describes the starting value (for instance, "e"), will be augmented to indicate how we reached the current value (for instance, "e.args[0].value").

Since we're no longer pretending to implement `fmt.Sprint`, we will use the `fmt` package to keep our example short.

```go
func display(path string, v reflect.Value) {
    switch v.Kind() {
    case reflect.Invalid:
        fmt.Printf("%s = invalid\n", path)
    case reflect.Slice, reflect.Array:
        for i := 0; i < v.Len(); i++ {
            display(fmt.Sprintf("%s[%d]", path, i), v.Index(i))
        }
    case reflect.Struct:
        for i := 0; i < v.NumField(); i++ {
            fieldPath := fmt.Sprintf("%s.%s", path, v.Type().Field(i).Name)
            display(fieldPath, v.Field(i))
        }
    case reflect.Map:
        for _, key := range v.MapKeys() {
            display(fmt.Sprintf("%s[%s]", path,
                formatAtom(key)), v.MapIndex(key))
        }
    case reflect.Ptr:
        if v.IsNil() {
            fmt.Printf("%s = nil\n", path)
        } else {
            display(fmt.Sprintf("(*%s)", path), v.Elem())
        }
    case reflect.Interface:
        if v.IsNil() {
            fmt.Printf("%s = nil\n", path)
        } else {
            fmt.Printf("%s.type = %s\n", path, v.Elem().Type())
            display(path+".value", v.Elem())
        }
    default: // basic types, channels, funcs
        fmt.Printf("%s = %s\n", path, formatAtom(v))
    }
}
```

Let's discuss the cases in order.

Slices and arrays: The logic is the same for both. The `Len` method returns the number of elements of a slice or array value, and `Index(i)` retrieves the element at index `i`, also as a `reflect.Value`; it panics if `i` is out of bounds. These are analogous to the built-in `len(a)` and `a[i]` operations on sequences. The `display` function recursively invokes itself on each element of the sequence, appending the subscript notation `"[i]"` to the path.

Although `reflect.Value` has many methods, only a few are safe to call on any given value. For example, the `Index` method may be called on values of kind `Slice`, `Array`, or `String`, but panics for any other kind.

Structs: The `NumField` method reports the number of fields in the struct, and `Field(i)` returns the value of the *i*-th field as a `reflect.Value`. The list of fields includes ones promoted from anonymous fields. To append the field selector notation ".f" to the path, we must obtain the `reflect.Type` of the struct and access the name of its *i*-th field.

Maps: The `MapKeys` method returns a slice of `reflect.Values`, one per map key. As usual when iterating over a map, the order is undefined. `MapIndex(key)` returns the value corresponding to key. We append the subscript notation "[key]" to the path. (We're cutting a corner here. The type of a map key isn't restricted to the types `formatAtom` handles best; arrays, structs, and interfaces can also be valid map keys. Extending this case to print the key in full is Exercise 12.1.)

Pointers: The `Elem` method returns the variable pointed to by a pointer, again as a `reflect.Value`. This operation would be safe even if the pointer value is `nil`, in which case the result would have kind `Invalid`, but we use `IsNil` to detect nil pointers explicitly so we can print a more appropriate message. We prefix the path with a "*" and parenthesize it to avoid ambiguity.

Interfaces: Again, we use `IsNil` to test whether the interface is nil, and if not, we retrieve its dynamic value using `v.Elem()` and print its type and value.

Now that our `Display` function is complete, let's put it to work. The `Movie` type below is a slight variation on the one in Section 4.5:

```go
type Movie struct {
    Title, Subtitle string
    Year            int
    Color           bool
    Actor           map[string]string
    Oscars          []string
    Sequel          *string
}
```

Let's declare a value of this type and see what `Display` does with it:

```go
strangelove := Movie{
    Title:    "Dr. Strangelove",
    Subtitle: "How I Learned to Stop Worrying and Love the Bomb",
    Year:     1964,
    Color:    false,
    Actor: map[string]string{
        "Dr. Strangelove":            "Peter Sellers",
        "Grp. Capt. Lionel Mandrake": "Peter Sellers",
        "Pres. Merkin Muffley":       "Peter Sellers",
        "Gen. Buck Turgidson":        "George C. Scott",
        "Brig. Gen. Jack D. Ripper":  "Sterling Hayden",
        `Maj. T.J. "King" Kong`:      "Slim Pickens",
    },
```

```
    Oscars: []string{
        "Best Actor (Nomin.)",
        "Best Adapted Screenplay (Nomin.)",
        "Best Director (Nomin.)",
        "Best Picture (Nomin.)",
    },
}
```

The call Display("strangelove", strangelove) prints:

```
Display strangelove (display.Movie):
strangelove.Title = "Dr. Strangelove"
strangelove.Subtitle = "How I Learned to Stop Worrying and Love the Bomb"
strangelove.Year = 1964
strangelove.Color = false
strangelove.Actor["Gen. Buck Turgidson"] = "George C. Scott"
strangelove.Actor["Brig. Gen. Jack D. Ripper"] = "Sterling Hayden"
strangelove.Actor["Maj. T.J. \"King\" Kong"] = "Slim Pickens"
strangelove.Actor["Dr. Strangelove"] = "Peter Sellers"
strangelove.Actor["Grp. Capt. Lionel Mandrake"] = "Peter Sellers"
strangelove.Actor["Pres. Merkin Muffley"] = "Peter Sellers"
strangelove.Oscars[0] = "Best Actor (Nomin.)"
strangelove.Oscars[1] = "Best Adapted Screenplay (Nomin.)"
strangelove.Oscars[2] = "Best Director (Nomin.)"
strangelove.Oscars[3] = "Best Picture (Nomin.)"
strangelove.Sequel = nil
```

We can use Display to display the internals of library types, such as *os.File:

```
Display("os.Stderr", os.Stderr)
// Output:
// Display os.Stderr (*os.File):
// (*(*os.Stderr).file).fd = 2
// (*(*os.Stderr).file).name = "/dev/stderr"
// (*(*os.Stderr).file).nepipe = 0
```

Notice that even unexported fields are visible to reflection. Beware that the particular output of this example may vary across platforms and may change over time as libraries evolve. (Those fields are private for a reason!) We can even apply Display to a reflect.Value and watch it traverse the internal representation of the type descriptor for *os.File. The output of the call Display("rV", reflect.ValueOf(os.Stderr)) is shown below, though of course your mileage may vary:

```
Display rV (reflect.Value):
(*rV.typ).size = 8
(*rV.typ).hash = 871609668
(*rV.typ).align = 8
(*rV.typ).fieldAlign = 8
(*rV.typ).kind = 22
(*(*rV.typ).string) = "*os.File"
```

```
(*(*(*rV.typ).uncommonType).methods[0].name) = "Chdir"
(*(*(*(*rV.typ).uncommonType).methods[0].mtyp).string) = "func() error"
(*(*(*(*rV.typ).uncommonType).methods[0].typ).string) = "func(*os.File) error"
...
```

Observe the difference between these two examples:

```
var i interface{} = 3

Display("i", i)
// Output:
// Display i (int):
// i = 3

Display("&i", &i)
// Output:
// Display &i (*interface {}):
// (*&i).type = int
// (*&i).value = 3
```

In the first example, Display calls reflect.ValueOf(i), which returns a value of kind Int. As we mentioned in Section 12.2, reflect.ValueOf always returns a Value of a concrete type since it extracts the contents of an interface value.

In the second example, Display calls reflect.ValueOf(&i), which returns a pointer to i, of kind Ptr. The switch case for Ptr calls Elem on this value, which returns a Value representing the *variable* i itself, of kind Interface. A Value obtained indirectly, like this one, may represent any value at all, including interfaces. The display function calls itself recursively and this time, it prints separate components for the interface's dynamic type and value.

As currently implemented, Display will never terminate if it encounters a cycle in the object graph, such as this linked list that eats its own tail:

```
// a struct that points to itself
type Cycle struct{ Value int; Tail *Cycle }
var c Cycle
c = Cycle{42, &c}
Display("c", c)
```

Display prints this ever-growing expansion:

```
Display c (display.Cycle):
c.Value = 42
(*c.Tail).Value = 42
(*(*c.Tail).Tail).Value = 42
(*(*(*c.Tail).Tail).Tail).Value = 42
...ad infinitum...
```

Many Go programs contain at least some cyclic data. Making Display robust against such cycles is tricky, requiring additional bookkeeping to record the set of references that have been followed so far; it is costly too. A general solution requires unsafe language features, as we will see in Section 13.3.

Cycles pose less of a problem for fmt.Sprint because it rarely tries to print the complete structure. For example, when it encounters a pointer, it breaks the recursion by printing the pointer's numeric value. It can get stuck trying to print a slice or map that contains itself as an element, but such rare cases do not warrant the considerable extra trouble of handling cycles.

Exercise 12.1: Extend Display so that it can display maps whose keys are structs or arrays.

Exercise 12.2: Make display safe to use on cyclic data structures by bounding the number of steps it takes before abandoning the recursion. (In Section 13.3, we'll see another way to detect cycles.)

12.4. Example: Encoding S-Expressions

Display is a debugging routine for displaying structured data, but it's not far short of being able to encode or *marshal* arbitrary Go objects as messages in a portable notation suitable for inter-process communication.

As we saw in Section 4.5, Go's standard library supports a variety of formats, including JSON, XML, and ASN.1. Another notation that is still widely used is *S-expressions*, the syntax of Lisp. Unlike the other notations, S-expressions are not supported by the Go standard library, not least because they have no universally accepted definition, despite several attempts at standardization and the existence of many implementations.

In this section, we'll define a package that encodes arbitrary Go objects using an S-expression notation that supports the following constructs:

```
42              integer
"hello"         string (with Go-style quotation)
foo             symbol (an unquoted name)
(1 2 3)         list   (zero or more items enclosed in parentheses)
```

Booleans are traditionally encoded using the symbol t for true, and the empty list () or the symbol nil for false, but for simplicity, our implementation ignores them. It also ignores channels and functions, since their state is opaque to reflection. And it ignores real and complex floating-point numbers and interfaces. Adding support for them is Exercise 12.3.

We'll encode the types of Go using S-expressions as follows. Integers and strings are encoded in the obvious way. Nil values are encoded as the symbol nil. Arrays and slices are encoded using list notation.

Structs are encoded as a list of field bindings, each field binding being a two-element list whose first element (a symbol) is the field name and whose second element is the field value. Maps too are encoded as a list of pairs, with each pair being the key and value of one map entry. Traditionally, S-expressions represent lists of key/value pairs using a single *cons* cell (key . value) for each pair, rather than a two-element list, but to simplify the decoding we'll ignore dotted list notation.

Encoding is done by a single recursive function, encode, shown below. Its structure is essentially the same as that of Display in the previous section:

gopl.io/ch12/sexpr
```go
func encode(buf *bytes.Buffer, v reflect.Value) error {
    switch v.Kind() {
    case reflect.Invalid:
        buf.WriteString("nil")

    case reflect.Int, reflect.Int8, reflect.Int16,
        reflect.Int32, reflect.Int64:
        fmt.Fprintf(buf, "%d", v.Int())

    case reflect.Uint, reflect.Uint8, reflect.Uint16,
        reflect.Uint32, reflect.Uint64, reflect.Uintptr:
        fmt.Fprintf(buf, "%d", v.Uint())

    case reflect.String:
        fmt.Fprintf(buf, "%q", v.String())

    case reflect.Ptr:
        return encode(buf, v.Elem())

    case reflect.Array, reflect.Slice: // (value ...)
        buf.WriteByte('(')
        for i := 0; i < v.Len(); i++ {
            if i > 0 {
                buf.WriteByte(' ')
            }
            if err := encode(buf, v.Index(i)); err != nil {
                return err
            }
        }
        buf.WriteByte(')')

    case reflect.Struct: // ((name value) ...)
        buf.WriteByte('(')
        for i := 0; i < v.NumField(); i++ {
            if i > 0 {
                buf.WriteByte(' ')
            }
            fmt.Fprintf(buf, "(%s ", v.Type().Field(i).Name)
            if err := encode(buf, v.Field(i)); err != nil {
                return err
            }
            buf.WriteByte(')')
        }
        buf.WriteByte(')')
```

```go
        case reflect.Map: // ((key value) ...)
            buf.WriteByte('(')
            for i, key := range v.MapKeys() {
                if i > 0 {
                    buf.WriteByte(' ')
                }
                buf.WriteByte('(')
                if err := encode(buf, key); err != nil {
                    return err
                }
                buf.WriteByte(' ')
                if err := encode(buf, v.MapIndex(key)); err != nil {
                    return err
                }
                buf.WriteByte(')')
            }
            buf.WriteByte(')')

        default: // float, complex, bool, chan, func, interface
            return fmt.Errorf("unsupported type: %s", v.Type())
        }
        return nil
    }
```

The `Marshal` function wraps the encoder in an API similar to those of the other encod-ing/... packages:

```go
    // Marshal encodes a Go value in S-expression form.
    func Marshal(v interface{}) ([]byte, error) {
        var buf bytes.Buffer
        if err := encode(&buf, reflect.ValueOf(v)); err != nil {
            return nil, err
        }
        return buf.Bytes(), nil
    }
```

Here's the output of `Marshal` applied to the `strangelove` variable from Section 12.3:

```
    ((Title "Dr. Strangelove") (Subtitle "How I Learned to Stop Worrying and Lo
    ve the Bomb") (Year 1964) (Actor (("Grp. Capt. Lionel Mandrake" "Peter Sell
    ers") ("Pres. Merkin Muffley" "Peter Sellers") ("Gen. Buck Turgidson" "Geor
    ge C. Scott") ("Brig. Gen. Jack D. Ripper" "Sterling Hayden") ("Maj. T.J. \
    "King\" Kong" "Slim Pickens") ("Dr. Strangelove" "Peter Sellers"))) (Oscars
    ("Best Actor (Nomin.)" "Best Adapted Screenplay (Nomin.)" "Best Director (N
    omin.)" "Best Picture (Nomin.)")) (Sequel nil))
```

The whole output appears on one long line with minimal spaces, making it hard to read. Here's the same output manually formatted according to S-expression conventions. Writing a pretty-printer for S-expressions is left as a (challenging) exercise; the download from gopl.io includes a simple version.

```
((Title "Dr. Strangelove")
 (Subtitle "How I Learned to Stop Worrying and Love the Bomb")
 (Year 1964)
 (Actor (("Grp. Capt. Lionel Mandrake" "Peter Sellers")
         ("Pres. Merkin Muffley" "Peter Sellers")
         ("Gen. Buck Turgidson" "George C. Scott")
         ("Brig. Gen. Jack D. Ripper" "Sterling Hayden")
         ("Maj. T.J. \"King\" Kong" "Slim Pickens")
         ("Dr. Strangelove" "Peter Sellers")))
 (Oscars ("Best Actor (Nomin.)"
          "Best Adapted Screenplay (Nomin.)"
          "Best Director (Nomin.)"
          "Best Picture (Nomin.)"))
 (Sequel nil))
```

Like the `fmt.Print`, `json.Marshal`, and `Display` functions, `sexpr.Marshal` will loop forever if called with cyclic data.

In Section 12.6, we'll sketch out the implementation of the corresponding S-expression decoding function, but before we get there, we'll first need to understand how reflection can be used to update program variables.

Exercise 12.3: Implement the missing cases of the encode function. Encode booleans as t and nil, floating-point numbers using Go's notation, and complex numbers like 1+2*i* as #C(1.0 2.0). Interfaces can be encoded as a pair of a type name and a value, for instance ("[]int" (1 2 3)), but beware that this notation is ambiguous: the `reflect.Type.String` method may return the same string for different types.

Exercise 12.4: Modify encode to pretty-print the S-expression in the style shown above.

Exercise 12.5: Adapt encode to emit JSON instead of S-expressions. Test your encoder using the standard decoder, `json.Unmarshal`.

Exercise 12.6: Adapt encode so that, as an optimization, it does not encode a field whose value is the zero value of its type.

Exercise 12.7: Create a streaming API for the S-expression decoder, following the style of `json.Decoder` (§4.5).

12.5. Setting Variables with `reflect.Value`

So far, reflection has only *interpreted* values in our program in various ways. The point of this section, however, is to *change* them.

Recall that some Go expressions like x, x.f[1], and *p denote variables, but others like x + 1 and f(2) do not. A variable is an *addressable* storage location that contains a value, and its value may be updated through that address.

A similar distinction applies to reflect.Values. Some are addressable; others are not. Consider the following declarations:

```
x := 2                         // value    type    variable?
a := reflect.ValueOf(2)        // 2        int     no
b := reflect.ValueOf(x)        // 2        int     no
c := reflect.ValueOf(&x)       // &x       *int    no
d := c.Elem()                  // 2        int     yes (x)
```

The value within a is not addressable. It is merely a copy of the integer 2. The same is true of b. The value within c is also non-addressable, being a copy of the pointer value &x. In fact, no reflect.Value returned by reflect.ValueOf(x) is addressable. But d, derived from c by dereferencing the pointer within it, refers to a variable and is thus addressable. We can use this approach, calling reflect.ValueOf(&x).Elem(), to obtain an addressable Value for any variable x.

We can ask a reflect.Value whether it is addressable through its CanAddr method:

```
fmt.Println(a.CanAddr()) // "false"
fmt.Println(b.CanAddr()) // "false"
fmt.Println(c.CanAddr()) // "false"
fmt.Println(d.CanAddr()) // "true"
```

We obtain an addressable reflect.Value whenever we indirect through a pointer, even if we started from a non-addressable Value. All the usual rules for addressability have analogs for reflection. For example, since the slice indexing expression e[i] implicitly follows a pointer, it is addressable even if the expression e is not. By analogy, reflect.ValueOf(e).Index(i) refers to a variable, and is thus addressable even if reflect.ValueOf(e) is not.

To recover the variable from an addressable reflect.Value requires three steps. First, we call Addr(), which returns a Value holding a pointer to the variable. Next, we call Interface() on this Value, which returns an interface{} value containing the pointer. Finally, if we know the type of the variable, we can use a type assertion to retrieve the contents of the interface as an ordinary pointer. We can then update the variable through the pointer:

```
x := 2
d := reflect.ValueOf(&x).Elem()      // d refers to the variable x
px := d.Addr().Interface().(*int)    // px := &x
*px = 3                              // x = 3
fmt.Println(x)                        // "3"
```

Or, we can update the variable referred to by an addressable reflect.Value directly, without using a pointer, by calling the reflect.Value.Set method:

```
d.Set(reflect.ValueOf(4))
fmt.Println(x) // "4"
```

The same checks for assignability that are ordinarily performed by the compiler are done at run time by the Set methods. Above, the variable and the value both have type int, but if the variable had been an int64, the program would panic, so it's crucial to make sure the value is assignable to the type of the variable:

```
d.Set(reflect.ValueOf(int64(5))) // panic: int64 is not assignable to int
```

And of course calling Set on a non-addressable reflect.Value panics too:

```
x := 2
b := reflect.ValueOf(x)
b.Set(reflect.ValueOf(3)) // panic: Set using unaddressable value
```

There are variants of Set specialized for certain groups of basic types: SetInt, SetUint, Set-String, SetFloat, and so on:

```
d := reflect.ValueOf(&x).Elem()
d.SetInt(3)
fmt.Println(x) // "3"
```

In some ways these methods are more forgiving. SetInt, for example, will succeed so long as the variable's type is some kind of signed integer, or even a named type whose underlying type is a signed integer, and if the value is too large it will be quietly truncated to fit. But tread carefully: calling SetInt on a reflect.Value that refers to an interface{} variable will panic, even though Set would succeed.

```
x := 1
rx := reflect.ValueOf(&x).Elem()
rx.SetInt(2)                     // OK, x = 2
rx.Set(reflect.ValueOf(3))       // OK, x = 3
rx.SetString("hello")            // panic: string is not assignable to int
rx.Set(reflect.ValueOf("hello")) // panic: string is not assignable to int

var y interface{}
ry := reflect.ValueOf(&y).Elem()
ry.SetInt(2)                     // panic: SetInt called on interface Value
ry.Set(reflect.ValueOf(3))       // OK, y = int(3)
ry.SetString("hello")            // panic: SetString called on interface Value
ry.Set(reflect.ValueOf("hello")) // OK, y = "hello"
```

When we applied Display to os.Stdout, we found that reflection can read the values of unexported struct fields that are inaccessible according to the usual rules of the language, like the fd int field of an os.File struct on a Unix-like platform. However, reflection cannot update such values:

```
stdout := reflect.ValueOf(os.Stdout).Elem() // *os.Stdout, an os.File var
fmt.Println(stdout.Type())                   // "os.File"
fd := stdout.FieldByName("fd")
fmt.Println(fd.Int()) // "1"
fd.SetInt(2)          // panic: unexported field
```

An addressable reflect.Value records whether it was obtained by traversing an unexported struct field and, if so, disallows modification. Consequently, CanAddr is not usually the right check to use before setting a variable. The related method CanSet reports whether a reflect.Value is addressable *and* settable:

```
fmt.Println(fd.CanAddr(), fd.CanSet()) // "true false"
```

12.6. Example: Decoding S-Expressions

For each Marshal function provided by the standard library's encoding/... packages, there is a corresponding Unmarshal function that does decoding. For example, as we saw in Section 4.5, given a byte slice containing JSON-encoded data for our Movie type (§12.3), we can decode it like this:

```
data := []byte{/* ... */}
var movie Movie
err := json.Unmarshal(data, &movie)
```

The Unmarshal function uses reflection to modify the fields of the existing movie variable, creating new maps, structs, and slices as determined by the type Movie and the content of the incoming data.

Let's now implement a simple Unmarshal function for S-expressions, analogous to the standard json.Unmarshal function used above, and the inverse of our earlier sexpr.Marshal. We must caution you that a robust and general implementation requires substantially more code than will comfortably fit in this example, which is already long, so we have taken many shortcuts. We support only a limited subset of S-expressions and do not handle errors gracefully. The code is intended to illustrate reflection, not parsing.

The lexer uses the Scanner type from the text/scanner package to break an input stream into a sequence of tokens such as comments, identifiers, string literals, and numeric literals. The scanner's Scan method advances the scanner and returns the kind of the next token, which has type rune. Most tokens, like '(', consist of a single rune, but the text/scanner package represents the kinds of the multi-character tokens Ident, String, and Int using small negative values of type rune. Following a call to Scan that returns one of these kinds of token, the scanner's TokenText method returns the text of the token.

Since a typical parser may need to inspect the current token several times, but the Scan method advances the scanner, we wrap the scanner in a helper type called lexer that keeps track of the token most recently returned by Scan.

gopl.io/ch12/sexpr
```
type lexer struct {
    scan  scanner.Scanner
    token rune // the current token
}

func (lex *lexer) next()        { lex.token = lex.scan.Scan() }
func (lex *lexer) text() string { return lex.scan.TokenText() }

func (lex *lexer) consume(want rune) {
    if lex.token != want { // NOTE: Not an example of good error handling.
        panic(fmt.Sprintf("got %q, want %q", lex.text(), want))
    }
    lex.next()
}
```

Now let's turn to the parser. It consists of two principal functions. The first of these, read, reads the S-expression that starts with the current token and updates the variable referred to by the addressable reflect.Value v.

```go
func read(lex *lexer, v reflect.Value) {
    switch lex.token {
    case scanner.Ident:
        // The only valid identifiers are
        // "nil" and struct field names.
        if lex.text() == "nil" {
            v.Set(reflect.Zero(v.Type()))
            lex.next()
            return
        }
    case scanner.String:
        s, _ := strconv.Unquote(lex.text()) // NOTE: ignoring errors
        v.SetString(s)
        lex.next()
        return
    case scanner.Int:
        i, _ := strconv.Atoi(lex.text()) // NOTE: ignoring errors
        v.SetInt(int64(i))
        lex.next()
        return
    case '(':
        lex.next()
        readList(lex, v)
        lex.next() // consume ')'
        return
    }
    panic(fmt.Sprintf("unexpected token %q", lex.text()))
}
```

Our S-expressions use identifiers for two distinct purposes, struct field names and the nil value for a pointer. The read function only handles the latter case. When it encounters the scanner.Ident "nil", it sets v to the zero value of its type using the reflect.Zero function. For any other identifier, it reports an error. The readList function, which we'll see in a moment, handles identifiers used as struct field names.

A '(' token indicates the start of a list. The second function, readList, decodes a list into a variable of composite type—a map, struct, slice, or array—depending on what kind of Go variable we're currently populating. In each case, the loop keeps parsing items until it encounters the matching close parenthesis, ')', as detected by the endList function.

The interesting part is the recursion. The simplest case is an array. Until the closing ')' is seen, we use Index to obtain the variable for each array element and make a recursive call to read to populate it. As in many other error cases, if the input data causes the decoder to index beyond the end of the array, the decoder panics. A similar approach is used for slices, except we must create a new variable for each element, populate it, then append it to the slice.

The loops for structs and maps must parse a (key value) sublist on each iteration. For structs, the key is a symbol identifying the field. Analogous to the case for arrays, we obtain the existing variable for the struct field using FieldByName and make a recursive call to populate it. For maps, the key may be of any type, and analogous to the case for slices, we create a new variable, recursively populate it, and finally insert the new key/value pair into the map.

```go
func readList(lex *lexer, v reflect.Value) {
    switch v.Kind() {
    case reflect.Array: // (item ...)
        for i := 0; !endList(lex); i++ {
            read(lex, v.Index(i))
        }

    case reflect.Slice: // (item ...)
        for !endList(lex) {
            item := reflect.New(v.Type().Elem()).Elem()
            read(lex, item)
            v.Set(reflect.Append(v, item))
        }

    case reflect.Struct: // ((name value) ...)
        for !endList(lex) {
            lex.consume('(')
            if lex.token != scanner.Ident {
                panic(fmt.Sprintf("got token %q, want field name", lex.text()))
            }
            name := lex.text()
            lex.next()
            read(lex, v.FieldByName(name))
            lex.consume(')')
        }

    case reflect.Map: // ((key value) ...)
        v.Set(reflect.MakeMap(v.Type()))
        for !endList(lex) {
            lex.consume('(')
            key := reflect.New(v.Type().Key()).Elem()
            read(lex, key)
            value := reflect.New(v.Type().Elem()).Elem()
            read(lex, value)
            v.SetMapIndex(key, value)
            lex.consume(')')
        }

    default:
        panic(fmt.Sprintf("cannot decode list into %v", v.Type()))
    }
}
```

```go
func endList(lex *lexer) bool {
    switch lex.token {
    case scanner.EOF:
        panic("end of file")
    case ')':
        return true
    }
    return false
}
```

Finally, we wrap up the parser in an exported function Unmarshal, shown below, that hides some of the rough edges of the implementation. Errors encountered during parsing result in a panic, so Unmarshal uses a deferred call to recover from the panic (§5.10) and return an error message instead.

```go
// Unmarshal parses S-expression data and populates the variable
// whose address is in the non-nil pointer out.
func Unmarshal(data []byte, out interface{}) (err error) {
    lex := &lexer{scan: scanner.Scanner{Mode: scanner.GoTokens}}
    lex.scan.Init(bytes.NewReader(data))
    lex.next() // get the first token
    defer func() {
        // NOTE: this is not an example of ideal error handling.
        if x := recover(); x != nil {
            err = fmt.Errorf("error at %s: %v", lex.scan.Position, x)
        }
    }()
    read(lex, reflect.ValueOf(out).Elem())
    return nil
}
```

A production-quality implementation should never panic for any input and should report an informative error for every mishap, perhaps with a line number or offset. Nonetheless, we hope this example conveys some idea of what's happening under the hood of the packages like encoding/json, and how you can use reflection to populate data structures.

Exercise 12.8: The sexpr.Unmarshal function, like json.Marshal, requires the complete input in a byte slice before it can begin decoding. Define a sexpr.Decoder type that, like json.Decoder, allows a sequence of values to be decoded from an io.Reader. Change sexpr.Unmarshal to use this new type.

Exercise 12.9: Write a token-based API for decoding S-expressions, following the style of xml.Decoder (§7.14). You will need five types of tokens: Symbol, String, Int, StartList, and EndList.

Exercise 12.10: Extend sexpr.Unmarshal to handle the booleans, floating-point numbers, and interfaces encoded by your solution to Exercise 12.3. (Hint: to decode interfaces, you will need a mapping from the name of each supported type to its reflect.Type.)

12.7. Accessing Struct Field Tags

In Section 4.5 we used struct *field tags* to modify the JSON encoding of Go struct values. The json field tag lets us choose alternative field names and suppress the output of empty fields. In this section, we'll see how to access field tags using reflection.

In a web server, the first thing most HTTP handler functions do is extract the request parameters into local variables. We'll define a utility function, params.Unpack, that uses struct field tags to make writing HTTP handlers (§7.7) more convenient.

First, we'll show how it's used. The search function below is an HTTP handler. It defines a variable called data of an anonymous struct type whose fields correspond to the HTTP request parameters. The struct's field tags specify the parameter names, which are often short and cryptic since space is precious in a URL. The Unpack function populates the struct from the request so that the parameters can be accessed conveniently and with an appropriate type.

gopl.io/ch12/search

```go
import "gopl.io/ch12/params"

// search implements the /search URL endpoint.
func search(resp http.ResponseWriter, req *http.Request) {
    var data struct {
        Labels     []string `http:"l"`
        MaxResults int      `http:"max"`
        Exact      bool     `http:"x"`
    }
    data.MaxResults = 10 // set default
    if err := params.Unpack(req, &data); err != nil {
        http.Error(resp, err.Error(), http.StatusBadRequest) // 400
        return
    }

    // ...rest of handler...
    fmt.Fprintf(resp, "Search: %+v\n", data)
}
```

The Unpack function below does three things. First, it calls req.ParseForm() to parse the request. Thereafter, req.Form contains all the parameters, regardless of whether the HTTP client used the GET or the POST request method.

Next, Unpack builds a mapping from the *effective* name of each field to the variable for that field. The effective name may differ from the actual name if the field has a tag. The Field method of reflect.Type returns a reflect.StructField that provides information about the type of each field such as its name, type, and optional tag. The Tag field is a reflect.StructTag, which is a string type that provides a Get method to parse and extract the substring for a particular key, such as http:"..." in this case.

gopl.io/ch12/params

```go
// Unpack populates the fields of the struct pointed to by ptr
// from the HTTP request parameters in req.
func Unpack(req *http.Request, ptr interface{}) error {
    if err := req.ParseForm(); err != nil {
        return err
    }

    // Build map of fields keyed by effective name.
    fields := make(map[string]reflect.Value)
    v := reflect.ValueOf(ptr).Elem() // the struct variable
    for i := 0; i < v.NumField(); i++ {
        fieldInfo := v.Type().Field(i) // a reflect.StructField
        tag := fieldInfo.Tag           // a reflect.StructTag
        name := tag.Get("http")
        if name == "" {
            name = strings.ToLower(fieldInfo.Name)
        }
        fields[name] = v.Field(i)
    }

    // Update struct field for each parameter in the request.
    for name, values := range req.Form {
        f := fields[name]
        if !f.IsValid() {
            continue // ignore unrecognized HTTP parameters
        }
        for _, value := range values {
            if f.Kind() == reflect.Slice {
                elem := reflect.New(f.Type().Elem()).Elem()
                if err := populate(elem, value); err != nil {
                    return fmt.Errorf("%s: %v", name, err)
                }
                f.Set(reflect.Append(f, elem))
            } else {
                if err := populate(f, value); err != nil {
                    return fmt.Errorf("%s: %v", name, err)
                }
            }
        }
    }
    return nil
}
```

Finally, Unpack iterates over the name/value pairs of the HTTP parameters and updates the corresponding struct fields. Recall that the same parameter name may appear more than once. If this happens, and the field is a slice, then all the values of that parameter are accumulated into the slice. Otherwise, the field is repeatedly overwritten so that only the last value has any effect.

The populate function takes care of setting a single field v (or a single element of a slice field) from a parameter value. For now, it supports only strings, signed integers, and booleans. Supporting other types is left as an exercise.

```go
func populate(v reflect.Value, value string) error {
    switch v.Kind() {
    case reflect.String:
        v.SetString(value)

    case reflect.Int:
        i, err := strconv.ParseInt(value, 10, 64)
        if err != nil {
            return err
        }
        v.SetInt(i)

    case reflect.Bool:
        b, err := strconv.ParseBool(value)
        if err != nil {
            return err
        }
        v.SetBool(b)

    default:
        return fmt.Errorf("unsupported kind %s", v.Type())
    }
    return nil
}
```

If we add the server handler to a web server, this might be a typical session:

```
$ go build gopl.io/ch12/search
$ ./search &
$ ./fetch 'http://localhost:12345/search'
Search: {Labels:[] MaxResults:10 Exact:false}
$ ./fetch 'http://localhost:12345/search?l=golang&l=programming'
Search: {Labels:[golang programming] MaxResults:10 Exact:false}
$ ./fetch 'http://localhost:12345/search?l=golang&l=programming&max=100'
Search: {Labels:[golang programming] MaxResults:100 Exact:false}
$ ./fetch 'http://localhost:12345/search?x=true&l=golang&l=programming'
Search: {Labels:[golang programming] MaxResults:10 Exact:true}
$ ./fetch 'http://localhost:12345/search?q=hello&x=123'
x: strconv.ParseBool: parsing "123": invalid syntax
$ ./fetch 'http://localhost:12345/search?q=hello&max=lots'
max: strconv.ParseInt: parsing "lots": invalid syntax
```

Exercise 12.11: Write the corresponding Pack function. Given a struct value, Pack should return a URL incorporating the parameter values from the struct.

Exercise 12.12: Extend the field tag notation to express parameter validity requirements. For example, a string might need to be a valid email address or credit-card number, and an integer might need to be a valid US ZIP code. Modify Unpack to check these requirements.

Exercise 12.13: Modify the S-expression encoder (§12.4) and decoder (§12.6) so that they honor the `sexpr:"..."` field tag in a similar manner to `encoding/json` (§4.5).

12.8. Displaying the Methods of a Type

Our final example of reflection uses `reflect.Type` to print the type of an arbitrary value and enumerate its methods:

gopl.io/ch12/methods

```
// Print prints the method set of the value x.
func Print(x interface{}) {
    v := reflect.ValueOf(x)
    t := v.Type()
    fmt.Printf("type %s\n", t)

    for i := 0; i < v.NumMethod(); i++ {
        methType := v.Method(i).Type()
        fmt.Printf("func (%s) %s%s\n", t, t.Method(i).Name,
            strings.TrimPrefix(methType.String(), "func"))
    }
}
```

Both `reflect.Type` and `reflect.Value` have a method called `Method`. Each `t.Method(i)` call returns an instance of `reflect.Method`, a struct type that describes the name and type of a single method. Each `v.Method(i)` call returns a `reflect.Value` representing a method value (§6.4), that is, a method bound to its receiver. Using the `reflect.Value.Call` method (which we don't have space to show here), it's possible to call `Value`s of kind `Func` like this one, but this program needs only its `Type`.

Here are the methods belonging to two types, `time.Duration` and `*strings.Replacer`:

```
methods.Print(time.Hour)
// Output:
// type time.Duration
// func (time.Duration) Hours() float64
// func (time.Duration) Minutes() float64
// func (time.Duration) Nanoseconds() int64
// func (time.Duration) Seconds() float64
// func (time.Duration) String() string

methods.Print(new(strings.Replacer))
// Output:
// type *strings.Replacer
// func (*strings.Replacer) Replace(string) string
// func (*strings.Replacer) WriteString(io.Writer, string) (int, error)
```

12.9. A Word of Caution

There is a lot more to the reflection API than we have space to show, but the preceding examples give an idea of what is possible. Reflection is a powerful and expressive tool, but it should
be used with care, for three reasons.

The first reason is that reflection-based code can be fragile. For every mistake that would
cause a compiler to report a type error, there is a corresponding way to misuse reflection, but
whereas the compiler reports the mistake at build time, a reflection error is reported during
execution as a panic, possibly long after the program was written or even long after it has
started running.

If the readList function (§12.6), for example, should read a string from the input while
populating a variable of type int, the call to reflect.Value.SetString will panic. Most
programs that use reflection have similar hazards, and considerable care is required to keep
track of the type, addressability, and settability of each reflect.Value.

The best way to avoid this fragility is to ensure that the use of reflection is fully encapsulated
within your package and, if possible, avoid reflect.Value in favor of specific types in your
package's API, to restrict inputs to legal values. If this is not possible, perform additional
dynamic checks before each risky operation. As an example from the standard library, when
fmt.Printf applies a verb to an inappropriate operand, it does not panic mysteriously but
prints an informative error message. The program still has a bug, but it is easier to diagnose.

```
fmt.Printf("%d %s\n", "hello", 42) // "%!d(string=hello) %!s(int=42)"
```

Reflection also reduces the safety and accuracy of automated refactoring and analysis tools,
because they can't determine or rely on type information.

The second reason to avoid reflection is that since types serve as a form of documentation and
the operations of reflection cannot be subject to static type checking, heavily reflective code is
often hard to understand. Always carefully document the expected types and other invariants
of functions that accept an interface{} or a reflect.Value.

The third reason is that reflection-based functions may be one or two orders of magnitude
slower than code specialized for a particular type. In a typical program, the majority of functions are not relevant to the overall performance, so it's fine to use reflection when it makes the
program clearer. Testing is a particularly good fit for reflection since most tests use small data
sets. But for functions on the critical path, reflection is best avoided.

13

Low-Level Programming

The design of Go guarantees a number of safety properties that limit the ways in which a Go program can "go wrong." During compilation, type checking detects most attempts to apply an operation to a value that is inappropriate for its type, for instance, subtracting one string from another. Strict rules for type conversions prevent direct access to the internals of built-in types like strings, maps, slices, and channels.

For errors that cannot be detected statically, such as out-of-bounds array accesses or nil pointer dereferences, dynamic checks ensure that the program immediately terminates with an informative error whenever a forbidden operation occurs. Automatic memory management (garbage collection) eliminates "use after free" bugs, as well as most memory leaks.

Many implementation details are inaccessible to Go programs. There is no way to discover the memory layout of an aggregate type like a struct, or the machine code for a function, or the identity of the operating system thread on which the current goroutine is running. Indeed, the Go scheduler freely moves goroutines from one thread to another. A pointer identifies a variable without revealing the variable's numeric address. Addresses may change as the garbage collector moves variables; pointers are transparently updated.

Together, these features make Go programs, especially failing ones, more predictable and less mysterious than programs in C, the quintessential low-level language. By hiding the underlying details, they also make Go programs highly portable, since the language semantics are largely independent of any particular compiler, operating system, or CPU architecture. (Not entirely independent: some details leak through, such as the word size of the processor, the order of evaluation of certain expressions, and the set of implementation restrictions imposed by the compiler.)

Occasionally, we may choose to forfeit some of these helpful guarantees to achieve the highest possible performance, to interoperate with libraries written in other languages, or to implement a function that cannot be expressed in pure Go.

In this chapter, we'll see how the unsafe package lets us step outside the usual rules, and how to use the cgo tool to create Go bindings for C libraries and operating system calls.

The approaches described in this chapter should not be used frivolously. Without careful attention to detail, they may cause the kinds of unpredictable, inscrutable, non-local failures with which C programmers are unhappily acquainted. Use of unsafe also voids Go's warranty of compatibility with future releases, since, whether intended or inadvertent, it is easy to depend on unspecified implementation details that may change unexpectedly.

The unsafe package is rather magical. Although it appears to be a regular package and is imported in the usual way, it is actually implemented by the compiler. It provides access to a number of built-in language features that are not ordinarily available because they expose details of Go's memory layout. Presenting these features as a separate package makes the rare occasions on which they are needed more conspicuous. Also, some environments may restrict the use of the unsafe package for security reasons.

Package unsafe is used extensively within low-level packages like runtime, os, syscall, and net that interact with the operating system, but is almost never needed by ordinary programs.

13.1. unsafe.Sizeof, Alignof, and Offsetof

The unsafe.Sizeof function reports the size in bytes of the representation of its operand, which may be an expression of any type; the expression is not evaluated. A call to Sizeof is a constant expression of type uintptr, so the result may be used as the dimension of an array type, or to compute other constants.

```
import "unsafe"
fmt.Println(unsafe.Sizeof(float64(0))) // "8"
```

Sizeof reports only the size of the fixed part of each data structure, like the pointer and length of a string, but not indirect parts like the contents of the string. Typical sizes for all non-aggregate Go types are shown below, though the exact sizes may vary by toolchain. For portability, we've given the sizes of reference types (or types containing references) in terms of words, where a word is 4 bytes on a 32-bit platform and 8 bytes on a 64-bit platform.

Computers load and store values from memory most efficiently when those values are properly *aligned*. For example, the address of a value of a two-byte type such as int16 should be an even number, the address of a four-byte value such as a rune should be a multiple of four, and the address of an eight-byte value such as a float64, uint64, or 64-bit pointer should be a multiple of eight. Alignment requirements of higher multiples are unusual, even for larger data types such as complex128.

For this reason, the size of a value of an aggregate type (a struct or array) is at least the sum of the sizes of its fields or elements but may be greater due to the presence of "holes." Holes are unused spaces added by the compiler to ensure that the following field or element is properly aligned relative to the start of the struct or array.

Type	Size
bool	1 byte
intN, uintN, floatN, complexN	$N/8$ bytes (for example, float64 is 8 bytes)
int, uint, uintptr	1 word
*T	1 word
string	2 words (data, len)
[]T	3 words (data, len, cap)
map	1 word
func	1 word
chan	1 word
interface	2 words (type, value)

The language specification does not guarantee that the order in which fields are declared is the order in which they are laid out in memory, so in theory a compiler is free to rearrange them, although as we write this, none do. If the types of a struct's fields are of different sizes, it may be more space-efficient to declare the fields in an order that packs them as tightly as possible. The three structs below have the same fields, but the first requires up to 50% more memory than the other two:

```
                            // 64-bit    32-bit
struct{ bool; float64; int16 }  // 3 words   4 words
struct{ float64; int16; bool }  // 2 words   3 words
struct{ bool; int16; float64 }  // 2 words   3 words
```

The details of the alignment algorithm are beyond the scope of this book, and it's certainly not worth worrying about every struct, but efficient packing may make frequently allocated data structures more compact and therefore faster.

The unsafe.Alignof function reports the required alignment of its argument's type. Like Sizeof, it may be applied to an expression of any type, and it yields a constant. Typically, boolean and numeric types are aligned to their size (up to a maximum of 8 bytes) and all other types are word-aligned.

The unsafe.Offsetof function, whose operand must be a field selector x.f, computes the offset of field f relative to the start of its enclosing struct x, accounting for holes, if any.

Figure 13.1 shows a struct variable x and its memory layout on typical 32- and 64-bit Go implementations. The gray regions are holes.

```
var x struct {
    a bool
    b int16
    c []int
}
```

The table below shows the results of applying the three unsafe functions to x itself and to each of its three fields:

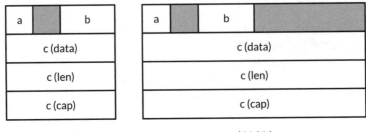

Figure 13.1. Holes in a struct.

```
Typical 32-bit platform:
Sizeof(x)   = 16  Alignof(x)   = 4
Sizeof(x.a) = 1   Alignof(x.a) = 1   Offsetof(x.a) = 0
Sizeof(x.b) = 2   Alignof(x.b) = 2   Offsetof(x.b) = 2
Sizeof(x.c) = 12  Alignof(x.c) = 4   Offsetof(x.c) = 4

Typical 64-bit platform:
Sizeof(x)   = 32  Alignof(x)   = 8
Sizeof(x.a) = 1   Alignof(x.a) = 1   Offsetof(x.a) = 0
Sizeof(x.b) = 2   Alignof(x.b) = 2   Offsetof(x.b) = 2
Sizeof(x.c) = 24  Alignof(x.c) = 8   Offsetof(x.c) = 8
```

Despite their names, these functions are not in fact unsafe, and they may be helpful for understanding the layout of raw memory in a program when optimizing for space.

13.2. unsafe.Pointer

Most pointer types are written *T, meaning "a pointer to a variable of type T." The unsafe.Pointer type is a special kind of pointer that can hold the address of any variable. Of course, we can't indirect through an unsafe.Pointer using *p because we don't know what type that expression should have. Like ordinary pointers, unsafe.Pointers are comparable and may be compared with nil, which is the zero value of the type.

An ordinary *T pointer may be converted to an unsafe.Pointer, and an unsafe.Pointer may be converted back to an ordinary pointer, not necessarily of the same type *T. By converting a *float64 pointer to a *uint64, for instance, we can inspect the bit pattern of a floating-point variable:

```
package math

func Float64bits(f float64) uint64 { return *(*uint64)(unsafe.Pointer(&f)) }

fmt.Printf("%#016x\n", Float64bits(1.0)) // "0x3ff0000000000000"
```

Through the resulting pointer, we can update the bit pattern too. This is harmless for a float-ing-point variable since any bit pattern is legal, but in general, unsafe.Pointer conversions let us write arbitrary values to memory and thus subvert the type system.

An unsafe.Pointer may also be converted to a uintptr that holds the pointer's numeric value, letting us perform arithmetic on addresses. (Recall from Chapter 3 that a uintptr is an unsigned integer wide enough to represent an address.) This conversion too may be applied in reverse, but again, converting from a uintptr to an unsafe.Pointer may subvert the type system since not all numbers are valid addresses.

Many unsafe.Pointer values are thus intermediaries for converting ordinary pointers to raw numeric addresses and back again. The example below takes the address of variable x, adds the offset of its b field, converts the resulting address to *int16, and through that pointer updates x.b:

gopl.io/ch13/unsafeptr

```
var x struct {
    a bool
    b int16
    c []int
}

// equivalent to pb := &x.b
pb := (*int16)(unsafe.Pointer(
    uintptr(unsafe.Pointer(&x)) + unsafe.Offsetof(x.b)))
*pb = 42

fmt.Println(x.b) // "42"
```

Although the syntax is cumbersome—perhaps no bad thing since these features should be used sparingly—do not be tempted to introduce temporary variables of type uintptr to break the lines. This code is incorrect:

```
// NOTE: subtly incorrect!
tmp := uintptr(unsafe.Pointer(&x)) + unsafe.Offsetof(x.b)
pb := (*int16)(unsafe.Pointer(tmp))
*pb = 42
```

The reason is very subtle. Some garbage collectors move variables around in memory to reduce fragmentation or bookkeeping. Garbage collectors of this kind are known as *moving GCs*. When a variable is moved, all pointers that hold the address of the old location must be updated to point to the new one. From the perspective of the garbage collector, an unsafe.Pointer is a pointer and thus its value must change as the variable moves, but a uintptr is just a number so its value must not change. The incorrect code above *hides a pointer* from the garbage collector in the non-pointer variable tmp. By the time the second statement executes, the variable x could have moved and the number in tmp would no longer be the address &x.b. The third statement clobbers an arbitrary memory location with the value 42.

There are myriad pathological variations on this theme. After this statement has executed:

```
pT := uintptr(unsafe.Pointer(new(T))) // NOTE: wrong!
```

there are no pointers that refer to the variable created by new, so the garbage collector is
entitled to recycle its storage when this statement completes, after which pT contains the
address where the variable was but is no longer.

No current Go implementation uses a moving garbage collector (though future implementations might), but this is no reason for complacency: current versions of Go do move *some*
variables around in memory. Recall from Section 5.2 that goroutine stacks grow as needed.
When this happens, all variables on the old stack may be relocated to a new, larger stack, so we
cannot rely on the numeric value of a variable's address remaining unchanged throughout its
lifetime.

At the time of writing, there is little clear guidance on what Go programmers may rely upon
after an unsafe.Pointer to uintptr conversion (see Go issue 7192), so we strongly recommend that you assume the bare minimum. Treat all uintptr values as if they contain the
former address of a variable, and minimize the number of operations between converting an
unsafe.Pointer to a uintptr and using that uintptr. In our first example above, the three
operations—conversion to a uintptr, addition of the field offset, conversion back—all
appeared within a single expression.

When calling a library function that returns a uintptr, such as those below from the reflect
package, the result should be immediately converted to an unsafe.Pointer to ensure that it
continues to point to the same variable.

```
package reflect

func (Value) Pointer() uintptr
func (Value) UnsafeAddr() uintptr
func (Value) InterfaceData() [2]uintptr // (index 1)
```

13.3. Example: Deep Equivalence

The DeepEqual function from the reflect package reports whether two values are "deeply"
equal. DeepEqual compares basic values as if by the built-in == operator; for composite values, it traverses them recursively, comparing corresponding elements. Because it works for
any pair of values, even ones that are not comparable with ==, it finds widespread use in tests.
The following test uses DeepEqual to compare two []string values:

```
func TestSplit(t *testing.T) {
    got := strings.Split("a:b:c", ":")
    want := []string{"a", "b", "c"}
    if !reflect.DeepEqual(got, want) { /* ... */ }
}
```

Although DeepEqual is convenient, its distinctions can seem arbitrary. For example, it doesn't
consider a nil map equal to a non-nil empty map, nor a nil slice equal to a non-nil empty one:

```
var a, b []string = nil, []string{}
fmt.Println(reflect.DeepEqual(a, b)) // "false"

var c, d map[string]int = nil, make(map[string]int)
fmt.Println(reflect.DeepEqual(c, d)) // "false"
```

In this section we'll define a function `Equal` that compares arbitrary values. Like `DeepEqual`, it compares slices and maps based on their elements, but unlike `DeepEqual`, it considers a nil slice (or map) equal to a non-nil empty one. The basic recursion over the arguments can be done with reflection, using a similar approach to the `Display` program we saw in Section 12.3. As usual, we define an unexported function, `equal`, for the recursion. Don't worry about the `seen` parameter just yet. For each pair of values x and y to be compared, `equal` checks that both (or neither) are valid and checks that they have the same type. The result of the function is defined as a set of switch cases that compare two values of the same type. For reasons of space, we've omitted several cases since the pattern should be familiar by now.

gopl.io/ch13/equal

```go
func equal(x, y reflect.Value, seen map[comparison]bool) bool {
    if !x.IsValid() || !y.IsValid() {
        return x.IsValid() == y.IsValid()
    }
    if x.Type() != y.Type() {
        return false
    }

    // ...cycle check omitted (shown later)...

    switch x.Kind() {
    case reflect.Bool:
        return x.Bool() == y.Bool()

    case reflect.String:
        return x.String() == y.String()

    // ...numeric cases omitted for brevity...

    case reflect.Chan, reflect.UnsafePointer, reflect.Func:
        return x.Pointer() == y.Pointer()

    case reflect.Ptr, reflect.Interface:
        return equal(x.Elem(), y.Elem(), seen)

    case reflect.Array, reflect.Slice:
        if x.Len() != y.Len() {
            return false
        }
        for i := 0; i < x.Len(); i++ {
            if !equal(x.Index(i), y.Index(i), seen) {
                return false
            }
        }
        return true
```

```
        // ...struct and map cases omitted for brevity...
        }
        panic("unreachable")
    }
```

As usual, we don't expose the use of reflection in the API, so the exported function Equal must call reflect.ValueOf on its arguments:

```
    // Equal reports whether x and y are deeply equal.
    func Equal(x, y interface{}) bool {
        seen := make(map[comparison]bool)
        return equal(reflect.ValueOf(x), reflect.ValueOf(y), seen)
    }

    type comparison struct {
        x, y unsafe.Pointer
        t    reflect.Type
    }
```

To ensure that the algorithm terminates even for cyclic data structures, it must record which pairs of variables it has already compared and avoid comparing them a second time. Equal allocates a set of comparison structs, each holding the address of two variables (represented as unsafe.Pointer values) and the type of the comparison. We need to record the type in addition to the addresses because different variables can have the same address. For example, if x and y are both arrays, x and x[0] have the same address, as do y and y[0], and it is important to distinguish whether we have compared x and y or x[0] and y[0].

Once equal has established that its arguments have the same type, and before it executes the switch, it checks whether it is comparing two variables it has already seen and, if so, terminates the recursion.

```
    // cycle check
    if x.CanAddr() && y.CanAddr() {
        xptr := unsafe.Pointer(x.UnsafeAddr())
        yptr := unsafe.Pointer(y.UnsafeAddr())
        if xptr == yptr {
            return true // identical references
        }
        c := comparison{xptr, yptr, x.Type()}
        if seen[c] {
            return true // already seen
        }
        seen[c] = true
    }
```

Here's our Equal function in action:

```
    fmt.Println(Equal([]int{1, 2, 3}, []int{1, 2, 3}))        // "true"
    fmt.Println(Equal([]string{"foo"}, []string{"bar"}))      // "false"
    fmt.Println(Equal([]string(nil), []string{}))             // "true"
    fmt.Println(Equal(map[string]int(nil), map[string]int{})) // "true"
```

It even works on cyclic inputs similar to the one that caused the `Display` function from Section 12.3 to get stuck in a loop:

```
// Circular linked lists a -> b -> a and c -> c.
type link struct {
    value string
    tail  *link
}
a, b, c := &link{value: "a"}, &link{value: "b"}, &link{value: "c"}
a.tail, b.tail, c.tail = b, a, c
fmt.Println(Equal(a, a)) // "true"
fmt.Println(Equal(b, b)) // "true"
fmt.Println(Equal(c, c)) // "true"
fmt.Println(Equal(a, b)) // "false"
fmt.Println(Equal(a, c)) // "false"
```

Exercise 13.1: Define a deep comparison function that considers numbers (of any type) equal if they differ by less than one part in a billion.

Exercise 13.2: Write a function that reports whether its argument is a cyclic data structure.

13.4. Calling C Code with cgo

A Go program might need to use a hardware driver implemented in C, query an embedded database implemented in C++, or use some linear algebra routines implemented in Fortran. C has long been the lingua franca of programming, so many packages intended for widespread use export a C-compatible API, regardless of the language of their implementation.

In this section, we'll build a simple data compression program that uses cgo, a tool that creates Go bindings for C functions. Such tools are called *foreign-function interfaces* (FFIs), and cgo is not the only one for Go programs. SWIG (swig.org) is another; it provides more complex features for integrating with C++ classes, but we won't show it here.

The `compress/...` subtree of the standard library provides compressors and decompressors for popular compression algorithms, including LZW (used by the Unix `compress` command) and DEFLATE (used by the GNU `gzip` command). The APIs of these packages vary slightly in details, but they all provide a wrapper for an `io.Writer` that compresses the data written to it, and a wrapper for an `io.Reader` that decompresses the data read from it. For example:

```
package gzip // compress/gzip

func NewWriter(w io.Writer) io.WriteCloser
func NewReader(r io.Reader) (io.ReadCloser, error)
```

The bzip2 algorithm, which is based on the elegant Burrows-Wheeler transform, runs slower than gzip but yields significantly better compression. The `compress/bzip2` package provides a decompressor for bzip2, but at the moment the package provides no compressor. Building one from scratch is a substantial undertaking, but there is a well-documented and high-performance open-source C implementation, the `libbzip2` package from `bzip.org`.

If the C library were small, we would just port it to pure Go, and if its performance were not critical for our purposes, we would be better off invoking a C program as a helper subprocess using the os/exec package. It's when you need to use a complex, performance-critical library with a narrow C API that it may make sense to wrap it using cgo. For the rest of this chapter, we'll work through an example.

From the libbzip2 C package, we need the bz_stream struct type, which holds the input and output buffers, and three C functions: BZ2_bzCompressInit, which allocates the stream's buffers; BZ2_bzCompress, which compresses data from the input buffer to the output buffer; and BZ2_bzCompressEnd, which releases the buffers. (Don't worry about the mechanics of the libbzip2 package; the purpose of this example is to show how the parts fit together.)

We'll call the BZ2_bzCompressInit and BZ2_bzCompressEnd C functions directly from Go, but for BZ2_bzCompress, we'll define a wrapper function in C, to show how it's done. The C source file below lives alongside the Go code in our package:

gopl.io/ch13/bzip

```c
/* This file is gopl.io/ch13/bzip/bzip2.c,          */
/* a simple wrapper for libbzip2 suitable for cgo. */
#include <bzlib.h>

int bz2compress(bz_stream *s, int action,
                char *in, unsigned *inlen, char *out, unsigned *outlen) {
  s->next_in = in;
  s->avail_in = *inlen;
  s->next_out = out;
  s->avail_out = *outlen;
  int r = BZ2_bzCompress(s, action);
  *inlen -= s->avail_in;
  *outlen -= s->avail_out;
  s->next_in = s->next_out = NULL;
  return r;
}
```

Now let's turn to the Go code, the first part of which is shown below.

```go
// Package bzip provides a writer that uses bzip2 compression (bzip.org).
package bzip

/*
#cgo CFLAGS: -I/usr/include
#cgo LDFLAGS: -L/usr/lib -lbz2
#include <bzlib.h>
#include <stdlib.h>
bz_stream* bz2alloc() { return calloc(1, sizeof(bz_stream)); }
int bz2compress(bz_stream *s, int action,
                char *in, unsigned *inlen, char *out, unsigned *outlen);
void bz2free(bz_stream* s) { free(s); }
*/
import "C"
```

```
import (
    "io"
    "unsafe"
)

type writer struct {
    w       io.Writer // underlying output stream
    stream *C.bz_stream
    outbuf [64 * 1024]byte
}

// NewWriter returns a writer for bzip2-compressed streams.
func NewWriter(out io.Writer) io.WriteCloser {
    const blockSize = 9
    const verbosity = 0
    const workFactor = 30
    w := &writer{w: out, stream: C.bz2alloc()}
    C.BZ2_bzCompressInit(w.stream, blockSize, verbosity, workFactor)
    return w
}
```

The import "C" declaration is special. There is no package C, but this import causes go build to preprocess the file using the cgo tool before the Go compiler sees it. During preprocessing, cgo generates a temporary package that contains Go declarations corresponding to all the C functions and types used by the file, such as C.bz_stream and C.BZ2_bzCompressInit. The cgo tool discovers these types by invoking the C compiler in a special way on the contents of the comment that precedes the import declaration.

The comment may also contain #cgo directives that specify extra options to the C toolchain. The CFLAGS and LDFLAGS values contribute extra arguments to the compiler and linker commands so that they can locate the bzlib.h header file and the libbz2.a archive library. The example assumes that these are installed beneath /usr on your system. You may need to alter or delete these flags for your installation.

NewWriter makes a call to the C function BZ2_bzCompressInit to initialize the buffers for the stream. The writer type includes another buffer that will be used to drain the decompressor's output buffer.

The Write method, shown below, feeds the uncompressed data to the compressor, calling the function bz2compress in a loop until all the data has been consumed. Observe that the Go program may access C types like bz_stream, char, and uint, C functions like bz2compress, and even object-like C preprocessor macros such as BZ_RUN, all through the C.x notation. The C.uint type is distinct from Go's uint type, even if both have the same width.

```
func (w *writer) Write(data []byte) (int, error) {
    if w.stream == nil {
        panic("closed")
    }
    var total int // uncompressed bytes written
```

```go
    for len(data) > 0 {
        inlen, outlen := C.uint(len(data)), C.uint(cap(w.outbuf))
        C.bz2compress(w.stream, C.BZ_RUN,
            (*C.char)(unsafe.Pointer(&data[0])), &inlen,
            (*C.char)(unsafe.Pointer(&w.outbuf)), &outlen)
        total += int(inlen)
        data = data[inlen:]
        if _, err := w.w.Write(w.outbuf[:outlen]); err != nil {
            return total, err
        }
    }
    return total, nil
}
```

Each iteration of the loop passes bz2compress the address and length of the remaining portion of data, and the address and capacity of w.outbuf. The two length variables are passed by their addresses, not their values, so that the C function can update them to indicate how much uncompressed data was consumed and how much compressed data was produced. Each chunk of compressed data is then written to the underlying io.Writer.

The Close method has a similar structure to Write, using a loop to flush out any remaining compressed data from the stream's output buffer.

```go
    // Close flushes the compressed data and closes the stream.
    // It does not close the underlying io.Writer.
    func (w *writer) Close() error {
        if w.stream == nil {
            panic("closed")
        }
        defer func() {
            C.BZ2_bzCompressEnd(w.stream)
            C.bz2free(w.stream)
            w.stream = nil
        }()
        for {
            inlen, outlen := C.uint(0), C.uint(cap(w.outbuf))
            r := C.bz2compress(w.stream, C.BZ_FINISH, nil, &inlen,
                (*C.char)(unsafe.Pointer(&w.outbuf)), &outlen)
            if _, err := w.w.Write(w.outbuf[:outlen]); err != nil {
                return err
            }
            if r == C.BZ_STREAM_END {
                return nil
            }
        }
    }
```

Upon completion, Close calls C.BZ2_bzCompressEnd to release the stream buffers, using defer to ensure that this happens on all return paths. At this point the w.stream pointer is no longer safe to dereference. To be defensive, we set it to nil, and add explicit nil checks to each method, so that the program panics if the user mistakenly calls a method after Close. Not only is writer not concurrency-safe, but concurrent calls to Close and Write could cause the program to crash in C code. Fixing this is Exercise 13.3.

The program below, bzipper, is a bzip2 compressor command that uses our new package. It behaves like the bzip2 command present on many Unix systems.

gopl.io/ch13/bzipper

```
// Bzipper reads input, bzip2-compresses it, and writes it out.
package main

import (
    "io"
    "log"
    "os"

    "gopl.io/ch13/bzip"
)

func main() {
    w := bzip.NewWriter(os.Stdout)
    if _, err := io.Copy(w, os.Stdin); err != nil {
        log.Fatalf("bzipper: %v\n", err)
    }
    if err := w.Close(); err != nil {
        log.Fatalf("bzipper: close: %v\n", err)
    }
}
```

In the session below, we use bzipper to compress /usr/share/dict/words, the system dictionary, from 938,848 bytes to 335,405 bytes—about a third of its original size—then uncompress it with the system bunzip2 command. The SHA256 hash is the same before and after, giving us confidence that the compressor is working correctly. (If you don't have sha256sum on your system, use your solution to Exercise 4.2.)

```
$ go build gopl.io/ch13/bzipper
$ wc -c < /usr/share/dict/words
938848
$ sha256sum < /usr/share/dict/words
126a4ef38493313edc50b86f90dfdaf7c59ec6c948451eac228f2f3a8ab1a6ed -
$ ./bzipper < /usr/share/dict/words | wc -c
335405
$ ./bzipper < /usr/share/dict/words | bunzip2 | sha256sum
126a4ef38493313edc50b86f90dfdaf7c59ec6c948451eac228f2f3a8ab1a6ed -
```

We've demonstrated linking a C library into a Go program. Going in the other direction, it's also possible to compile a Go program as a static archive that can be linked into a C program or as a shared library that can be dynamically loaded by a C program. We've only scratched the surface of cgo here, and there is much more to say about memory management, pointers, callbacks, signal handling, strings, errno, finalizers, and the relationship between goroutines and operating system threads, much of it very subtle. In particular, the rules for correctly passing pointers from Go to C or vice versa are complex, for reasons similar to those we discussed in Section 13.2, and not yet authoritatively specified (see Go issue 12416). For further reading, start with `https://golang.org/cmd/cgo`.

Exercise 13.3: Use `sync.Mutex` to make `bzip2.writer` safe for concurrent use by multiple goroutines.

Exercise 13.4: Depending on C libraries has its drawbacks. Provide an alternative pure-Go implementation of `bzip.NewWriter` that uses the `os/exec` package to run `/bin/bzip2` as a subprocess.

13.5. Another Word of Caution

We ended the previous chapter with a warning about the downsides of the reflection interface. That warning applies with even more force to the `unsafe` package described in this chapter.

High-level languages insulate programs and programmers not only from the arcane specifics of individual computer instruction sets, but from dependence on irrelevancies like where in memory a variable lives, how big a data type is, the details of structure layout, and a host of other implementation details. Because of that insulating layer, it's possible to write programs that are safe and robust and that will run on any operating system without change.

The `unsafe` package lets programmers reach through the insulation to use some crucial but otherwise inaccessible feature, or perhaps to achieve higher performance. The cost is usually to portability and safety, so one uses `unsafe` at one's peril. Our advice on how and when to use `unsafe` parallels Knuth's comments on premature optimization, which we quoted in Section 11.5. Most programmers will never need to use `unsafe` at all. Nevertheless, there will occasionally be situations where some critical piece of code can be best written using `unsafe`. If careful study and measurement indicates that `unsafe` really is the best approach, restrict it to as small a region as possible, so that most of the program is oblivious to its use.

For now, put the last two chapters in the back of your mind. Write some substantial Go programs. Avoid `reflect` and `unsafe`; come back to these chapters only if you must.

Meanwhile, happy Go programming. We hope you enjoy writing Go as much as we do.

Index

!, negation operator 63
%, remainder operator 52, 166
&&, short-circuit AND operator 63
&, address-of operator 24, 32, 94, 158, 167
&, implicit 158, 167
&^, AND-NOT operator 53
&^, bit-clear operator 53
' quote character 56
*, indirection operator 24, 32
++, increment statement 5, 37, 94
+, string concatenation operator 5, 65
+, unary operator 53
+=, -=, etc., assignment operator 5
-, unary operator 53
--, decrement statement 5, 37
... argument 139, 142
... array length 82
... parameter 91, 142, 143, 172
... path 292, 299
/*...*/ comment 25
// comment 5, 25
:= short variable declaration 5, 31, 49
<<, left shift operator 54
==, comparison operator 40, 63
>>, right shift operator 54
^, bitwise complement operator 53
^, exclusive OR operator 53
_, blank identifier 7, 38, 95, 120, 126, 287
` backquote character 66
| in template 113
|, bitwise OR operator 166, 167
||, short-circuit OR operator 63

Abstract Syntax Notation One (ASN.1) 107
abstract type 24, 171
abstraction, premature 216, 316, 317
ad hoc polymorphism 211
address of local variable 32, 36
address of struct literal 103
addressable expression 159, 341
addressable value 32
address-of operator & 24, 32, 94, 158, 167
aggregate type 81, 99
Alef programming language xiii
algorithm
    breadth-first search 139, 239
    depth-first search 136
    Fibonacci 37, 218
    GCD 37
    insertion sort 101
    Lissajous 15
    slice rotation 86
    topological sort 136
aliasing, pointer 33
alignment 354
allocation
    heap 36
    memory 36, 71, 89, 169, 209, 322
    stack 36
anchor element, HTML 122
AND operator &&, short-circuit 63
AND-NOT operator &^ 53
animation, GIF 13
anonymous
    function 22, 135, 236
    function, defer 146
    function, recursive 137

struct field 104, 105, 106, 162
API
    encoding 213, 340
    error 127, 152
    package 284, 296, 311, 333, 352
    runtime 324
    SQL 211
    system call 196
    template 115
    token-based decoder 213, 215, 347
APL programming language xiii
append built-in function 88, 90, 91
appendInt example 88
argument
    ... 139, 142
    command-line 4, 18, 33, 43, 179, 180, 290, 313
    function 119
    pointer 33, 83
    slice 86
arithmetic expression evaluator 197
array
    comparison 83
    length, ... 82
    literal 82, 84
    type 81
    underlying 84, 88, 91, 187
    zero value 82
ASCII 56, 64, 66, 67, 305
ASN.1 (Abstract Syntax Notation One) 107
assembly line, cake 234
assertion
    function 316
    interface type 208, 210

test 306
type 205, 211
assignability 38, 175
assignability, interface 175
assignment
    implicit 38
    multiple-value 37
    operator +=, -=, etc. 5
    operators 36, 52
    statement 5, 7, 36, 52, 94, 173
    tuple 31, 37
associativity, operator 52
atomic operation 264
attack, HTML injection 115
attack, SQL injection 211
autoescape example 117

back-door, package 315
back-off, exponential 130
backquote character, ` 66
bank example package 258, 261, 263
bare return 126
basename example 72
behavior, undefined 260
Benchmark function 302, 321
bidirectional to unidirectional
    channel conversion 231
binary
    operators, table of 52
    semaphore 262
    tree 102
bit vector 165
bit-clear operator &^ 53
bit-set data type 77
bitwise
    complement operator ^ 53
    operators, table of 53
    OR operator | 166, 167
black-box test 310
blank identifier _ 7, 38, 95, 120, 126,
    287
blank import 287
block
    file 46
    lexical 46, 120, 135, 141, 212
    local 46
    package 46
    universe 46
blocking profile 324
Blog, Go xvi, 326
boiling example 29
bool type 63
boolean
    constant, false 63
    constant, true 63
    zero value 30
breadthFirst function 139
breadth-first search algorithm 139,
    239

break statement 24, 46
break statement, labeled 249
brittle test 317
broadcast 251, 254, 276
Brooks, Fred xiv
btoi function 64
buffered channel 226, 231
bufio package 9
bufio.NewReader function 98
bufio.NewScanner function 9
(*bufio.Reader).ReadRune
    method 98
bufio.Scanner type 9
(*bufio.Scanner).Err method 97
(*bufio.Scanner).Scan method 9
(*bufio.Scanner).Split method
    99
bufio.ScanWords function 99
+build comments 296
build constraints 296
build tags 296
building packages 293
built-in function
    append 88, 90, 91
    cap 84, 232
    close 226, 228, 251
    complex 61
    copy 89
    delete 94
    imag 61
    len 4, 54, 64, 65, 81, 84, 233
    make 9, 18, 88, 94, 225
    new 34
    panic 148, 149
    real 61
    recover 152
built-in interface, error 196
built-in type, error 11, 128, 149,
    196
byte slice to string conversion 73
byte type 52
ByteCounter example 173
bytes package 71, 73
bytes.Buffer type 74, 169, 172, 185
(*bytes.Buffer).Grow method
    169
(*bytes.Buffer).WriteByte
    method 74
(*bytes.Buffer).WriteRune
    method 74
(*bytes.Buffer).WriteString
    method 74
bytes.Equal function 86
bzip C code 362
bzip example package 363
bzipper example 365

C++ programming language xiv, xv,
    361

C programming language xii, xv, 1,
    6, 52, 260, 361
cache, concurrent non-blocking 272
cache, non-blocking 275
cake assembly line 234
call
    by reference 83
    by value 83, 120, 158
    interface method 182
    ok value from function 128
calling C from Go 361
camel case 28
cancellation 251, 252
cancellation of HTTP request 253
cap built-in function 84, 232
capacity, channel 226, 232, 233
capacity, slice 88, 89
capturing iteration variable 140
capturing loop variable 141, 236,
    240
case in type switch 212
case, select 245
Celsius type 39
CelsiusFlag function 181
cf example 43
cgo tool 361, 363
<-ch, channel receive 18, 225, 232
ch<-, channel send 18, 225, 232
chaining, method 114
chan type 225
channel
    buffered 226, 231
    capacity 226, 232, 233
    close 228, 251
    closing a 225
    communication 225, 245
    comparison 225
    conversion, bidirectional to
        unidirectional 231
    draining a 229, 252
    make 18, 225
    nil 246, 249
    polling 246
    range over 229
    receive <-ch 18, 225, 232
    receive, non-blocking 246
    receive, ok value from 229
    send ch<- 18, 225, 232
    synchronous 226
    type 18
    type <-chan T, receive-only 230
    type chan<- T, send-only 230
    type, unidirectional 230, 231
    unbuffered 226
    zero value 225, 246
character conversion 71
character test 71
charcount example 98
chat example 254

chat server 253
CheckQuota function 312, 313
client, email 312
client, SMTP 312
clock example 220, 222
clock server, concurrent 219
close built-in function 226, 228, 251
close, channel 228, 251
closer goroutine 238, 250
closing a channel 225
closure, lexical 136
cmplx.Sqrt function 61
code
    format 3, 6, 9, 48
    point, Unicode 67
    production 301
ColoredPoint example 161
comma example 73
command, testing a 308
command-line argument 4, 18, 33, 43, 179, 180, 290, 313
comment
    /*...*/ 25
    // 5, 25
    doc 42, 296
    // Output 326
comments, +build 296
communicating sequential processes (CSP) xiii, 217
communication, channel 225, 245
comparability 9, 38, 40, 53, 86, 93, 97, 104
comparison
    array 83
    channel 225
    function 133
    interface 184
    map 96
    operator == 40, 63
    operators 40, 93
    operators, table of 53
    slice 87
    string 65
    struct 104
compilation, separate 284
complement operator ^, bitwise 53
complex built-in function 61
complex type 61
composite literal 14
composite type xv, 14, 81
composition, parallel 224
composition, type xv, 107, 162, 189
compress/bzip2 package 361
compression 361
conceptual integrity xiv
concrete type 24, 171, 211, 214
concurrency 17, 217, 257
    excessive 241, 242

safe 275
safety 256, 257, 272, 365
    with shared variables 257
concurrent
    clock server 219
    directory traversal 247
    echo server 222
    non-blocking cache 272
    web crawler 239
confinement, serial 262
confinement, variable 261
consistency, sequential 268, 269
const declaration 14, 75
constant
    false boolean 63
    generator, iota xiii, 77
    time.Minute 76
    time.Second 164
    true boolean 63
    types, untyped 78
constants, precision of 78
constraints, build 296
contention, lock 267, 272
context switch 280
continue statement 24, 46
continue statement, labeled 249
contracts, interfaces as 171
control flow 46
conversion
    bidirectional to unidirectional channel 231
    byte slice to string 73
    character 71
    implicit 79
    narrowing 40, 55
    numeric 79
    operation 40, 55, 64, 71, 78, 79, 173, 187, 194, 208, 231, 353, 358
    rune slice to string 71
    rune to string 71
    string 71
    string to byte slice 40, 73
    string to rune slice 71, 88
    unsafe.Pointer 356
copy built-in function 89
countdown example 244, 245, 246
counting semaphore 241
coverage, statement 318, 320
coverage, test 318
coverage_test example 319
CPU profile 324
crawl example 240, 242, 243
crawler, concurrent web 239
crawler, web 119
critical section 263, 270, 275
cross-compilation 295
cryptography 55, 83, 121, 325
crypto/sha256 package 83
customSort example 190

cyclic data structure 337
cyclic test dependency 314

data
    race 259, 267, 275
    structure, cyclic 337
    structure, recursive 101, 102, 107
    type, bit-set 77
database driver, MySQL 284
database/sql package 211, 288
daysAgo function 114
deadbeef 55, 80
deadlock 233, 240, 265
declaration
    const 14, 75
    func 3, 29, 119
    import 3, 28, 42, 284, 285, 363
    method 40, 155
    package 2, 28, 41, 285
    package-level 28
    scope 45, 137
    shadowing 46, 49, 206, 212
    short variable 5, 7, 30, 31
    statement, short variable 7
    struct 99
    type 39
    var 5, 30
declarations, order of 48
decode example, S-expression 347
decoder API, token-based 213, 215, 347
decoding, S-expression 344
decoding, XML 213
decrement statement -- 5, 37
dedup example 97
deep equivalence 87, 317, 358
default case in select 246
default case in switch 23
default case in type switch 212
defer anonymous function 146
defer example 150, 151
defer statement 144, 150, 264
deferred function call 144
delete built-in function 94
depth-first search algorithm 136
dereference, implicit 159
diagram
    helloworld substring 69
    pipeline 228
    slice capacity growth 90
    slice of months 84
    string sharing 65
    struct hole 355
    thumbnail sequence 238
digital artifact example 178
Dijkstra, Edsger 318
Dilbert 100
directed acyclic graph 136, 284
directory traversal, concurrent 247

discriminated union 211, 213, 214
Display function 333
display example 333
display function 334
displaying methods of a type 351
Distance function 156
doc comment 42, 296
doc.go doc comment file 42, 296
documentation, package 296
domain name, import path 284
dot . in template 113
downloading packages 292
Dr. Strangelove 336
draining a channel 229, 252
du example 247, 249, 250
dup example 9, 11, 12
duplicate suppression 276
dynamic dispatch 183
dynamic type, interface 181

echo example 5, 7, 34, 309
echo test 309
echo server, concurrent 222
echo_test.go 310
effective tests, writing 316, 317
email client 312
embarrassingly parallel 235
embedded struct field 161
embedding, interface 174
embedding, struct 104, 161
Employee struct 100
empty
    interface type 176
    select statement 245
    string 5, 7, 30
    struct 102
encapsulation 168, 284
encoding API 213, 340
encoding, S-expression 338
encoding/json package 107
encoding/xml package 107, 213
end of file (EOF) 131
enum 77
environment variable
    GOARCH 292, 295
    GOMAXPROCS 281, 321
    GOOS 292, 295
    GOPATH xvi, 291, 295
    GOROOT 292
equal function 87, 96
equality, pointer 32
equivalence, deep 87, 317, 358
error built-in interface 196
error built-in type 11, 128, 149, 196
error API 127, 152
error.Error method 196
errorf function 143
error-handling strategies 128, 152,
    310, 316

errors package 196
errors.New function 196
escape
    hexadecimal 66
    HTML 116
    octal 66
    sequence 10
    sequences, table of 66
    Unicode 68, 107
    URL 111
escaping variables 36
eval example 198
event multiplexing 244
events 227, 244
Example function 302, 326
example
    autoescape 117
    basename 72
    boiling 29
    ByteCounter 173
    bzipper 365
    cf 43
    charcount 98
    chat 254
    clock 220, 222
    ColoredPoint 161
    comma 73
    countdown 244, 245, 246
    coverage_test 319
    crawl 240, 242, 243
    customSort 190
    dedup 97
    defer 150, 151
    digital artifact 178
    display 333
    du 247, 249, 250
    dup 9, 11, 12
    echo 5, 7, 34, 309
    eval 198
    fetch 16, 148
    fetchall 18
    findlinks 122, 125, 139
    ftoc 29
    github 110, 111
    graph 99
    helloworld 1, 2
    http 192, 194, 195
    intset 166
    issues 112
    issueshtml 115
    issuesreport 114
    jpeg 287
    lissajous 14, 22, 35
    mandelbrot 62
    memo 275, 276, 277, 278, 279
    methods 351
    movie 108, 110
    netcat 221, 223, 227
    netflag 78

nonempty 92
outline 123, 133
package, bank 258, 261, 263
package, bzip 363
package, format 332
package, geometry 156
package, http 192
package, links 138
package, memo 273
package, params 348
package, storage 312, 313
package, tempconv 42
package, thumbnail 235
palindrome 303, 305, 308
params 348
Parse 152
pipeline 228, 230, 231
playlist 187
rev 86
reverb 223, 224
server 19, 21
sexpr 340
S-expression decode 347
sha256 83
sleep 179
spinner 218
squares 135
sum 142
surface 59, 203
tempconv 39, 180, 289
temperature conversion 29
tempflag 181
test of word 303
thumbnail 236, 237, 238
title 153
topoSort 136
trace 146
treesort 102
urlvalues 160
wait 130
word 303, 305, 308
xmlselect 215
appendInt 88
exception 128, 149
excessive concurrency 241, 242
exclusion, mutual 262, 267
exclusive lock 263, 266, 270
exclusive OR operator ^ 53
exponential back-off 130
export of struct field 101, 106, 109,
    110, 168
export_test.go file 315
Expr.Check method 202
expression
    addressable 159, 341
    evaluator 197
    method 164
    receive 225
Expr.Eval method 199

extending a slice 86
Extensible Markup Language (XML) 107
external test package 285, 314

Fahrenheit type 39
failure message, test 306
fallthrough statement 23, 212
false boolean constant 63
fetch example 16, 148
fetchall example 18
fib function 37, 218
Fibonacci algorithm 37, 218
field
　anonymous struct 104, 105, 106, 162
　embedded struct 161
　export of struct 101, 106, 109, 110, 168
　order, struct 101, 355
　selector 156
　struct 15, 99
　tag, omitempty 109
　tag, struct 109, 348
figure
　Lissajous 13
　Mandelbrot 63
　3-D surface 58, 203
File Transfer Protocol (FTP) 222
file
　block 46
　export_test.go 315
　name, Microsoft Windows 72
　name, POSIX 72
　_test.go 285, 302, 303
findlinks example 122, 125, 139
fixed-size stack 124
flag package 33, 179
flag
　go tool -bench 321
　go tool -benchmem 322
　go tool -covermode 319
　go tool -coverprofile 319
　go tool -cpuprofile 324
　go tool -nodecount 325
　go tool -text 325
　go tool -web 326
　godoc -analysis 176
　go list -f 315
　go -race 271
　go test -race 274
　go test -run 305
　go test -v 304
flag.Args function 34
flag.Bool function 34
flag.Duration function 179
flag.Parse function 34
flag.String function 34
flag.Value interface 179, 180

floating-point
　number 56
　precision 56, 57, 63, 78
　truncation 40, 55
fmt package 2
fmt.Errorf function 129, 196
fmt.Fprintf function 172
fmt.Printf function 10
fmt.Println function 2
fmt.Scanf function 75
fmt.Sscanf function 180
fmt.Stringer interface 180, 210
for scope 47
for statement 6
forEachNode function 133
foreign-function interface (FFI) 361
format, code 3, 6, 9, 48
format example package 332
formatAtom function 332
framework, web 193
ftoc example 29
func declaration 3, 29, 119
function
　anonymous 22, 135, 236
　append built-in 88, 90, 91
　argument 119
　assertion 316
　Benchmark 302, 321
　body, missing 121
　breadthFirst 139
　btoi 64
　bufio.NewReader 98
　bufio.NewScanner 9
　bufio.ScanWords 99
　bytes.Equal 86
　call, deferred 144
　call, ok value from 128
　cap built-in 84, 232
　CelsiusFlag 181
　CheckQuota 312, 313
　close built-in 226, 228, 251
　cmplx.Sqrt 61
　comparison 133
　complex built-in 61
　copy built-in 89
　daysAgo 114
　delete built-in 94
　Display 333
　display 334
　Distance 156
　equal 87, 96
　errorf 143
　errors.New 196
　Example 302, 326
　fib 37, 218
　flag.Args 34
　flag.Bool 34
　flag.Duration 179
　flag.Parse 34

flag.String 34
fmt.Errorf 129, 196
fmt.Fprintf 172
fmt.Printf 10
fmt.Println 2
fmt.Scanf 75
fmt.Sscanf 180
forEachNode 133
formatAtom 332
gcd 37
handler 19, 21, 152, 191, 194, 195, 348
html.Parse 121, 125
http.DefaultServeMux 195
http.Error 193
http.Get 16, 18
http.Handle 195
http.HandleFunc 19, 22, 195
http.ListenAndServe 19, 191
http.NewRequest 253
http.ServeMux 193
hypot 120
imag built-in 61
image.Decode 288
image.RegisterFormat 288
incr 33
init 44, 49
intsToString 74
io.Copy 17, 18
ioutil.ReadAll 16, 272
ioutil.ReadDir 247
ioutil.ReadFile 12, 145
io.WriteString 209
itob 64
json.Marshal 108
json.MarshalIndent 108
json.NewDecoder 111
json.NewEncoder 111
json.Unmarshal 110, 114
len built-in 4, 54, 64, 65, 81, 84, 233
links.Extract 138
literal 22, 135, 227
log.Fatalf 49, 130
main 2, 310
make built-in 9, 18, 88, 94, 225
math.Hypot 156
math.Inf 57
math.IsInf 57
math.IsNaN 57
math.NaN 57
multi-valued 11, 30, 37, 96, 125, 126
mustCopy 221
net.Dial 220
net.Listen 220
new built-in 34
nil 132
os.Close 11

os.Exit 16, 34, 48
os.Getwd 48
os.IsExist 207
os.IsNotExist 207
os.IsPermission 207
os.Open 11
os.Stat 247
panic built-in 148, 149
parameter 119
params.Unpack 349
png.Encode 62
PopCount 45
real built-in 61
recover built-in 152
recursive anonymous 137
reflect.TypeOf 330
reflect.ValueOf 331, 337
reflect.Zero 345
regexp.Compile 149
regexp.MustCompile 149
result list 119
runtime.Stack 151
SearchIssues 111
sexpr.Marshal 340
sexpr.readList 347
sexpr.Unmarshal 347
signature 120
sort.Float64s 191
sort.Ints 191
sort.IntsAreSorted 191
sort.Reverse 189
sort.Strings 95, 137, 191
Sprint 330
sqlQuote 211, 212
strconv.Atoi 22, 75
strconv.FormatInt 75
strconv.Itoa 75
strconv.ParseInt 75
strconv.ParseUint 75
strings.Contains 69
strings.HasPrefix 69
strings.HasSuffix 69
strings.Index 289
strings.Join 7, 12
strings.Map 133
strings.NewReader 289
strings.NewReplacer 289
strings.Split 12
strings.ToLower 72
strings.ToUpper 72
template.Must 114
template.New 114
Test 302
time.After 245
time.AfterFunc 164
time.Now 220
time.Parse 220
time.Since 114
time.Tick 244, 246

title 144, 145
type 119, 120
unicode.IsDigit 71
unicode.IsLetter 71
unicode.IsLower 71
unicode.IsSpace 93
unicode.IsUpper 71
unsafe.AlignOf 355
unsafe.Offsetof 355
unsafe.Sizeof 354
url.QueryEscape 111
utf8.DecodeRuneInString 69
utf8.RuneCountInString 69
value 132
variadic 142, 172
visit 122
WaitForServer 130
walkDir 247
zero value 132

garbage collection xi, xiii, 7, 35, 230,
    353, 357
garbage collector, moving 357
GCD algorithm 37
gcd function 37
geometry example package 156
geometry.Point.Distance method
    156
getter method 169
GIF animation 13
GitHub issue tracker 110
github example 110, 111
Go
    Playground xvi, 326
    Blog xvi, 326
    issue 110, 112, 358, 366
go tool 2, 42, 44, 290
go tool -bench flag 321
go tool -benchmem flag 322
go tool -covermode flag 319
go tool -coverprofile flag 319
go tool -cpuprofile flag 324
go tool -nodecount flag 325
go tool pprof 325
go tool -text flag 325
go tool -web flag 326
go tool cover 318, 319
go doc tool 25
go statement 18, 218
GOARCH environment variable 292,
    295
go build 2, 286, 293, 294
go doc 296
godoc -analysis flag 176
godoc tool xvi, 25, 297, 326
go env 292
gofmt tool 3, 4, 44, 286
go get xvi, 2, 292, 293
go help 290

goimports tool 3, 44, 286
go install 295
golang.org/x/net/html package
    122
golint tool 292
go list 298, 315
go list -f flag 315
GOMAXPROCS environment variable
    281, 321
GOOS environment variable 292, 295
GOPATH environment variable xvi,
    291, 295
gopl.io repository xvi
go -race flag 271
GOROOT environment variable 292
goroutine 18, 217, 233, 235
    closer 238, 250
    identity 282
    leak 233, 236, 246
    monitor 261, 277
    multiplexing 281
    vs. OS thread 280
go run 2, 294
go test 301, 302, 304
go test -race flag 274
go test -run flag 305
go test -v flag 304
goto statement 24
graph example 99
GraphViz 326
Griesemer, Robert xi
growth, stack 124, 280, 358
guarding mutex 263

half-open interval 4
handler function 19, 21, 152, 191,
    194, 195, 348
"happens before" relation 226, 257,
    261, 277
"has a" relationship 162
hash table 9, 93
Haskell programming language xiv
heap
    allocation 36
    profile 324
    variable 36
helloworld example 1, 2
helloworld substring diagram 69
hexadecimal escape 66
hexadecimal literal 55
hidden pointer 357
Hoare, Tony xiii
hole, struct 354
HTML
    anchor element 122
    escape 116
    injection attack 115
    metacharacter 116
    parser 121

html.Parse function 121, 125
html/template package 113, 115
HTTP
  GET request 21, 127, 272, 348
  POST request 348
  request, cancellation of 253
  request multiplexer 193
http example 192, 194, 195
http example package 192
(*http.Client).Do method 253
http.DefaultClient variable 253
http.DefaultServeMux function
  195
http.Error function 193
http.Get function 16, 18
http.Handle function 195
http.HandleFunc function 19, 22,
  195
http.Handler interface 191, 193
http.HandlerFunc type 194, 203
http.ListenAndServe function 19,
  191
http.NewRequest function 253
http.Request type 21, 253
(*http.Request).ParseForm
  method 22, 348
http.ResponseWriter type 19, 22,
  191, 193
http.ServeMux function 193
hypot function 120

identifier _, blank 7, 38, 95, 120, 126,
  287
identifier, qualified 41, 43
identity, goroutine 282
IEEE 754 standard 56, 57
if, initialization statement in 22,
  206
if-else scope 47
if-else statement 9, 22, 47
imag built-in function 61
image manipulation 121
image package 62, 287
image/color package 14
image.Decode function 288
image/png package 288
image.RegisterFormat function
  288
imaginary literal 61
immutability 261
immutability, string 65, 73
implementation with slice, stack 92,
  215
implicit
  & 158, 167
  assignment 38
  conversion 79
  dereference 159
import declaration 3, 28, 42, 284,

285, 363
import
  blank 287
  path 284
  path domain name 284
  renaming 286
incr function 33
increment statement ++ 5, 37, 94
index operation, string 64
indirection operator * 24, 32
infinite loop 6, 120, 228
information hiding 168, 284
init function 44, 49
initialization
  lazy 268
  package 44
  statement in if 22, 206
  statement in switch 24
initializer list 30
injection attack, HTML 115
injection attack, SQL 211
in-place slice techniques 91
insertion sort algorithm 101
int type 52
integer
  literal 55
  overflow 53, 113
  signed 52, 54
  unsigned 52, 54
integration test 314
interface
  assignability 175
  comparison 184
  dynamic type 181
  embedding 174
  error built-in 196
  flag.Value 179, 180
  fmt.Stringer 180, 210
  http.Handler 191, 193
  io.Closer 174
  io.Reader 174
  io.Writer 15, 22, 172, 174, 186,
    208, 209, 309
  JSON 110
  method call 182
  nil 182
  pitfall 184
  ReadWriteCloser 174
  ReadWriter 174
  satisfaction 171, 175
  sort.Interface 186
  type 171, 174
interface{} type 143, 176, 331
interface
  type assertion 208, 210
  type, empty 176
  value 181
  with nil pointer 184
  zero value 182

interfaces as contracts 171
internal package 298
intset example 166
intsToString function 74
invariants 159, 169, 170, 265, 284,
  311, 352
io package 174
io.Closer interface 174
io.Copy function 17, 18
io.Discard stream 22
io.Discard variable 18
io.EOF variable 132
io/ioutil package 16, 145
io.Reader interface 174
iota constant generator xiii, 77
ioutil.ReadAll function 16, 272
ioutil.ReadDir function 247
ioutil.ReadFile function 12, 145
io.Writer interface 15, 22, 172,
  174, 186, 208, 209, 309
io.WriteString function 209
"is a" relationship 162, 175
issue, Go 110, 112, 358, 366
issue tracker, GitHub 110
issues example 112
issueshtml example 115
issuesreport example 114
iteration order, map 95
iteration variable, capturing 140
itob function 64

Java programming language xv
JavaScript Object Notation (JSON)
  107, 338
JavaScript programming language
  xv, 107
jpeg example 287
JSON
  interface 110
  interface, Open Movie Database
    113
  interface, xkcd 113
  marshaling 108
  unmarshaling 110
json.Decoder type 111
json.Encoder type 111
json.Marshal function 108
json.MarshalIndent function 108
json.NewDecoder function 111
json.NewEncoder function 111
json.Unmarshal function 110, 114

keyword, type 212
keywords, table of 27
Knuth, Donald 323

label scope 46
label, statement 46
labeled

break statement 249
continue statement 249
statement 46
layout, memory 354, 355
lazy initialization 268
leak, goroutine 233, 236, 246
left shift operator << 54
len built-in function 4, 54, 64, 65,
    81, 84, 233
lexical block 46, 120, 135, 141, 212
lexical closure 136
lifetime, variable 35, 46, 135
links example package 138
links.Extract function 138
Lisp programming language 338
Lissajous algorithm 15
Lissajous figure 13
lissajous example 14, 22, 35
list, initializer 30
literal
    array 82, 84
    composite 14
    function 22, 135, 227
    hexadecimal 55
    imaginary 61
    integer 55
    map 94
    octal 55
    raw string 66
    rune 56
    slice 38, 86
    string 65
    struct 15, 102, 106
local
    block 46
    variable 29, 141
    variable, address of 32, 36
    variable scope 135
locating packages 291
lock
    contention 267, 272
    exclusive 263, 266, 270
    mutex 102, 263, 264, 324
    non-reentrant 265
    readers 266
    shared 266
    writer 266
log package 49, 130, 170
log.Fatalf function 49, 130
lookup m[key], map 94
lookup, ok value from map 96
loop
    infinite 6, 120, 228
    range 6, 9
    variable, capturing 141, 236, 240
    variable scope 141, 236
    while 6

main function 2, 310

main, package 2, 285, 310
make built-in function 9, 18, 88, 94,
    225
make channel 18, 225
make map 9, 18, 94
make slice 88, 322
Mandelbrot figure 63
Mandelbrot set 61
mandelbrot example 62
map
    as set 96, 202
    comparison 96
    element, nonexistent 94, 95
    iteration order 95
    literal 94
    lookup m[key] 94
    lookup, ok value from 96
    make 9, 18, 94
    nil 95
    range over 94
    type 9, 93
    with slice key 97
    zero value 95
marshaling JSON 108
math package 14, 56
math/big package 63
math/cmplx package 61
math.Hypot function 156
math.Inf function 57
math.IsInf function 57
math.IsNaN function 57
math.NaN function 57
math/rand package 285, 308
memo example 275, 276, 277, 278,
    279
memo example package 273
memoization 272
memory allocation 36, 71, 89, 169,
    209, 322
memory layout 354, 355
metacharacter, HTML 116
method
    (*bufio.Reader).ReadRune 98
    (*bufio.Scanner).Err 97
    (*bufio.Scanner).Scan 9
    (*bufio.Scanner).Split 99
    (*bytes.Buffer).Grow 169
    (*bytes.Buffer).WriteByte 74
    (*bytes.Buffer).WriteRune 74
    (*bytes.Buffer).WriteString
        74
    call, interface 182
    chaining 114
    declaration 40, 155
    error.Error 196
    Expr.Check 202
    expression 164
    Expr.Eval 199
    geometry.Point.Distance 156

getter 169
    (*http.Client).Do 253
    (*http.Request).ParseForm 22,
        348
    name 156
    net.Conn.Close 220
    net.Listener.Accept 220
    (*os.File).Write 183
    path.Distance 157
    promotion 161
    receiver name 157
    receiver parameter 156
    receiver type 157
    reflect.Type.Field 348
    reflect.Value.Addr 342
    reflect.Value.CanAddr 342
    reflect.Value.Interface 331,
        342
    reflect.Value.Kind 332
    selector 156
    setter 169
    String 40, 166, 329
    (*sync.Mutex).Lock 21, 146, 263
    (*sync.Mutex).Unlock 21, 146,
        263
    (*sync.Once).Do 270
    (*sync.RWMutex).RLock 266
    (*sync.RWMutex).RUnlock 266
    (*sync.WaitGroup).Add 238
    (*sync.WaitGroup).Done 238
    template.Funcs 114
    template.Parse 114
    (*testing.T).Errorf 200, 304,
        306
    (*testing.T).Fatal 306
    time.Time.Format 220
    value 164
    (*xml.Decoder).Token 213
methods example 351
methods of a type, displaying 351
Microsoft Windows file name 72
missing function body 121
m[key], map lookup 94
mobile platforms 121
Modula-2 programming language
    xiii
modularity 283
monitor 264, 275
monitor goroutine 261, 277
movie example 108, 110
moving garbage collector 357
multimap 160, 193
multiple-value assignment 37
multiplexer, HTTP request 193
multiplexing, event 244
multiplexing, goroutine 281
multithreading, shared-memory
    217, 257
multi-valued function 11, 30, 37, 96,

125, 126
mustCopy function 221
mutex 145, 163, 256, 269
  guarding 263
  lock 102, 263, 264, 324
  read/write 266, 267
mutual exclusion 262, 267
MySQL database driver 284

name
  method 156
  method receiver 157
  package 28, 43
  parameter 120
  space 41, 156, 283
named
  result 120, 126
  result zero value 120, 127
  type 24, 39, 40, 105, 157
naming convention 28, 169, 174,
    289
naming, package 289
NaN (not a number) 57, 93
narrowing conversion 40, 55
negation operator ! 63
net package 219
netcat example 221, 223, 227
net.Conn type 220
net.Conn.Close method 220
net.Dial function 220
netflag example 78
net/http package 16, 191
net.Listen function 220
net.Listener type 220
net.Listener.Accept method 220
net/smtp package 312
net/url package 160
networking 121, 219
new built-in function 34
new, redefining 35
nil
  channel 246, 249
  function 132
  interface 182
  map 95
  pointer 32
  pointer, interface with 184
  receiver 159, 185
  slice 87
non-blocking
  cache 275
  cache, concurrent 272
  channel receive 246
  select 246
nonempty example 92
nonexistent map element 94, 95
non-reentrant lock 265
non-standard package 121
number, floating-point 56

number zero value 5, 30
numeric
  conversion 79
  precision 55, 78
  type 51

Oberon programming language xiii
object 156
object-oriented programming
    (OOP) 155, 168
octal escape 66
octal literal 55
ok value 37
ok value from channel receive 229
ok value from function call 128
ok value from map lookup 96
ok value from type assertion 206
omitempty field tag 109
Open Movie Database JSON
    interface 113
operation, atomic 264
operation, conversion 40, 55, 64, 71,
    78, 79, 173, 187, 194, 208, 231,
    353, 358
operator
  +=, -=, etc., assignment 5
  &, address-of 24, 32, 94, 158, 167
  &^, AND-NOT 53
  &^, bit-clear 53
  ^, bitwise complement 53
  |, bitwise OR 166, 167
  ==, comparison 40, 63
  ^, exclusive OR 53
  *, indirection 24, 32
  <<, left shift 54
  !, negation 63
  %, remainder 52, 166
  >>, right shift 54
  &&, short-circuit AND 63
  ||, short-circuit OR 63
  +, string concatenation 5, 65
  -, unary 53
  +, unary 53
  associativity 52
  precedence 52, 63
  s[i:j], slice 84, 86
  s[i:j], substring 65, 86
operators
  assignment 36, 52
  comparison 40, 93
  table of binary 52
  table of bitwise 53
  table of comparison 53
optimization 264, 321, 323
optimization, premature 324
OR operator ||, short-circuit 63
order of declarations 48
order, struct field 101, 355
organization, workspace 291

OS thread vs. goroutine 280
os package 4, 206
os.Args variable 4
os.Close function 11
os.Exit function 16, 34, 48
*os.File type 11, 13, 172, 175, 185,
    336
os.FileInfo type 247
(*os.File).Write method 183
os.Getwd function 48
os.IsExist function 207
os.IsNotExist function 207
os.IsPermission function 207
os.LinkError type 207
os.Open function 11
os.PathError type 207
os.Stat function 247
outline example 123, 133
// Output comment 326
overflow, integer 53, 113
overflow, stack 124

package declaration 2, 28, 41, 285
package
  API 284, 296, 311, 333, 352
  back-door 315
  bank example 258, 261, 263
  block 46
  bufio 9
  bytes 71, 73
  bzip example 363
  compress/bzip2 361
  crypto/sha256 83
  database/sql 211, 288
  documentation 296
  encoding/json 107
  encoding/xml 107, 213
  errors 196
  external test 285, 314
  flag 33, 179
  fmt 2
  format example 332
  geometry example 156
  golang.org/x/net/html 122
  html/template 113, 115
  http example 192
  image 62, 287
  image/color 14
  image/png 288
  initialization 44
  internal 298
  io 174
  io/ioutil 16, 145
  links example 138
  log 49, 130, 170
  main 2, 285, 310
  math 14, 56
  math/big 63
  math/cmplx 61

math/rand 285, 308
memo example 273
name 28, 43
naming 289
net 219
net/http 16, 191
net/smtp 312
net/url 160
non-standard 121
os 4, 206
params example 348
path 72
path/filepath 72
reflect 330
regexp 149
runtime 151
sort 95, 186, 189
storage example 312, 313
strconv 22, 71, 75
strings 7, 71, 72, 289
sync 237, 263
syscall 196, 208
tempconv example 42
testing 285, 302
text/scanner 344
text/tabwriter 188
text/template 113, 300
thumbnail example 235
time 18, 77, 183
unicode 71
unicode/utf8 69
unsafe 354
package-level declaration 28
packages
    building 293
    downloading 292
    locating 291
    querying 298
palindrome 191
palindrome example 303, 305, 308
panic 64, 152, 253
panic built-in function 148, 149
paradoxical race 267
parallel composition 224
parallel, embarrassingly 235
parallelism 217
parameter
    ... 91, 142, 143, 172
    function 119
    method receiver 156
    name 120
    passing 120
    unused 120
params example 348
params example package 348
params.Unpack function 349
parentheses 4, 6, 9, 52, 63, 119, 146,
    158, 285, 335, 345
Parse example 152

parser, HTML 121
Pascal programming language xiii
path, ... 292, 299
path package 72
path.Distance method 157
path/filepath package 72
Pike, Rob xi, xiii, 67, 107
pipeline example 228, 230, 231
pipeline 227
pipeline diagram 228
pitfall, interface 184
pitfall, scope 140
platforms, mobile 121
Playground, Go xvi, 326
playlist example 187
png.Encode function 62
pointer 24, 32, 34
    aliasing 33
    argument 33, 83
    equality 32
    hidden 357
    nil 32
    receiver 158, 167
    to struct 100, 103
    zero value 32
polling channel 246
polymorphism, ad hoc 211
polymorphism, subtype 211
PopCount function 45
Portable Network Graphics (PNG)
    62
POSIX file name 72
POSIX standard xi, 55, 72, 197
precedence, operator 52, 63
precision
    floating-point 56, 57, 63, 78
    numeric 55, 78
    of constants 78
predeclared names, table of 28
premature abstraction 216, 316, 317
premature optimization 324
Printf %% 10
Printf verbs, table of 10
Printf %b 10, 54, 75
Printf %c 10, 56
Printf %d 10, 55
Printf %e 10, 57
Printf %f 10, 57
Printf %g 10, 57
Printf %[n] 56
Printf %o 10, 55
Printf %q 10, 56, 97
Printf %s 10
Printf %*s 134
Printf %T 10, 80, 83, 184, 331
Printf %t 10, 83
Printf %#v 106, 207
Printf %v 10, 11
Printf % x 71

Printf %#x 56
Printf %x 10, 55, 83
production code 301
profile
    blocking 324
    CPU 324
    heap 324
profiling 324
programming language
    Alef xiii
    APL xiii
    C++ xiv, xv, 361
    C xii, xv, 1, 6, 52, 260, 361
    Haskell xiv
    Java xv
    JavaScript xv, 107
    Lisp 338
    Modula-2 xiii
    Oberon xiii
    Pascal xiii
    Python xv, 193
    Ruby xv, 193
    Scheme xiii
    Squeak, Newsqueak xiii
promotion, method 161
protocol buffers 107
Python programming language xv,
    193

qualified identifier 41, 43
querying packages 298
quote character, ' 56

race
    condition 21, 257, 258, 259
    detector 271, 274
    paradoxical 267
randomized testing 307
range loop 6, 9
range over channel 229
range over map 94
range over string 69, 88
{{range}} template action 113
raw string literal 66
reachability 36
read, stale 268
readers lock 266
read/write mutex 266, 267
ReadWriteCloser interface 174
ReadWriter interface 174
real built-in function 61
receive
    <-ch, channel 18, 225, 232
    expression 225
    non-blocking channel 246
    ok value from channel 229
receive-only channel type <-chan T
    230
receiver

name, method 157
nil 159, 185
parameter, method 156
pointer 158, 167
type, method 157
recover built-in function 152
recursion 121, 124, 247, 333, 339, 345, 359
recursive
    anonymous function 137
    data structure 101, 102, 107
    type 48
redefining new 35
reference
    call by 83
    identity 87
    type 9, 12, 93, 120
reflect package 330
reflection 329, 352, 359
reflect.StructTag type 348
reflect.Type type 330
reflect.Type.Field method 348
reflect.TypeOf function 330
reflect.Value type 331, 342
reflect.Value zero value 332
reflect.Value.Addr method 342
reflect.Value.CanAddr method 342
reflect.Value.Interface method 331, 342
reflect.Value.Kind method 332
reflect.ValueOf function 331, 337
reflect.Zero function 345
regexp package 149
regexp.Compile function 149
regexp.MustCompile function 149
regular expression 66, 149, 305, 321
relation, "happens before" 226, 257, 261, 277
relationship, "has a" 162
relationship, "is a" 162, 175
remainder operator % 52, 166
renaming import 286
rendezvous 234
replacement character �, Unicode 70, 98
repository, gopl.io xvi
request
    HTTP GET 21, 127, 272, 348
    HTTP POST 348
    multiplexer, HTTP 193
result list, function 119
result, named 120, 126
return, bare 126
return statement 29, 120, 125
rev example 86
reverb example 223, 224
right shift operator >> 54
Ruby programming language xv,

193
rune literal 56
rune type 52, 67
rune slice to string conversion 71
rune to string conversion 71
runtime package 151
runtime API 324
runtime scheduler 281
runtime.Stack function 151

satisfaction, interface 171, 175
Scalable Vector Graphics (SVG) 58
scheduler, runtime 281
Scheme programming language xiii
scope
    declaration 45, 137
    for 47
    if-else 47
    label 46
    local variable 135
    loop variable 141, 236
    pitfall 140
    short variable declaration 22, 48
    switch 47
search algorithm, breadth-first 139, 239
search algorithm, depth-first 136
SearchIssues function 111
select case 245
select, default case in 246
select, non-blocking 246
select statement 244, 245
select{} statement 245
selective recovery 152
selector, field 156
selector, method 156
semaphore, binary 262
semaphore, counting 241
semicolon 3, 6
send ch<-, channel 18, 225, 232
send statement 225
send-only channel type chan<- T 230
separate compilation 284
sequence diagram, thumbnail 238
sequential consistency 268, 269
serial confinement 262
server example 19, 21
server
    chat 253
    concurrent clock 219
    concurrent echo 222
set, map as 96, 202
setter method 169
sexpr example 340
S-expression
    decode example 347
    decoding 344
    encoding 338

sexpr.Marshal function 340
sexpr.readList function 347
sexpr.Unmarshal function 347
SHA256 message digest 83
sha256 example 83
shadowing declaration 46, 49, 206, 212
shared
    lock 266
    variables 257
    variables, concurrency with 257
shared-memory multithreading 217, 257
shift operator <<, left 54
shift operator >>, right 54
short
    variable declaration 5, 7, 30, 31
    variable declaration scope 22, 48
    variable declaration statement 7
short-circuit
    AND operator && 63
    evaluation 63
    OR operator || 63
signature, function 120
signed integer 52, 54
s[i:j], slice operator 84, 86
s[i:j], substring operator 65, 86
simple statement 6, 22
Sizeof table 354
sleep example 179
slice 4
    argument 86
    capacity 88, 89
    capacity growth diagram 90
    comparison 87
    extending a 86
    key, map with 97
    literal 38, 86
    make 88, 322
    nil 87
    of months diagram 84
    operator s[i:j] 84, 86
    rotation algorithm 86
    techniques, in-place 91
    type 84
    used as stack 123
    zero length 87
    zero value 74, 87
SMTP client 312
socket
    TCP 219
    UDP 219
    Unix domain 219
sort algorithm, topological 136
sort package 95, 186, 189
sort.Float64s function 191
sort.Interface interface 186
sort.Ints function 191
sort.IntsAreSorted function 191

sort.IntSlice type 191
sort.Reverse function 189
sort.Strings function 95, 137, 191
spinner example 218
Sprint function 330
SQL API 211
SQL injection attack 211
sqlQuote function 211, 212
squares example 135
Squeak, Newsqueak programming
    language xiii
stack
    allocation 36
    fixed-size 124
    growth 124, 280, 358
    implementation with slice 92, 215
    overflow 124
    slice used as 123
    trace 149, 253
    variable 36
    variable-size 124
stale read 268
standard
    IEEE 754 56, 57
    POSIX xi, 55, 72, 197
    Unicode 2, 27, 52, 66, 67, 69, 97
statement
    --, decrement 5, 37
    ++, increment 5, 37, 94
    assignment 5, 7, 36, 52, 94, 173
    break 24, 46
    continue 24, 46
    coverage 318, 320
    defer 144, 150, 264
    fallthrough 23, 212
    for 6
    go 18, 218
    goto 24
    if-else 9, 22, 47
    label 46
    labeled 46
    return 29, 120, 125
    select{} 245
    select 244, 245
    send 225
    short variable declaration 7
    simple 6, 22
    switch 23, 47
    tagless switch 24
    type switch 210, 212, 214, 329
    unreachable 120
storage example package 312, 313
Strangelove, Dr. 336
strategies, error-handling 128, 152,
    310, 316
strconv package 22, 71, 75
strconv.Atoi function 22, 75
strconv.FormatInt function 75
strconv.Itoa function 75

strconv.ParseInt function 75
strconv.ParseUint function 75
stream, io.Discard 22
String method 40, 166, 329
string
    concatenation operator + 5, 65
    conversion 71
    immutability 65, 73
    index operation 64
    literal 65
    literal, raw 66
    range over 69, 88
    sharing diagram 65
    test 71
    to byte slice conversion 40, 73
    to rune slice conversion 71, 88
    zero value 5, 7, 30
    comparison 65
strings package 7, 71, 72, 289
strings.Contains function 69
strings.HasPrefix function 69
strings.HasSuffix function 69
strings.Index function 289
strings.Join function 7, 12
strings.Map function 133
strings.NewReader function 289
strings.NewReplacer function 289
strings.Reader type 289
strings.Replacer type 289
strings.Split function 12
strings.ToLower function 72
strings.ToUpper function 72
struct declaration 99
struct
    comparison 104
    embedding 104, 161
    Employee 100
    empty 102
    field 15, 99
    field, anonymous 104, 105, 106,
        162
    field, embedded 161
    field, export of 101, 106, 109, 110,
        168
    field order 101, 355
    field tag 109, 348
    hole 354
    hole diagram 355
    literal 15, 102, 106
    literal, address of 103
    pointer to 100, 103
    type 15, 24, 99
struct{} type 227, 241, 250
struct type, unnamed 163
struct zero value 102
substitutability 193
substring operator s[i:j] 65, 86
subtype polymorphism 211
sum example 142

surface example 59, 203
surface figure, 3-D 58, 203
SVG 58
SWIG 361
Swiss army knife 290
switch, default case in 23
switch, initialization statement in
    24
switch scope 47
switch statement 23, 47
switch statement, tagless 24
switch statement, type 210, 212,
    214, 329
switch, context 280
sync package 237, 263
synchronous channel 226
sync.Mutex type 263, 269
(*sync.Mutex).Lock method 21,
    146, 263
(*sync.Mutex).Unlock method 21,
    146, 263
sync.Once type 270
(*sync.Once).Do method 270
sync.RWMutex type 266, 270
(*sync.RWMutex).RLock method
    266
(*sync.RWMutex).RUnlock method
    266
sync.WaitGroup type 237, 250, 274
(*sync.WaitGroup).Add method
    238
(*sync.WaitGroup).Done method
    238
syscall package 196, 208
syscall.Errno type 196, 197
system call API 196

table of
    binary operators 52
    bitwise operators 53
    comparison operators 53
    escape sequences 66
    keywords 27
    predeclared names 28
    Printf verbs 10
    UTF-8 encodings 67
table, Sizeof 354
table-driven testing 200, 306, 319
tag, struct field 109, 348
tagless switch statement 24
tags, build 296
TCP socket 219
techniques, in-place slice 91
tempconv example 39, 180, 289
tempconv example package 42
temperature conversion example 29
tempflag example 181
template API 115
template

| in 113
action, {{range}} 113
dot . in 113
template.Funcs method 114
template.HTML type 116
template.Must function 114
template.New function 114
template.Parse method 114
Test function 302
test
  black-box 310
  brittle 317
  character 71
  coverage 318
  dependency, cyclic 314
  echo 309
  failure message 306
  integration 314
  of word example 303
  package, external 285, 314
  string 71
  white-box 311
  assertion 306
_test.go file 285, 302, 303
testing package 285, 302
testing
  a command 308
  randomized 307
  table-driven 200, 306, 319
testing.B type 321
testing.T type 302
(*testing.T).Errorf method 200, 304, 306
(*testing.T).Fatal method 306
tests, writing effective 316, 317
text/scanner package 344
text/tabwriter package 188
text/template package 113, 300
Thompson, Ken xi, 67
thread 218, 280
thread-local storage 282
3-D surface figure 58, 203
thumbnail example 236, 237, 238
thumbnail example package 235
thumbnail sequence diagram 238
time package 18, 77, 183
time.After function 245
time.AfterFunc function 164
time.Duration type 76, 179
time.Minute constant 76
time.Now function 220
time.Parse function 220
time.Second constant 164
time.Since function 114
time.Tick function 244, 246
time.Time type 114
time.Time.Format method 220
title example 153
title function 144, 145

token-based decoder API 213, 215, 347
token-based XML decoding 213
tool
  cgo 361, 363
  go 2, 42, 44, 290
  go doc 25
  godoc xvi, 25, 297, 326
  gofmt 3, 4, 44, 286
  goimports 3, 44, 286
  golint 292
topological sort algorithm 136
topoSort example 136
trace example 146
trace, stack 149, 253
tree, binary 102
treesort example 102
true boolean constant 63
truncation, floating-point 40, 55
tuple assignment 31, 37
type declaration 39
type keyword 212
type
  abstract 24, 171
  aggregate 81, 99
  array 81
  assertion 205, 211
  assertion, interface 208, 210
  assertion, ok value from 206
  bool 63
  bufio.Scanner 9
  byte 52
  bytes.Buffer 74, 169, 172, 185
  Celsius 39
  chan 225
  channel 18
  <-chan T, receive-only channel 230
  chan<- T, send-only channel 230
  complex 61
  composite xv, 14, 81
  composition xv, 107, 162, 189
  concrete 24, 171, 211, 214
  displaying methods of a 351
  empty interface 176
  error built-in 11, 128, 149, 196
  Fahrenheit 39
  function 119, 120
  http.HandlerFunc 194, 203
  http.Request 21, 253
  http.ResponseWriter 19, 22, 191, 193
  int 52
  interface{} 143, 176, 331
  interface 171, 174
  interface dynamic 181
  json.Decoder 111
  json.Encoder 111
  map 9, 93

method receiver 157
mismatch 55
named 24, 39, 40, 105, 157
net.Conn 220
net.Listener 220
numeric 51
*os.File 11, 13, 172, 175, 185, 336
os.FileInfo 247
os.LinkError 207
os.PathError 207
recursive 48
reference 9, 12, 93, 120
reflect.StructTag 348
reflect.Type 330
reflect.Value 331, 342
rune 52, 67
slice 84
sort.IntSlice 191
strings.Reader 289
strings.Replacer 289
struct{} 227, 241, 250
struct 15, 24, 99
switch, case in 212
switch, default case in 212
switch statement 210, 212, 214, 329
sync.Mutex 263, 269
sync.Once 270
sync.RWMutex 266, 270
sync.WaitGroup 237, 250, 274
syscall.Errno 196, 197
template.HTML 116
testing.B 321
testing.T 302
time.Duration 76, 179
time.Time 114
uint 52
uintptr 52, 354, 357
underlying 39
unidirectional channel 230, 231
unnamed struct 163
unsafe.Pointer 356
url.URL 193
types, untyped constant 78

UDP socket 219
uint type 52
uintptr type 52, 354, 357
unary operator + 53
unary operator - 53
unbuffered channel 226
undefined behavior 260
underlying array 84, 88, 91, 187
underlying type 39
Unicode
  code point 67
  escape 68, 107
  replacement character � 70, 98

standard 2, 27, 52, 66, 67, 69, 97
unicode package 71
unicode.IsDigit function 71
unicode.IsLetter function 71
unicode.IsLower function 71
unicode.IsSpace function 93
unicode.IsUpper function 71
unicode/utf8 package 69
unidirectional channel type 230, 231
union, discriminated 211, 213, 214
universe block 46
Unix domain socket 219
unmarshaling JSON 110
unnamed struct type 163
unnamed variable 34, 88
unreachable statement 120
unsafe package 354
unsafe.AlignOf function 355
unsafe.Offsetof function 355
unsafe.Pointer conversion 356
unsafe.Pointer type 356
unsafe.Pointer zero value 356
unsafe.Sizeof function 354
unsigned integer 52, 54
untyped constant types 78
unused parameter 120
URL 123
URL escape 111
url.QueryEscape function 111
url.URL type 193
urlvalues example 160
UTF-8 66, 67, 98
UTF-8 encodings, table of 67
utf8.DecodeRuneInString function
    69
utf8.RuneCountInString function
    69
utf8.UTFMax value 98

value
    addressable 32
    call by 83, 120, 158
    function 132
    interface 181
    method 164
    utf8.UTFMax 98
var declaration 5, 30
variable
    confinement 261
    heap 36
    http.DefaultClient 253
    io.Discard 18
    io.EOF 132
    lifetime 35, 46, 135
    local 29, 141
    os.Args 4
    stack 36
    unnamed 34, 88
variables, escaping 36

variables, shared 257
variable-size stack 124
variadic function 142, 172
vector, bit 165
vendoring 293
visibility 28, 29, 41, 168, 297
visit function 122

wait example 130
WaitForServer function 130
walkDir function 247
web
    crawler 119
    crawler, concurrent 239
    framework 193
while loop 6
white-box test 311
Wilkes, Maurice 301
Wirth, Niklaus xiii
word example 303, 305, 308
word example, test of 303
workspace organization 291
writer lock 266
writing effective tests 316, 317

xkcd JSON interface 113
XML decoding 213
XML (Extensible Markup Language)
    107
(*xml.Decoder).Token method
    213
xmlselect example 215

zero length slice 87
zero value
    array 82
    boolean 30
    channel 225, 246
    function 132
    interface 182
    map 95
    named result 120, 127
    number 5, 30
    pointer 32
    reflect.Value 332
    slice 74, 87
    string 5, 7, 30
    struct 102
    unsafe.Pointer 356